Guide to
Small Town
Escapes

Guide to
Small Town
Escapes

**NATIONAL
GEOGRAPHIC**
WASHINGTON, D.C.

The OLD HOMESTEAD
NO· FOOD
DRINKS
PETS
STROLLERS
VISA
Vintage
LINENS
OLD
BOOKS

Contents

Front cover: Tunbridge Fair, Vermont *Page 1:* Architectural detail, Port Townsend, Washington *Pages 2-3:* Avalon on Santa Catalina Island, California *Opposite:* Shop in Eureka Springs, Arkansas

Small Town Escapes

Lost in Time

Swaying on a rocker on the porch of Lewisburg, West Virginia's General Lewis Inn one spring twilight not long ago, I was chatting with another guest when it dawned on me: My only worries were where to eat dinner that night and how to spend the next day—rafting down the Greenbrier River, visiting a cluster of covered bridges, stopping by the venerable Greenbrier Inn in White Sulphur Springs for high tea, or simply poking into the picturesque town's many antique shops and art galleries.

Along a mail route

This is the essence of a small town escape—the chance to briefly slip away from the hectic 21st century into a quieter realm, where life seems simpler, less pressured, even calming. I love the fact that, for one weekend, my only task is to discover what special things a place has to offer. There are no set agendas; I have the choice of doing everything—or nothing. And, in the pursuit of relaxation, I never know what will unfold. I have special memories of watching a sublime performance of *The King and I* in a century-old barn in New Hope, Pennsylvania, chancing upon a beautiful old rocking chair in a wayside antique store in New Castle, Delaware, dining by candlelight in a creaky, 18th-century tavern in Abingdon, Virginia. In California, I have pounded abalones taken fresh from the sea in Mendocino and hiked to the top of the Sierra Buttes near Downieville. I have tapped my toes to the rambunctious strains of an oompah band in Hermann, Missouri, watched a scarlet sun slip into glimmering aqua waters near Petoskey, Michigan, and sampled dandelion wine in the Amana Colonies, Iowa. Fond memories, indeed.

Perhaps even more alluring are the opportunities small towns offer for pampering yourself: the fun of spending a couple of days in exquisite surroundings, with bright blooming gardens, feather beds, and crackling fires. You may be treated to a sumptuous breakfast and dine on some local specialty by candlelight—or in the company of locals down by the fishing pier. At the end of the day await sweet-smelling bubbles in a claw-foot tub.

Enchanting places lost in time, delicious tonics to modern-day stress, small towns close enough to home for an easy escape, and yet they're worlds—or centuries—away. So what are you waiting for? *Barbara A. Noe*

About This Guide

National Geographic Guide to Small Town Escapes presents 77 of America's most charming, out-of-the-way small towns. They range from tiny hamlets such as Medford, New Jersey, to the historic cores of larger cities, such as Fredericksburg, Virginia, and include an array of fishing villages, mountain resorts, island retreats, historic religious settlements, Old West towns, and more. We selected the towns based on their authenticity and tranquility. At the same time, each one provides enough activities to keep you occupied, if you so desire.

To assist us in whittling down the endless possibilities, we consulted local authorities, as well as our own regional travel writers. The final selections are only a sampling—a starting point for your getaway planning.

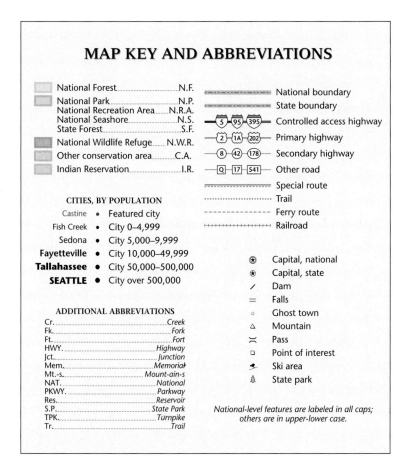

MAP KEY AND ABBREVIATIONS

National Forest............N.F.
National Park............N.P.
National Recreation Area......N.R.A.
National Seashore............N.S.
State Forest............S.F.
National Wildlife Refuge....N.W.R.
Other conservation area..........C.A.
Indian Reservation..........I.R.

CITIES, BY POPULATION

Castine • Featured city
Fish Creek • City 0–4,999
Sedona • City 5,000–9,999
Fayetteville • City 10,000–49,999
Tallahassee • City 50,000–500,000
SEATTLE • City over 500,000

ADDITIONAL ABBREVIATIONS

Cr.............Creek
Fk.............Fork
Ft.............Fort
HWY.............Highway
Jct.............Junction
Mem.............Memorial
Mt.-s.............Mount-ain-s
NAT.............National
PKWY.............Parkway
Res.............Reservoir
S.P.............State Park
TPK.............Turnpike
Tr.............Trail

National boundary
State boundary
Controlled access highway
Primary highway
Secondary highway
Other road
Special route
Trail
Ferry route
Railroad

⊛ Capital, national
⊛ Capital, state
∕ Dam
= Falls
○ Ghost town
△ Mountain
≍ Pass
◻ Point of interest
⚡ Ski area
🛆 State park

National-level features are labeled in all caps; others are in upper-lower case.

Our seasoned travel writers know the towns inside and out and share their knowledge in evocative narratives; they guide you to their favorite places and fill you in on local history and lore. A Travelwise section accompanies each town narrative, highlighting popular activities, major festivals, unique shops (including local specialties that make fantastic take-home souvenirs), must-see sights (both in the town and nearby), inns, and restaurants. This section also suggests the best seasons to visit and provides sources for further information. Locator maps guarantee you will find each town.

All information has been checked and, to the best of our knowledge, is correct as of publication. However, it is always advisable to phone ahead when possible, since information can change. Be warned that area codes change often. In addition to the stated days of closure, many sites close on national holidays.

Price Ranges

RESTAURANTS
An indication of the cost of one entrée, without beverage, dessert, or tip, is given by $ signs with the following ranges:

$	0-$10
$$	$10-$25
$$$	Over $25

LODGINGS
An indication of the cost of a double room in high season is given by $ signs, with the following ranges:

$	0-$75
$$	$75-$150
$$$	Over $150

NEW ENGLAND

Castine

Follow the tangle of back roads down the Blue Hill Peninsula, past white wooden villages and wildflower-dotted meadows, to a point where dark blue waters merge with emerald green land, and here you'll find Castine. Overlooking Penobscot Bay, this picturesque little town is one of the most authentic New England fishing villages you will ever encounter, complete with trim historic houses, elm-shaded streets, a village green, and a working harbor.

Sailing lessons

Despite an early bit of confusion over the actual name of this place—the possibilities ranged from Majabagaduce and Passageewakeag (Place of Spirits) to Fort Pentagöet—Castine is firmly rooted in its seafaring traditions. The most obvious manifestation is the 650-student **Maine Maritime Academy,** perched high on the hill above the bay. The state's only merchant-marine college, the academy was founded in 1941 and has continued to prepare men and women for careers as ship captains, naval architects, and marine engineers.

Once you're used to the clusters of big-bicepped, crew-cut cadets from the academy strolling the streets here, you can begin to focus on Castine's real charms. They spread abundantly from the heart of the town, with its creaky clapboard and brick stores at Main and Water Streets, way out to **Dyce Head Lighthouse,** recently refurbished by the state at enormous expense. The lighthouse may eventually be used as a museum, although no one seems too sure about that.

What the locals are very certain about, however, is their pride in the whole white-paint and green-shuttered ambience and timeless charm of their delightful community. For an excellent do-it-yourself guided tour, read the hundred or so historical markers around town, or pick up a copy of the "Walking Tour of Castine" brochure identifying 50 key buildings and other sites (not bad for a town of barely a thousand people), and you'll enjoy a delightful couple of hours strolling along immaculately kept streets and superbly restored houses. Obviously, money has been pumped in by people "from away," but Castine still maintains the authenticity that comes from a core population of multigenerational residents.

Take a walk down Main Street, and you'll discover outstanding examples of late Victorian architecture, with all the trim, in the form of the **Castine Inn** and the **Pentagöet Inn.** More recently, the post office (housed in the old 1893 Customs House) has also shown remarkable initiative by repainting its own Victoriana edifice in the original colors of oxblood and beige. (The Victorians

Castine's harbor

did not necessarily use white; that's a modern minimalist trend.) At **Bah's Bakehouse** in the center of town, the locals slurping mugs of coffee or sipping Bah's famous haddock "chowdah" can still get pretty worked up about such an assertive choice of color. To some of them, it's "ridiculous" or "ugly," but to others it's "historically correct" or "nice to see something different for a change." Tradition is serious in Castine.

Up the hill a little way from "downtown" (four stores, two restaurants, a bakery, and a pub), you find the town's other "heart" in the form of a perfect village green surrounded by a church, a library, an elegant school, and the town museum and historical society, all shaded by enormous trees and all in the oh-so-familiar white walls and green trim. This Rock-wellian grouping exhibits all the orderly sensibilities and clarity of purpose of early settlers here. This is actually quite remarkable, because no other town in Maine has experienced such a convoluted and complex history as little Castine.

You begin to get an idea of Castine's complicated past when you first drive into town: You'll pass the substantial earthwork remains of **Fort George** on the high bluffs above the academy (just by the golf course—an 1897

Pentagöet Inn

creation), and then lower down, right on the seashore, you'll see a similar grouping at the smaller **Fort Madison.** In fact, if you look carefully, you'll find the remains of four forts. A French trading post was built here in 1613, and in the years following its establishment, the site was occupied by four different warring factions—French, British, Dutch, and American. It was occupied and reoccupied on more than ten occasions, until things finally settled down under British rule in 1759. Considering the town's history, it's not surprising that a proud resident would describe Castine as "a tough little place and not half so pretty as it looks today."

Enthusiasts for "odd museums" will be more than satisfied with the **Wilson Museum,** which not only preserves a smattering of local records but also offers an eclectic mishmash of prehistoric artifacts, ship models, dioramas, and even Bali masks, Zulu artifacts, and pre-Inca pottery. It's the lifelong collection of John Howard Wilson, a geologist-anthropologist who first visited Castine in 1891. A little more focused on Castine itself is the **Castine Historical Society,** housed in the gracious three-story 1859 **Abbott School,** classic Italianate in design and complete with a delicate cupola. The most prominent display is the 24-foot-long bicentennial quilt assembled for the town's 200th anniversary in 1996.

One of Castine's curiosities is the **British Canal** in the northern part of the town. This old waterway was dug with amazing fortitude by the British when they reoccupied the town for the fifth time during the War of 1812. Essentially it created an island fortress of Castine, restricted the escape of deserters, made tax collection and population control easier, and generally messed up the local economy until the British left for good on April 15, 1815. The walk along the canal's banks is pleasant, if slightly wet, and the best time to go is at low tide.

Ghosts of the old warring days still float around Castine. Some claim that in late summer, if you listen really well, you'll hear a drummer boy up on the earthen ramparts of Fort George. There's certainly no doubt that this now endearingly tranquil place was once the site of almost constant conflict, desperate ignominy, and tortured loyalties. Maybe that eerie shrieking the wind makes as it rushes through the spruce forests here is just that—the wind. Or…maybe not. Only the spirits of Castine know for certain.   *David Yeadon*

Travelwise

GETTING THERE

Castine is in south-central Maine, 45 miles south of Bangor on the Blue Hill Peninsula. The peninsula has no public transportation. Planes service Bangor. By car, drive south on Me. 15 to Bucksport, follow US 1 east to Orland, then Me. 175 and 166 to Castine.

GENERAL INFORMATION

Summer and fall are the best times to visit: The sun is out, blueberries are ripe, and temperatures are warm. Castine has no local information office, but businesses and lodgings have copies of the **Castine Merchants Association**'s visitor brochure/map and walking tour. Or contact the association ahead of time (*P.O. Box 329, Castine 04421. 207-326-4884*). For additional information go to the **Castine Town Office** (*Emerson Hall, Court St., Castine 04421. 207-326-4502. Closed Sat.-Sun. www.castine.org*).

THINGS TO SEE AND DO

Castine Historical Society (*Abbott School Bldg., Castine Town Common. 207-326-4118. July–Labor Day Tues.-Sun.; adm. fee*) Located in the former high school (1859), the society has a small museum with relics from bygone days.

Forts The British captured **Fort George** (*Battle Ave.*) in the American Revolution and the War of 1812. At **Fort Madison** (*Perkins St. at the bay*), picnic tables dot the remains of the 18th-century British stronghold. Observe excavations at **Fort Pentagöet** (*Perkins St., by Castine Harbor Lodge*), an early French fort that is a national historic landmark.

Maine Maritime Academy (*Main St. 207-326-2206 or 800-227-8465*) Tours can be arranged at the Admissions Office.

Wilson Museum (*12 Perkins St. 207-326-8545. Mem. Day–Sept. Tues.-Sun. p.m.; adm. fee*) You'll find anthropologist J. Howard Wilson's mix of relics from his many travels.

WHERE TO EAT

Bah's Bakehouse (*Water St. 207-326-9510. $*) This local hangout is famous for its cinnamon buns, clam chowder, sandwiches, and "very creative flour arrangements."

Water Street Cafe (*108 Water St. 207-326-2008. $$*) Owner/chef Brenda Hunt mixes Thai, Indian, French, and Italian flavors.

WHERE TO STAY

Castine Harbor Lodge (*Perkins St. 207-326-4335. $$*) The 1893 mansion offers 16 ocean-view guest rooms, a fine restaurant, a honeymoon cottage, and boat moorings.

Castine Inn (*Main St. 207-326-4365. May-Oct. $*) This restored 1890s summer hotel offers 20 light, airy rooms.

Manor Inn (*Battle Ave. 207-326-4861. $$*) This large 1895 English manor-style beauty is set on a hillside overlooking the coast.

Pentagöet Inn (*Main St. 207-326-8616 or 800-845-1701. May-Oct. $*) This Victorian includes turrets, gables, and a wraparound porch. Rooms are unusually shaped but cozy.

Bethel

There's a distinct irony in Bethel. The summers here are remarkably peaceful, despite the fact that this delightful place appears to have everything a rural resort town should have—a gorgeous mountain-and-forest setting; classic antique residences; an enticing collection of arts, crafts, and other specialty shops; an "on-premises" pottery; and an array of Victorian inns that are the envy of many New England wannabe hot spots. Winter's a different matter, of course, with all the flurry that accompanies its wide array of skiing opportunities and snow-related frolicking in the adjoining Sunday River and White Mountains regions. So, if peace is what you seek, avoid the blackfly season in June and bask in summer solace in this lovely place.

First impressions are distinctly unimpressive. A quick look around reveals a weedy, windy plain that was once a railroad stockyard; weathered billboards proclaim some grand development scheme that seems to have petered out after the construction of what? A hotel? No. Apparently a rather odd cinema, a bank, and a **Chamber of Commerce Information Center** occupy what seems to be a cutesy version of a 19th-century railroad station.

But persevere. Don't dismiss Bethel as some kind of forlorn, past-its-prime regional transportation hub. For, believe it or not, just a short distance up Main Street, with its pottery, crafts stores, and ornate Victorian inns, hides pure magic—a Brigadoon-like haven for the weary traveler. Pause for a while and allow time to pass more slowly in this vast bowl bound by the **White Mountains** and **Oxford Hills** to the south and the outdoor recreation paradise of the **Sunday River** ski area to the north.

Even at the top of Main Street, at the cusp of the hill, you have no real idea of what awaits you until suddenly you emerge at the side of the little library on a gently sloping green at the **Common**. Complete with fountain and bandstand, it's set on the edge of a ridge that drops abruptly to reveal glorious vistas of wild uplands coated with deep green forests and buffeted by pine-perfumed breezes. This is the heart of town and, with the exception of a sortie or two down to the nearby crafts stores and inns on Main Street, the Common is where you'll find all the best that Bethel has to offer.

"It's the focal point of the town," says Stanley Howe, Bethel historian and executive director of the Bethel Historical Society. The society is housed in the **O'Neil Robinson House** and the neighboring **Dr. Moses Mason House** (1813) overlooking the Common. "The Common is quintessentially New England. I am privileged to work and live with such a fine view of the special place."

And that's precisely what the affluent, mover-shaker patients (including the occasional Vanderbilt) of Dr. John George Gehring, the "miracle man of Bethel," must have thought when they traveled to Bethel at the turn of the

20th century on lengthy pilgrimages. Their destination was his haven for "nervous disorders" therapy and recuperation in the ornate mansion he built at the end of Broad Street, just a few houses south of the Common, in 1896.

Today, Gehring's pioneering practice in soothing and stimulating the psyche is being continued at the same mansion by the **NTL Institute for Applied Behavioral Science** *(800-777-5227)*, a cutting-edge organization devoted to developing new approaches to human dynamics in the professional world. "There's so much competition out there—people are always on 'screech,'" said Christine Greenleaf, an administrator at the institute. "Vacations are still stupidly short in the U.S.A., and many people still don't take them! We all need far more time for soul-nurturing…that's why some of our sessions are open to anyone."

Bethel barn

And, as luck would have it, one of the most hedonistic centers for soul-nurturing (as well as tummy-nurturing, health-nurturing, and golf game-nurturing) is barely a stone's throw away from Gehring's mansion: The prestigious **Bethel Inn & Country Club** was founded in 1913 by the good doctor and five of his more visionary patients, all of whom are honored by an ornate Tiffany bronze plaque displayed proudly in the lobby. This now-extensive complex built around the original hotel, painted canary yellow and white, has experienced a number of economic crises despite support over a number of years by one of Gehring's most notable clients, William Bingham, the "wealthiest man in Maine" and prime benefactor of the town's renowned Gould Academy. The hotel used to close periodically for the winter, but after new management took over in 1978, it reemerged bigger and better, eventually growing into today's high-ranking travel destination. It boasts 200 acres, 57 rooms, 40 condos, an 18-hole championship golf course, a conference center, a health club, a ski center, a boating center, and elegant dining.

Although they are smaller and have far fewer facilities, a couple of inns down Main Street are renowned for personal pampering and excellent dining. The **Victoria Inn** is decorated in painted-lady, purple-and-lavender splendor on upper Main Street and is a decadently delicious haven of Old World comforts and suites, particularly the new ones in the remodeled annex where luxury reigns. Down the road, the more modestly appointed **Sudbury Inn** *(151 Main St. 207-824-2174)* caters to a different clientele, featuring fine dining in its restaurant and offering an array of over 25 on-tap beers in the **Suds Pub**.

Eating well is guaranteed in and around this lovely, peaceful place. Besides the fine restaurants at the local inns, you'll also find the **Sunday River Brewing Co.** *(US 2 and Sunday River Access Rd. 207-824-3541)*, which is located a couple of miles out of town. There you can wash big pub-platters down with a selection of Sunday River beers and watch the actual process unfold. The glassed-in brewery specializes in classic India Pale Ale, Redstone Red Ale, and a Black Bear Porter that was lovingly described by the barman in oenophile terms. In his own words, it was "big-bodied, malty, almost a molasses-coffee flavor—don't you think?—with a superb hoppy finish." What can you do when faced with such erudition except nod enthusiastically and order another pint?

And what else can you do in Bethel, when faced with such a plethora of pleasures, but accept the advice of the NTL administrator, relax, and take time out for a little soul-nurturing.   *David Yeadon*

Travelwise

GETTING THERE
Bethel is in southwestern Maine, about 50 miles northwest of Auburn and I-495. Plane service is to Bangor and Portland (closer). From Portland, take I-495 north to Me. 26 north.

GENERAL INFORMATION
While winter is prime time here, summer (avoid the blackfly season in June) is less hectic and an ideal time to enjoy Bethel's small town ambience. Abundant information, including the walking tour brochure, is available from the **Bethel Area Chamber of Commerce** (30 Cross St., P.O. Box 1247, Bethel 04217. 207-824-2282. www .bethelmaine.com). Stores and inns also provide information.

THINGS TO SEE AND DO
Dr. Moses Mason House (On the Common. 207-824-2908 or 800-824-2910. July–Labor Day Tues.-Sun., by appt. rest of year) Exhibits on 19th-century life occupy this 1813 home and the adjoining 1821 **O'Neil Robinson House,** where a room is dedicated to the memory of Mollyockett. An herbal healer, the Pequawket Indian is credited with saving the life of baby Hannibal Hamlin in 1809, who grew up to become Abraham Lincoln's first vice president.

Outdoor Activities Golf, fly-fishing, skiing, and horseback riding can be arranged by the Bethel Inn. Bethel Outdoor Adventure and Campground (207-824-4224) offers guided hiking and kayak and canoe trips. For llama treks, call the Telemark Inn (207-836-2703).

ANNUAL EVENTS
Bethel Art Fair (1st Sat. in July. On the Common. 207-824-2282) See exceptional talent at this great village arts and crafts event.

Mollyockett Day (3rd Sat. in July. On the Common. 207-824-2282) A parade, races, fiddlers, and frog-jumping contests honor the Pequawket healer.

WHERE TO EAT
The inns are the best bet, but a snack at the **Bottle and Bag** (E of village on US 2. 207-824-3673. $), a local hangout, can be interesting.

WHERE TO STAY
Bethel Inn & Country Club (On the Common, 1 Broad St. 207-824-2175 or 800-654-0125. $$$) Upmarket guests at this New England resort enjoy golf, cross-country skiing, a health club, tennis, and gourmet dining.

Summit Hotel (4 miles N on US 2, on Sunday River Access Rd. 207-824-3500. $$$) This ultra-luxury mountain resort is ideal for Sunday River skiing and laid-back pampering.

Victoria Inn (32 Main St. 207-824-8060 or 888-774-1235. $$) This elegant inn invites guests to "step back in time to a bygone era of elegant, unhurried gracious living and dining."

Littleton

At the threshold of New Hampshire's rugged White Mountains stands a former manufacturing center that's been reborn as an attractive home base for North Country travelers. In many places, Littleton would be a small town that time had passed by. But here in New Hampshire's upper Connecticut Valley, it's become the lively center of a recreation wonderland.

Climb up to the cupola of **Thayers Inn**, a colonnaded landmark that has been greeting travelers since 1850, and you'll soon see why the town of Littleton is here. Below you is the Ammonoosuc River, foaming over its granite bed as it makes its way from Mount Washington to the Connecticut. Without the Ammonoosuc, there would be no bustling Main Street in the view from the opposite cupola window. Littleton, now an attractively sited service town for the **Franconia Notch** and western **White Mountains** regions, began life as a manufacturing center powered by the waters of that swift little river.

Littleton's woolen mills once produced cloth that became uniforms for the Union Army in the Civil War. Distillers, carriage makers, and a buckskin glove manufacturer thrived here. But Littleton's signature industry was one pointing the way toward exploitation of the natural resource that powers its economy today—scenery. Back before the 20th century ushered in the era of electronic entertainment, Benjamin Kilburn established the Kilburn Stereoscopic View Manufactory in Littleton; it became the world's largest producer of stereographs—those dual-image prints that were placed in a viewer called a stereoscope to create a 3-D illusion. Kilburn's first love was photographing mountain vistas.

The White Mountains first brought visitors to Littleton, and the town's location just north of scenic Franconia Notch, site of the rock outcropping known as the **Old Man of the Mountain,** still makes it a perfect base for exploring White Mountain National Forest. But unlike many vacation retreats lying in the shadow of Mount Washington and the Presidential Range, Littleton has a lot going in its own right. In fact, you could easily pass up a day's hiking in the hills for a walk down lively Main Street. Within a few blocks are boutiques, bookstores, restaurants, and the **Littleton Historical Museum** with its recollections of, among other things, Ben Kilburn's stereograph industry.

Robert Frost

One of the area's most celebrated residents came here because he wanted "to be a plain New Hampshire farmer." Of course, Robert Frost had a bit more in mind during the five years he owned the Franconia farm now known as the **Frost Place.** Even after he sold it, Frost rented the farm for the next 18 summers. The 1859 farmhouse is now a museum featuring memorabilia and first editions. Each year a resident poet and five other nationally known poets give readings at a midsummer festival.

Thayers Inn

Tucked just a block off Main Street, on the banks of the Ammonoosuc, is the **Littleton Grist Mill,** dating from 1798 and ranking as northern New Hampshire's oldest commercial building. At the mill, a waterwheel more than 20 feet in diameter drives two 4-foot grinding stones through a system of wooden gears. At the hands-on museum, you can watch wheat and other grains being ground into meal and flour. The mill's commercially produced flours and meals are for sale right on the premises. The complex also houses an exhibit of artifacts that turned up during the restoration of the ancient building, as well as a delightful sandwich shop.

Thayers Inn is perhaps Main Street's greatest success story. It's unusual for a 150-year-old hostelry this size to still be in business, let alone thriving. The four-story, white Greek Revival building, now on the National Register of Historic Places, has hosted presidents from Franklin Pierce to Jimmy Carter;

Ulysses Grant gave a speech from the balcony. Actress Bette Davis stayed here for the world premiere of *The Great Lie*. The inn's guest rooms are thoroughly up-to-date, but one has been preserved as a museum piece, with furnishings as they would have been at the time it opened (you can't sleep in it).

Head east out of Littleton via US 302 to **Bethlehem,** a favored summer retreat since the 1860s. Once known as a refuge for hay fever sufferers, the town occupies a plateau with splendid White Mountain views. A century ago, wealthy summer sojourners built majestic mansions, several of which are now inns and B&Bs, along Bethlehem's Main Street. During the late 1940s and early 1950s, several hotels began to attract a Hasidic Jewish clientele, and bearded, black-garbed vacationers still share the town's sidewalks with golfers headed toward its two championship courses.   *William G. Scheller*

Travelwise

GETTING THERE
Littleton is just off I-93 at the Vermont border. The nearest major airports are in Manchester, New Hampshire, and Burlington, Vermont. Concord Trailways *(800-639-3317)* services the town. Dave's Taxi *(603-444-0407)* provides local transportation.

GENERAL INFORMATION
Littleton is at its prettiest June through October, but if you're a skier you may prefer the winter months. For information contact the **Littleton Area Chamber of Commerce** *(120 Main St., Littleton 03561. 603-444-6561);* **Bethlehem Chamber of Commerce** *(2178 Main St., Bethlehem 03574. 603-869-3409);* and **White Mountains Attractions** *(P.O. Box 10, North Woodstock 03262. 800-346-3687).*

THINGS TO SEE AND DO
Littleton Grist Mill *(18 Mill St. 603-444-7478 or 888-28GRIST)* Still grinding grain, a waterwheel at the restored, 200-year-old, water-powered grist mill on the Ammonoosuc is the centerpiece of the hands-on museum located in the mill.

Littleton Historical Museum *(1 Cottage St. 603-444-6435. July–mid-Oct. Wed. and Sat. p.m., by appt. rest of year)* Memorabilia and photographs depict Littleton's history.

Walking and Hiking The Littleton Conservation Commission *(2 Union St., Littleton 03561)* maintains three areas: **The Dells,** with well-marked walking trails around a pond; **Pine Hill Trail,** a 1-mile, round-trip walk through the woods past

numerous glacial erratics; and **Kilburn Crags,** a 0.7-mile hike to the summit and panoramic views of the Ammonoosuc River Valley.

ENTERTAINMENT
Littleton Opera House *(2 Union St. 603-444-3996, ext. 60. Adm. fee for some events)* The year-round program includes dances, concerts, and plays.

Weathervane Theatre *(US 3 N, P. O. Box 127, Whitefield 03598. 603-837-9322. July-Aug.; adm. fee)* New Hampshire's only professional alternating repertory company performs.

ANNUAL EVENTS
Art Show/Crafts Fair *(4th Sat. in Sept. 603-444-6561)* See local arts and crafts on display.

Christmas Celebration and Parade *(Late Nov. 603-444-6561)* The three-day celebration begins the day after Thanksgiving.

Connecticut River Valley vista

WHERE TO EAT

Flying Moose Cafe (2 W. Main St. 603-444-2661 or 888-616-BEAL. $$) Fine contemporary cuisine, with a specialty in wood-grilling, is served in a historic inn.

Littleton Diner (145 Main St. 603-444-3994. $) Good solid fare in a genuine diner.

Topic of the Town (25 Main St. 603-444-6721. $) This casual eatery has two slogans: "Where the Locals Go to Dine" and "Where People Never Leave Hungry." Both are true.

WHERE TO STAY

Adair Country Inn (80 Guilder Ln., Bethlehem. 603-444-2600 or 888-444-2600. $$$) A Georgian colonial revival estate with dramatic mountain views. Nine guest rooms.

Beal House Inn (2 W. Main St. 603-444-2661 or 888-616-BEAL. $$) The 1833 inn features an enclosed porch and seven cozy rooms, most with four-poster beds.

Mulburn Inn at Bethlehem (2370 Main St., Bethlehem. 603-869-3389 or 800-457-9440. $$) Seven spacious guest rooms in an elegant Victorian mansion. Cary Grant and Barbara Hutton honeymooned in the Adams Room.

Thayers Inn (111 Main St. 603-444-6469 or 800-634-8179. $) Enjoy moderate rates, nice accommodations, and a downtown location.

NEARBY PLACES

Franconia Notch State Park (10 miles S on I-93. 603-823-8800. Adm. fee to some sights) Within the park are the Old Man of the Mountain, Echo Lake, the Cannon Mountain Aerial Tramway, and Flume gorge.

Frost Place (Off N.H. 116, Franconia. 603-823-5510. Mem. Day–June Sat.-Sun. p.m., July–mid-Oct. Wed.-Mon. p.m.; adm. fee) The farmhouse where Robert Frost lived off and on for 23 years is filled with memorabilia; the half-mile Poetry Nature Trail winds through the woods out back.

Mount Washington Auto Road (N.H. 16, Pinkham Notch. 603-466-3988. Weather permitting; adm fee) Drive 8 miles to the top of the Northeast's highest peak.

Mount Washington Cog Railway (Off US 302, Bretton Woods. 603-278-5404 or 800-922-8825. May–early Nov., weather permitting; fare) The three-hour round-trip journey on a steam-powered, cog-driven railway climbs 3 miles to the top of Mount Washington.

Hanover

The Appalachian Trail wriggles through the center of Hanover, hidden above a great curl in the Connecticut River north of Lebanon, New Hampshire, and away from all the bustle of the interstate intersection (89 and 91) near White River Junction, Vermont. The town possesses an air of academic aloofness coupled with the charm of a neoclassic campus enveloping an enormous green—focal point of the community. The place radiates culture, with its theater and galleries offering an array of soul-nurturing delights.

The Orozco Frescoes

Stirring and powerful, the murals on the walls of the Baker Library were created from 1932 to 1934, when José Clemente Orozco, one of Mexico's leading artists, was artist-in-residence at Dartmouth. "The Epic of American Civilization" is a 3,000-square-foot masterwork that dramatically depicts the pre- and post-Columbian eras. In it, the artist emphasizes the evil aspects of power—the horrors of human sacrifice; the quagmires of superstition, fear, and exploitation; the cold austerity of the machine age; and the "false gods" of the modern world.

On a fine crisp New Hampshire day this stately college town, set on a high plateau above the east bank of the Connecticut River, is within viewing distance of Vermont's Green Mountains to the west and the soaring massifs of the White Mountains to the east. Its 9,000 residents (and another 5,250 or so students) celebrate educational excellence, taking great pride in world-renowned **Dartmouth College,** the prime feature of the town.

The towering neoclassic facades of the campus buildings encompass the enormous green, the heart of the community. Along the south side of the green the neo-Georgian **Hanover Inn** sprawls languorously, anchoring the collection of stores in the compact downtown. In many college towns, one might expect to see shops selling punk-ware and Goth-paraphernalia; what you'll find in Hanover is a Gap store. Instead of beer-blast hangouts and junk food establishments, you'll discover interesting pubs (**Murphy's on the Green** often features ostrich entrées and unusual homemade sauces), restaurants, and bakeries. In lesser college towns, stores with cheap posters and trinkets might predominate; Hanover, however, boasts its **League of New Hampshire Craftsmen,** featuring creations by many of the finest craftspeople in the state and in northern New England.

Hanover is definitely different, and it has been that way ever since the founding of Dartmouth College in 1769. First, this noble institution was funded largely by Britain's King and other donors, including the Earl of Dartmouth (a rather unique bequest in those anti-British, revolutionary days), and founded by the Reverend Eleazar Wheelock with the primary purpose of instructing "the Youth of the Indian Tribes…English Youth and any others." Second, it has one of the

At Dartmouth College

most elegant campuses in the eastern states and one of the largest greens of any small community in the nation. And third, the town possesses a vast creative legacy, which is possibly the reason for Hanover's regional prominence. One example is Mexican artist José Clemente Orozco's powerful murals, on display in the basement of the campus's most prominent spired building, the mammoth 1927 **Baker Library** (see sidebar p. 24). That creativity is also expressed in the abundant performances and workshops in theater, film, dance, classical music, opera, and jazz, and in the all-encompassing art dynamics of the **Hopkins Center,** known lovingly as "the Hop." Just one glance at the posters for upcoming events at the Hop makes you realize that this is no mere regional "rep" center. It is a focal point of national performance excellence offering artistic expression for curious and cultivated audiences.

A stroll around the soaring galleries of the **Hood Museum of Art,** with its eclectic displays and ever changing exhibits, is enriching in the extreme, especially if you allow yourself time to pause and ponder the intricacies of the famed Assyrian reliefs from the Palace of King Ashurnasirpal II (883-859 B.C.) in his capital of Nimrud (northern Iraq). Once highly colored, these large panels are now the original warm tan color of the stone, and the grace and confidence of the sculptor's line gives them enormous power and resonance. "If you sit long enough, they seem to come alive—especially that one," said an elderly visitor to her companion. She pointed to the figure of the king who had named himself the King of the World. "Oh yes," said the other, "He's definitely the boss!"

A little "coming alive" is what you'll feel after taking the self-guided walking tour of the college: **Dartmouth Row,** on the east side of the green, is said to be one of the finest groupings of early college buildings in the country; **Webster Hall** is named after one of Dartmouth's most famous sons—Daniel Webster (class of 1801); and the towered bulk of **Rollins Chapel** is an unusual example of stone-built Romanesque-Revival Victorian architecture. This is merely the historic inner core, but it's enough to justify a stop for sustenance at the **Dirt Cowboy Café** across Wheelock Street. Try the Dirt Cowboy espresso topped with steamed half-and-half. On South Main, consider ordering one of the deli-style delights at **Lou's** diner or perhaps an enormous gourmet burger at **Molly's Restaurant & Bar.** You might also try a touch of eastern-exotic cuisine at one of the town's Indian, Thai, or Chinese restaurants.

And just when you're thinking you can rest before the evening concert at the Hop, someone comes along and mentions the enticing little villages of **Lyme** and **Orford** just to the north of town. You could also take in the lively **Alliance for Visual Arts Gallery** in a renovated overalls factory in **Lebanon,** 5 miles to the south, and the plays and dance performances at the opera houses in Lebanon and **White River Junction.** For true culture-buffs, there's the beautiful **Saint-Gaudens National Historic Site** in nearby Cornish. Whoever said small town exploration was easy?   *David Yeadon*

Travelwise

GETTING THERE

Hanover is on the east bank of the Connecticut River in west-central New Hampshire, 5 miles north of the intersection of I-89 and I-91 near White River Junction, Vermont. The closest major airports are in Manchester, New Hampshire, and Burlington, Vermont. From Manchester, drive north on I-93 and I-89. From Burlington it's a clear run south on I-89. Vermont Transit (*802-864-6811*) has direct service to Boston and connecting services from New York and Hartford to White River Junction.

GENERAL INFORMATION

While Hanover is definitely an all-season town, fall (for viewing the colorful leaves) and

winter (for the great skiing) tend to be the most popular times to visit. Abundant information on the town, college tours, and the region is available at the information booth on the green (*June-Sept.*). You can also contact the **Hanover Area Chamber of Commerce** (*P.O. Box 5105, Hanover 03755. 603-643-3115. www.hanoverchamber.org*).

THINGS TO SEE AND DO

Canoeing For rentals and day and overnight trips contact North Star Canoe Rentals (*RR 2, Box 894, Cornish, NH 03745. 603-542-5802*).

Dartmouth College An impressive array of attractions around the green includes the **Baker Library** (N. Main St. 603-646-2560), the **Dartmouth Row** of outstanding neoclassic college buildings, the **Hood Museum of Art** (Wheelock St. 603-646-2808. Closed Mon.), and the **Hopkins Center** (Wheelock St. 603-646-2422).

Fishing For guided trips and fly-fishing instruction, contact the Lyme Angler in Hanover (8 S. Main St. 603-643-1263).

Skiing The nearest skiing is at Whaleback (S of Lebanon. 603-448-1489) and Dartmouth Skiway (N of Hanover off N.H. 10. 603-795-2143). Contact the Vermont Chamber of Commerce (802-223-3443) and the New Hampshire Office of Travel and Tourism (603-271-2666) for further information.

Walking Scores of trails are maintained around the town, reflecting Hanover's care for its public lands.

ENTERTAINMENT

Hopkins Center (Wheelock St. 603-646-2422) A wellspring of creativity in almost every performance arena. And then, of course, there's the student nightlife scene at the pubs and restaurants around town (see below).

SHOPPING

Dartmouth Bookstore (33 S. Main St. 603-643-3616) Run by the Storrs family since 1872, this is a definite must-see and justifies its title as Rural New England's Classic Bookstore with more than 120,000 titles—and no cappuccino!

League of New Hampshire Craftsmen (13 Lebanon St. 603-643-5050) On display is a remarkable array of crafts. The League also offers classes and workshops.

ANNUAL EVENT

Dartmouth's Winter Carnival (2nd weekend in Feb. Call the Dartmouth Office of Public Affairs 603-646-3661) This three-day bacchanal of winter sports, ice sculptures, concerts, and theater is a highlight of the year and also the nation's oldest collegiate carnival, first held in 1911.

WHERE TO EAT

Café Buon Gustaio (72 S. Main St. 603-643-5711. Closed Mon. $$) Intimate

Italian dining offers a familiar menu plus an extensive array of grilled vegetables.

Lou's (30 S. Main St. 603-643-3321. $) Serving deli-style fare, Lou's is only open for breakfast and lunch. The place is always lively—and occasionally loud.

Murphy's on the Green (11 S. Main St. 603-643-4075. $$) This great student hangout prepares generous bar-food platters and unusual eclectic specials.

WHERE TO STAY

Hanover Inn (Corner of Wheelock and Main Sts. 603-643-4300 or 800-443-7024. $$$) You can't miss the Hanover. After 200 years of expansion, the inn dominates the south side of the green and is definitely priced for the wealthy parents of students. The restaurants are topflight, too, especially the Daniel Webster Room.

Trumbull House Bed & Breakfast (40 Etna Rd. 603-643-2370 or 800-651-5141. $$$) This B&B offers five "luxury country" guest rooms, a serene setting, and breakfasts that are sumptuous.

NEARBY PLACES

Alliance for Visual Arts Gallery (11 Bank St., Lebanon. 603-448-3117) The alliance presents excellent and ever changing exhibitions of works by numerous New Hampshire and Vermont artists.

Montshire Museum of Science (1 Montshire Rd., Norwich, VT. 802-649-2200. Adm. fee) This wonderful science education center, located in a modern structure just across the river from Hanover, is ideal for children of all ages. The exhibits are very hands-on; the 110-acre site includes nature trails.

Saint-Gaudens National Historic Site (Saint-Gaudens Rd., off N.H. 12A, Cornish. 603-675-2175. Late May–late Oct.; adm. fee) At this site, you'll find a magnificent restoration of Augustus Saint-Gaudens's residence from 1885 until his death in 1907. The New Gallery has a particularly charming Roman-style atrium and pool. The main 1804 house, **Aspet,** contains furnishings collected by the world-famous sculptor on his extensive travels.

Woodstock

Follow the path taken by Rockefellers and ski pioneers to an exquisitely preserved village in the foothills of the Green Mountains. In this lovely part of the Connecticut River Valley, you'll discover Vermont's only national historical park, a 19th-century model farm, and a cosmopolitan array of restaurants, shops, and inns.

In the post office at Woodstock, a mural neatly sums up the history of the town and, in many respects, the history of all of Vermont. The painting depicts the evolution of the area, from the days of its earliest settlers to the era of the ski industry. Woodstock is where Vermont first learned that two of its most profitable commodities are gravity and winter.

At an inn near the slopes of nearby Mount Tom, in 1934, a group of skiers from New York came up with the idea of chipping in to fund the building of Vermont's first rope tow, a rudimentary device powered by a Ford Model T truck engine. The men spent $500, seed money for the multi-million-dollar Vermont ski industry of today.

It would be too easy to say that skiing put Woodstock on the map, because this handsome little village was already there. The town was first settled in 1765 by emigrants from southern New England who saw the advantage of its location on the Ottauquechee River, a stream that once powered local woolen mills; the river continued to power other businesses well into the 20th century. In fact, Woodstock had even seen an earlier tourist influx, associated with the discovery of "curative" local mineral springs in the late 1800s.

No one, of course, ever "designed" a New England village in the 18th and 19th centuries. But looking at Woodstock, it's hard to believe that no master plan was employed. At its center is a compact commercial district, and although largely given nowadays to galleries and boutiques, it is still presided over by the wonderfully eclectic **F. H. Gillingham & Sons,** a rambling emporium where you can buy a pound of pâté with ease. A Richardsonian Romanesque library, the courthouse, and the post office with its expressive mural are all downtown, as is **Teagle's Landing,** a charming vest-pocket park along the banks of Kedron Brook, which flows beneath Central Street on the way to the Ottauquechee.

Just west of the business center is one of Vermont's grandest town greens, a village common that serves as the perfect foil for the immaculately kept federal, Greek Revival, and Victorian houses that surround it. Several of these homes have been converted into lovely inns. (A word of advice: A perennial item of contention stems from Woodstock's location on US 4, a primary east-west route through Vermont. Local merchants and innkeepers have been trying to keep a lid on increased truck traffic, but they are always being reminded that "you can't stop progress." Keeping this in mind, you might ask for a room in the back if your inn is on Central Street).

The grandest of Woodstock's hostelries stands at the southern end of the green and out of the range of vehicular noise. This is the posh **Woodstock**

Country lane near Woodstock

Inn, long known as one of Vermont's grandest destination resorts. It's renowned for its quietly elegant accommodations and public rooms, the imaginatively updated New England cuisine featured in its gracious dining room, and its comprehensive sports offerings, including tennis, an 18-hole golf course, and the small but challenging **Suicide Six** ski area, located just outside of town.

Woodstock's history has been enriched, and its range of attractions broadened, by a remarkable string of professional and family associations dating back to the mid-19th century. Area native Frederick Billings made a fortune with the Northern Pacific Railroad in the 1870s and '80s, and when he chose to establish a model farm on his estate in Woodstock, he was inspired by the writings of George Perkins Marsh, a Woodstock-born U.S. congressman and diplomat who was one of the pioneers of the conservation movement. Marsh's book *Man and Nature* taught Billings the importance of forest reclamation. Billings adopted reclamation practices and left as part of his legacy the beautiful stands of trees on what is today **Marsh-Billings-Rockefeller National Historical Park,** located on the outskirts of town.

The Rockefeller connection came about when Laurance S. Rockefeller (grandson of John D. Rockefeller, Sr.), a resort developer whose properties include the Woodstock Inn, married Billings's granddaughter, Mary. The

Rockefellers set up part-time residence on the Billings family estate. Several years ago they announced that they would donate the roughly 555-acre tract to the National Park Service. Laurance S. Rockefeller relinquished his life tenancy after the death of his wife, and today, park visitors can tour both the Billings-Rockefeller Mansion and the impeccably managed woodlands that surround it.

Frederick Billings's model farm is now called the **Billings Farm & Museum.** It continues as a working farm, maintaining a prize-winning dairy herd as well as sheep, work horses, and poultry. It also offers visitors seasonal demonstrations that highlight farm activities of days gone by. Four connecting 19th-century barns on the property have been converted into Vermont's finest museum of rural life. Also on site is the home of Billings's farm manager. This comfortable Queen Anne-style residence incorporated the very latest in 1890s technology.

Some Vermonters will tell you that a town like Woodstock is a model village in much the same way that the Billings operation is a model farm: The town is attractive to look at, but it is not representative of everyday life in the Green Mountains. This place is no stage set, either. Woodstock took a long time to become what it is, and what that happens to be is just about the prettiest place in the state to spend a leisurely weekend.   *William G. Scheller*

Travelwise

GETTING THERE

Woodstock is near the I-89/I-91 junction in eastern Vermont, 12 miles west of White River Junction via US 4. The closest major airports are in Burlington, Vermont, and Manchester, New Hampshire. Vermont Transit runs from Boston, New York, and points in between. Amtrak *(800-USA-RAIL)* services White River Junction.

GENERAL INFORMATION

To learn the best times to visit, contact the **Woodstock Area Chamber of Commerce** *(18 Central St., Woodstock 05091. 802-457-3555 or 888-4WOODST. www.woodstockvt.com).* The information booth on the green is open from June to October *(802-457-1042).*

THINGS TO SEE AND DO

Billings Farm & Museum *(Vt. 12 and River Rd. 802-457-2355. Daily May-Oct., select weekends Nov. and Dec., call for hours; adm. fee)*

This living museum and working farm showcases 19th-century life in rural Vermont.

Dana House *(26 Elm St. 802-457-1822. May-Oct.; adm. fee)* The Woodstock Historical Society's 1807 house is decorated with furnishings dating from ca 1800 through 1900.

Horseback Riding To view Woodstock from atop a horse, contact Kedron Valley Stables *(South Woodstock. 802-457-1480).*

Marsh-Billings-Rockefeller National Historical Park *(Vt. 12. 802-457-3368. Mem. Day–Oct.)* Vermont's only national property focuses on conservation.

Vermont Institute of Natural Science (VINS) and Vermont Raptor Center *(Church Hill Rd. 802-457-2779. Daily June-Oct., weekends May, call for winter hours; adm. fee)* Visiting this nature preserve, living museum, and rehabilitation facility for raptors is an interesting experience.

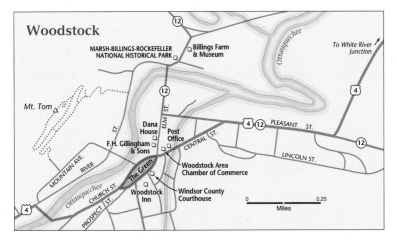

Walking and Hiking Follow marked and mapped trails in the village *(call Chamber of Commerce for information)* and at VINS. The Appalachian and Long Trails are nearby.

Walking Tours Walking tours of the village *(802-457-1042)* can be arranged during summer and the fall foliage season.

ENTERTAINMENT

Brown Bag Concerts *(On the green. 888-4WOODST)* Free lunchtime performances are held every other week in summer.

Pentangle Council on the Arts *(31 The Green. 802-457-3981)* Regional, national, and international artists perform in the Town Hall Theatre and at outdoor venues.

SHOPPING

F. H. Gillingham & Sons *(16 Elm St. 800-344-6668)* It's a general store/hardware store/gourmet grocer—all under one roof.

Stephen Huneck Gallery *(49 Central St. 802-457-3206 or 800-449-2580)* The folk artist displays whimsical animals on prints, sculptures, and furniture.

ANNUAL EVENT

Winter Carnival *(Begins Presidents' Day weekend. 802-457-1502. Some fees)* The week-long celebration includes concerts, sleigh rides, and a torchlight ski parade.

WHERE TO EAT

Pane e Salute *(61 Central St. 802-457-4882. $)* The bakery prepares Italian breads and serves hearty regional specialties. Breakfast

and lunch are served daily in summer; dinner on Fri. and Sat. Call for winter hours.

The Prince and the Pauper *(24 Elm St. 802-457-1818 $$)* Modern French and American cuisine has a Vermont accent. Dinner (no lunch) is served by candlelight.

WHERE TO STAY

Kedron Valley Inn *(Vt. 106, South Woodstock. 802-457-1473 or 800-836-1193. $$$)* Just a few minutes from Woodstock, this elegant and romantic inn offers superb accommodations and gourmet dining.

Three Church Street Bed & Breakfast *(The Green. 802-457-1925. $$)* Choose from 11 guest rooms in a lovely Georgian home with spacious sitting rooms, pool, and tennis court.

Woodstock Inn & Resort *(14 The Green. 802-457-1100 or 800-448-7900. $$$)* The resort has 144 luxurious rooms and suites, a golf course, and a health and fitness center.

NEARBY PLACES

President Calvin Coolidge State Historic Site *(Vt. 100 A, Plymouth Notch. 802-672-3773. Late May–mid Oct.; adm. fee)* The 30th President's birthplace and boyhood home is one of the best preserved presidential homes.

Quechee The 165-foot-deep, mile-long **Quechee Gorge** *(7 miles E of Woodstock on US 4. Quechee Chamber of Commerce 800-295-5451)* is a must-see. Hiking trails run along its sides.

Weston

On the northeastern edge of the Green Mountain National Forest and surrounded by some of the greatest skiing locations in Vermont is a tiny hamlet with all the features of a typical small town in New England: a tree-shaded green (with bandstand), quaint stores and galleries, museums, superb B&Bs, and an atmosphere of time-honored Old World ways. The place is Weston, home of the legendary Vermont Country Store company, and there's magic to be found here.

Farrar-Mansur House

Although this delightful museum near the village green has limited hours (802-824-6624. July-Aug. Wed.-Sun. p.m. and fall weekends; adm. fee), it's worth exploring. Inside the 1797 home and tavern are a 1841 Rawson shelf clock, grain-painted furniture, silver creations by Bailey of Woodstock, and portraits by folk artists Asahel Powers and Aaran Dean Fletcher. But the most popular features are the 1930s-era murals by WPA artist Roy Williams in the ladies' parlor. They recall Weston in the 1820s, when it looked much like today's town.

It's not really the kind of thing one expects to come across by chance but, then again, chance discoveries are really what makes exploring small towns along back roads so interesting. Just north of the village of Weston, a small sign reads **Weston Priory,** and at the end of a drive that winds past a pond and gardens stands a large, timber barnlike structure. Inside, a group of 50 or so locals and travelers are gathered for prayer, listening reverently as 12 Benedictine monks in simple white robes sit in a circle and sing beautiful plainsong-like melodies to the accompaniment of a monk-guitarist. (Many of the melodies were composed by one or more of the brothers.) The gentle, echoing sounds of the monks' blended voices float out across the nearby gardens and meadows and into the shadowy woodlands—cathedrals of silence—all around. And then there is silence. Utter silence. And you can sense the almost tangible, bonding spirit of the music and the stillness. There are smiles and deep sighs as the next melody begins.

A tiny card pinned to a wall informs its readers that recordings are available at the gift shop (along with priory-produced apples and maple syrup) inside the adjoining monastery. Other more serious displays of photographs and leaflets draw attention to the work of the Benedictines with people living in poverty in Mexico and Guatemala. It is an uplifting place, a soul-nurturing haven in the hills, a welcome surprise.

And Weston itself is full of surprises, too. Although it appears to be a blink-and-you're-through-it kind of place, Weston boasts excellent museums, intriguing stores, talented craftspeople, outstanding inns and B&Bs, two elegant churches, and a theater with its own restaurant—all huddled around

The Vermont Country Store

a perfect green that comes complete with shade maples, a bandstand, and a chuckling stream. Add a cradling of wooded hills and it's so "New England" it's virtually Rockwellian.

"I definitely don't do Rockwell," laughed Robert Todd, artist-in-residence and owner with his wife, Karin, of the **Todd Gallery** at the edge of town. Actually, some of his Vermont landscapes have more of a Wyeth flavor. Robert's gallery is like most of the village stores—small and richly packed with a wide range of delights; in this instance, the holdings included works from eight or more additional artists, plus wooden ware, pottery, baskets, and other Vermont handmade crafts. "I'm doing the only thing I've ever wanted to do, in one of the most artistic little communities in the state. Just take a look at some of the work: the glass of Vitriesse, Wick Ahren's carved whales next to the Fudge Shop, some of the crafts in the Village Store. Keeps you on your toes, all this artistry! Keeps you pushin'. I've never finished a painting I'm really satisfied with yet. If I did, I'd probably never paint again!"

Robert's attitude also seems to have inspired the motto of the town's biggest attraction—the huge bulging barn of the famous **Vermont Country Store,** founded in 1946 by Vrest Orton. This ever expanding national "Voice of the Mountains" catalog business and the opening of new nostalgia-nuanced stores reflects a never satisfied, always do better attitude. And this tribute to Yankee shopkeeping around the potbellied stove has certainly put Weston on the map. In fact, it could have wrecked the place, smothering it Wal-Mart-style. But it didn't. There's still very much a thriving community spirit here, a great pride in things local.

Take this example, overheard outside the Farrar-Mansur House museum: "I'm so sorry the museum is closed today," an elderly resident whispered sadly to a family of disappointed travelers. "I think Edith is a little under the weather. I could call and see if someone would come and open it for you." And, believe it or not, someone did. Now that's pride and caring.

The 1797 **Farrar-Mansur House,** furnished with Weston family heirlooms and telling an intriguing history of the community, is evidence of even more local pride (see sidebar p. 32). The adjoining **Old Mill Museum** displays 19th-century water-powered tools, and the Crafts Building houses the Weston Coronet Band Wagon and the Craft Shop at the Millyard, which sells and demonstrates Vermont crafts.

But it's the building closer to the village green that seems to attract most attention. Who would have thought that a small community of 425 or so people could support something as grandiose as the elegantly columned **Weston Playhouse?** Since 1935 it has been the home of Vermont's oldest professional theater, whose main season typically offers a mélange of Shakespeare, Rodgers and Hammerstein, maybe a Bernstein or Sondheim musical, and a cutting-edge contemporary play. Recent shows have included TV and film star Christopher Lloyd (*Back to the Future*) and Alley Mills (*The Wonder Years).* Weston's community is a showcase for unique Yankee ingenuity. An unusual amount of individual creative spirit and energy surges through this town, making it a place you shouldn't miss.   *David Yeadon*

Travelwise

GETTING THERE

Weston is at the northeastern edge of Green Mountain NF approximately 20 miles west of I-91, 20 miles west of the Connecticut River near Bellows Falls, and 15 miles east of US 7 at Manchester. Trains and planes service Albany to the west and Boston to the east.

GENERAL INFORMATION

The popularity of the Vermont Country Store, the theater, the nearby skiing centers, and the riotous fall colors of the Green Mountains ensure year-round appeal for Weston. Local brochures and maps are available nearly everywhere in town, on the web *(www.westonvt.com),* and from the **Woodstock Historical Society** *(P.O. Box 246, Weston 05161),* the local **Chamber of Commerce** *(802-824-5606),* and the **Vermont Department of Tourism and Marketing** *(134 State St., Montpelier 05602. 800-VERMONT).*

THINGS TO SEE AND DO

Farrar-Mansur House and Old Mill Museums (see sidebar p. 32)

Vermont Country Store *(802-824-3184. Closed Sun.)* In 1946, a mail-order-catalog empire was born here. Today it's a bonanza for browsers and seekers of serendipity.

Weston Priory *(4 miles N near intersection of Vt. 100 and Vt. 155. 802-824-5409)* Services most days at this small, secluded Benedictine community and Sunday masses all feature liturgical music written by the brothers.

ENTERTAINMENT

Weston Playhouse *(Vt. 100, on the village green. 802-824-5288. Late June–mid-Oct.)* The oldest professional theater in the state, the Greek Revival playhouse has its own restaurant and after-hours cabaret.

SHOPPING

Weston is a potpourri of galleries and craft shops, many featuring the work of local artists and artisans.

Todd Gallery *(614 Main St. 802-824-5606)* This gallery displays watercolors from Vermont and Ireland, as well as paintings, prints, sculptures, and photographs.

ANNUAL EVENTS

Chamber Music Concerts *(July. Kinhaven School of Music. 802-824-3365)* This famous local school presents quality recitals.

Weston Craft Show *(Columbus Day weekend. 802-824-3576)* This juried show featuring 50 top-ranking Vermont artisans takes over all three floors of the Weston Playhouse. Quality ware includes woven baskets, bird carvings, and doll clothing.

WHERE TO EAT

In addition to excellent cuisine at the inns, try **Downstairs at The Playhouse** *(Village green. 802-824-5288. $$)*, which has a convenient location on the banks of the picturesque Weston Falls. Nearby **Grafton** and **Newfane** also offer outstanding dining options (see right).

WHERE TO STAY

Darling Family Inn *(815 Vt. 100. 802-824-3223. $$)* This 170-year-old farmhouse is filled with American and English country antiques, including an 18th-century spinet and four-poster beds.

Inn at Weston *(Vt. 100, 802-824-6789. $$$)* Two 19th-century homes and a barn sit on 6 acres. The inn offers fine dining.

Wilder Homestead Inn *(25 Lawrence Hill Rd. 802-824-8172. $$)* The McKay family from Britain has recently taken over this

elegant 1827 brick inn. Available are 7 unique rooms, most with private baths and some with original Moses Eaton stenciling. The inn offers big farm breakfasts, gourmet dinners, and the chef's menu of the day (3-course set meal).

NEARBY PLACES

Chester *(Chamber of Commerce 802-875-2939)* A lovely, laid-back "walking" town on Pattacork Brook, Chester has excellent antique and crafts stores.

Autumn stroll in a Weston park

Grafton *(Information Center 802-843-2255)* This quintessential Vermont village is home to the 1801 **Old Tavern at Grafton** *(820-843-2231)*, a superb inn; and the famous **Grafton Village Cheese** *(820-843-2221 or 800-472-3866)*, which has long been producing excellent cheeses.

Newfane *(Town Office 802-365-7772)* One of Vermont's most photographed villages.

Ski Centers Stratton Mountain is one of the largest, but there are also Magic Mountain, Bromley, and Okemo. Call 800-VERMONT for general information. For sales and rentals of skis, snowboards, and other equipment, contact Equipe Sport *(10 miles from Weston in Rawsonville, at Vt. 30 and 100. 800-282-6665)*.

Williamstown

Residents call this the Village Beautiful, and it is a well-deserved title, particularly if you approach this demure little college town from the Taconic Range east of Petersburg, New York. From high on the forested ridges, you can peer out between the trees and catch fleeting glimpses of the towers and spires of one of New England's most charming communities, set in a wooded bowl with vistas extending eastward to North Adams and beyond. This is the quintessential Berkshire village, saturated in culture, art, theater, dance, and litera-ture. It reflects many of the utopian dreams of our forefathers, specifically the purity of rural academia well away from the worldly distractions of coastal cities.

"It would be no small advantage if every college were thus located at the base of a mountain," wrote Henry David Thoreau in 1839 in favor of placing institutions of higher learning well away from the distractions of urban environ-ments. And it would be equally advantageous if other college communities could offer as many cultural delights to their students and visitors as Williamstown, with barely 8,000 residents.

At first glimpse the little town seems to be all academia, with its great campus comprising vast lawns and greens and abundant temples and cloisters of learning (an idealized blend of Oxford and Harvard that would make many of our forefathers smile). Moving downhill, though, the scene gradually changes: From the sprawling Williams Inn, at the key intersection of Mass. 2 and US 7, the town extends across the Green River and merges with a commercial strip that stretches eastward toward the old industrial town of North Adams. Beyond that eyesore of a strip the town is embraced by rolling foothills dotted with farms and elegant houses, a superb golf course, and the playing fields and stadia of the university.

Oldest Observatory
East of the Williams College Museum of Art is a little stone building with odd proportions and a diminutive white dome. You can easily miss it if you're driving on streets crowded with jaywalking students, but try to find it because this is the 1838 **Hopkins Observatory and Mehlin Museum of Astronomy,** the oldest working observatory in the United States. Besides planetarium shows and telescope viewings, the observatory offers a fascinating collection of exhibits on the history of astronomy. Call 413-597-2188 for details.

"The whole place is built on the gifts of alumni," said Ed Fauteaux, owner of the Library Antiques store on Spring Street in a downtown that looks as though it was deliberately tucked away on a side street. "It's amazing how many people move back here to retire after a life of movin' and shakin' in the

Along the Appalachian Trail near Williamstown

law, or government, or money markets. I guess this little town leaves its mark. Even as a 'comer-in'—a flatlander—I can feel it, too. One alumnus, a real famous guy in sports, just gave 20 million dollars for a new dance center at the bottom of the street."

And Ed's obviously right. Everywhere in this model enclave of rural academia are plaques honoring the generosity of alumni and other admirers who have found something of enduring value in the hills and meadows of the northern Berkshires.

Col. Ephraim Williams, a hero of the French and Indian War, also loved this place. With money from his will, the Free School was founded in 1791, and in accordance with his wishes, it was renamed **Williams College** a couple of years later. Or maybe the town fathers thought better of the original name, West Hoosuck (or Hoosac). After all, who wants to be labeled a Hoosucker?

Over two centuries, the glorious intertwining of town and gown has produced one of the nation's most respected liberal arts schools, whose prime attractions are the envy of larger, more cosmopolitan centers. And prime attraction number one—again, the creation (indirectly) of an alumnus—is the **Sterling and Francine Clark Art Institute** on South Street. Sterling's grandfather, Williams alumnus Edward Clark, was a lawyer and partner of sewing-machine king Isaac Singer. With the inheritance he received from his successful grandfather, Sterling invested a fortune in art from around the world. He started conservatively with accredited old masters, but as his confidence and taste evolved, his collection grew to include works by Turner (in his later "light-is-everything" mode), Sargent, Remington, Homer, and the Impressionists—with emphasis on Renoir. He also bought works by such lesser known artists as Alma-Tadema, whose ultra-realistic works luxuriate in the forms of well-endowed handmaidens and nubile slave girls. As they bathe, you can almost smell the perfumed waters, and the painter's light is so tactile you may think you can feel its heat.

Of course, to honor his grandfather's alma mater, Sterling Clark chose Williamstown as the place to build his series of galleries in the 1950s. Their neoclassic exteriors are adorned in gleaming white marble, and at first one expects self-serving ostentation. But, happily, the mood within is restrained, and the rooms are modest in size. Visitors enter galleries shaped by the mind of a world-class collector, whose taste for artistic excellence was perhaps inspired by an overriding theme described by one awed woman: "Light. It's the light he loved in all these artworks."

And she's right. You leave here gleaming and glowing.

And the glow continues—challenged by some of the more exacting requirements of modern art appreciation—at the town's second exceptional repository of creativity, the **Williams College Museum of Art.** This rather dour-looking structure is across Main Street from the **Thompson** (another alumnus) **Memorial Chapel,** which boasts high Gothic splendor and a famed Tiffany window. Once inside the museum, however, the mood changes to a free-flowing, contemporary space of 14 galleries. The emphasis is on 18th- to 20th-century art and includes works by Hopper, Rivers, and Warhol, as well as Gainsborough, Copley, Romney, and—in the portrait gallery—Gilbert Stuart.

Williams College

(The cadre of Williams College alumni who were collectors and donors became such a notable influence on the art scene that they were dubbed the Williams Mafia!)

If the contemporary element appeals to you, then an absolute "must" when you leave Williamstown is a visit to the **Massachusetts Museum of Contemporary Art** in adjoining North Adams, a struggling remnant of "a factory city from central casting" (according to one writer). Housed in a seemingly endless sprawl of former industrial structures, this is the nation's, if not the world's, largest center for contemporary, visual, and performing art. Where else, for example, would you find a quarter-mile-long work of art by Rauschenberg!

But don't rush away from Williamstown too quickly. This is a place that rewards the dawdler, so take time to stroll around town or enjoy a guided tour of the college campus, attend a play at the **Adams Memorial Theater** *(413-597-2342)*, gaze at the enormous collection of some 50,000 rare books and other documents in the **Chapin Library,** or peruse the odd collections in the **House of Local History** *(1095 Main St. 413-458-2160)* at the town library. (If you think all of this is just a little too urbane for your tastes, remember that among the prime "annoyances" in Williamstown are the regular forays by bears and bobcats into neighborhood gardens!) And then watch where the students hang out in the evening. The food won't be flashy, as in many of the town's finer restaurants and inns, but the fun's for free. *David Yeadon*

Travelwise

GETTING THERE

Williamstown is in northwestern Massachusetts, where Mass. 2 intersects US 7. Pittsfield is approximately 20 miles south and North Adams 5 miles east.

GENERAL INFORMATION

Visitor brochures and town maps are available at the booth on the town green (*Jct. of Mass. 2 and US 7*), or contact the **Williamstown Chamber of Commerce** (*P.O. Box 357, Williamstown 01267. 413-458-9077. www.williamstownchamber.com*). For college information, contact the **Office of Public Affairs, Williams College** (*413-597-4277*).

THINGS TO SEE AND DO

Chapin Library (*Stetson Hall, off Main St. 413-597-2462*) Over 50,000 books and manuscripts date back as far as the ninth century.

Sterling and Francine Clark Art Institute (*225 South St. 413-458-9545. Daily July-Aug., Tues.-Sun. rest of year; adm. fee*) This magnificent private art collection features American masters and French Impressionists.

Williams College Museum of Art (*Lawrence Hall, Main St. 413-597-2429. Closed Mon.*) Powerful spaces encompass 20th-century American art and an array of changing exhibits.

ANNUAL EVENT

Williamstown Theater Festival (*Late June–late Aug. Adams Memorial Theater. 413-597-3399. Adm. fee*) The town's major event.

WHERE TO EAT

College towns tend to favor pubby snack places, and they're here too—**Canterbury's Pub, Savories, Mezze Bistro,** and **Hobson's Choice**—but there's fine dining, too.

Le Jardin (*2 miles S on Mass. 2 and US 7. 413-458-8032. $$*) It's renowned for duckling with bing cherry sauce and salmon dijonnaise.

Mill on the Floss (*US 7, New Ashford. 413-458-9123. $$*) This rustic setting offers great French-inspired cuisine and outstanding rack of lamb.

WHERE TO STAY

Field Farm Guest House (*554 Sloan Rd. 413-458-3135. $$*) Artworks abound at this former home of noted art collector

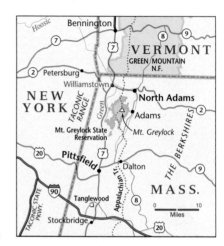

Lawrence Bloedel. The interior is spartan Danish with exquisite detailings.

Orchards (*222 Adams Rd. 413-458-9611 or 800-225-1517. $$$*) Despite its location on the town's mini-strip, this is a magnificent hotel with a quiet court and fine restaurant.

River Bend Farm (*643 Simonds Rd., off US 7. 413-458-3121. $$*) The restored 18th-century "farm" offers a taproom and enormous hearths.

NEARBY PLACES

The Berkshires This mountainous enclave south of town is a cornucopia of cultural and recreational delights focused on **Tanglewood** and the charms of **Stockbridge,** Norman Rockwell's home for decades and now the site of a museum dedicated to his work. For general information, call the Massachusetts Office of Travel and Tourism (*800-227-6277*).

Massachusetts Museum of Contemporary Art (*87 Marshall St., North Adams. 413-662-2111. Closed Mon.*) One of the world's largest collections of modern art.

Mount Greylock State Reservation (*S of North Adams via Notch Rd. to the summit road. 413-499-4262*) The state's highest point (3,491 feet) is ideal for walking, cycling, fishing, camping, and snowmobiling; the mountaintop Bascom Lodge is a fine overnighter (*winter 413-443-0011, summer 413-743-1591*).

Chatham

Head to the town known as the "first stop of the East Wind" for a taste of a quieter, older Cape Cod, where gulls wheel above the lobster fleet and a solitary beacon casts its beam 28 miles out to sea. Discover sophisticated shopping, snug inns in old sea captains' mansions, and a wildlife refuge that lies at the juncture of sand, sky, and sea.

There aren't many places in the United States where, on the same day, you can watch the sun come up and go down over the ocean. One such place is Chatham, located on the "elbow" of arm-shaped Cape Cod. Stroll down to **Chatham Lighthouse** before dawn, and watch the day begin over the open Atlantic. At dusk, head over to **Hardings Beach,** where you can see the sun dip into Nantucket Sound.

The first European to set foot on Chatham's shores was France's peripatetic explorer, Samuel de Champlain (a plaque on Stage Harbor Road, just past Bridge Street, marks his landing spot). But the English were the first to set down roots. English settlement dates from the 1650s, and Chatham mariners have been going out in their fishing boats for nearly as long. Head to the **Fish Pier** just off Shore Road, north of downtown, and you can still see the fleet

Plum Island, near Chatham

Chatham Lighthouse

bringing in its catch. For a taste, stop in at **Nickerson Fish and Lobster,** located right on the pier; they will cook your lobster to order in the summer.

For all the salty flavor of its fish pier, however, Chatham, like many of Cape Cod's towns, is a thriving tourist town. This is not to say that Chatham resembles Provincetown, its flamboyant neighbor to the north. Like P-town, Chatham has gleaming white sea captains' houses, beach roses climbing across salt-silvered shingles, and gorgeous blue hydrangeas in almost every front yard. But the town at the elbow has no raffish veneer, and at night, you can hear a fish bone drop in the sand.

Take a stroll along downtown Chatham's Main Street, which is lined with enough shops for a whole day's browsing. You can buy handblown art glass at **Chatham Glass Company,** a seascape or two from **Struna Galleries,** and outrageously delicious chocolates from **Chatham Candy Manor.**

Wander off Main Street for a taste of the area's history at the Chatham Historical Society's **Old Atwood House** on Stage Harbor Road. Built in 1752, the house has been restored and filled with 18th- and 19th-century furnishings and artifacts relating to the area's domestic life and maritime trades. One room is dedicated to local resident Joseph C. Lincoln, a popular early 20th-century author whose novels, such as *Galusha the Magnificent* and *Rugged Water,* featured sea captains and other Cape Cod characters. Lincoln memorabilia and first editions are on display.

Just behind the Old Atwood House, an annex contains a series of murals by Alice Stallknecht Wight, who moved to Chatham in the early 1900s and depicted her neighbors at work, at a church supper, assembled to listen to Christ—the surprise being that all of them are in their workaday modern dress, and Christ is a contemporary fisherman preaching from a dory.

The artist's metaphor was appropriate, because in Chatham nearly all roads lead to the sea. The town boasts eight saltwater beaches (more if you count out-of-the-way spots); **South** and **Hardings Beaches** are standouts not only for bathing, but because of the opportunities they offer for long walks on the sand. There are plenty of ways to get out on the water, too. Seal- and bird-watching cruises are popular, as are fishing charters. Fascinating ocean excursions go out to the beautifully desolate **Monomoy Island** (actually two islands since it was split by a 1978 storm) in Monomoy National Wildlife Refuge. Birding here can be spectacularly rewarding.

As Henry David Thoreau said of Cape Cod itself, here you can stand and "put all America behind you."   *William G. Scheller*

Onandaga Saga

On January 13, 1907, the steamship *Onandaga* ran aground off Chatham. All on board were saved, but the *Onandaga* was stranded for three months. To lighten the ship so that she could be towed off the bar by tugboats, residents were hired to transfer her cargo to shore. Among the items on the bill of lading were shoes and bushels of potatoes, not all of which could be accounted for later. According to some stories, people in Chatham were well shod and well fed that winter.

Travelwise

GETTING THERE

Chatham is located on Cape Cod. Over the Sagamore Bridge, follow US 6 to Mass. 137 south to Mass. 28 into Chatham. The Barnstable Municipal Airport at Hyannis *(508-775-2020)* services Cape Cod. Plymouth & Brockton Bus Line *(508-778-9767)* runs between Boston and Hyannis. Cape Cod Transit Authority *(508-385-8311)* provides bus transportation from Hyannis to Chatham.

GENERAL INFORMATION

Chatham is most popular in spring, summer, and fall. In winter, the town offers a tranquil retreat. The **Chatham Chamber of Commerce** *(P.O. Box 793, Chatham 02633. 508-945-5199 or 800-715-5567)* maintains an information booth at 533 Main Street.

THINGS TO SEE AND DO

Beaches Chatham has numerous beaches for swimming, including **Hardings Beach** *(Nantucket Sound. Parking fee)* and **South Beach** *(Chatham Harbor and the Atlantic. Private taxi shuttle, no parking).*

Boating For cruises and seal-watching charters, contact Beachcomber Boat Tours *(508-945-5265)* or Chatham Water Tours *(508-432-5895).* For boat rentals, try Oyster River Boatyard *(508-945-0736).*

Fishing Charters Get in touch with Chatham Charters *(508-945-7806)* or Booby Hatch *(508-430-2312).*

Monomoy National Wildlife Refuge *(Headquarters on Morris Island. 508-945-0594)* For an island tour, contact the Massachusetts Audubon Society in Wellfleet *(508-349-2615).*

Old Atwood House *(347 Stage Harbor Rd. 508-945-2493. Mid-June–mid-Sept. Tues.-Fri.; adm. fee)* On display are period furniture, household artifacts, seafaring tools, and murals by Alice Stallknecht Wight.

Sailboarding and Windsurfing Rent equipment at Monomoy Sail & Cycle *(508-945-0811 or 800-824-0201).*

SHOPPING

Chatham Candy Manor *(484 Main St. 508-945-0825 or 800-221-6497)* Try the heavenly homemade candies and hand-dipped chocolates.

Chatham Glass Company *(758 Main St. 508-945-5547)* Contemporary art glass by artists Jim Holmes and Deborah Doane.

Nickerson Fish and Lobster *(Chatham Fish Pier. 508-945-0145)* Lobster is cooked to order Memorial Day to Labor Day, and weekends to Columbus Day.

Struna Galleries *(436 Main St. 508-945-5713)* View a local artist's representations of traditional Cape Cod scenes.

WHERE TO EAT

Pate's *(Mass. 28. 508-945-9777. $$)* Enjoy prime rib carved tableside and delicious seafood specialties.

Vining's Bistro *(595 Main St. 508-945-5033. $$)* The creative international fare sometimes includes an excellent Bangkok fisherman's stew.

WHERE TO STAY

Chatham Bars Inn *(Shore Rd. 508-945-0096 or 800-527-4884. $$$)* Many of this resort's lovely rooms and suites have waterfront views. Cottages are also available. The oceanfront restaurant has fireside dining.

Chatham Wayside Inn *(512 Main St. 508-945-5859 or 800-391-5550. $$$)* Choose from 56 luxurious rooms—some with balconies, fireplaces, and whirlpool tubs; fine dining.

Moses Nickerson House *(364 Old Harbor Rd. 508-945-5859 or 800-628-6972. $$$)* This 1839 sea captain's home, Chatham's most photographed B&B, offers 7 beautifully appointed guest rooms.

Little Compton

Some call it Fogland. But don't be misled, because the fogs are rare. What most visitors remember are broad vistas, lazy days, blonde sand beaches, patchwork-quilt farms, colonial-era cottages, and Little Compton itself, set neatly around its green and church and deeply steeped in history. The people here are proud of their little hidden corner of the world and see no reason to change anything.

Beach roses

Sunset glow on Sakonnet Harbor

"Keep Little Compton Little" is the motto of many residents who worry about the influence of outsiders. "Oh, don't take it too seriously," said the grinning summer-job girl at the Little Compton general store. "People are real friendly once you get to know them. They're just a bit protective is all. They like what they've got and don't see a reason to mess with it."

And, as New Yorkers might say, "What's not to like!?" Indeed, quite a few of them make this area their home-away-from-home for the summer; it's a haven of shingle-roof cottages, low-lying farms, and meadows bound by field-stone walls and interspersed with woodlands and reed-bound marshlands.

The village of Little Compton is clustered around its green, or the **Commons;** its cemetery; and a large white **Congregational church.** The history of this sleepy place is more vivid than most visitors expect: There were disputes with the Sakonnet (Sokognates or Soughkonnets) Indians over land, and then a sudden surge of new wealth developed when the famed Rhode Island Red chicken was first reared here in 1854 and the town rapidly became the largest poultry center in the nation. Around the same time, Portuguese settlers from the Azores began arriving. The Azoreans were whalers and farmers and found the land similar to their native soil. Working first as menial laborers, they eventually amassed enough money to buy local farms and become an active part of this increasingly cosmopolitan village.

"The winters are quiet enough and the village settles back into itself, but the summers are getting a little—just a little—Hamptonesque," said Bernard Shapiro, owner of the 1850 **Bodington House** B&B. He didn't seem to be concerned, though; in fact, nobody's really concerned. The place has hardly changed at all in over a century—"and if we ever forget the way things used to be we just nip down the road to our **Wilbor House Museum,** and we're right back in the 1600s!" said the lively librarian at the library adjoining the Bodington House. "Our roots go deep y'know—all the way back to Plymouth Plantation," she added.

Beyond the village, salty sea breezes waft in across **Sakonnet Point,** frisking the ocean around the old 1884 light on Little Cormorant Rock, a dumpy structure 66 feet high and relighted as an active beacon in 1997 after 42 years of inactivity. From the tip of the point, on a strange spit encompassing tidal pools, pebble beaches, and odd rock outcroppings, you can peer back at the land and see what looks like a gray warehouse. But it's not really a warehouse; it's a rather salubrious institution known as the **Stone House Club,** celebrated for its excellent food, early American tavern, and eclectic accommodations.

Many things in Little Compton are not quite what they appear to be, and maybe the fog has something to do with it, blurring the boundaries and creating an illusionary state—a state all too readily experienced if you overdo the tastings at nearby **Sakonnet Vineyards.** Here, a dream of Earl and Susan Samson came to fruition in 1987 when they purchased an already operating vineyard and winery. Within a decade, they created New England's most productive winery, renowned for its excellent Vidal Blanc, Gewürztraminer, Chardonnay, and Fumé Vidal "estate" wines.

Yet another fascinating blurring of reality occurs a few miles up the road at **Tiverton Four Corners.** On the edge of this little artists' enclave, you'll see what appears to be huge slabs of rough lumber scattered by the roadside. But pause and ponder, and you'll realize you've entered the realm of Michael Higgins's **Magic Garden of Tiverton.**

And there is indeed a sense of magic here. A young man at the Wilbor House summed it up with a sly smile: "You won't find many visitors here after Labor Day. S'all very quiet, but it's then you can feel the mystery creeping back in." Anne Carpenter, selling fresh fish at a farmer's stand on R.I. 77 to Tiverton (including a couple of striped bass she caught at 2:30 that morning) added, also with a smile: "Oh yes! I miss them when they've gone. Trade isn't the same, but then we're back to our 'Little Fogland' again, and that's the way we kinda like it!"   *David Yeadon*

Magic Garden

Michael Higgins's world of carved creatures includes a 10-foot-long caterpillar wearing seven pairs of size-14 Reeboks, a "Terror Tree" with enormous fangs, Vinnie the Vulture wrapped in rough-bark wings, a birch-bark fruit fly, and dragons in a variety of sizes. The work of a 44-year-old man with a long black ponytail and a chain saw, they are usually on display at Tiverton Four Corners. "It's kinda whittling on a grand scale," claims Michael, "but kids love to see the creatures appear from a dead lump of wood, so I'm traveling a lot now and doing 'demos.' Someone called me the 'da Vinci of the chain saw!' That's crazy; I'm just a carver-cartoonist who loves what he does—every minute!"

Travelwise

GETTING THERE

Little Compton is located in southeastern Rhode Island, 15 miles south of I-195 at Fall River, Massachusetts, and 25 miles southeast of Providence, Rhode Island. Public transportation is limited, and a car is essential for exploring the region and reaching the beaches.

GENERAL INFORMATION

Late spring to fall is the best time to visit Little Compton. The beaches and ocean are warm, and the farm stands are brimming with local produce. A regional information map produced by the **Coastal Village Cooperative** (www.coastalvillages.com) is available free from most stores and restaurants. For more information, contact the **Town Hall** (P.O. Box 226, Little Compton 02837. 401-635-4400) or the **Newport County Convention and Visitor's Bureau** (23 America's Cup Ave., Newport 02840. 800-976-5122. www.gonewport.com).

THINGS TO SEE AND DO

Fishing For chartered trips of up to six people, call the Oceaneer at Sakonnet Point Marina (401-635-4292).

Kayaking For rentals, instruction, and guided tours, contact the Sakonnet Boathouse (169 Riverside Drive, Tiverton. 401-624-1440).

Sakonnet Vineyards (162 W. Main Rd. 401-635-8486) New England's largest winery offers excellent estate wines and a stylish tasting room.

South Shore Beach and Goosewing Beach (Daily and weekly fees for nonresidents) The beaches are superb and relatively uncrowded even in midsummer.

Walking Wilbor Woods, Sakonnet Point, Round Pond, and Tappers Beach are easy, peaceful walks from the Stone House Club. Pick up a leaflet there or locally.

Wilbor House Museum (548 W. Main Rd. 401-635-4035. Late June-Aug. Thurs.-Mon. p.m., weekends in Sept.; adm. fee) See a well-restored 1690 farmhouse, a barn, a carriage house, a peaked-top schoolhouse, and even a small catboat, *Peggoty,* converted to a thatched-roof garden studio in 1915 for famed local artist Sidney R. Burleigh. An unusual feature of the house is the Portuguese Room, with its display of Azorean artifacts.

SHOPPING

Fried Glass Studios (37 Old Stone Church Rd. 401-635-4044) Offering a delightful range of handblown glass artifacts, Lora and Ian Silvia welcome "viewers" to this backwater village. It has an operating grist mill and was the notorious Valley of Sin during the old rum-running days.

Tiverton Four Corners This hamlet teems with galleries, workshops, and crafts outlets, most notably Michael Higgins's **Magic Garden of Tiverton** (401-625-1344), **The Courtyards,** and the **Art and Education Center,** which hosts summer concerts and classes.

WHERE TO EAT

Four Corners Grille (3841 Main Rd., Tiverton Four Corners. 401-624-1510. $$) The cheery diner-style place is famous for Maryland crab cakes, lobster bisque, English fish-and-chips, chicken pot pie, whole fried clams, and the Mayflower Burger with Angus beef on an English muffin.

WHERE TO STAY

Little Compton is home to many charming B&Bs, including **Bodington House** (46 The Commons. 401-635-2069), **Lands End** (410B Long Hwy. 401-635-9557), **Harmony Home** (456 Long Hwy. 401-635-2283), and the **Roost at Sakonnet Vineyards** (170 W. Main Rd. 401-635-8486), all in the $80 range for a double. And then there is the graceful and expansive **Stone House Club** by the ocean (122 Sakonnet Point Rd. 401-635-2222. $$$). It boasts an authentic tavern, eclectic rooms, and equally eclectic restaurant. The only annoyance is that membership fee.

Washington

While places like Woodbury and Southbury become more developed and "commuteristic," Washingtonians retain their own flavor, that of the more northern northwest corner of Connecticut. And yes, indeed, Connecticut is graced with many other small towns that keep their character despite the creeping commuter-land tentacles stretching from New York, Hartford, and the coastal cities. But how can one ignore little Washington—as pristine and polished as some movie sets and happily situated in an area offering a wealth of potential discoveries for back-road travelers? Well, quite obviously, one can't.

The valleys run deep in this area, originally named Judea after a parish that stood in the Washington area. The forests are silent and dark, full of tales about ancient Native American lifeways and lusty with the lore of a young America and the revolutionary era. Despite signs of encroaching

Lake Waramaug canoes

commuterism in nearby towns, in Washington you can sense enormous pride in its local history, enduring folklore, and colonial-era mores. And residents have good reason to be proud. In 1779 the village became the fifth such place to be named in honor of George Washington (the great man briefly paused for breakfast at Squire Cogswell's Tavern in New Preston on Friday, May 25, 1781). "As perfectly manicured as a New York socialite," according to one journalist, Washington perches on a plateau high above the Shepaug River; its white clapboard houses, all adorned with dark green shutters, are scattered around a verdant green and the 1801 **First Congregational Church,** whose flock first gathered in 1741. That bulwark of Yankee independence, the town meeting, is still the official legislative body here. And surely there must be a

historic inn in this idyllic place? Of course there is. When you enter the **Mayflower,** set below the green and alongside a stream in superb Elizabethan-style stepped gardens, you come face-to-pocketbook with one of the nation's top-ranked inns. (Prices reflect the level of indulgence you can enjoy in sumptuous rooms and top-flight cuisine.) Take a stroll through the gardens, the dining room, the terraces, and the clubby bar. In the library borrow a copy of one of Shakespeare's many works, in keeping with the inn's theme,

First Congregational Church

which is based on the Bard and the Elizabethan era. Try the English-style afternoon tea, complete with dainty sandwiches, tiny cakes, and fine porcelain, if only to see how well the well-heeled traveler can exist in this part of New England. "There is nothing which has yet been contrived by man by which so much happiness is produced as by a good inn," patriot Samuel Johnson once said, and his adage still holds true in this remarkable and affluent place.

It's possible to sense affluence—and its many benefits—everywhere in the village. Washington's most notable institution, for instance, is the **Gunnery School** (*Conn. 47, on the green*) whose sprawling campus occupies most of the valley side below the green. Founder Frederick W. Gunn was born here in 1816, and this later proponent of temperance and the abolishment of slavery established his school in 1850 on the premise that social, physical, and moral development is as important to human evolution as intellectual ability. The relationship between the school and affluence started in the 1880s when former students began building their summer retreats in Washington, transforming it from a small farming village into a place with broader class and cultural qualities.

The celebrated man's name is found everywhere, most notably at the **Gunn Memorial Library and Museum,** comprising a historic house and the village library. The charming 1781 house displays 19th-century room furnishings and a superb collection of historic costumes and textiles; the library's reading room features a painted ceiling that would be the pride of any church.

Referred to by one librarian as "our little Sistine," the style of H. Siddons Mowbray's notable work, richly adorned in gold leaf and sparkling in vivid scarlets and blues, will be immediately recognizable to admirers of New York's Pierpont Morgan Library. Although this work is far more modest than Mowbray's Manhattan murals, it's still a remarkable find in such a secluded village. (The original part of the library was designed in 1908 by Ehrick Rossiter, who designed the first shingle-style mansions.)

But there's more: Seth Warner, who was Ethan Allen's sturdy companion and one of the infamous Green Mountain Boys during the Revolution, was born nearby and is buried beneath a large memorial on the green in nearby Roxbury. Another local notable, William Hamilton Gibson, is commemorated in the library for *Pastoral Days* and *Strolls by Starlight and Sunshine*, superbly illustrated books that reflect his great understanding and love of nature; much of that wisdom and caring was gleaned and developed during hikes through this still wild region.

"It really is great hiking country," said Dominic DeVietro, the new owner of the **Washington Green Deli,** while preparing sandwiches of marinated portobello mushrooms and curried chicken salad. Among the best places to go, according to Dominic and many others, are **Hidden Valley,** an area along the Shepaug River just north of here, and the **Steep Rock Reservation,** near the Institute for American Indian Studies south of town. Just north of all the antique stores at New Preston is **Lake Waramaug,** where you can pause from your walk to fish for a while; the nearby winery also makes a nice visit.

Also worthwhile is the side trip down the steep hill from the green into **Washington Depot,** a rather haphazard huddle of antique shops, bookstores, gas stations, and an oversize Town Hall. Once the "ax-handle capital" of New England, this place is now a thriving art center where you will find, located in one of the few buildings to survive a horrific 1955 flood, the **Washington Art Association,** a charming complex of galleries and studio spaces.

With all their town has to offer, Washingtonians seem to love living here. "If you can find a place nowadays that's affordable!" chimed in one young woman at the Washington Art Association. Well, any place with an inn like the Mayflower and half a dozen or so expensive private schools scattered about the hills is obviously going to have a higher cost of living. In the words of Dominic at the deli, "You pay for what you get 'round here. And what you get is definitely worthy paying for!"   *David Yeadon*

Native American Heritage

Vast gallery spaces, full-scale displays of Algonquian lifeways, a medicine wheel garden, and permanent exhibits on Connecticut Indian history are among the delights at the **Institute for American Indian Studies.** Visitors can see a replicated Algonquian village with tree-bark wigwams and a tribal longhouse, and at the exceptional museum store they can choose from diverse offerings. Unfortunately, much of the institute's collection still sits in vaults. An expansion is under way, but limited funds are frustrating progress.

Travelwise

GETTING THERE

Washington is located in western Connecticut, 45 miles west of Hartford, via US 44 and US 202. The nearest major airport is in Hartford.

GENERAL INFORMATION

Summer and fall are ideal for visits, but late spring and early winter are quieter. Abundant information can be obtained from Washington Depot's **City Hall** (*2 Bryan Plaza, Washington Depot 06794. 860-868 2786*) or the **Washington Business Association** (*P.O. Box 91, Washington Depot 06794. www.washington-ct.com*).

THINGS TO SEE AND DO

Gunn Memorial Library and Museum (*5 Wykeham Rd., on the green. Library 860-868-7586, museum 860-868-7756. Thurs.-Sun p.m.*) Offerings include 19th-century room furnishings, local history exhibits, costumes, and a ceiling mural by H. Siddons Mowbray.

Institute for American Indian Studies (*Curtis Rd., off Conn. 199. 860-868-0518. Call for hours; adm. fee*) See sidebar p. 51.

Walking Contact Steep Rock Association (*860-868-9131*) for information on **Shelter Rock** and **Hidden Valley,** hard-to-find tracts of land that are beloved by locals.

Washington Art Association (*4 Bryan Plaza, Washington Depot. 860-868-2878*) This lively commercial gallery offers studio classes and frequently changing exhibits of works by regional artists.

WHERE TO EAT

Most upscale cuisine is found at the local inns, but the **Washington Green Deli** (*5 Kirby Rd. 860-868-7324. $*) offers gourmet sandwiches and snacks, and the **G.W. Tavern** in Washington Depot (*20 Conn. 47. 860-868-6633. $$*) has a familiar American menu that features excellent hamburgers.

WHERE TO STAY

Boulders (*East Shore Rd., New Preston. 860-868-0541. $$$*) Set below Pinnacle Mountain, the inn's Main House is made out of boulders. It features a lake-view restaurant serving regional cuisine, rooms adorned with antique furnishings, wood-burning fireplaces, and a private lakefront.

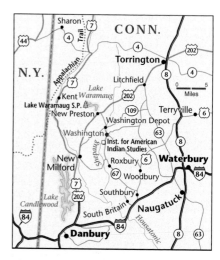

Hopkins Inn (*22 Hopkins Rd., New Preston. 860-868-7295. $$*) The yellow-and-white Italianate inn, with a German-flavored restaurant and menu, sits on a ridge overlooking **Lake Waramaug.** You can even select your own wines from the adjoining **Hopkins Vineyards** (*860-868-7954*).

The Mayflower (*Conn. 47. 860-868-9466. $$$*) In 1920 Harry Van Sinderen used family inheritances to convert his old alma mater, the 1894 Ridge School, into one of the nation's best country inns. It is renowned for its gardens, sumptuous rooms and suites, and gourmet restaurant.

NEARBY PLACES

Kent (*15 miles NW of Washington on US 7. Chamber of Commerce 860-927-1463*) Visit the intriguing **Sloane-Stanley Museum** (*860-927-3849. Mid-May–late Oct. Wed.-Sun.; adm. fee*). Much of the collection contains early American tools gathered by Eric Sloane.

Litchfield (*15 miles NE on US 202. Chamber of Commerce 860-482-6586*) In this wonderfully preserved 18th-century village, see the **Litchfield Historical Society Museum** (*7 South St. 860-567-4501*) and the **Tapping Reeve House and Law School** (*82 South St. 860-567-4501*), America's first law school.

Woodbury Antique Dealers Assoc. (*9 miles SE on Conn. 47*) Stores offer Americana, oriental rugs, antiques, and more.

Sharon

Blessed with broad vistas, this enchanting little community is laid out along a linear village green on a forested ridge. Residents and visitors can look to the west, across valleys and ranges, toward New York State's great Hudson River. Sharon hides its graces modestly. You have to seek to find its theater and museum, its inns and restaurants, and even the celebrated wildlife sanctuary created by the Audubon Society almost half a century ago. But seek you should.

Country road near Sharon

Every year a big debate resumes about the best New England location in which to enjoy fall's colors as they spread southward from Maine into the Connecticut Valley and across the glorious **Litchfield Hills** in the northwestern corner of the state. Here in the Litchfields, a dramatic region of deep forests and tumultuous hills, fall's leaves are deemed spectacular. So, consider this area an ideal base for your fall rambles, and if heritage is also important to you, there are few parts of New England where Yankee history and ingenuity are so evident and so tangible.

Despite the demure and quiet charms of present-day Sharon (incorporated in 1739), the town was a little hotbed of industry and guerrilla-like activities during the Revolution. At a forge a few miles from the village, the redoubtable

Along a Sharon lane

Ethan Allen cast cannon for the Continental Army and gathered together a band of men he called "as good a regiment of marksmen and scalpers as America can afford."

The forges at Sharon turned out a boggling array of products in the heyday of the iron industry in the area. The community's economy was always more diversified than that of adjoining settlements, however, and at one time it produced not only cigars, shoes, and wooden mousetraps but also the famed Hotchkiss rifled cannon projectile; it even briefly raised silkworms on the white mulberry trees that still line Main Street.

Wealth proliferated in this dandified haven of high society, and many citizens became so affluent that they imported stonemasons from Italy to construct exquisitely detailed mansions. Take a stroll from the top of **Main Street,** where the road curves by a small cluster of stores and meanders northward to Lakeville and Salisbury, down the long tree-shaded green. Pass the town hall, the spired church, the small library richly detailed in the Richardsonian Romanesque style, and the Gay-Hoyt House Museum, and you'll be amazed by the showcase of 19th-century architecture, in a range of styles from filigree carpenter-Gothic to dainty Queen Anne and elegant Italianate. You'll complete this first part of the walk at one of the town's most prominent sites, the 1885 **Memorial Clocktower.** Another splendid example of the craftsmanship of those Italian stonemasons, the clocktower is in the same proudly pompous style as the library. But don't end here. The green continues as a broad swath of lawn and trees, with even larger mansions set back in landscaped estates, redolent with wealth and privilege.

"Oh, there's money here," said the spritely lady at the tax collector's office in the town hall across the long green from the library (*very* long—actually over a mile and a half in length). "Lots of celebrity-people, famous artists and actors and whatnot…. They're all big supporters of our theater, just down the hill from the clocktower."

The exhibits at the circa 1775 **Gay-Hoyt House Museum** (one of the few brick houses in town), in addition to its permanent collection of 18th- and 19th-century decorative arts, provide an interesting overview of Sharon's transformation from wild forest to today's quiet town. Since Sharon's earliest days as a town, one feature has remained constant—the gorgeous, linear green that sets the community apart from New England towns having more traditional greens with square layouts.

At one point in its history, Sharon was a frantic little manufacturing center, but that is no longer the case. Today's relatively peaceful, mellow town is a comfort to frazzled outsiders and lovers of small towns. It's an ideal place to while away a day or two, and such dawdling could include a trip to nearby **Salisbury,** a historic community with a large village green and the **White Hart.** Described as a "fabulous lodging" by *Gourmet* magazine, this hotel includes an Olde English-style tavern. Once renowned as the arsenal of the Revolution, Salisbury's Mount Riga produced America's finest iron ore during the 18th century and was a great seething mining camp for more than a century. The camp attracted Swiss and Russian immigrants whose impact on the region, often depicted in legends about black magic and evil-doings, still permeates the town; today, local mishaps and strange sightings are sometimes blamed on the spirits of the early settlers. But like Sharon, Salisbury has left its industrial heritage far behind and now attracts travelers and "comers-in" with its many charms.

A second must-see place on the outskirts of Sharon is the **Sharon Audubon Center,** a 758-acre wildlife sanctuary. It is precisely what Keyo and Clement Ford envisioned when they donated their Bog Meadow Farm—an estate of forests, streams, ponds, and old fields—over 40 years ago. Now there are 11 miles of trails through the various habitats; herb, wildflower, and butterfly and hummingbird gardens; and numerous school and adult-oriented programs. The most popular "live animal" activity is the Wild Bird Rehabilitation Program, which treats as many as 200 injured or orphaned birds annually and returns them to the wild. "Gets pretty lively round here," said one of the docents, "but it's so peaceful you can't help but relax." The same could be said of Sharon itself!   *David Yeadon*

West Cornwall

Amid this cozy crafts enclave near Sharon is a covered bridge that dates back to 1837. Drive through its shadowy interior and you'll come out by Ian Ingersoll's woodworking shop and showroom. He and his handful of craftsmen construct the fine, Shaker-influenced furniture that is his trademark. "This town is always either closing down or crammed with new businesses," Ian observed. "We just lost our Brookside Bistro and a couple of other stores." So, go enjoy this little cluster of houses, stores, and shops while there's still something left to enjoy!

Travelwise

GETTING THERE

Sharon sits on a high ridge in northwest
Connecticut, about 25 miles northwest of
Torrington via Conn. 4. The Taconic Parkway
in New York State is 20 miles southwest,
through Amenia and Millbrook. The closest
major airports are in Albany, New York, and
Hartford, Connecticut.

GENERAL INFORMATION

Summer and fall are the best times to
visit, although the Litchfield Hills possess
year-round charm and are also ideal for
nonpeak-season sojourns in the spring.
Abundant information on the region is
readily available at stores, hotels, and
restaurants and from the **Litchfield Hills
Visitors Bureau** *(P.O. Box 968, Litchfield
06759. 860-567-4506. www.litchfieldhills.com).*
More specific information on Sharon
can be obtained from the **Northwest
Connecticut's Chamber of Commerce**
(860-482-6586).

THINGS TO SEE

Beardsley Gardens *(157 Gay St.
860-364-0727. Closed Jan.-Feb.)* More than
1,500 varieties of plants exist in a lovely
setting that is utterly enticing to the
gardener in us all.

Gay-Hoyt House Museum *(18 Main St.
860-364-5688. Call for hours; adm. fee)*
Remarkable tools, paintings, furniture, and
other 18th- and 19th-century artifacts are on
display in this lovely 1775 brick colonial house.
Also take time to see the enchanting garden.

Sharon Audubon Center *(325 Conn. 4,
860-364-0520. Adm. fee)* This peaceful and
varied wildlife sanctuary features a bird
rehabilitation program that cares for injured
and orphaned birds and returns them to
wild. The center also maintains ponds,
woodlands, and 11 miles of trails.

WHERE TO EAT

Bulls Bridge Inn *(US 7, Kent. 860-927-1000.
$$)* Near a historic covered bridge, the inn
features grilled entrées, a salad bar, and a
taproom that is rich in Old World ambience.

Fife 'n' Drum *(US 7, Kent. 860-927-3509.
$$)* Enjoy the celebrated American cuisine
served up here.

WHERE TO STAY

1890 Colonial Bed and Breakfast
(150 Gay St. 860-364-0436. $$) An elegant
B&B, this 1890 home has 5 acres and a
remarkably eclectic decor of Japanese,
Indian, and Etruscan artifacts.

Fairland Bed and Breakfast *(27 S. Main
St. 860-364-0081. $)* This 1840 home is
surrounded by 18 scenic acres.

White Hart *(Village green, Salisbury. 860-435-
0030 or 800-832-0041. $$)* The quintessential
country hotel is renowned for outstanding
cuisine at the American Grill, its luxury
accommodations, and its Olde English tavern.

NEARBY PLACES

Housatonic Meadows State Park *(1 mile
N of Conn. 4 on US 7. 860-672-6772)* Trails
wind through pristine woodlands. Fly-fishers
will want to head straight for the shallow,
cold, and swift Housatonic River.

Kent Falls State Park *(US 7.
860-927-3238. Parking fee)* See the
magnificent 200-foot-high falls and enjoy
hiking, picnicking, and fishing opportunities.

Macedonia Brook State Park *(Conn. 341,
4 miles NW of Kent off US 7. 860-927-3238)*
Go hiking, fishing, picnicking, and camping
amid the park's 2,000 acres.

West Cornwall (See sidebar p. 55)
Workshops at this crafts enclave include
Ian Ingersoll's *(860-672-6334),* for Shaker-
inspired furniture; and the **Cornwall Bridge
Pottery** *(860-672-6545).*

MID-ATLANTIC

Cutchogue

Leave the traffic jams and congestion behind as you head east along Long Island's quiet North Fork, a thin strip of land surrounded on three sides by water. Residents have long made their living off the land and the sea, and tiny Cutchogue is typical of the villages here. Its main road (N.Y. 25) is dotted with wineries, farm stands, and antique shops. Its back roads, which wind down to Long Island Sound and the sea, offer visitors a hidden world of tidal estuaries and shallow creeks teeming with birds and marine life.

Fort Corchaug

Thanks to noted anthropologist Dr. Ralph Solecki, who lived in Cutchogue when he was a boy in the 1930s, we know much about Fort Corchaug—the Fort Knox of its era. A rectangular area about 210 feet by 160 feet, the fort was surrounded by tree trunks embedded in shallow trenches. The wall nearest the creek was double-palisaded for much of its length. During his excavations, Dr. Solecki unearthed articles indicating that the Corchaug Indians, who lived in the most important wampum-producing region of 17th-century America, traded with Europeans long before the town was founded.

Throughout the town's 350-year history, its fortunes have ebbed and flowed like the tides of Peconic Bay and Long Island Sound, which border it. Over the years its people made their living scalloping, oystering, crabbing, and potato farming. Then, in the early '70s, Alex and Louisa Hargrave planted a crop that changed the face of Cutchogue, as well as much of the rest of the East End's North Fork. Following in the footsteps of Moses Fournier (aka "Moses the Frenchman"), who operated a thriving vineyard here in colonial times, they planted 17 acres of their former potato farm with Cabernet Sauvignon grapes. Today, six of the North Fork's 21 vineyards are in Cutchogue, and the potato has been eclipsed by the grape.

One reason vineyards thrive on the North Fork is the sandy soil, which permits excellent drainage. The other reason is what has made Long Island's East End a tourist mecca for many years: The island has about 220 days of sun each year, the most on the northeastern seaboard. Until recently, most vacationers had flocked to upscale South Fork resorts such as the Hamptons and Montauk. But now they're discovering that tiny towns like Cutchogue, along Long Island's North Fork, offer more tranquil, and often less costly, alternatives.

The wineries along N.Y. 25—Cutchogue's main road—and County Rd. 48 are major attractions. Most offer tours and have tasting rooms (several, such as Hargrave and Bedell Cellars, greet visitors for tastings in converted potato barns). There are few nicer ways to spend a summer's afternoon than drifting from one winery to another, sampling vintages and then sitting in the sun, nibbling cheese, and watching grapes ripen on the vines.

Long Island Sound

The wineries range in size and offerings, and visitors without a hollow leg might want to pick a few to visit in advance. The "Wine Press," available at liquor stores, chambers of commerce, the local tourist information center, or by mail, describes many of them and tells what varieties they specialize in. Jo-Ann Perry, owner and operator of **Vintage Tours,** can help visitors who are undecided about which wineries to tour, or who just want to sit back, enjoy the scenery, and see the sights: She tailors her tours according to individual interests and tastes, and she can even include an elegant picnic lunch.

First-time visitors to Cutchogue often get so caught up in winery-hopping that they forget the town has many other fascinating places to explore. When the first Europeans—a small band of Puritans—arrived on the North Fork in 1640, they were greeted by the Corchaug Indians, who had settled here many years before and built a sturdy fort on present-day Downs' Creek, just to the southwest of the village. There's talk of preserving what little remains of the fort, but you'll have to rely heavily on your imagination as you look over Downs' Creek Estuary where it once stood. Today's inhabitants include numerous species of waterfowl, including ospreys, green herons, and egrets; and because it's a migratory flyway, the estuary is a favorite spot for bird-watchers throughout the year.

The Corchaug Indians harvested whelk shells and clam shells here to make wampum, and today the waters are still a good spot to go clamming (be sure to get a license at the Town Hall, *631-765-1800*). If you want to explore the estuary by canoe or kayak, give **Eagle's Neck Paddling Company** or **Matt-A-Mar Marina** a call. They can provide a car carrier for your rented craft or deliver it to the spot.

The Old House, Cutchogue

Cutchogue's oldest house—and one of the oldest English houses in New York State—was actually built 5 miles down the road, in Southold, in 1649, by an English immigrant; it was moved piecemeal to its present site in 1660. Today **The Old House,** a national historic landmark, anchors a complex of buildings on the village green. The 1840s **Old School House,** Cutchogue's first district school, holds mementos from a bygone era, as does the circa 1701 restored **Wickham Farmhouse.** In **The Old Burying Ground,** 18th-century stones record family names from Cutchogue's earliest days.

Wickham has long been a popular name in these parts: Three generations of Wickhams lived in The Old House. Today their descendants own **Wickham's Fruit Farm,** just the place to pick up supplies for a picnic lunch. Another might be **Braun's Seafood Company,** the East End's leading distributor of seafood. The company, which processes as much as 100,000 pounds of fresh fish and 30,000 lobsters each week in summer, boils shrimp and lobster to go.

One of the most delightful spots to picnic is on the small beach in New Suffolk overlooking Robins Island. A marker on First Street, near the beach, designates the spot where, in 1899, modern submarine inventor John Philip Holland tested the S.S. *Holland VI,* which the U.S. Navy purchased in 1900 to inaugurate its submarine fleet. Peconic Bay's most productive scallop beds were established nearby, and baymen brought their harvest to the numerous scallop houses here. If you do not have the time to assemble a picnic, **Legends** serves up delicious fresh fish (the steamed clams are succulent) and desserts that have become legendary.

If you're looking for potatoes, you can find farmers who still grow the famous spuds. And if you're looking for Long Island's answer to Napa Valley, you've certainly come to the right place. Add striking seascapes and some colorful local history, and you're in for a wonderful escape.   *William G. Scheller*

Travelwise

GETTING THERE

Cutchogue is on the North Fork of Long Island, about 100 miles from New York City via I-495 (Long Island Expressway) and N.Y. 25 (Main Rd.). Trains and buses service the town. Cross Sound Ferry, Inc. *(Dock Rd., Orient Point. 631-323-2743)* operates between Orient Point, at the tip of the North Fork, and New London, Connecticut. The nearest airport is Long Island MacArthur in Islip.

GENERAL INFORMATION

Cutchogue is lovely year-round. Contact the **North Fork Promotion Council** *(Box 1865, Southold 11971. 631-298-5757. www.northfork.org).* The **Cutchogue-New Suffolk Historical Council** *(P.O. Box 361, Cutchogue 11935. 631-734-7122)* has a good walking tour brochure.

THINGS TO SEE AND DO

Boat Rentals Contact Eagle's Neck Paddling Company *(49295 Main Rd., Southold. 631-765-3502)* for kayaks and canoes. Capt. Marty's *(1st St. and King St., New Suffolk. 631-734-6852)* rents aluminum skiffs. Matt-A-Mar Marina *(Wickham Rd., Mattituck. 631-298-4739)* has rentals and tours. Strong's Marine *(Camp Mineola Rd., Mattituck. 631-298-4770)* offers powerboats, skiing, and tubing packages.

Helicopter Rides Fly over Long Island's East End with Eastern Flight Services *(2111 Smithtown Ave., Ronkonkoma. 631-588-2780).*

The Old House Society and the Cutchogue/New Suffolk Historic Council *(Village green, Main Rd., Cutchogue. 631-734-7122. Late June–early Sept., tours Sat., Sun., and Mon. p.m.)* Featured are five historic buildings, including the 1649 Old House.

Wineries Try Bedell Cellars *(Main Rd. 631-734-7537),* Gristina Vineyards *(24385 Main Rd. 631-734-7089),* and Pellegrini Vineyards *(23005 Main Rd. 631-734-4111).* Jo-Ann Perry at Vintage Tours *(P.O. Box 143, Peconic 11958. 631-765-4689)* offers customized van tours of the vineyards and the area. Each winery in Cutchogue sells its special vintages.

SHOPPING

The North Fork is dotted with antique shops, such as **Antiques & Old Lace** *(31935 Main St., Cutchogue. 631-734-6462),*

with more than 7,000 square feet of antiques.

Braun's Seafood Company *(Main Rd., Cutchogue. 631-734-6700)* Be sure to try their steamed lobster and clams.

Wickham's Fruit Farm *(Main Rd. 631-734-6441. Closed Sun.)* Vegetables and berries in season, as well as baked goods.

ANNUAL EVENT

Garden Tour *(Early June. Cutchogue-New Suffolk Chamber of Commerce 631-734-2335. Adm. fee)* The local tour books up well in advance.

WHERE TO EAT

Cutchogue Diner *(Main Rd., Cutchogue. 631-734-9056. $)* Three meals daily and delicious homemade desserts.

Legends *(835 1st St., New Suffolk. 631-734-5123. $$)* Fresh fish, sweet clams, and legendary desserts.

WHERE TO STAY

Top O' The Mornin' *(26350 Main Rd., Cutchogue. 631-734-5143. $$)* This historic farmhouse offers three charming rooms and Irish hospitality.

NEARBY PLACES

Greenport *(North Fork Promotion Council 631-298-5757)* In the North Fork's largest town, you can ride the antique carousel, then take the ferry to **Shelter Island** *(Chamber of Commerce 631-749-0399).* This little island retreat remains secluded from modern times. Splendid beaches sprawl along its western shore, and the **Mashomack Nature Preserve** is on its eastern side.

Cold Spring

Travel up the storied Hudson River to a town that loomed large in colonial times and during the Revolutionary and Civil Wars. Although the U.S. Military Academy at West Point stands just across the river, Cold Spring has long since beaten its swords into plowshares. It has become a favorite weekend retreat for antique lovers and enthusiasts of Hudson Valley lore.

In the 19th century, the roar of artillery resounded through the Hudson Highlands for almost 50 years as workers from Cold Spring's West Point Foundry tested their cannon by firing across the Hudson at Storm King Mountain on the western shore. Today's Highlands echo with the whistles of trains streaking along the eastern shore to and from New York City, stopping at Cold Spring to pick up and discharge commuters and visitors. The entire picturesque downtown of this village is a national historic district, and its Victorian Main Street is lined with antique shops that sell everything from spittoons to shillelaghs.

Cold Spring itself is something of an antique, albeit a very nicely polished one. It husbands its history carefully, proud of the days when it was one of the chief armorers of the United States. Cold Spring was once an obscure colonial hamlet whose name supposedly derives from a spring that provided drinking water for passing ships; there are those who say, though, that George Washington christened the site after enjoying a satisfying draught.

In 1817, Cold Spring's fortunes began to rise with the establishment of West Point Foundry by Gouverneur Kemble, who became known as the Father of Cold Spring. (Gouverneur was his first name, not his title.) Although the foundry turned out iron and brass products as varied as dumb-bells, window weights, structural and ornamental ironwork, and even America's first steam locomotive, *The Best Friend*, it was primarily a manufacturer of heavy ordnance for the U.S. military.

Its most famous product was the Parrott Gun, invented by foundry superintendent Robert T. Parrott, who applied the principle of rifling—the spiraling grooves in rifle barrels that give spin and increased accuracy to bullets—to large field pieces. A reproduction Parrott

Presidential Visit

Back when Cold Spring's West Point Foundry was turning out Parrott Guns for the Union Army, President Abraham Lincoln visited the facility on an inspection tour. Anxious to demonstrate the impressive distance and accuracy of the cannon that bore his name, Col. Robert Parrott fired across the river at a formation called Crow's Nest on Storm King Mountain. But the President had probably been impressed enough for one day: "I'm confident you can hit that mountain over there," he reportedly told Colonel Parrott, "so suppose we get something to eat. I'm hungry."

Storm King Mountain from Stony Point

Gun overlooks the Hudson at a riverfront park on West Street across from the Hudson House Inn.

The foundry's success made Cold Spring a company town. Society revolved around the foundry's proprietors and their Army officer colleagues, a fact borne out in one of the most famous paintings of the Hudson River school, "A Pic-Nic on the Hudson" by Thomas Pritchard Rossiter. This splendidly composed grouping of Cold Spring's Civil War-era, military-and-industrial complex now hangs in the town's **Julia L. Butterfield Memorial Library.** It includes both Gouverneur Kemble and Robert Parrott, as well as an unidentified woman believed by some historians to be Emily Warren, who later married Brooklyn Bridge builder George Washington Roebling and helped see the great span to completion. The Roeblings are buried in **Cold Spring Cemetery.**

Business at the foundry fell off after the Civil War, and it closed for good in 1911. Cold Spring remained in the economic doldrums for many years, but it put itself back on the map in the 1980s when it became a magnet for antique dealers. Today there are more than 20 shops, among them dealers specializing in period prints and maps, many relating to the Hudson River; mission oak furniture; restored trunks and telephones; 19th-century lighting fixtures; American Victorian sterling silver; and beads and country crafts. Antiquing is hungry work, and downtown Cold Spring is liberally supplied with places to catch a bite between finds.

Visitors can also learn about Cold Spring's history without buying pieces of it. The Putnam County Historical Society oversees the **Foundry School Museum** in the original foundry schoolhouse. The main exhibit focuses on the West Point Foundry, about which there is an excellent film. The museum also offers exhibits on other aspects of local history and a collection of Hudson River school paintings, including "The Gun Foundry" by John Ferguson Weir.

Not far away, adjacent to the National Audubon Society's **Constitution Marsh Wildlife Sanctuary,** are the grounds of the foundry itself, part of the 85-acre Foundry Cove Historic Preserve. The only surviving structure is the 1865 Office Building, which is undergoing gradual restoration by Scenic Hudson, a nonprofit group. The preserve encompasses **Foundry Cove,** providing wonderful views of the river and nearby Constitution Island.

Close by is the 1833 **Greek Revival Chapel of Our Lady of Restoration,** built by foundry workers on land given by Gouverneur Kemble for a place of worship. It is now used for nondenominational services, memorials, and musicals.

About a mile south of town stands **Boscobel,** a historic house museum recalling the days of the old Dutch landed aristocracy. Begun in 1804 and completed four years later, the federal-style mansion originally stood 15 miles away in Montrose, New York. Nearly demolished in the 1950s (it was sold to a wrecker for $35!), Boscobel was moved to its present location through the efforts of local preservationists. Its sumptuous furnishings offer a glimpse of the life enjoyed by Hudson Valley grandees two centuries ago.

Cold Spring has meant different things to different eras: a place where sailors plying America's Rhine picked up fresh water; a state-of-the-art link in a young nation's defense industry; a getaway for today's sight-seers and antiquers.

William G. Scheller

Travelwise

GETTING THERE

Cold Spring is located in the mid-Hudson Valley, north of New York City. From I-84 take US 9 south to N.Y. 301 into town. The Metro-North Hudson Railroad *(800-METRO-INFO)* services the eastern shore. The village is within walking distance of the train station. For transportation, call 914-265-TAXI. The nearest major airport is JFK in New York City.

GENERAL INFORMATION

The town is at its loveliest and liveliest in spring, summer, and fall. For information, contact the **Cold Spring/Garrison Area Chamber of Commerce** *(Box 36, Cold Spring 10516. 914-265-3200)* and **Putnam County Visitors Bureau** *(110 Old Route 6, Building #3, Carmel 10512. 914-225-0381).* "A Heritage Way Walking Tour" is available at the Foundry School Museum.

Cold Spring's main thoroughfare

THINGS TO SEE AND DO

Boat Tours Contact Outdoor Sports *(141 Main St.. 914-265-2048)* for supervised kayak tours of the Hudson and Constitution Marsh, sailing lessons, and boat rides. Hudson River Adventures *(Newburgh Landing, Newburgh. 914-782-0685)* offers river tours on the *Pride of the Hudson.* The two-hour tour offered by Constitution Island Association *(914-446-8676. June–late Oct. Wed.-Thurs.)* includes a visit to Constitution Island, departing from South Dock, West Point.

Boscobel *(1601 N.Y. 9D. 914-265-3638. Guided tours April-Dec. daily except Tues.; adm. fee)* A 19th-century mansion that has been superbly restored and richly furnished, it sits on magnificent grounds.

Foundry School Museum *(63 Chestnut St. 914-265-4010. Call for schedule. Closed Jan.-Feb.; adm. fee)* Well-prepared exhibits focus on local history.

Hiking The former home and landscaped grounds of industrial designer Russell Wright, **Manitoga** *(N.Y. 9D, 6 miles S of town. 914-424-3812)* has 4 miles of paths. **Hudson Highlands State Park** *(Off N.Y. 9D)* is an undeveloped 5,700-acre wilderness preserve that offers miles of trails, including one to Breakneck Ridge, with views of the valley. The **Appalachian Trail** is only a few miles away.

Julia L. Butterfield Memorial Library *(Morris Ave. 914-265-3040. Call for schedule)* Be sure to take a moment to view "A Pic-Nic on the Hudson," a well-known painting by Thomas Pritchard Rossiter.

Walking Tours Members of the Putnam County Historical Society host walking tours of the town every Sunday from May to mid-November. The tours leave from 72 Main Street. Donations are welcome.

SHOPPING

Country Clocks *(142 Main St. 914-265-3361)* A unique collection of clocks are for sale. On weekends, many of them can be heard chiming on the hour.

Oh Fudge! *(5 Stone St. 914-265-4493)* This establishment prepares homemade chocolates and fudge. Visitors relax on the outdoor patio, enjoying delicious varieties of chocolate-flavored, coffee-based lattes and frozen drinks.

ANNUAL EVENTS

Hudson Valley Shakespeare Festival *(1601 N.Y. 9D, Boscobel. 914-265-7858)*

During July and August, a professional summer stock troupe performs on the grounds of the Boscobel mansion.

WHERE TO EAT

Cathryn Dolcigno Tuscan Grill *(91 Main St. 914-265-5582. $$)* The menu features northern Italian cuisine.

Northgate at Dockside Harbor *(1 North St. 914-265-5555. Early May–late Oct. Tues.-Sun.; $$)* This restaurant's specialty is seafood that is served at the water's edge.

Plumbush Inn *(N.Y. 9D. 914-265-3904. Jan.-March Thurs.-Sun., Wed.-Sun. rest of year; $$)* Fine continental cuisine with Swiss touches is served in eight cozy dining rooms, three of them furnished with wood-burning fireplaces.

WHERE TO STAY

Hudson House Inn *(2 Main St. 914-265-9355. $$$)* New York's second oldest hostelry, the inn overlooks the Hudson River and offers up-to-date amenities and an excellent dining room. Some rooms have balconies.

Pig Hill Inn *(73 Main St. 914-265-9247. $$$)* This village B&B offers nine rooms, some with private baths and working fireplaces. Guests can enjoy breakfast, lunch, and tea served in the gardens.

NEARBY PLACES

Clarence Fahnestock Memorial State Park *(N.Y. 301, Carmel. 914-225-7207)* The park's 10,000-plus acres encompass an extensive trail system and several lakes for fishing and swimming.

Constitution Island *(Ferry leaves from South Dock, at bottom of Williams Rd., West Point. 914-446-8676)* Visitors with an interest in literature will enjoy seeing the 15-room Victorian home of writers Susan and Anna Warner, while history buffs will want to take in the ruins of Revolutionary War fortifications.

Constitution Marsh Wildlife Sanctuary *(914-265-2601)* This 270-acre preserve is home to a variety of wildlife; a trail offers Hudson River views.

United States Military Academy *(West Point. 914-938-4011)* Highlights include the museum, Revolutionary War Fort Putnam, and concerts by the academy's band.

Cooperstown

Head to the south shores of New York State's Otsego Lake, source of the Susquehanna River, to find a town honored as the source of America's National Pastime. Make a sumptuous inn your headquarters as you immerse yourself in baseball past and present, step into a time capsule of rural life circa 1840, and pay homage to the roots of American art and literature.

Victorian-style lamp post

By now, it's almost beside the point whether the game of baseball was devised by Abner Doubleday at Cooperstown, New York, in 1839. Few scholars today doubt that baseball was played, in one form or another, long before Doubleday—later a Civil War general—and his friends took to the fields around Cooperstown with a bat and ball. What matters more is that a century after that first game was supposedly played, Cooperstown became the home of the National Baseball Hall of Fame and Museum, America's best-loved sports shrine.

It's difficult to imagine a more appropriate setting in which to celebrate the quintessentially American sport of baseball. Cooperstown personifies the small town environment in which the summer game evolved. All the glories of the big leagues ultimately hearken back to places like this.

Of course, there was a Cooperstown before baseball. This village set in the rolling hills of upcountry New York State has close affiliations with yet another facet of American iconography and myth: It is named for William Cooper, father of eminent American novelist James Fenimore Cooper. The elder Cooper moved here from New Jersey in the early 19th century, and the future novelist spent his boyhood wandering through the woods he later immortalized in his *Leatherstocking Tales*. (He also chose to retire here, after many years away.) The "Glimmerglass" of the tales is, in fact, Otsego Lake, whose wooded shores Cooper might not find unfamiliar today—except for the thriving town at its southern end that bears his family's name.

For all the federal and Greek Revival houses—many of them sumptuous inns—in its residential neighborhoods, downtown Cooperstown has the look of a bustling small town of the early 1900s. Three- and four-story brick buildings line the main streets, and from their appearance you would expect their ground-level facades to house drugstores, soda fountains, dry goods shops, hardware stores, and a Frank Capra–style bank or two. Look closer. The merchants of Cooperstown seem almost obsessively devoted to a single commodity: baseball memorabilia. Hoping to find a Brooks Robinson rookie card, a ball autographed by Pete Rose, a Brooklyn Dodgers cap, a jersey from a long-gone Negro League team, or a genuine Louisville Slugger? They're all

Cooperstown on Otsego Lake

here, within the space of a few blocks.

The memorabilia and collectible shops are just a prelude to the main event, however. The **National Baseball Hall of Fame and Museum** occupies a stately Georgian Revival home on Main Street, flanked, appropriately, by an old-fashioned scoreboard carrying the latest major league scores. The Hall of Fame is truly a place that is more than the sum of its parts. It would be easy to catalog its impressive holdings: the bats, gloves, and balls associated with the Olympian records of the sport; exhibits chronicling the evolution of rules, playing styles, dominant teams, ballparks, and uniforms; and such interesting artifacts as the trusty Underwood typewriter of sportswriter Grantland Rice. But this place isn't baseball's "attic"; it is baseball's cathedral, where the spirit of the sport lives. At its heart, of course, is the hall of bronze plaques bearing the names, likenesses, and accomplishments of the game's greatest players.

What if you're not one of Cooperstown's Main Street throng, suited up in the colors of your favorite team as if the game were just about to start? No matter; you'll find more than baseball here. Head out past the stately **Otesaga hotel,** with its broad apron of lawn sloping toward the lake, to the Farmers' Museum and the Fenimore Art Museum. The **Farmers' Museum** offers an

accurate re-creation of upstate life 150 years ago. Period structures collected from throughout the region were moved here to form a working village, complete with print shop, general store, tavern, smithy, pharmacy, farm buildings, and more. Craftspeople demonstrate their skills, and the barnyard is filled with rare heritage breeds of farm animals. You can also visit a Seneca log house, circa 1780, that originally stood on New York's Tonawanda Indian Reserve. It's furnished with the belongings of a typical Seneca family of the era. A special attraction at the museum is the Cardiff Giant, the enormous stone figure fobbed off as a petrified prehistoric man in a 19th-century hoax.

Across the street, the **Fenimore Art Museum** occupies the Fenimore House, a 1930s mansion built on the site of James Fenimore Cooper's home. Inside you'll find a trove of art and Americana, including the Thaw Collection of American Indian arts; 200,000 prints documenting a century of work by New York photographers; a series of busts made from the life masks of prominent early 19th-century Americans; and one of the best collections of Hudson River school and genre paintings anywhere.

All in all, there's so much to see and do in Cooperstown that you might want to take your trip into extra innings.   *William G. Scheller*

Travelwise

GETTING THERE

Cooperstown, in south-central New York State, is 70 miles west of Albany and just 30 miles south of the New York State Thruway (I-90). Adirondack Trailways/Pine Hill Trailways *(800-858-8555)* serves Cooperstown. Major airports are in Albany, Syracuse, and Binghamton.

GENERAL INFORMATION

Spring, summer, and fall draw the most crowds. Winter can be a magical time: The town decorates lavishly for Christmas and hosts a Winter Carnival each February on the Presidents' birthday weekend. The **Cooperstown Chamber of Commerce** *(31 Chestnut St., Cooperstown 13326. 607-547-9983)* has a wealth of information on the region, as does the **Otsego County Chamber of Commerce** *(12 Carbon St., Oneonta 13820. 800-843-3394).* Parking is at a premium in Cooperstown: A Village Trolley transports visitors to major points of interest from free perimeter parking areas on N.Y. 28 and 80.

THINGS TO SEE AND DO

Boat Tours and Rentals Lake Otsego Boat Tours *(Lake Front Park. 607-547-5295. May–mid-Oct.)* takes visitors aboard a fully restored, turn-of-the-20th-century, hand-crafted boat. Sam Smith's Boatyard *(West Lake Rd., off N.Y. 80. 607-547-2543. April-Sept.)* rents boats from skiffs to pontoon barges.

Farmers' Museum *(N.Y. 80. 607-547-1450 or 888-547-1450. Daily June-Sept., Tues.-Sun. April-May and Oct.-Nov.; adm. fee)* See living history exhibits.

Fenimore Art Museum *(Lake Rd., N.Y. 80. 607-547-1400 or 888-547-1450. Daily June-Sept., Tues.-Sun. April-May and Oct.-Dec.; adm. fee)* View a superb collection of American art.

National Baseball Hall of Fame and Museum *(Main St. 607-547-7200 or 888-Hall-of-Fame. Adm. fee)* The greatest players and moments in baseball are honored.

Train Rides The Cooperstown & Charlotte Valley Railroad *(N.Y. 28. 607-432-2429)* offers a 16-mile, round-trip ride through the countryside to Milford.

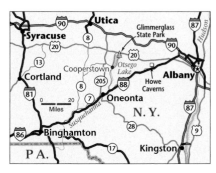

ANNUAL EVENTS

National Baseball Hall of Fame Game and Induction *(3rd weekend in July. 607-547-9983)* The ceremony, which is free to the public, is followed by the Hall of Fame game at Doubleday Field.

Governor Clinton Canoe Regatta *(Mem. Day weekend. 607-547-9983)* The 70-mile race begins here at the headwaters of the Susquehanna River and ends in Bainbridge, New York.

WHERE TO EAT

Blue Mingo Grill *(Sam Smith's Boatyard, West Lake Rd., off N.Y. 80. 607-547-7496. Closed in winter. $$)* Inspired international cuisine is served lakeside at lunch and dinner.

Gabriella's on the Square *(161 Main St. 607-547-8000. $$)* A creative menu features Continental favorites served in a casual yet elegant setting.

WHERE TO STAY

Cooper Inn *(Main St. at Chestnut St. 607-547-2567 or 800-348-6222. $$$)* This handsome, early 1800s federal-style manor house includes 15 rooms and suites. Guests can use facilities at the Otesaga.

Landmark Inn *(64 Chestnut St. 607-547-7225. $$)* This elegantly appointed, 1857 Victorian is just a short walk from downtown and the National Baseball Hall of Fame and Museum. Breakfast is a standout.

The Otesaga *(60 Lake St. 607-547-9931 or 800-348-6222. $$$)* Overlooking Lake Otsego, the 1909 resort has two fine restaurants, a renowned golf course, a pool, and canoes.

Wellsboro

Set amid the Endless Mountains and serving as an ideal base for trips and hikes to nearby Pine Creek Gorge (Pennsylvania's Grand Canyon), Wellsboro comes as a welcome interlude along the narrow, winding, and hectic US 6. Here among Victorian houses and a main street reminiscent of the 1950s, you can pause, stroll across the manicured town green, and slip into a soda fountain and bobbysocks serendipity, *Mayberry*-style. There's a small town ambience you'll carry with you as you explore the forested worlds beyond.

At the Wellsboro Diner

Surrounded by superb natural features and boasting a spacious green and maple-lined main street graced by retro gas lamps, Wellsboro is a bit of an anachronism. At first glance the 19th-century **Penn Wells Hotel,** the coy green **Wellsboro Diner** (an authentic 1939 creation) on the corner of East Avenue, the fifties flavor of **Dunhan's** department store, and the Victorians rising beyond the columned courthouse suggest a place content to nestle among the wooded hills away from the traffic on nearby US 6. Closer inspection, however, reveals a cluster of motels, garish gas stations, and junk food outlets at the edge of town. The modern world is obviously trying to muscle its way in, but, as an elderly resident remarked over huge hamburgers at the diner: "Nothing much really changes in Wellsboro. The town was settled by a bunch of stubborn New Englanders back in the early 1800s at a time when this area was a popular haven for Utopian pioneer cults. Seems what was good enough for them is fine with us."

Pine Creek Gorge

And that's what most outsiders sense—all those "flatlanders" and "ridgerunners" who flock through the town on their way to enjoy trout fishing, wild turkey hunting, and the glories of the Endless Mountains and the Pine Creek Gorge. Those who decide to rest here a while are calmed and coddled by the town's many charms, some of them rather curious. In the middle of the elm-shaded green, for example, edged by churches, small houses, and B&Bs (one visitor called the richly adorned interior of Nelle Rounsaville-Provost's **La Petite Auberge** a "Francophile connoisseur's dream") stands a large fountain sculpture of Wynken, Blynken, and Nod bouncing through the "sea of dew" in their wooden shoe. This delightfully unexpected relief from traditional town-green adornments of long-forgotten notables, stern and censorial in bronze poses on marble plinths, was apparently given to the town by an admirer back in the '30s, and it has become one of Wellsboro's beloved icons. No vandalism, no graffiti here, just the words of that evocative poem and the look of excitement on the three little faces.

There's also an unusual memorial on the green. Characters unfettered by the chains of conventional society are not usually the subject of town park plaques, but a welcome exception was made in the case of Nessmuk. To an admiring biographer, George Washington Sears—Nessmuk's real name—was a Thoreau-spirited adventurer, woodsman, canoeist, seaman, cobbler, writer, poet, and conservationist; he was a protester "against social injustice, yet a dedicated American patriot…his was a voice in the wilderness, the voice of a rebel in the woods." Nessmuk's verbal and published tirades, usually directed at 19th-century social and environmental degradations, became increasingly focused on lumbering practices that denuded mountains of pine and hemlock and decimated their trout streams. Turn-of-the-20th-century photographs confirm the devastation: The land for miles around Pine Creek was stark and lunarlike. Fortunately, the subsequent collapse of local lumbering allowed the natural regrowth of forests into today's splendid neo-wilderness, but the words of Nessmuk's poem "October" remind us of the ongoing need to nurture our natural wonders:

> *For brick and mortar breed filth and crime*
> *And death stalks in on the struggling crowd*
> *But he shuns the shadow of oak and pine.*

You can still sense Nessmuk's spirit in today's town. Careful conservation has enabled the retention of most of the fine Victorians, particularly along Main Street. Some have been converted into attractive B&Bs, most notably the **Blue Moon Inn,** where famous folk artist Susan Clickner has her studio and gallery. Chester Place has been reincarnated as the **Green Free Library** at 134 Main (beside it is the contemporary **Gmeiner Art and Cultural Center**); the **Robinson House,** residence of the local bank's founder, is now home to the Tioga County Historical Society's exhibits and period room displays. The elegant 1887 **Jesse Robinson Manor** *(120 Main St.)* was the town's original B&B. The 1885 **Walrath and Coolidge House** *(126 Main St.),* built for law offices, has been maintained since 1976 as the local funeral home.

Wellsboro is an easy place to know and like. The diner is still the focal point of town for chatting and gossiping, as it has been for over 60 years. Across the road, the stately dining rooms and low buffet prices of the Penn Wells Hotel appeal to businessmen and flatlanders. Next door, the **Arcadia Theater**—in 1929 the first in the state to show talkies—is a community-owned operation offering popular weekend dinner shows. At the Howey Family's **Steak House,** which offers a huge Porterhouse, you might hear someone discussing the last "really big" crime—the robbery of the Robinson's First National Bank of Wellsboro on September 16, 1874.

One elderly resident summed it up neatly: "To us Wellsboroans, New York and those other East Coast cities are another universe."   *David Yeadon*

Pennsylvania's Grand Canyon

Ten miles from town you're deep in the Endless Mountains and woodlands protected by an array of state parks and forests. To the north and east of town are lake area and valley area scenic routes, but the prime attractions here are vista points at the **Leonard Harrison** and **Colton Point State Parks:** They look out over a 1,200-foot-deep section of the 50-mile-long Pine Creek Gorge—Pennsylvania's Grand Canyon. Young geologically, the gorge formed a mere 15,000 years ago when waters dammed by the great Wisconsin ice sheet were released.

Travelwise

GETTING THERE

Wellsboro is in north-central Pennsylvania, at the junction of US 6 and Pa. 287, approximately 50 miles north of Williamsport and 100 miles west of Scranton. Closest major airports are at Pittsburgh and Philadelphia. Capital Trailways buses (717-233-7673) run from Harrisburg to Mansfield, 12 miles east; local public transportation is available from there.

GENERAL INFORMATION

Late spring is best for avoiding crowds. Watch out for "no vacancy" conditions during the Laurel Festival in mid-June and when fall colors peak in early October. Information from the **Wellsboro Area Chamber of Commerce** (114 Main St., Wellsboro 16901. 570-724-1926) includes excellent walking/driving maps. The **Tioga County Visitors Bureau** (570-724-0635) is in the same building.

THINGS TO SEE AND DO

Arcadia Theater (50 Main St. 570-724-4957) Weekend dinner shows.

Gmeiner Art and Cultural Center (134 Main St. 570-724-1917. Closed a.m.) Visitors enjoy regularly changing exhibitions.

Outdoor Activities For rafting, canoeing, bicycling, or hiking in canyon country, contact Pine Creek Outfitters (10 miles W of Wellsboro on US 6. 570-724-3003). If a wilderness adventure on horseback or in a covered wagon interests you, call Mountain Trail Horse Center (RR 2. 570-376-5561).

Tioga County Historical Society Museum (Robinson House, 120 Main St. 570-724-6116. Mon.-Fri. p.m.) Furnished Victorian parlor, plus late 19th-century displays and a genealogical library.

ANNUAL EVENTS

Dickens of a Christmas (Early Dec. 570-376-5561) In this Victorian romp, the town offers craft and food vendors, street performers, wagon rides, and a tree-lighting ceremony.

Pennsylvania State Laurel Festival (Mid-June. 570-376-5561) Enjoy concerts, a carnival, a craft show, international foods, a pageant, and more.

WHERE TO EAT

Penn Wells Hotel (62 Main St. 570-724-2111. $$) At this old-fashioned hostelry, the "big fish" enjoy inexpensive buffets or elegant meals in a large dining room filled with local legends.

Steak House (29 Main St. 570-724-9092. $$) Take advantage of large portions and fair prices at this tavern-restaurant.

Wellsboro Diner (19 Main St. 570-729-3992. $) The real thing! In continuous operation since 1939, the diner offers a typical menu with interesting specials.

WHERE TO STAY

Blue Moon Inn (129 Main St. 570-724-0942. $$) Home of folk artist Susan Clickner and her Stonewall Folk Art Gallery, the Victorian villa combines old-time ambience with modern features.

La Petite Auberge (3 Charles St. 570-724-3288. $$) Dripping with antiques and collectibles, this B&B offers a full gourmet breakfast.

NEARBY PLACES

Colton Point State Park (12 miles W of Wellsboro on US 6 to Ansonia, then 5 miles S on Colton Rd. 570-724-3060) Overlooks on the Pine Creek Gorge's east rim are popular in the summer.

Leonard Harrison State Park (9 miles SW of Wellsboro, on RR 660 W. 570-724-3061) Enjoy superb views of Pine Creek Gorge or take the Turkey Path Trail to the bottom.

Pennsylvania Lumber Museum (5660 US 6 W, Galeton. 814-435-2652. Mid-May–Nov.; adm. fee) Glimpse the old lumber days.

Doylestown

Plush green hills and sprightly streams, stone farmhouses and weathered covered bridges: This is the fabled pastoral landscape of Bucks County, the muselike inspiration for scores of writers and artists. James Michener, Oscar Hammerstein, Pearl S. Buck, and eccentric Henry Mercer, to name just a few, all made their homes in this corner of eastern Pennsylvania, residing in or around charming Doylestown. Now this upscale town, with its specialty boutiques and fine restaurants, celebrates the legacy of those geniuses with first-rate museums, three unusual concrete castles, a working tile factory, and more.

It all began in 1745, when William Doyle built a public house where two wagon roads intersected in the wilderness. A quiet town named for Doyle grew up around the crossroads, remaining a simple place until 1810, when the county seat was moved here from Newton. Then doctors, lawyers, surveyors, and other professionals moved in, and by 1900 a community of 3,000 was prospering. The downtown's cheery mix of colonial, federal, and Victorian architecture, all lovingly preserved and lived in, reflects its moneyed heritage.

Henry Mercer's mod-medieval Fonthill

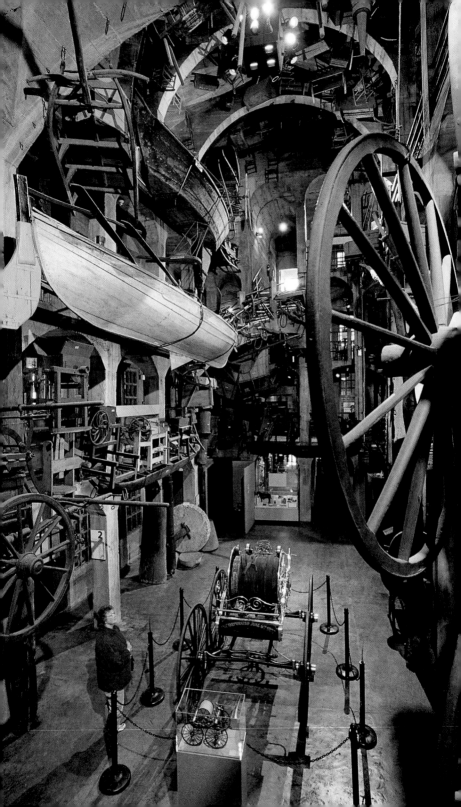

Doyle's Tavern is long gone, its spot in this flower-bedecked town now taken by the **Fountainhouse,** a bulky, green-and-white edifice housing an upscale Starbucks and law offices. From here, it's fun to stroll the pretty, tree-shaded streets, wandering in and out of shops, chatting with locals, sipping a cup of specialty coffee at Coffee 'n' Cream. You can't miss the art deco **County Theatre,** a restored, community-based theater that still shows films. Nearby stands the old **Doylestown Inn,** with a sidewalk café perfect for lunch. David Frame is an artist in residence whose poetic works portray the beauty of the surrounding Bucks County countryside. Also of interest is the stretch of East Court Street, across from the Bucks County Courthouse, known as **Lawyers Row**—modest federal houses dating from the early 1800s.

Then head to **Fonthill,** one of the town's most fantastic monuments, where you'll learn about a man who added idiosyncrasy to Doylestown's charm. Henry Chapman Mercer was, among other things, an artist who in the late 1800s became interested in the forgotten tradition of Pennsylvania German pottery and adapted it to tilemaking—a style that greatly influenced the American Arts and Crafts movement. He built **Mercer's Moravian Pottery and Tileworks,** and soon his tiles were being demanded by such places as Grauman's Chinese Theatre in Hollywood and the National Press Club in Washington, D.C.

In 1908 Mercer began building Fonthill, his dream house, a veritable fun house. Using no blueprint, he sketched what he wanted his

At the Michener Art Museum

workers to accomplish each day, improvising techniques as they went along. Almost everything is made of concrete, including desks, chairs, and window frames, and each of the 44 rooms is smothered with tiles—some his own, some from his vast historical collection. Windows don't match, stairways coil out of nowhere then disappear, hallways are suffocating mazes leading who knows where. The result is a garish, asymmetrical, mod-medieval castle that you have to see to believe. Nearby you can also tour the tileworks, still producing tiles in the Mercer way. A gift shop purveys an array of these singular works of art.

Mercer was also a self-taught archaeologist who spent decades studying cultures around the world. When he returned to Doylestown in the late 1800s, he realized that down the road, archaeologists would be interested in the early American tools and handicrafts made obsolete by the Industrial Revolution. Mercer spent 25 years collecting all kinds of, well, junk: broken spinning wheels and dilapidated wagons, archaic dental tools and mousetraps. To house his 50,000-piece collection, he built another concrete castle: the **Mercer Museum** on Pine Street. This jam-packed ensemble of goods—a Conestoga wagon here, a whaling boat there, a gallows in the far corner, even chairs and steamer trunks suspended from the four-story atrium—represents 40 differ-

Inside the relic-filled Mercer Museum

ent crafts and trades. Wandering through the chilly rooms (it's all concrete, after all), you feel as if you've stumbled into an overstuffed attic.

The story goes that, as Mercer celebrated the completion of his concrete Fonthill by igniting a pile of kerosene-soaked lumber atop his roof late one night in 1912, the washerwoman who lived across the street rushed, terrified, to her adopted son's bedside. This little boy, Jim Michener, grew up to be the celebrated and prize-winning writer of scores of tomes, including *Hawaii, The Covenant,* and *Centennial.* Michener was also a benefactor of the **James A. Michener Art Museum,** located across the street from the Mercer Museum. One room of this impressive gallery is devoted to his life, complete with an old typewriter and the original manuscript of *The Novel.* Other rooms celebrate other local artists and writers, with the most famous work being "Peaceable Kingdom" by Edward Hicks, probably America's finest 19th-century naive artist. A multimedia display in the back provides a roundup of the area's most famous talents. You can listen to the lyrics of Oscar Hammerstein, including those from *The King and I* and *Showboat.* A living-room-like setting is devoted to playwrights George S. Kaufman and Moss Hart, with Hart's guest book open to an entry signed by an incensed Alexander Woollcott: "This is to certify that, on my first visit to Moss Hart's house, I had one of the most unpleasant evenings I can recall…" Hart responded that at least he hadn't broken a leg and was forced to stay for weeks, a remark that became the kernel for *The Man Who Came For Dinner.* Author Dorothy Parker, painter Edward Redfield, and Harlem Renaissance author Jean Toomer are among others represented. The most revealing section probably is the one dedicated to Pearl S. Buck, winner of the Pulitzer Prize for *The Good Earth,* a novel about peasant life in China. The exhibit is filled with images of Amerasian children, all of whom were helped by the Pearl S. Buck Foundation.

To learn more about this multifaceted woman, visit her 60-acre homestead north of Doylestown. She lived in China for 42 years before moving to **Green Hills Farm,** and her 1835 farmhouse is filled with a mélange of Chinese and American antiques. You see the desk where she wrote *The Good Earth,* as well as her favorite vases, silk robes, intricately carved wooden paintings, and family photos. Her typewriter sits near the picture window where she perched many a day, seeking inspiration from a green landscape that has inspired generations of artists and writers, and which will doubtlessly inspire generations more. *Barbara A. Noe*

Covered Bridges

Twelve covered bridges (11 at least a century old; one rebuilt after a fire) dot the Bucks County countryside. A pleasant afternoon can be spent visiting the five nearest North River Road:

- Loux Covered Bridge, Wismer Road, Plumsteadville
- Cabin Run Covered Bridge, Covered Bridge Road, Plumsteadville
- Frankenfield Covered Bridge, Hollow Horn and Cafferty Road, Tinicum
- Erwinna Covered Bridge, Geiger Hill Road, Erwinna
- Uhlerstown Covered Bridge, Uhlerstown Road, Uhlerstown

Travelwise

GETTING THERE

Doylestown is off I-95 in southeastern Pennsylvania, about 25 miles north of Philadelphia and 85 miles south of New York City. Major airports are Philadelphia International and Newark International.

GENERAL INFORMATION

The best seasons to visit are spring, with its flowering gardens, and autumn, when the foliage ignites. Summer is hot and humid, while winter can be cold and snowy. For a free visitors guide, contact the **Bucks County Conference & Visitors Bureau** *(152 Swamp Rd., Doylestown 18901. 215-345-4552. www.bccvb.org).*

THINGS TO SEE AND DO

Fonthill Museum *(E. Court St. and Pa. 313. 215-348-9461. Adm. fee)* Henry Mercer's castle-home is set on 70 acres ideal for picnicking.

James A. Michener Art Museum *(138 S. Pine St. 215-340-9800. Closed Mon.; adm. fee)* Local artists and writers are celebrated.

Mercer Museum *(84 S. Pine St. 215-345-0210. Adm. fee)* This seven-story Tudoresque castle houses Mercer's collection of over 40,000 early American tools.

Mercer's Moravian Pottery and Tileworks *(130 Swamp Rd./Pa. 313. 215-345-6722. Adm. fee)* Henry Mercer's tilemaking techniques live on at this working museum.

Pearl S. Buck House *(520 Dublin Rd., Perkasie. 215-249-0100 or 800-220-2825. Closed Mon. and Jan.-Feb.; adm. fee)* See the 60-acre homestead of the Nobel and Pulitzer Prize winner.

WHERE TO EAT

Black Walnut *(80 W. State St. 215-348-0708. $$)* Enjoy excellent Continental cuisine such as sesame-crusted salmon and beef tenderloin au poivre with white truffles.

Inn on Blueberry Hill *(Pa. 611 and Almhouse Rd. 215-491-1777. Closed Mon. and lunch. $$$)* The historic Victorian serves French Continental cuisine.

Paganini Trattoria *(81 W. State St. 215-348-5922. $$)* Featuring Italian staples like carpaccio and specials like *maccheroncini alla vodka.*

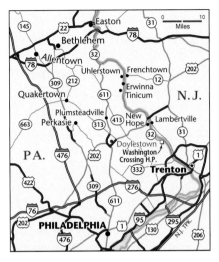

Sign of the Sorrel Horse *(4424 Old Easton Rd. 215-230-9999)* A 1714 gristmill provides the setting for gourmet dining.

WHERE TO STAY

Doylestown Inn *(18 W. State St. 215-345-6610. $$$)* A downtown landmark for nearly a century, the inn has 20 simple guest rooms and a restaurant, tavern, and sidewalk café.

Inn at Fordhook Farm *(105 New Britain Rd. 215-345-1766. $$$)* Once the home of W. Atlee Burpee and the mail-order seed company, the stone mansion is set on 60 acres of grass, gardens, and woods.

NEARBY PLACES

To the east of town lies the great Delaware River, separating Pennsylvania from New Jersey, perhaps most famous for the crossing by George Washington in 1776. **Washington Crossing Historic Park** *(Pa. 32 and 532, Washington Crossing. 215-493-4076)* marks the historic event. Along the river's banks you'll find the somewhat touristy town of **New Hope** *(215-862-5880),* with its eclectic mix of boutiques and the historic **Bucks County Playhouse** *(70 S. Main St. 215-862-2041. Mid-April–Dec. Wed.-Sun.).* Just across the river in New Jersey is charming **Lambertville** *(Chamber of Commerce 609-397-0055),* featuring more antique and art boutiques, and to the north lies **Frenchtown,** yet another enchanting town.

Medford

Pine garlands and twinkling white lights provide a Victorian touch to tiny Medford in early December, when the whole township crowds Main Street for the annual Dickens celebration. A cool, northerly wind sends aloft the sweet aroma of steaming apple cider and cinnamon, as bundled-up revelers—carolers, characters from *A Christmas Carol,* and musicians alike—greet familiar faces, of which there are many. For that's the kind of place Medford is: a friendly, tight-knit community where everyone knows everyone.

But should you arrive during nonfestival time, you'll probably be struck by how quiet Medford is. Indeed, its lovingly restored residences—beautiful old federal and Victorian clapboards—are silent monuments to a time when the small town bristled with the goings-on of bog-iron furnaces, a busy gristmill, a glass factory, and cranberry bogs. Those industries are mostly gone now, leaving Medford a perfect place in which to seek a slower pace—a place where little girls feed kittens on begonia-splashed porches, new mothers push prams beneath centuries-old branches, and brides pose at the picturesque town gazebo.

Standing at the corner of Main and Union, you can peer a hundred years into the past, to a time when horse-drawn wagons loaded with strawberries, blueberries, cranberries, and other Medford produce trundled by a similar scene on their way to Philadelphia markets. Nearly all of the buildings that line Main Street were built during Medford's heyday, between the late 1700s and 1850. The township has erected informative plaques outside the most significant edifices, making for a pleasant and interesting stroll. Blossom-draped lamp posts and postage-stamp gardens add colorful flourishes to the quintessential small town scene.

At this same intersection sits the green-and-yellow **Indian Chief Tavern,** dating from 1810 and once providing weary travelers with supper and a place to sleep; it now houses a luncheonette and a couple of shops. Down the way, across the street, you can make out the old-style sign for **Braddock's Tavern,** a darkly lit, frame-and-clapboard eating establishment built in 1844, where dark, cozy rooms illuminated by flickering candles seem straight out of colonial times. Among Main Street's picture-perfect houses, once home to many of the town's most influential early families, be sure to seek out the **Riley/Garwood House** (*53 S. Main St.*), a classic 18th-century Georgian with a Flemish bond facade. Riley was the village cabinetmaker who, like all other cabinetmakers of the time, also was the village undertaker. The first floor of the **William Dyer House** (*63-65 S. Main St.*), built in the Greek Revival style in 1841, was once a general store run by William Dyer and William Braddock, who stocked everything from perfume and liquor to salt pork and cheese. The **Stratton/Braddock House** (*70 S. Main St.*), all white and gray, is another house with Flemish bond brick, built circa 1760.

Medford's charming main street

While Medford is foremost a residential town, a spattering of antique shops and craft boutiques occupy Main Street's walls, purveying century-old dolls and country-style armoires, handmade wooden toys and Victorian vases. In between these shops are a couple of establishments that whisper modern-day, providing an unexpected contemporary flair to the underlying old-time spirit. **Health Haven II**, which features natural foods, is run by a certified nutritional consultant and shiatsu specialist. And **Cafe Noelle** is a tiny, cheery bistro serving up some truly cosmopolitan fare—perhaps lobster-filled ravioli with diced shrimp and crabmeat, or sautéed veal in veloute sauce.

But the past is what defines this town, so be sure to investigate its earliest years. Drive north on Main Street and turn left on N.J. 70, where development is just encroaching upon sprawling fields. A right on Jennings Road brings you down a tree-shaded, wildflower-scented lane and past the **Nail House.** This is where Mark Reeve, in the early 1800s, reputedly produced and sold the first machine-cut nails in America (sadly for him, he never patented his invention). Reeve is responsible for Medford's name—he successfully petitioned to change its former appellation (Upper Evesham) after an impressionable trip to Medford, Massachusetts—and also for the town plot that remains little changed today. Nearby, the **John Haines House** *(26 Fostertown Rd.)* is the town's oldest extant house;

Harvesting Pine Barren cranberries

the Haines family built the area's first milling community, known as Haines Mill and later renamed Kirby's Mill.

Picturesque **Kirby's Mill** still straddles the South Branch Rancocas River northeast of town, the scene of a spirited apple festival in autumn. With foundations dating from 1778, this water-powered mill once worked overtime as a sawmill, gristmill, and cider mill, as well as a blacksmith and wheelwright shop. Currently being restored, it sits prettily among the trees and beckons for a picnic; or rent a punt and paddle on its dark, glassy pond.

From here you can plunge into the **Pine Barrens,** a dark, mysterious swath of pitch pines and oaks crossed with slow-moving creeks and sandy, aimless roads. This 1.1-million-acre realm, designated an international biosphere reserve by the United Nations in 1983, was long the domain of the Pineys, reclusive folk who eked a living from the land—some of whom are said to still reside in the backwoods. You probably won't see them; instead, the greatest glimpse you'll get of the old times are probably the cranberry bogs that still produce abundant fruit (during harvest time in October, don't be surprised if every conversation you hear in Medford concerns cranberries), and an old glass and iron company town that is open for tours.

Perhaps it's this association with the past that gives the barrens its disconcerting restlessness. Strike out into the wilderness, perhaps to hike a sandy trail or paddle one of the tea-colored streams, and you'll note right away the utter silence. An uneasy silence punctuated by puzzling rustlings in the underbrush that give credence to wild tales, the most frightening of which concerns a monster called the Jersey devil: It isn't out to hurt anybody—so it's said—but it has been blamed for a good deal of destruction nonetheless. At the end of the day, you will be content to return to Medford and curl up in the comfort of a safe, warm B&B. *Barbara A. Noe*

Travelwise

GETTING THERE

Medford is in southern New Jersey, 18 miles east of Philadelphia. From the New Jersey Turnpike, follow N.J. 70 east, then go south on County Rd. 541 (Main Street). The nearest major airport is in Philadelphia.

GENERAL INFORMATION

Heat and humidity prevail in summertime, while spring and fall are pleasant. Blueberries are picked July to mid-August, and October brings the cranberry harvest. For more information, contact the **Historic Medford Village Business Association** (P.O. Box 1363, Medford 08055. 609-714-8811) or the **Medford Historical Society** (P.O. Box 362, Medford 08055. 609-654-2608). The **New Jersey Office of Travel and Tourism** (609-292-2470) can provide information on the surrounding area.

THINGS TO SEE AND DO

Blueberry Picking For a list of farms where you can pick fresh fruits, call 609-625-0056.

Canoeing Popular rivers include the Oswego, Wading, Batsto, and Mullica. Contact the New Jersey Office of Travel and Tourism for rental and guided trip information.

Cranberry Harvesting During the harvest you can watch commercial companies at work from roadsides along County Rd. 563 near Chatsworth or in **Double Trouble State Park** (Toms River exit off Garden State Pkwy. 732-341-6662).

Hiking (Lebanon SF 609-726-1191, Wharton SF 609-561-3262, Bass River SF 609-296-1114) The most popular trail is the **Batona Trail**, a 50-mile sandy, level pathway through the heart of the Pine Barrens, connecting the Lebanon, Wharton, and Bass River State Forests. Contact the New Jersey Office of Travel and Tourism for other trail possibilities.

Kirby's Mill (275 Church Rd. off Cty. Rd. 541. 609-654-0768. Sun. June-Aug., by appt. rest of year) Artifacts relating to carpentry, farming, and cranberry harvesting are on display.

Lebanon State Forest (Near the jct. of N.J. 70 and N.J. 72. 609-726-1191) Pakim Pond was once a reservoir for cranberry bogs. The forest offers cabins and campsites.

Wharton State Forest (Cty. Rd. 542 in Batsto or US 206 in Atsion. 609-561-3262. Adm. fee to some sites and some parking fees) New Jersey's largest state forest (120,000 acres) boasts an extensive network of sandy trails, including the **Batsto Pond Nature Trail,** which explores a microcosm of several pinelands habitats. Here, too, is **Historic Batsto Village,** an 1880s glass and iron company town, and the ghost town of **Atsion Village,** a former iron forge. The state forest offers swimming, canoeing, cabins, and campsites.

Woodford Cedar Run Wildlife Refuge (6 Sawmill Rd. 856-983-0326. Closed Mon.-Tues.; donation) Dedicated to preserving the Pine Barrens and educating people about its wildlife, the refuge offers hands-on exhibits for children, small live animals to see and touch, and a 1-mile trail around Cedar Run Lake. Ask about scheduled outdoor programs in the Pine Barrens.

WHERE TO EAT

Braddock's Tavern (39 S. Main St. 609-654-1604. $$) Fine dining in a colonial setting. Hearty fare includes seafood, veal, and poultry.

Cafe Noelle (20 S. Main St. 609-953-1155. $$) Creative pastas, fish, and more.

WHERE TO STAY

Main Stay B&B (45 S. Main St. 609-654-7528. $$) Queen Anne Victorian with nine cozy rooms.

New Castle

Tucked in a strategic bend of the Delaware River, New Castle was founded as a fort in the 1600s, with enough subsequent bustle and flurry to promise eventual major city status. Indeed, throughout the 1700s, it served as an important port midway between the North and South, a place well known to George Washington, Thomas Jefferson, and other luminaries of the day. New Castle flourished as Delaware's colonial capital, then state capital, but metropolism was not to be. The town slipped into gradual economic decline—losing all hope for wider renown—after a series of losses, the most critical being the naming of Dover as the state capital in 1777, and missing out on long-distance railroad lines in 1840. Thanks to those misfortunes, New Castle remains a delightfully forgotten place, where centuries-old houses and fragrant boxwood gardens, candlelit taverns and clapboard B&Bs provide a picturesque backdrop far away from modern day.

Peter Stuyvesant, governor of the Dutch colonies, claimed the area and constructed Fort Casimir here in 1651. Located on the wide Delaware—a major waterway linking the Chesapeake Bay with Philadelphia—the settlement drew more than admiring glances from many colonizing forces: Over the next 30 years, it was seized by the Swedes, the Dutch (again), the English, the Dutch (again), and the English (again). Then, in 1682, the Duke of York gave a substantial land grant to William Penn, which included present-day Pennsylvania and Delaware. Well, the people of Delaware, now a mix of Swedes, Dutch, and English, didn't have much in common with the Pennsylvanians, mostly Quakers. They fought for their own assembly and in 1704 achieved it. As the colony's largest city, New Castle became its capital.

The best way to experience old New Castle is to stroll its shady streets, buckled with the ancient roots of oaks, elms, and sycamores and lined with beautifully maintained historic residences. Stuyvesant platted the town in 1655, a plan that remains true to its original form, with the most important buildings centered around a public green where early residents grazed sheep and cattle.

The green's most prominent building is the **New Castle Court House,** from whose balcony flutter the four different flags of the town's rulers. The courthouse was built in 1732, and it was here on June 15, 1776, that the assembly voted to separate from Great Britain and Pennsylvania, establishing the state of Delaware with New Castle as the capital. On July 24 of that same year, the Declaration of Independence was read from the courthouse's balcony to the citizens of Delaware. Two months later, on September 20, the first state constitution was adopted here. Inside, the sunny, open courtroom and assembly room, beautifully restored in spartan colonial style complete with Wind-

Immanuel Episcopal Church

Italianate flourishes in New Castle

sor chairs and feather pens, make it easy to picture those consequential days.

Vendors once gathered to purvey their wares at **Market Square,** across Market Street from the courthouse. The old **town hall,** built in 1823, stands at the foot of the empty, fenced-in square, while a statue of William Penn reminds passersby that the first steps the religious-freedom advocate took in the New World were at New Castle in 1682. At the far end of the green, the sleek white steeple of **Immanuel Episcopal Church** rises above a crumbling stone wall. Following a fire in 1980, the church was rebuilt according to original records. The tower is original, as is the cemetery, dating back to the church's founding in 1689; here, time-lustered tombstones belonging to early residents demand quiet contemplation on the passage of time. Among the prominent citizens resting in peace is George Read—The Signer, as locals proudly allude to his role in the Declaration of Independence.

Bordering the green to the west, Third Street holds some of the town's most interesting buildings, mostly dating from the 18th and 19th centuries. The **Old Library Museum,** an unusual octagonal structure built in 1892, is the block's youngest building. Down the way is the circa 1700 **Old Dutch House,** considered the town's oldest structure—fairly evident by its ancient sloping eaves. Inside, sweet checkered curtains and embroidery samplers are humble attempts to soften small, austere rooms where plain, bulky furniture and rudimentary utensils bring to life the hardships of immigrants fleeing religious persecution in their homeland. Perhaps the most intimate items here are the ornately painted courting bench by the window, where young lovers once sat under watchful family eyes, and an original Dutch oven that former residents left behind.

Life improved some decades later: The **Amstel House,** a genteel, Georgian-style residence on nearby Fourth Street, was the town's most elegant house when it was built in 1738. Governor Van Dyke once lived here, and George

Washington attended the wedding reception of the governor's daughter in the parlor in 1784 (he's said to have stood by the fireplace and kissed all the pretty girls, "as was his wont").

The Strand was the heart of old New Castle, a bustling waterfront street filled with taverns, brothels, and inns. Given today's medley of stately trees and fine houses, it's a little hard to imagine how chaotic it must have been. You can find one glimpse at tiny **Packet Alley,** midway down the street. This little lane was long ago a busy passageway for travelers heading north and south. Among the street's elegant houses, the one that catches the eye is the **George Read II House,** constructed in 1801 in the federal style. This grandiose, redbrick mansion is famous for its Palladian windows and silver-plated hardware on solid mahogany doors. Members of the prominent Read family lived here until 1975; since restored in its original style, it provides a fascinating look at the privileged lifestyle of one colonial family.

At the foot of Delaware Street, the old **town wharf** seems insignificant, just a platform overlooking the river. But in bygone days, this niche was crowded with sailing vessels. Enjoy the river view along the paved 1.2-mile hiker-biker trail, which takes off to the right through grassy **Battery Park.** Follow the trail past boats bobbing in the harbor, beaches strewn with shells, and a bird-filled marsh, to earthwork terraces of early fortifications, built to ward off pirate attack.

Slip back into the present along **Delaware Street,** where several taverns and cafés offer standard fare. Then you have all the time in the world to explore the various antique shops and other boutiques. Nodding off in one of the town's cozy B&Bs—far away from car horns, most certainly atop a down mattress, perhaps in the same room where Penn once slept—you are guaranteed good old-fashioned sweet dreams.   *Barbara A. Noe*

Travelwise

GETTING THERE

New Castle lies in northeastern Delaware, 3 miles south of the Delaware Memorial Bridge (I-295) via Del. 9. The nearest airport is in Philadelphia, 35 miles northwest via I-95.

GENERAL INFORMATION

Spring and summer promise the most pleasant weather, with gardens boasting a riot of vibrant blossoms. Summer can be hot and humid, with frequent afternoon thunderstorms. Though winter can be cold, December brings festive decorations and candlelight tours. For recorded information, contact the Historic New Castle Visitors Bureau (*P.O. Box 465, New Castle 19720. 302-322-8411 or 800-758-1550. www.visitnew castle.com*). The Mayor's Office (*302-322-9802*) and New Castle Court House (*302-323-4453*) can answer questions. Brochures and maps are available at all shops.

THINGS TO SEE AND DO

Amstel House (4th and Delaware Sts. 302-322-2794. Adm. fee) One of New Castle's most elegant houses, it is maintained as a colonial house museum.

Antiquing There are many shops on and off Delaware Street. Jenny Lind and Enrico Caruso once sang at the **Opera House** (308 Delaware St.), since converted into a grandiose antique emporium.

Battery Park Fronting the Delaware River, this grassy expanse offers a playground for children, a bike trail, picnic tables, and tennis courts. Concerts are held every Wednesday night between late June and mid-August.

George Read II House (42 The Strand. 302-322-8411. March-Dec. Tues.-Sun., Jan.-Feb. Sat.-Sun., and by appt.; adm. fee) This 19th-century mansion was restored as a house museum; gardens retain much of their 1840s plan.

Immanuel Episcopal Church (100 Harmony St. 302-328-2413) Founded in 1689 as Delaware's first Anglican church, Immanuel is open daily and visitors are invited to services.

New Castle Court House Museum (211 Delaware St. 302-323-4453. Closed Mon.) The cupola of this historic building was used as the center of the 12-mile radial circle that formed Delaware's northern boundary. Informative tours offered.

Old Dutch House (32 E. 3rd St. 302-322-2794. March-Dec. Tues.-Sun., Jan.-Feb. Sat.-Sun.; adm. fee) Typical early Dutch residence furnished with period antiques. Guided tours.

Old Library Museum (40 E. 3rd St. 302-322-2794. Closed Mon.-Wed.) The second home of the New Castle Library is where the historical society now resides; temporary exhibits.

ANNUAL EVENTS

A New Castle Christmas (1st Sun. in Dec. 800-758-1550) Tour the museums, churches, and public buildings decked out for the Christmas season.

Separation Day (1st Sat. in June. Mayor's Office 302-322-9802) Delaware separated from Great Britain on June 15, 1776. Watch reenactments and fireworks at Battery Park.

WHERE TO EAT

The Arsenal at Old New Castle (30 Market St. 302-328-1290. $$) Spirited historic dining in rooms commemorating the Revolutionary and Civil Wars and War of 1812.

David Finney Inn (216 S. Delaware St. 302-322-6367 or 800-324-4476. $$) Fine dining in a romantic setting.

Jessop's Tavern and Restaurant (114 Delaware St. 302-322-6111. $$) English, Dutch, and Swedish specialties are served in a renovated 1724 colonial tavern.

Opera House Victorian Tea Room (308 Delaware St. 302-326-1211. Open weekends. $$) High tea includes Devonshire cream, lemon curd, tea sandwiches, and pastries.

WHERE TO STAY

Armitage Inn (2 The Strand. 302-328-6618. $$) Built in 1732 and once owned by a patriot during the Revolutionary War, the inn overlooks the Delaware River and Battery Park. Five guest rooms.

David Finney Inn (216 S. Delaware St. 302-322-6367 or 800-324-4476. $$$) The elegant colonial-style inn offers four suites.

Fox Lodge at Lesley Manor (123 W. 7th St. 302-328-0768. $$/$$$) Victorian Gothic Revival inn dating from 1855. Three guest rooms.

Terry House (130 Delaware St. 302-322-2505. $$) The double porches of this four-story federal town house overlook Battery Park and the Delaware River. Four guest rooms.

William Penn Guest House (206 Delaware St. 302-328-7736. $$) In this 1682 restored guest house, William Penn reputedly once stayed overnight. Four guest rooms.

NEARBY PLACES

Longwood Gardens (US 1, Kennett Sq., Penn. 610-388-1000. Adm. fee) The estate of Pierre S. du Pont includes 1,050 acres of inside and outside gardens and water fountains comparable to those at Versailles.

Winterthur Museum, Gardens & Library (6 miles NW of Wilmington on Del. 52. 302-888-4600 or 800-448-3883. Adm. fee) The world-famous American decorative arts and furniture collection (1640-1860) of Henry Francis du Pont are housed in his former estate.

Oxford

There may not be another town like it on the East Coast. Oxford is a maze of narrow streets with tumbledown houses standing next to renovated cottages of weekend yachtsmen and boatyards specializing in custom small craft. Wandering its hummocked brick sidewalks, you'll never hit a bevy of upscale boutiques—just a couple of plank-floored grocery stores filled with the soft Eastern Shore drawl. And on days when the Methodist church organ pipes hymns across the town, even swans on the Tred Avon River look up from their shoreline dabbling.

Oxford's waterfront

Despite its unpretentious ease, little Oxford is justifiably proud of its roots, which date back to the mid-17th century. The town's heyday, though, was in the early 18th, when George Washington authorized it as the first port of entry to collect taxes. A reproduction of the tiny clapboard **customhouse** from that era still stands overlooking the river, manned by a volunteer who will happily explain that the original customhouse is actually situated across the Tred Avon, on land owned by the colonial customs agent. The guide may add wryly that the agent had gout and didn't want to row over to Oxford to collect tariffs. The blocks just behind the customhouse on **Morris Street** are dotted with vintage buildings, all now private houses. A stroll up the street will take you past sedate **Academy House** (once for officers of the now defunct

Chesapeake blue crabs

Maryland Military Academy), **Barnaby House** (a gabled, late 18th-century cottage), and the imposing clapboard **Grapevine House** (so named for the gnarled grapevine twining in front, brought from the Isle of Jersey in 1810). Keep walking and you'll soon come to "downtown": four or five storefront shops and offices clustered together across from Town Waterfront Park. Remarkable among this modest collection is **Americana Antiques,** whose 18th- and early 19th-century furniture, portraiture, and silver are as fine as you'd spot in a big-city gallery. Around the corner, the small, volunteer-operated **Oxford Museum** has the usual array of memorabilia, most of it concerned with the town's days as a booming tobacco port and later as a boatbuilding and packing center.

The British ships that sailed to Oxford's shores have been replaced by private sloops, and on breeze-blessed weekends the river itself seems in full sail, while the marinas lining Town Creek chorus with the ring of rigging against mast. The **Tred Avon Yacht Club** has been a town fixture since 1931. It's a members-only establishment, so most visitors congregate at the regionally famous **Robert Morris Inn.** The original (north) side of the structure was built by ship's carpenters in 1710, but in 1730, an English trading company bought it and ensconced their agent Robert Morris there. Though the charming rooms go quickly, there's always room at the inn's colonialesque dining room, where true Maryland fare is served with an elegant flourish. James Michener, who lived on a nearby inlet while writing *Chesapeake,* declared the inn's crab cakes the best on the Eastern Shore.

Just outside the inn, the **Oxford-Bellevue Ferry** ties up every half hour amid the ducks paddling at the foot of Morris Street. The ferry traces its ancestry back to a colonial one that began plying the Tred Avon in the 1680s; thus, the current version claims to be the "oldest privately operated ferry in the country." Be that as it may, it's a nice way to get out on the river. It's also a quick way to reach charming **St. Michaels** and its acclaimed **Chesapeake Bay Maritime Museum.** While only 20 minutes away, St. Michaels has what Oxford lacks: boutiques, tourists, and predictability. If your taste runs to bygone times, however, and to the sounds of church hymns, swans dabbling, and wind in the rigging, Oxford is your kind of town.   *K. M. Kostyal*

Travelwise

GETTING THERE

About 90 miles east and south of Washington, D.C., Oxford lies on Maryland's Eastern Shore, at the confluence of the Tred Avon River and Town Creek. Take US 50 to the Easton Parkway (Md. 322), then Md. 333 south 10 miles to Oxford. Or you can take the Oxford-Bellevue Ferry across the Tred Avon, boarding on Bellevue Rd. or at the foot of Morris St. Nearby airports include Baltimore-Washington International, Dulles International, and Reagan National.

GENERAL INFORMATION

Spring through fall are fine seasons here, with sailboats on the river and the smell of salt marshes in the air. In spring and fall, migratory waterfowl congregate on the shoreline; in summer, diners enjoy delicacies such as blue crabs and oysters. In winter some inns and businesses close down. Though Oxford has no chamber of commerce or visitor center, maps of town sites are available at local businesses, as well as at the Oxford Museum and Library, or by contacting the **Oxford Business Association** (*P.O. Box 544, Oxford 21654. 410-226-5730.www.oxfordmd.com/oba*). "Oxford, Maryland," available free from local businesses, highlights historic buildings and other sites. Jane Tucker's "Port of Entry" booklet offers a more detailed look.

THINGS TO SEE AND DO

Charter Boats Sailing and motorized are available from operators throughout the area. Contact the Easton Visitor Center (*210 Marlboro Ave. 410-822-4606*) for information.

Oxford Custom House (*N. Morris St. and The Strand. April–late fall weekends*) This small replica of the original colonial customhouse has guides on hand to explain Oxford's history as a major port.

Oxford Museum (*Morris and Market Sts. 410-226-0191. Mid-April–mid-Oct. Fri., Sat., and Sun. p.m.*) The local history museum features memorabilia from the town's illustrious past.

Oxford-Bellevue Ferry

(*Foot of N. Morris St. March-Nov.; fare*) A pleasant way to get out on the Tred Avon River and the quickest way to get to St. Michaels, the ferry makes the crossing between Oxford and Bellevue in about 25 minutes.

SHOPPING

Americana Antiques
(*111 S. Morris St. 410-226-5677*) Superb regional antiques are available in this shop.

WHERE TO EAT

Chatterbox Café (*103 Mill St. 410-226-0044. $$*) This old-fashioned café is famous among locals for its hearty weekend breakfasts. Lunches feature fat deli sandwiches and pastas.

Robert Morris Inn (*314 N. Morris St. 410-226-5111. $$*) Seafood is king. Try the shore platters, which come with several homemade vegetable dishes and an entrée.

WHERE TO STAY

Nichols House (*217 S. Morris St. 410-226-5799. $$*) In the heart of town, this cozy guest house cottage sits in the pleasant garden of a larger Victorian.

Robert Morris Inn (*314 N. Morris St. 410-226-5111. Reserve well in advance. $$/$$$*) A regional gem, the small, intimate inn is decorated in colonial period decor and overlooks the Tred Avon River.

NEARBY PLACES

St. Michaels This thriving waterfront village is noted for its **Chesapeake Bay Maritime Museum** (*Mill St. 410-745-2916. Adm. fee*). Small shops, seafood restaurants, and several inns crowd the town's small streets.

Easton (*Talbot Chamber of Commerce, 210 Marlboro Ave. 410-822-4606*) The Historical Society of Talbot County (*25 S. Washington St. 410-822-0773*) maintains two early 19th-century houses and a Quaker meetinghouse for public tours.

New Market

Gracious, federal-style buildings edge New Market's tree-shaded Main Street, composing one of the nation's most pristine collections of 19th-century architecture. As charming as the buildings are, people don't come to this wisp of a village in north-central Maryland to admire their exteriors. Rather, they come to see the interiors or, more explicitly, what their interiors contain. For virtually every other house harbors an antique shop, filled with such treasures as French provincial armoires, antique beer steins, authentic rope beds, federal tables, and all other manner of furnishings from the past. There are 30-odd antique shops in town, all rubbing shoulders with one another along the mile-long main street—hence, New Market's self-proclaimed sobriquet of "antiques capital of Maryland."

Things weren't always antiques. New Market began in 1793 as a tiny crossroads. Its location on the old Baltimore Pike (which later became the National Road, the first federal highway) made it a perfect overnight stopping place for Conestoga-driving travelers, who sought food and lodging in its eight hotels and taverns. Wheelwrights, blacksmiths, tanneries, as well as button and shoe factories and a wrought-iron nail shop, sprang up to meet the various needs of travelers and the surrounding farming community. Beyond the hotels, cattle and sheep grazed on rolling pastures before eventually being herded to markets in Baltimore.

The first antique dealer, Stoll Kemp arrived on July 4, 1936, and stayed for 50 years. Today many residents of the still-one-street town are retirees who moved here to start second careers. They reside in the picturesque buildings, perhaps setting up shops on the first floors, in the basements, or in the backyard barns. The large concentration of antique dealers makes for an interesting community. The owner of **Antiques Folly,** for instance, laughs that in any other town, eyebrows might arch if a neighbor came home late at night. "Here," she says, "people just think it must have been a good antique show."

The town is quiet on weekdays, when few stores are open and residents go about their daily business. Children attend school, firefighters hang out at the fire station, and some people commute to Frederick or Washington, D.C., for office jobs. But when the weekend comes, the town buzzes with activity as more than 500 outsiders converge here to rummage through the shops. It seems that each establishment specializes in something different, from wooden boxes to cast iron furniture to sports antiques. **Grange Hall Antiques** features Steiff animals and fishing tackle, while **Victorian Manor Jewelry** showcases breathtaking 19th-century accessories, and **Thirsty Knight Antiques** specializes in antique beer steins. And that's just a start. With such variety, most shop owners agree, competition is nonexistent.

New Market's General Store

The best strategy is to pick up from one of the stores a map that details shop specialties, and then study it for the places that suit your interests. Or, for the true antique connoisseurs, just begin at one end of the street, follow its length, cross the street, and head back. If you stop at every shop, this will be a daylong—or possibly two-day—pursuit.

For those who aren't into antiques, New Market holds few other attractions. You can take a pleasant stroll to **Messanelle Memorial Park,** filled with box-woods and benches. Taking tea at the **Village Tea Room** is an agreeable way to spend an hour or so. Otherwise, you have plenty of surrounding sights to enjoy.

Just 8 miles west is **Frederick,** a stately town that began as a wayside stop for wagon trains making the first trips west across the Allegheny Mountains. A 33-street historic district brims with colonial and federal architecture, and guided and self-guided walking tours begin at the **visitor center.** Francis Scott Key, who wrote "The Star-Spangled Banner," worshiped at **All Saints Episcopal Church,** while both his law office and his residence stand nearby. Among the town's other renowned residents was Barbara Fritchie, a 95-year-old widow who defiantly flew the American flag in the face of invading Confederate troops. The **Barbara Fritchie House and Museum** was built from original materials after the house was destroyed by a flood and torn down in 1868. (For antiquers not yet exhausted, Frederick has more than 300 antique dealers.)

Just north of Frederick sprawls **Catoctin Mountain Park,** the site of fabled Camp David. You can't visit the President's Shangri-la, of course, but in the park peaceful paths wander among maples and oaks, leading to eye-catching vistas of Frederick Valley's green-and-gold patchwork of fields and farms—a niche about as far away as you can get from New Market's hullabaloo.   *Barbara A. Noe*

Travelwise

GETTING THERE

New Market lies in north-central Maryland, 8 miles east of Frederick off I-70. The nearest international airports are Baltimore-Washington International, about 40 miles southeast, and Dulles International, some 50 miles southwest.

GENERAL INFORMATION

All shops are open on weekends. Hours vary during the week; a flying flag in front of a shop means it is open for business. For more information, contact the **New Market General Store** *(301-865-6313)* or the **Tourism Council of Frederick County** *(19 E. Church St., Frederick 21701. 301-663-8687 or 800-999-3613. www.newmarketmd.com or www.visitfrederick.org).*

ANNUAL EVENTS

Christmas in New Market *(1st weekend in Dec. 301-865-6313)* Decorated houses and antique shops recall a bygone era. Carolers, a tree lighting, visits with Santa, and more.

New Market Days *(Last weekend in Sept. 301-865-5544)* The annual fall festival celebrates the town's 18th-century heritage with crafts, entertainers, and regional cuisine.

WHERE TO EAT

Mealey's for Fine Food *(8 W. Main St. 301-865-5488. Closed Mon. $$)* Popular with locals, Mealey's is really the only restaurant in town. Good American cuisine includes prime rib of beef, hickory shrimp, Maryland crab cakes, and fried fantail shrimp.

New Market General Store *(26 W. Main St. 301-865-6313. Closed Wed. $)* Simple soups and sandwiches are served in a very casual setting, perfect for a quick bite between shops. The turn-of-the-19th-century general store purveys gourmet gifts, antiques, general merchandise, collectibles, and furniture.

Village Tea Room *(81 W. Main St. 301-865-3450. Closed Mon. $)* For a light lunch and afternoon tea, this is the place to go.

WHERE TO STAY

While New Market has only one place to stay, Frederick offers many more choices.

Strawberry Inn Bed & Breakfast *(17 W. Main St. 301-865-3318. $$)* Guests can choose from five rooms in this restored farmhouse in the center of New Market.

NEARBY PLACES

Frederick *(Visitor center, 19 E. Church St. 301-663-8687 or 800-999-3613. Guided tours weekends April-Dec.; fee for tours)* The 33-street historic district includes such venerable structures as the **All Saints Episcopal Church** *(106 W. Church St.)* and the **Barbara Fritchie House and Museum** *(154 W. Patrick St. 301-698-0630. April-Nov. Thurs.-Mon.; adm. fee)*. Nearby is **Catoctin Mountain Park** *(Visitor center on Md. 77. 301-663-9343)*, a mountainous, trail-crossed escape.

Fredericksburg

It's surprising for a city that has seen as much war as this one to end up so charming. But despite its Civil War hardships, this little burg on the banks of the Rappahannock River cultivates its small town, everybody-seems-to-know-everybody friendliness, as well as its deep, sometimes dark, past. Spilling across the rolling hills of the Virginia piedmont, the town tumbles toward the riverside downtown, where café owners, antique dealers, and craftsfolk speak to just about anybody who walks through their doors. The redbrick facades of the old colonial and federal buildings have been buffed up in recent years, and a number of the structures have been turned into creditable museums that celebrate a past longer than the nation's.

On any given weekend, the streets of Old Town Fredericksburg fill with both locals and urbanites escaping the sprawl and harried pace of nearby Washington, D.C. But here the capital's shenanigans seem far away, and the

Kenmore, home of George Washington's sister, Betty

town's mild ambience almost conjures the long-ago days when James Monroe and young George Washington walked the streets. Monroe was a lawyer here, and Washington spent his childhood on a farm just across the Rappahannock. Washington's sister, Betty, became Fredericksburg's grande dame, with her husband, Fielding Lewis, exerting much influence in the town's early commercial development. The Lewises were enthroned at **Kenmore,** a sprawling plantation whose holdings once included much of Fredericksburg. The remains of that former grandeur—just a few well-shaded acres surrounding the stately old manor house—are now embedded on a quiet residential street. A couple of blocks away stands the small clapboard **Mary Washington House,** where George and Betty's mother, said to have been stern but loving, spent the last 17 years of her life. The town's longtime institution of higher learning, **Mary Washington College,** bears her name. Its genteel excess of redbrick Georgian buildings overlooks campus greenswards and stately walkways at the west end of town.

If you happen to be in Fredericksburg any day but Sunday, you'll find it's well worth a stop at the local **farmers' market** on Prince Edward Street: Sample the bountiful seasonal produce of the Northern Neck, as this northernmost Virginia peninsula is called. From here, as you head into the heart of Old Town, you'll pass what seems like a historic museum on just about every block. The small **James Monroe Museum** memorializes the early lawyering days of the fifth President; the stolid **National Bank Museum** (*900 Princess Anne St.*) occupies one room in the National Bank building, notable for the almost two centuries of banking that have been conducted inside it. Nearby, **Masonic Lodge No. 4** (*803 Princess Anne St.*) once claimed young Mason George Washington and now also houses a museum relating to his membership.

The Washington trail continues one street over, at the **Hugh Mercer Apothecary Shop.** A friend of Washington, Mercer also bought the great man's boyhood home and died while fighting for independence under Washington's command. A couple of blocks up is the **Rising Sun Tavern.** The building was originally the home of Washington's youngest brother, Charles, and later it became a colonial tavern. Though you cannot dine here, you'll find that you wouldn't want to eat here anyway after you take the pass-the-spoon tour offered by contemporary tavern wenches. For a good overview of the Washington family's strong connection to this town—and the centuries that followed the Washington reign—stop by the **Fredericksburg Area Museum.**

Civil War Clash Point

About halfway between the Union capital in Washington, D.C., and the Confederate capital at Richmond, Virginia, Fredericksburg and its environs were major Civil War battle sites. The first fighting took place in the heart of the city in December 1862, and the following spring, armies clashed at Chancellorsville, about 10 miles to the west. The Southern victory there cost the South its Stonewall (Jackson). In May 1864, war raged again, this time at the Wilderness and Spotsylvania Court House, west and southwest of town.

Old Town Fredericksburg

If you grow tired of visiting museums, you can always fill the day with antiquing and crafting. Antique shops are plentiful along Caroline and William Streets, while waterfront Sophia Street has been claimed by the crafts crowd. In the barnlike **Waterfront Shoppes** *(718 Sophia St. 540-371-2799),* artisans sporting colonial garb sell handmade colonial-era lanterns that have been electrified for easy use, as well as cloaks and other clothing.

When your wanderings have caused you to work up an appetite, stop in at the local knoshing spot, **Sammy T's,** for a hearty sandwich. The eatery's alfresco patio seating lets you take in the changing street scene.

Aside from the weekend browsers who descend on the town, the place is also a mecca for history buffs, who know it as a major clash point for Union and Confederate Armies who fought bloody battles here during the Civil War. Four times troops descended in the Fredericksburg area, wreaking havoc each time. A few spots in the heart of town recall those hard days, including the **Old Stone Warehouse,** a strategic site from which Southern snipers kept the Union Army at bay as it tried to cross the Rappahannock. Over on the river's far bank, one of the places where Union generals holed up was **Chatham,** a Georgian-style mansion now open to the public and used as headquarters by the **Fredericksburg and Spotsylvania National Military Park.** Its main visitor center, where films recount the battles and park employees field questions from Civil War buffs, is located in town at the foot of **Marye's Heights,** where the Confederate line decimated Union troops charging out of town below. Walking up the grassy terraced heights today, you can still feel the ghosts of Robert E. Lee and his boys watching your approach, trying to determine if you are friend or foe. —*K. M. Kostyal*

Travelwise

GETTING THERE

Fredericksburg is located on I-95, 50 miles south of the nation's capital and 50 miles north of Virginia's capital of Richmond. The nearest major airports are Reagan National, Dulles International, and Richmond International.

GENERAL INFORMATION

Spring and fall are the best seasons; summers are hot and humid; winters damp and cold. For information, contact the **Fredericksburg Visitor Center** *(706 Caroline St. 22401. 540-373-1776 or 800-678-4748. www.fredericksburgva.com).*

THINGS TO SEE AND DO

Belmont *(224 Washington St., Falmouth. 540-654-1015. Adm. fee)* Officially known as Belmont, the Gari Melchers Estate and Memorial Gallery, this 18th-century clapboard house in the village across the river was the final home of a prominent early 20th-century American artist. The studio houses portraits and impressionist landscapes.

Fredericksburg and Spotsylvania National Military Park *(Main Visitor Center, 1013*

Lafayette Blvd. at Sunken Rd. 540-373-6122. Adm. tickets sold here; maps and literature on all battlefield sites available) The park encompasses four battlefields and associated sites within a 17-mile radius. The immediate Fredericksburg vicinity includes **Marye's Heights,** the hill that gave the South the advantage in December 1862; the adjacent Fredericksburg National Cemetery holding graves of over 15,000 men who fell in battle; **Chatham** *(120 Chatham Ln. 540-373-0802),* an 18th-century Georgian mansion used as Union headquarters in 1862; and **Old Salem Church,** an 1844 brick structure associated with both the 1862 and 1863 battles.

Fredericksburg Area Museum and Cultural Center *(907 Princess St. 540-371-3037. Adm. fee)* The museum documents the townsite's long and varied past.

Horse-drawn Carriage Tours *(Tickets at visitor center)* These 45-minute rides clomp along the streets of Old Town.

Hugh Mercer Apothecary Shop *(1020 Caroline St. 540-373-3362. Adm. fee)* A restored apothecary offers a look at colonial medicine.

James Monroe Museum and Memorial Library *(908 Charles St. 540-654-1043. Adm. fee)* Fifth President James Monroe began his law practice on this site. On display are many of his documents and Louis XVI furniture he used during his White House years.

Kenmore *(1201 Washington Ave. 540-373-3381. Adm. fee)* Home of George Washington's sister, Betty, this elegant colonial mansion is adorned with elaborate plasterwork; its dining room is considered among the 100 most beautiful rooms in America.

Mary Washington College *(1301 College Ave. 540-654-1000)* Founded in 1908, the campus includes neo-Georgian brick buildings.

Mary Washington House *(1200 Charles St. 540-373-1569. Adm. fee)* The small clapboard was the home of George's mother from 1772 until her death 17 years later. Some of her belongings are still here.

Rising Sun Tavern *(1304 Caroline St. 540-371-1494)* Tavern "wenches" offer lively tours of this structure from the 1760s.

River Activities Canoeing, tubing, and kayaking on the Rappahannock can be arranged through Clore Bros. Outfitters *(540-786-7749)* or Rappahannock Outdoors Educational Center *(540-371-5085).*

SHOPPING

Fredericksburg's Old Town is chockablock with antique stores and gift shops, and toward the riverfront a number of artists and artisans maintain studios and galleries.

ANNUAL EVENTS

Annual Outdoor Antiques Fair *(Late Sept. 540-373-1776 or 800-678-4748. Adm. fee)* Dealers are here from throughout the eastern United States.

Fielding Lewis Market Day *(2nd Sat. in May. Caroline St. 540-373-1776 or 800-678-4748)* Colonial crafts, costumes, and merchandise recall bustling port days.

Fredericksburg Day of Historic Garden Week *(3rd weekend in April. 540-373-1776 or 800-678-4748. Adm. fee)* This statewide festival celebrates Virginia's fine homes and gardens, and one day is devoted to Fredericksburg.

Fredericksburg Music Festival *(Early June. 540-373-1776 or 800-678-4748. Adm. fee)* World-class musicians play Celtic, jazz, and classical music; ballets; and more.

WHERE TO EAT

La Petite Auberge *(311 William St. 540-371-2727. $$)* Hearty French country cooking is offered at reasonable prices.

Sammy T's *(801 Caroline St. 540-371-2008. $)* A local hangout, Sammy's offers generous sandwiches, salads, and other favorites.

WHERE TO STAY

Braehead B&B *(123 Lee Dr. 540-899-3648. $$)* During the 1862 battle, Robert E. Lee breakfasted at this 1859 brick home; three guest rooms with private baths.

Kenmore Inn *(1200 Princess Anne St. 540-371-7622. $$)* Dating from the 1780s, this historical inn boasts columns, arched entryways, a dining room, and 12 guest rooms decorated with antiques.

Richard Johnston Inn *(711 Caroline St. 540-899-7606. $$)* The stately brick building dates from 1770 and now offers six bedrooms and two suites decorated with antiques.

Abingdon

As the sun sets on the misty blue landscape of southwest Virginia, sending long shadows on tree-carpeted mountains and velvety pastures, all is quiet. All is quiet, that is, but in the little highland town of Abingdon, where the Barter Theatre is in full swing. Perhaps George and Emily are falling in love in *Our Town,* or Heathcliff is yearning for Catherine in *Wuthering Heights.* Maybe Pablo Picasso and Albert Einstein are deliberating in *Picasso at the Lapin Agile,* or Nazi Germany's boisterous side is being played out in *Cabaret.* Whatever the story being told, you can bet its production will be first-class, for the Barter is the State Theater of Virginia, and it remains the home of one of the oldest, still extant professional resident acting companies in America. But there's more to Abingdon than theater: Genteel B&Bs, candlelit restaurants, boutiques, artists' studios, a four-star historic hotel, and a wonderful rail-trail all combine to create a vibrant destination deep in the heart of the southern Appalachians.

Remote and wild, this mountainous niche came to life in the 1700s, as people heading west on the nearby Wilderness Road began passing through. In the 1760s, Daniel Boone visited while on a Kentucky surveying expedition. After wolves attacked his dogs one night, the legendary frontiersman christened the place Wolf Hills, a name that stuck until 1774. That year, Joseph Black built a fort to protect the growing number of townspeople from Indian attack, and the settlement became known as Black's Fort. The name was finally changed to Abingdon in 1778, when the town was incorporated, in honor of Martha Washington's ancestral parish in England.

Today, as long ago, **Main Street** is the town's major thoroughfare, if you can call it major. All red brick and shutters, colonial and federal edifices grace the tree-shaded street, their walls filled with boutiques and galleries, cafés and residences. You'll note right away that this is not a town of house museums, clinging desperately to the past. These stately structures are lived and worked

A Bartering Theater

A native Virginian, Robert Porterfield came up with the idea of a bartering theater when he brought a troupe of out-of-work New York City actors to Abingdon during the Great Depression. They accepted food for pay—"ham for Hamlet," they called it, though they also accepted corn, cakes, apples, even haircuts. Although a ham won't get you through the doors any longer, cash or plastic certainly will; and it's worth every penny for the highly skilled performances.

The Martha Washington's reception room

The venerable Barter Theatre

and played in, very much a part of today. For anyone interested in history, the Old Abingdon Association has placed informational plaques on the most significant structures.

The town's oldest building is **The Tavern,** constructed in 1779 to serve stagecoach travelers and still serving up hearty meals. Inside, glimmering candlelight casts dancing shadows on ancient wooden walls, evoking the days when such illustrious guests as President Andrew Jackson and King Louis-Philippe of France stopped by. Across the street is the **Adam Hickman House,** built in 1857 and now the **Cave House,** purveyor of fine local craftwork; the wolves that attacked Daniel Boone's dogs lived in the caves behind. Strolling west on Main Street, keep an eye out for the 1869 **Washington County Courthouse,** with its towering columns; the **Judge John A. Campbell House** *(116 E. Main St.),* built in 1847 and where Elliott Roosevelt, the father of First Lady Eleanor Roosevelt, once rented a room; and the lovely **Abingdon United Methodist Church,** built in 1883 and adorned with stunning stained-glass windows.

You can't miss the imposing **Martha Washington Inn** across the street from the Barter Theatre, its white wicker rockers swaying gently on the wide front porch. Gen. Francis Preston built the central brick core in 1832, and though the structure has been greatly renovated, much of its architectural integrity remains. The original living room is now the inn's main lobby, draped in swags and tassels, ribbons and bunting, and the polished-wood floors creak and groan with age. Beginning in 1858, the house became an elite girls school, then during the Civil War a makeshift field hospital for soldiers wounded in local skirmishes. There's one endearing tale of a girl named Beth who took care of a captured Union captain. Late one night as he lay dying, she serenaded him with a southern violin melody; her sweet notes can still be heard, it's said, on full-moon nights. After the school closed in 1932, the structure metamorphosed three years later into the grand, southern, four-star inn that survives today.

The single house open to the public, the **Fields-Penn 1860 House Museum,** is a block west from the hotel, a gracious Georgian constructed at the brink of the Civil War by James Fields, who built many of Abingdon's fine houses. Dolls, painted bowls, an authentic period kitchen, and vintage clothes are displayed just as if the occupants have left for a moment. Providing a glimpse into the lives of the second owners—the Penn family— are mother Estelle's exquisitely painted porcelain bowls and her daughter's fine paintings.

As you get to know Abingdon, you will sense its underlying artistic flair. There's the professional theater, of course, but there are also painters, sculptors, and weavers who keep local art galleries full. The unofficial command center is the **Starving Artist Cafe,** where works of art hang on the walls and some dishes are named for local artists. Across the street, resident artists work in large, airy studios at the **Arts Depot,** housed in the 19th-century freight station. And huge, colorful sculptures dot the grounds of the **William King Regional Arts Center,** poised on a nearby hill. A partner of the Virginia Museum of Fine Arts, this fabulous entity houses three large galleries.

From this hill you can see why artists are drawn here: Misty ridges, trout-filled streams, rhododendron thickets, cow-dotted pastures, and fields of goldenrod compose a sublime wilderness mosaic—a bounty of inspiration, indeed. Artist or not, enjoy this natural splendor from the **Virginia Creeper National Recreation Trail,** a converted rail-trail that winds, curves, and twists 34 miles from Green Spring Road up Whitetop Mountain. So quickly the street sounds are replaced by gurgling creeks and chirping crickets, rhapsodizing warblers and lowing cows. Here you find the essence of Abingdon, a cultural nook amid the isolated Blue Ridge Highlands. *Barbara A. Noe*

Travelwise

GETTING THERE

Abingdon is located in southwest Virginia, off I-81, about 130 miles west of Roanoke, Virginia, and about 130 miles east of Knoxville, Tennessee. Major airlines serve both Roanoke and Knoxville.

GENERAL INFORMATION

The best time to visit Abingdon is in the spring or early fall, when the surrounding landscape is colored with blooming or changing foliage and the temperatures are mild. Winter weather can be harsh. The **Abingdon Convention & Visitors Bureau** (335 Cummings St., Abingdon 24210. 540-676-2282 or 800-435-3440. www.abingdon.com) provides walking tour maps of historic areas, as well as other helpful information.

THINGS TO SEE AND DO

Arts Depot (314 Depot Sq. 540-628-9091. Thurs.-Sat. p.m. and by appt.) Watch studio artists at work and stroll through the Spotlight Gallery.

Barter Theatre (133 E. Main St. 540-628-3991 for reservations and ticket information. www.BarterTheatre.com) The official State Theater of Virginia, the Barter Theatre produces seasonal performances of first-class shows. Alumni include Gregory Peck, Ned Beatty, Kevin Spacey, and Patricia Neal.

Cave House Craft Shop (279 E. Main St. 540-628-7721) The 130-member Holston Mountain Arts and Crafts Cooperative sells works made regionally.

Fields-Penn 1860 House Museum (208 W. Main St. 540-676-0216. Wed.-Sat. p.m. and by appt.; donation) Guided tours portray town and family life in the late 1800s.

Virginia Creeper National Recreation Trail (Visitors Bureau 540-676-2282 or 800-435-3440) This gorgeous, 34-mile-long trail for hiking, biking, and horseback riding links downtown Abingdon with Whitetop Mountain. The best approach is to begin up the mountain, a downhill journey for almost all of the way back to Abingdon. Several companies offer bike rentals and shuttle services, including Blue Blaze Bike & Shuttle Service (540-475-5095 or 800-475-5095).

William King Regional Arts Center (415 Academy Dr. 540-628-5005. Closed Mon.; donation) Three galleries, working studios, and a sculpture garden showcase regional artists.

ANNUAL EVENTS

Plumb Alley Day (Sat. before Mem. Day. 800-435-3440) A local alley blooming with lilacs and dogwoods comes alive with music, antiques, and good food.

Virginia Highlands Festival (1st 2 weeks of Aug. 800-435-3440) This festival celebrates the area's cultural heritage.

WHERE TO EAT

Hardware Company Restaurant (260 W. Main St. 540-628-1111. $$) Seafood, pastas, steaks, and more are served up in one of Abingdon's popular hangouts.

Starving Artist Cafe (134 Wall St. at Depot Sq. 540-628-8445. $$) Eat gourmet sandwiches, fresh seafood, pasta, and vegetarian entrées; view local art exhibits on the walls.

The Tavern (222 E. Main St. 540-628-1118. $$) Considered the oldest building in Abingdon, the Tavern features classic American cuisine.

WHERE TO STAY

Martha Washington Inn (150 W. Main St. 540-628-3161 or 800-555-8000. $$$) One of the South's loveliest inns features 61 beautiful rooms, some with canopy beds.

Silversmith Inn (102 E. Main St. 540-676-3924. $$) This charming 1871 home, with four magnificently decorated rooms and a suite, was built on the site of a silversmith shop.

Summerfield Inn (101 W. Valley St. 540-628-5905 or 800-668-5905. $$) The gracious 20th-century home offers seven bedrooms.

Lewisburg

Deep in the heart of West Virginia's Allegheny Mountains, Lewisburg seems out of place, a cultural and recreational enclave in a land known for poverty and struggle. Here, residents—artists, retirees, shopkeepers—inhabit tidy colonial buildings on tree-shaded streets and shop in quaint boutiques filled with upscale art, New Age remedies, and handmade crafts. They dine at notable restaurants and

Carnegie Hall

attend performances at a veritable Carnegie Hall, donated by the great industrialist himself. Though this town works hard to polish its contemporary face, it still retains an old-fashioned allure—a place where summer afternoons are best lulled away with rocking chairs and ice-cold lemonade.

Perhaps the nicest spot to while away some time is the **General Lewis Inn,** perched high on a knoll above Washington Street. Southern charm permeates this genteel hotel's creaky rooms, each carefully decorated with local antiques. Plenty of history has taken place here: The oldest section dates back to 1834,

and during the Civil War, it survived a skirmish in its own backyard. The inn itself, established in 1929, was named for the town's founder, Andrew Lewis. Wander into the sitting room and you'll surely meet the owners, Mary Noel and Jim Morgan. Ask Mr. Morgan how he fell in love with the "innkeeper's daughter" many years back; hear how their daughter and son, Nan and Jim, now run the place with verve. Then take a seat in one of the high-backed rockers lining the veranda and quietly watch the world go by as the house cat, Butterscotch, purrs against your legs.

Old Hardware Gallery, on Washington Street

At some point you'll have to get up to see the town and its medley of colonial and federal buildings, all edging quiet lanes and shaded by ancient trees. Begin a stroll at the town square, dominated by the white-columned **Carnegie Hall,** Carnegie's gift in 1902 to the Lewisburg Female Institute. Squeaking hallways lead to a variety of artist and dance studios, the crown jewel being the 398-seat performance hall. This stately, green-and-red room recently underwent a one-million-dollar restoration, and it gleams. From September through May, classical music, bluegrass, dance troupes, and touring theaters lure patrons from far and wide.

Nearby stands the **Old Stone Presbyterian Church,** reputedly the oldest church in continuous use west of the Alleghenies. Constructed of native limestone in 1796, its interior includes what once were slave galleries. In the cemetery out back, the names of some of the area's earliest settlers are etched into now crumbling tombstones—among them Capt. Matthew Arbuckle, a woodsman and early explorer; and Dick Pointer, a black slave who distinguished himself at the 1778 Battle of Fort Donnally. More history lies across the square at the **John A. North House Museum,** built in 1820 and characterized by finely carved woodwork. A guide leads you through rooms filled with china, furniture, vintage clothing, and other relics from the early town. In one room a series of locally crafted dioramas depicts local sites, all peopled with clay figures of real townfolk. Ask your guide to point out some of the favorites, perhaps the General Store, where locals gather around a pot-bellied stove.

Down the street in Andrew Lewis Park you'll find **Lewis Spring,** where it all began. Back in 1751, a young surveyor named Andrew Lewis camped out here. With Indian uprisings prevalent in the surrounding Greenbrier River Valley, the camp was soon fortified into Fort Savannah. From here, Lewis—now a general—led an expedition of Virginia militiamen against the Shawnee, Mingo, Omaha, and Delaware, culminating in the Battle of Point Pleasant on the Ohio River. The Indian threat was greatly reduced and, in tribute, the settlement around Lewis Spring was named Lewisburg.

Between the spring and your chair at the General Lewis Inn lies the town's core, a bustling mix of urbane boutiques and restaurants. Continue your stroll, stopping now and then to chat with locals, browsing what there is to see. Upscale **Robert's Antiques** *(120 E. Washington St.)* always features a jaw-dropping window display, a unique horse-drawn hearse or some other artifact that Robert's meticulous searching has dug up. Housed in the old general store, **Mattie's** *(109 E. Washington St.)* is a New York–style roastery where pungent coffee aromas and classical notes mingle with fresh flowers and local artwork. **Edith's Health and Specialty Store** *(128 W. Washington St. 304-645-7998)*, purveyor of New Age and homeopathic wares, is a place where pierced youths and overall-clad elders alike seek out herbal remedies. And much excitement surrounds the old department store, which is being transformed into the new **Greenbrier Valley Theater** *(304-645-3838)*.

For all its big-town flair, Lewisburg is still a down-home place where people smile and nature is never far away. The town snuggles in the lush Greenbrier River Valley, a countryscape of tree-carpeted hills, stone-strewn streams, and rustic covered bridges. Showcasing this beauty best is the 76-mile **Greenbrier River Trail,** an abandoned rail corridor along the Greenbrier River popular with bikers, hikers, horseback riders, and cross-country skiers alike. Beginning just east of Lewisburg, it ambles north through supreme wilderness to Cass, a restored railroading town. If biking or hiking seems a bit too much, consider floating the river by raft or canoe. With wildflower-dotted banks moving slowly past and puffy clouds drifting across the bright blue sky above, you will have discovered the secret to a perfectly languid weekend. *Barbara A. Noe*

Battle of Lewisburg

A southern outpost for most of the Civil War, Lewisburg's only battle ended in a Union victory. Early on May 23, 1862, Confederates attacked Union troops occupying the town. In an hour-long skirmish, the inexperienced Northerners fought like veterans, and the Southerners were forced to retreat. The final losses: 80 Confederates, 13 Northerners. You can visit the Confederate Cemetery on McElhenney Rd. The Union casualties were buried at the National Cemetery in Staunton. Ask the visitors bureau for a battle tour brochure.

Travelwise

GETTING THERE

Lewisburg is off I-64 in southeastern West Virginia. The nearest major airport is Yaeger Airport in the capital city of Charleston.

GENERAL INFORMATION

The best time is spring, when wildflowers are in bloom, and fall, when the trees display rich colors. The **Lewisburg Convention and Visitors Bureau** (*105 Church St. 24901. 304-645-1000 or 800-833-2068. www.greenbrierwv.com*), housed in Carnegie Hall, has walking tour brochures and information on driving tours.

THINGS TO SEE AND DO

Andrew Lewis Spring (*Andrew Lewis Park, on Jefferson St.*) Discovered and named by early settler Andrew Lewis, the spring is enclosed in a stone springhouse more than 200 years old.

Carnegie Hall (*105 Church St. 304-645-7917*) This Greek Revival performance hall was built in 1902.

Greenbrier County Courthouse (*200 N. Court St.*) Last of several courthouses in Lewisburg, and typical of early Virginia courthouses with its red brick structure and white columns, this building was constructed in 1837.

Greenbrier River Trail (*304-799-4087 or 800-CALL-WVA. Take US 60 E for 3 miles, turn left just before bridge at Greenbrier River, follow Stone House Rd. about 1.5 miles*) Originally part of the Chesapeake & Ohio rail system, this 76-mile hike-and-bike trail runs along the Greenbrier River from North Caldwell to Cass. Bike rentals and transport services are available in Lewisburg.

Greenbrier Valley Theatre (*304-645-3838*) Live musicals, drama, and comedy on Wednesday through Saturday from mid-June to early August at the Old Barn at the Greenbrier Valley Airport. Additional performances are occasionally given in Greenbrier Valley Theatre on Washington Street.

John A. North House Museum (*301 W. Washington St. 304-645-3398. Closed Sun.; adm. fee*) Built in 1820, this house museum

contains the collection of the Greenbrier Historical Society.

Old Stone Presbyterian Church (*200 Church St.*) Lewisburg's most famous landmark dates from 1796, making it the oldest church west of the Alleghenies that has remained in continuous use.

WHERE TO EAT

Clingman's Market (*102 E. Washington St. 304-645-1990. Closed Sun. and dinner. $*) This local luncheon oddity hasn't changed much since its days as a pre-Depression meat market; farmers and businessmen alike sit at folding tables, their menu choices being generous portions of "meat" and "no meat."

Julian's Restaurant & Coffee Bar (*102 S. Lafayette St. 304-645-4145. Wed.-Sat. $$*) At Stephen Jackendoff's fine restaurant, favorites include pan-seared salmon with feta cheese and mushrooms; prime angus beef; and soft shell crabs.

WHERE TO STAY

General Lewis Inn (*301 E. Washington St. 304-645-2600 or 800-628-4454. $$*) The inn is furnished with locally collected antiques, and all beds in its 26 rooms are at least a century old. The inn's restaurant features southern-style cooking (*$$*).

The Greenbrier (*9 miles E of Lewisburg, in White Sulfur Springs. 304-536-1110. $$$*) One of the world's most famous and elegant resorts.

THE SOUTHEAST

Berea

Tucked into the Cumberland foothills where Kentucky's bluegrass brushes up against the mountains, this little town claims a big reputation. As folk arts and crafts capital of the state, Berea acts as a kind of year-round fair of woodwork, ceramics, weaving, wrought iron, and broomcraft. Some 100 artisans sell their work in 40 galleries scattered about town, and, as if that weren't enough, three major annual crafts festivals draw on talent from around the region and the nation. But the heart of the community lies in historic Berea College, where many students continue to learn traditional Appalachian crafts.

Good Woods

Turning a tree into a table involves a number of steps, and one of the main ones is choosing the right wood. Many artisans like wild cherry, for example, because it darkens naturally with age. Instrumentmakers prefer the deep, rich tones produced by cherry and fine-grained black walnut over, say, poplar, which produces a bright, ringing sound. Burls, swirls, and color variations are often left untouched to show off the individuality of a piece of wood. Before making a purchase, talk with the craftsman to find out what choices he or she made and why.

The tree-shaded campus of **Berea College** makes a good starting point for a tour of Berea. You can join a guided tour at Boone Tavern or pick up a map at the Admissions Building on Chestnut Street and Ky. 595. You won't find the college an intimidating maze of buildings and streets. The enrollment here is a mere 1,500, so parking and walking are a breeze. Yet it's worth noting that Berea has been ranked among the very top liberal arts colleges in the South.

In 1853 abolitionist Cassius Clay donated a tract of land in what was then called the Glade to establish a base for his antislavery movement. Despite a shaky start, the tiny village of Berea held on, and the forerunner of Berea College opened in 1855 on an equal basis to blacks and whites, men and women. That unprecedented display of egalitarianism did not sit well with the state legislature, so it passed a law in 1904 forbidding interracial education. The college then began focusing its efforts on educating less fortunate whites from the mountains. Some of the students brought handmade coverlets as tuition, and to capitalize on a growing national interest in Appalachian culture the school began to market handmade crafts. Berea and Asheville, North Carolina, became leaders in the revival of American crafts in the late 1920s. To this day, all students are on full scholarship, working ten to fifteen hours a week in the crafts areas or as employees in other college-run facilities.

One of the places you'll see student workers is across Main Street at the white-columned **Boone Tavern Hotel of Berea College.** Built in 1909, this

Boone Tavern Hotel of Berea College

gracious southern hostelry is a great place to plop into a student-made, cane-bottomed chair and sit for a spell. Or you can take a meal in the elegant yet casual dining room. Boone Tavern anchors **College Square,** home to a number of shops and restaurants. One that shouldn't be missed, even if you don't plan to buy, is **Warren May's** *(110 Center St.)*. For more than two decades he has been turning cherry, walnut, poplar, and other local woods into exquisite furniture. But he is best known for his elegant dulcimers. Listen to him play and you could easily end up plunking down $300 for one.

In a triangle between Center Street and US 25, you'll find the **Log House Craft Gallery,** where you can buy the best of hand-crafted pieces. Don't expect a bargain, though; these products reflect expert work. Brooms with

Cumberland foothills

carved walnut handles, wrought-iron candelabras, and stools made of woven sea grass are a few of the items for sale here; you can also find toys and non-traditional things. Sign up here for a tour of the college crafts program: Seeing students at work in the weaving cottage and in broomcraft and woodcraft shops gives you a real appreciation for the finished products in the stores.

From the Log House it's a short drive, or a 15-minute walk, out to **Churchill Weavers,** which has been around since 1922. You can take a self-guided wander back through the busy loom house where workers toil over hand-operated looms turning raw fiber into finished fabrics. Churchill prefers that you not talk to the weavers while they work, but you can learn more about the whole process by watching a demonstration video out front in the stylish gift shop.

The other main shopping area, **Old Town,** is a clutch of low-lying buildings along Broadway and Adams. **Berea's Welcome Center,** housed in a restored 1917 railroad depot, is located here and well worth a stop. Among shops, one highlight is **Weaver's Bottom Craft Studio** *(140 N. Broadway).* Unlike the offerings in most area shops, everything here is made by the people who run the store. Mary Colmer's cornshuck dolls have distinguishing regional touches—the ribbons and knots, for example; bedspreads and throws are made on the loom in the corner by her husband Neil.

Take a peek in the other stores: Each has something different to offer. With your trunk full of finely crafted works of wood, pottery, and weaving, you can feel good not only that you're bringing authentic pieces of the country back home, but that you're supporting a long tradition of mountain craftsmanship. *John M. Thompson*

Travelwise

GETTING THERE

Berea lies in central Kentucky, off I-75. It is 40 miles south of Lexington, which is accessible by plane or bus.

GENERAL INFORMATION

Spring and fall are the best times for a visit to Berea. Daytime temperatures can be delightful, but the evening air may be a bit chilly. Summer is generally hot and humid, and winter is unpredictable. For more information, contact the **Berea Welcome Center** (201 N. Broadway, Berea 40403. 606-986-2540 or 800-598-5263).

THINGS TO SEE AND DO

Berea College (Craft tours depart from Log House Craft Gallery, 210 Center St. 606-986-9341. Mon.-Fri., twice daily. Campus tours depart from Boone Tavern Hotel Mon.-Fri., four times daily) One-hour tours of the college and of the crafts program provide visitors with a good overview of Berea and its tradition of education.

Churchill Weavers (0.75 mile N of College Square off US 25, follow signs. 606-986-3126. Loom house tours Mon.-Fri.) You can spend some time watching weavers work in the old-fashioned way. Afterward, visit the elegant store out front where you can purchase their products.

SHOPPING

In addition to the shops mentioned previously, there are numerous other places where you can buy handmade products; most of them sell a variety of wares and gifts. Old Town has several shops that specialize in jewelry, glass art, Shaker furniture, and similar items.

ANNUAL EVENTS

Kentucky Guild of Artists & Craftsmen Fairs (3rd weekend in May and 2nd weekend in Oct. Indian Fort Theater, 3 miles E on Ky. 21. 606-986-3192. Adm. fee) With live music filling the air, more than 120 artisans from around the region display and sell their creations.

WHERE TO EAT

Note: Berea is a dry town. The nearest liquor store is in Richmond, Kentucky, about 15 miles to the north.

Boone Tavern Hotel of Berea College (100 Main St. 606-986-9358 or 800-366-9358. $$) The elegant southern fare with a tastefully casual ambience includes such specials as "chicken flakes in a bird's nest," spoon bread, and Jefferson Davis pie.

Papaleno's (108 Center St. 606-986-4497. $) This lively hangout for college students stays open late. Pizzas are the specialty of the house, but there are also good pasta dishes, sandwiches, and salads.

Sweet Betty's (Berea exit off I-75. 606-986-3824. $) The place to go for good home-style country cooking. Load up at the buffet, but save room for a piece of Betty's famous pie.

WHERE TO STAY

Boone Tavern Hotel of Berea College (100 Main St. 606-986-9358 or 800-366-9358. $$) This comfortable old hotel, with its stately columns and southern hospitality, has been a tradition here since 1909. Boone Tavern's guest rooms have been decorated with furniture handcrafted by students attending Berea College.

Doctor's Inn of Berea (617 Chestnut St. 606-986-3042. $$) A relaxed and homey atmosphere fills this handsome B&B, which features a grand piano, happy hour, and a full country-style breakfast.

NEARBY PLACE

White Hall State Historic Site (20 miles N of town, at White Hall Boonesborough exit off I-75. 606-623-9178. April-Oct. Wed.-Sun.; adm. fee) A tour of the 1798 home and estate of eccentric abolitionist Cassius Marcellus Clay—whose land grant was the start of Berea—gives visitors a fascinating glimpse of a colorful character.

Jonesborough

Set in the picturesque hill country of eastern Tennessee, the state's oldest town is a time capsule of early America. From the top of Main Street, you can behold dozens of restored, early 19th-century brick buildings, punctuated by the white spires of churches. Shopfronts and sidewalks wear seasonal decorations, while locals and tourists alike rest on benches outside the courthouse. Jonesborough combines country style with polish, and its pulse is easy to take. A weekend getaway at one of the many elegant B&Bs can quickly restore you to a saner rhythm and revise your concept of small town Appalachia.

Jonesborough has only come into its own within the last few decades. The raw material was there—historic buildings, pioneer heroes, and a pleasant setting—but by the late 1960s, a slow economy and the sprawling growth of nearby Johnson City were drying up Jonesborough's fortunes. Then two things happened. Citizens got their town listed on the National Register of

Main Street, Jonesborough

Historic Places, a first for the state. And in 1973, the National Storytelling Festival was born here, an annual event that some local merchants claim generates almost half their income.

If you pick up a walking-tour brochure at the **Visitor Center** and head to Main Street, you'll enter a small but thriving downtown. Lamp posts, brick sidewalks, and the lack of overhead wires lend an air of old times. Buildings sport large windows, ornamental cornices, and a large concentration of stepped gables. Founded in 1779 as a county seat in western North Carolina, Jonesborough five years later became the capital of the breakaway state of Franklin. But after a brief battle, the town returned to the fold and became part of Tennessee when the new state was formed in 1796. Andrew Jackson was a judge here, Davy Crockett was born about 10 miles away, and Daniel Boone hunted in the nearby woods.

Andrew Jackson, the town's most prominent early citizen, stayed at the **Chester Inn** *(116 1/2 Main St.)*. The rambling 1790s building, with a breezy second-floor veranda, also hosted two other presidents, James Polk and Andrew Johnson. It now houses the offices of Storytelling Foundation International; a store on the ground floor sells books and tapes. When completed in the fall of 2000, the Storytelling Center will contain exhibits, an auditorium, and classrooms where business leaders and others can learn effective

Flower-bedecked storefronts

storytelling. The national revival of the oral tradition is due in part to Jonesborough's annual October weekend drawing some 10,000 visitors.

Another ancient structure, the **Rees-Hawley House,** is documented as the "oldest house in Tennessee's oldest town." It operates as a B&B and is open for tours if you call ahead. The original chestnut log structure, dating from 1793, was augmented with a frame addition and wide front porch. The painstaking attention to historical accuracy in the furnishings and restoration is typical of the care given to old houses in Jonesborough. Check out the old-fashioned basement kitchen, for instance, with its working fireplace and antique implements. Friendly hostess Marcy Hawley will supply you with details on the house and the town—historic and current.

A stone's throw away, the 1840s **Salt House** at 127 Fox Street supplied salt to locals during the Civil War; now you can buy gifts and collectibles here. Walk back to Main to poke around other old buildings open to the public. **Mauk',** one of the oldest pharmacies in the state, is now a grab bag of tasteful crafts and souvenirs, but it maintains a few shelves of vitamins and nostrums. And don't miss the adjacent **Mail Pouch Building,** which dates from 1888; it's now a gift shop.

At the end of the day, feel free to join the locals at the **Cranberry Thistle,** a delightful den of flavored coffees, healthful sandwiches, and delicious cakes and brownies. Sit back in a rocking chair, introduce yourself, and catch up on the latest gossip and news. Whether the discussion centers on the rezoning of a street or on something said by somebody's grandfather in church one day, you'll find small town America at its most essential here. When there's a good-size crowd, the proprietors sometimes pass around a plate of fresh goodies.

Recent years have seen the steady return of people who had left town after growing up here. Perhaps people need to go away to really appreciate the quality of life, one member of the historic zoning commission says. "Since I've been here, I've never lost my keys, because I leave them in the car, and there's no key to the house," she says. She has a neighbor who walks her dog at two o'clock in the morning, hearing only the rumble of trains and the chiming of the courthouse clock. The price for such freedom is the relative isolation, but more and more people are thinking that's not a bad price at all. *John M. Thompson*

Travelwise

GETTING THERE

Jonesborough is in the northeast corner of Tennessee, 90 miles northeast of Knoxville and 10 miles south of I-81 via Tenn. 81. There is bus service to Johnson City, about 10 miles east, and Tri-Cities Regional Airport is about 20 miles north, just south of Kingsport.

GENERAL INFORMATION

Spring, summer, and fall are all good times for a visit. Storytelling weekend in October attracts the biggest crowds. For more information contact the **Historic Jonesborough Visitor Center** (*117 Boone St., Jonesborough 37659. 423-753-1010 or 800-400-4221*).

THINGS TO SEE AND DO

Jonesborough Repertory Theater (*Main St.*) For a schedule, call 423-753-0781.

Time and Tales Tour (*Visitor Center, 117 Boone St. 423-753-1013. Fee*) Groups of six or more can arrange escorted walking or bus tours of churches and private, still-lived-in, historic houses. Tours are in storytelling form.

Visitor Center (*117 Boone St. 423-753-1010*) Besides distributing free literature about the area, the Visitor Center sells books, storytelling tapes, and a walking-tour brochure; it also shows a short film. Under the same roof, the **Jonesborough-Washington County History Museum** (*423-753-1016. Adm. fee*) has exhibits on Andrew Jackson, the state of Franklin, and the abolitionist movement popular in this part of the state. Recently moved from Knob Creek, 7 miles north, the **one-room schoolhouse** out back offers a look at rural 1890s education. Pine floors, a working bell, and a dunce cap add authenticity. Students and teachers are in period dress, writing with quill pens and studying original texts.

Wetlands Water Park (*1523 Persimmon Ridge Rd. 423-753-1558 or 888-622-1885. Summer; adm. fee*) Cool off in a 200-foot water slide, 155-foot tubing river, children's play area, and large pool.

SHOPPING

Jonesborough specializes in country crafts such as quilts, preserves, and landscape paintings, as well as stuff found in area attics

and basements. The biggest antique shop is **Jonesborough Antique Mart** (*115 E. Main St. 423-753-8301*).

ANNUAL EVENTS

Historic Jonesborough Days (*Early July. 423-753-5281*) Games, crafts, music, a parade, and fireworks.

National Storytelling Festival (*1st weekend in Oct. Various downtown venues. 423-753-2171 or 800-952-8392. Fee*) More than 30 raconteurs from around the country gather here, at the grandaddy of all story events.

WHERE TO EAT

Main Street Cafe (*117 W. Main St. 423-753-2460. Closed Sun. $*) This genial eatery with its high pressed-tin ceiling and wood floors and booths makes you want to stay a while.

Parson's Table (*102 Woodrow Ave. 423-753-8002. Closed Mon. and Jan. $$*) Southern-French fare in an 1874 Gothic church building.

WHERE TO STAY

Blair-Moore House B&B (*201 W. Main St. 423-753-0044 or 888-453-0044. $$*) This 1832 Greek Revival-style house offers a lovely garden and tasteful furnishings. Each of three rooms has its own decor—Victorian, Western, and early American.

Hawley House B&B (*114 E. Woodrow Ave. 423-753-8869 or 800-753-8869. $$*) This handsome log-and-frame lodge has three rooms furnished with late 18th- and early 19th-century antiques.

Highlands

Here you enter one of the East Coast's most entrancing regions, a land of deeply forested mountains cut by canyons, mesmerizing waterfalls, and narrow back roads. To the Cherokee who lived here for generations before being forced to walk the Trail of Tears, this land was their treasured Hills in the Sky. Today a similar pride is felt by the residents of Highlands, an intriguing town set on a 4,000-foot-high plateau near the towering cliffs of Whiteside Mountain, where bald eagles and peregrine falcons soar under ringing blue skies and duck-down clouds.

The wild mountains that cradle Highlands are in Blue Ridge country, on the southern fringes of North Carolina's Great Smokies and the vast Cherokee and Nantahala National Forests. Starting with tightly packed ridges and hollows in the southern foothills, the landscape becomes thickly wooded as you move up into the mountains, a remote niche with scattered, kudzu-covered

Blue Ridge prospect from the Millstone Inn

shacks that hint at former occupancy. When you at last hit the high spots, you are rewarded with vistas of wavelike parallel mountain ridges.

Highlands is without doubt the highlight of the region. The Cherokee revered its pleasant prospect, and early explorers considered it a botanical wonderland. The town is not entirely unknown today: While Highlands has only 3,000 or so residents, its population can climb to more than 15,000 during the summer season. Even so, at the height of its tourist season, this tight-knit community somehow maintains the ambience of an early 1900s hill village and keeps to its laid-back, laconic ways. The result is precisely not what Samuel T. Kelsey and Clinton C. Hutchinson had in mind when they purchased 839 acres on this high mountain plateau in the mid-1870s and published a brochure proclaiming that there was "no better climate in the world for health, comfort and enjoyment." Kelsey and Hutchinson had a truly grand vision of a new megalopolis where two key map lines intersected: The first line extended from Chicago to Savannah, and the second stretched from New York to New Orleans. Highlands, they believed, would become the "next great center of national commerce"—not the little mountain health-resort that it has turned out to be.

A quiet retreat in Nantahala National Forest

Edged by the dense **Nantahala National Forest,** in which the spring rush of scarlet and white rhododendron blossoms softens an otherwise wild nature, Highlands maintains the relatively refined air of a resort: Cocktails are at six o'clock (it's strictly BYO in this dry county); dinner is at eight (jacket and tie are preferred in some establishments); and sidewalks are all neatly "rolled up" by ten in preparation for a tomorrow filled with more fishing, mountain drives, hikes, and picnics at one of more than 200 magnificent waterfalls that tumble and cascade through the canyons of Macon, Jackson, and Transylvania Counties.

"Don't let the funky old storefronts of our little town fool you," said Pat Benton. She and her husband Rip own the handsomely restored **Highlands Inn,** which dates from 1880 and is situated in the center of town directly across the street from the equally appealing 1878 **Old Edwards Inn.** "This little place has got it all—fancy shopping, antique bookstores, art galleries, live theater, antiques, handmade jewelry, crafts stores, and some of the best eatin' in all the mountains around here!" Obviously Pat's biased, but she's also accurate. Highlands has big-city sophistication in a distinctly rural guise, and that's its appeal. It also enjoys all the real benefits of bucolic rurality: The air sparkles, the summers are cool with low humidity, and nature trails from the **Highlands Nature Center** and its botanical gardens meander through lush woodlands. Waiting to be explored, the surrounding forests offer deep peace and cathedral silences just beyond the edge of town.

Be careful, though, if you decide to see the area by car, because you may find that it's not an easy drive following the seemingly endless, winding roads that climb and descend through this ancient land. The mountains here hold layer upon layer of rocks that were buckled, bowed, and eroded for more than 200 million years, long before the geologically youthful Rockies and Sierras began to rise. Two or three decades ago you would have had this place pretty much to yourself, and even today—despite the recent popularity of mountain country clubs, golf courses, and lakeside developments, as well as ostentatious trophy homes—you'll still find long, empty stretches of road within easy distance of tiny Highlands.

Probably the most beautiful drive leaves town via US 64 west. Paralleling the Cullasaja River and its spectacular, 300-foot gorge, the forested byway takes you past a series of crashing waterfalls. You can walk behind **Dry Falls** into a dry cave; and a portion of old US 64 allows you to drive beneath **Bridal Veil Falls.** Wet and lush, you probably won't be surprised to learn that this woodlands is actually a rain forest—it sees more than 90 inches of rain a year, making it the second wettest spot in the United States.

Eighteen miles later awaits the little town of **Franklin.** At first glance, this place seems to be little more than an old-fashioned main street set atop a steep hill and surrounded by fast food outlets, auto dealers, and garish gas stations. But look more closely: Franklin is Gem City, where you'll find a collection of gem stores, a gem museum (including Scottish Tartans for some reason), and gem-hunters galore. The nearby Cowee Valley, or Valley of Rubies, was once thought to be among the nation's richest repositories of rubies, sapphires, garnets, and rhodolites. Commercial mining operations gave up decades ago, but that doesn't discourage the thousands who flock here in search of the ever elusive "big one."

As regions go, this whole area is a gem. It's a wonderworld of waterfalls, lakes, towering mountains, deep valleys, canyons—and dreams.   *David Yeadon*

Travelwise

GETTING THERE

Highlands is located in the southwest corner of North Carolina, about 45 miles west of the I-26 and N.C. 280 intersection, then west on US 64 via Brevard and Cashiers. A slower but splendidly scenic drive is via the Blue Ridge Parkway to N.C. 215 and US 64 west from Rosman. The closest major airport is in Atlanta.

GENERAL INFORMATION

All seasons have their delights here, but late spring and early fall are ideal for mid-range temperatures and low humidity. Highlands has a small **Chamber of Commerce** office *(P.O. Box 404, Highlands 28741. 828-526-2112)* at Oak and 4th Streets, with abundant information on the town and region.

THINGS TO SEE AND DO

Bascom-Louise Gallery *(554 Main St. 828-526-4949. Closed Sun.-Mon.)* This modest nonprofit gallery located within the excellent Hudson Library features the works of local and regional artists.

Center for Life Enrichment *(Crosby Community Services Ctr., 348 S. 5th St. 828-526-9381)* The center's offerings include cabarets and more serious educational courses.

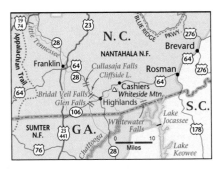

Fly-fishing Instruction and guides can be arranged by contacting Main Stream Outfitters *(173 Right Sq. 828-526-5649).*

Highlands Nature Center *(Horse Cove Rd. 828-526-2623. Call for hours)* The center contains a fascinating array of local Native American items, plants and animals of the southern Appalachians, and geological specimens. The adjoining botanical gardens and hiking trail is open year-round, and miles of local trails link up key sites around the town. Most dramatic is the **Sunset Rocks Overlook,** a 20-minute hike from the center.

Highlands Playhouse *(Oak and 4th Sts. 828-526-2695)* While not exactly a hot spot for hypernightlife, the playhouse celebrates almost 60 years of nationally acclaimed seasonal theater by putting on occasional cutting-edge productions.

SHOPPING

A recent rapid increase in commercial development here reflects the tastes of a discriminating upmarket clientele of residents and visitors. Particularly notable is a wide range of antique stores, art galleries, and craft stores on Main Street and Wright Square. **Cyrano's Bookshop** (390 Main St. 828-1526-5488) sells "books for the mind, heart and soul." **Masterworks of Highlands** (141 Wright Sq. 828-526-2633) and **Mountain Heritage** (371 Main St. 828-526-5519) both feature what they call the works of America's finest artisan-craftsmen.

ANNUAL EVENT

Highlands Chamber Music Festival (Summer. 828-526-9060. Adm. fee) This well-established program offers superlative regional and national chamber music ensembles.

WHERE TO EAT

Nationally acclaimed for its fine dining, Highlands has many restaurants from which to choose. In addition to the hotel restaurants, other notable places include the following establishments:

Lakeside Restaurant (Smallwood Ave. 828-526-9419. $$) This eatery is known as a casual restaurant with serious cuisine and has large portions of Continental dishes. It is possible to order wine here, and there is a "Brown Bag" license for beer and spirits—rather important in this dry region.

On the Verandah (1536 Franklin Rd. 828-526-2338. $$) Fine eclectic contemporary American cuisine is served in a splendidly scenic indoor/outdoor setting overlooking Lake Sequoyah.

Wolfgang's on Main (474 E. Main St. 828-526-3807. Call for hours. $$) A historic home setting with garden pavilion, deck, and fireside dining features New Orleans specialties by Chef Wolfgang, formerly of Brennan's.

WHERE TO STAY

Chandler Inn (US 64 E and Martha's Ln. 828-526-5992. $$) The inn is pure rusticity, with three barn-sided buildings that surround

a central courtyard. Guests enjoy porches with swings and rocking chairs; flowers and plants that seem to be everywhere; cozy romantic rooms—some with fireplaces; and beds adorned with brass headboards.

Highlands Inn (Main St. 828-526-9380 or 800-964-6955. $$) Recently celebrating its 120th year as a hotel, this extensively renovated favorite exudes pure country charm and boasts a fine restaurant, Kelsey Place.

Millstone Inn (7 miles E on US 64, in Cashiers. 828-743-2737. $$$) A timber-frame hotel with 11 rooms and astounding views.

Old Edwards Inn (4th and Main Sts. 828-526-9319. $$) This sturdy stone and brick hostelry dates from 1878 and features antique-decorated rooms and fine contemporary wall-stenciling by local artist, Donna Feltman. It also serves up a generous amount of true southern hospitality.

Toad Hall (61 Sequoyah Point Way, off US 64 W. 828-526-3889 or 888-891-3889. $$$) Enjoy total seclusion on a lakebound peninsula with great vistas, antique-filled rooms, and canoes for exploring Lake Sequoyah.

NEARBY PLACES

Cliffside Lake (4.5 miles W of town on US 64) Follow lake-loop trails and take an interpretive hike describing shrubs and trees along the cliff-top Vista Trail.

Franklin (Chamber of Commerce 704-524-3161 or 800-336-7829) This unassuming town is known for the precious and semiprecious stones mined in the area. This wealth of natural resources is celebrated during the **Macon County Gemboree** in late July.

Glen Falls (2 miles S on N.C. 106, turn L a mile on Glen Falls Rd.) An exciting dirt road drive culminates in three lovely falls on Overflow Creek.

Nantahala National Forest (U.S. Forest Service 828-526-3765) Call for general information on the vast array of natural recreational features in the Highlands area.

Whiteside Mountain (6 miles E on US 64) A 2-mile hike offers spectacular vistas from a 2,100-foot ridge on 4,900-foot Whiteside Mountain. This mountain boasts the highest vertical cliffs in the eastern United States.

Beaufort

Once disparaged as "fish town," beautiful little Beaufort (BO-furt) still has an air of working-class sturdiness despite its renown as an architectural showplace. Edged up against Taylor's Creek, its perfect grid of shaded streets is blessed by the salty breath of the nearby Atlantic and chockablock with more than a hundred well-preserved Greek Revival, federal, and Victorian gems, some built by the yesteryear sea captains who inhabited this town. Now given over to countless B&Bs, the houses seem like town personalities, here long before their current owners and destined to be overseeing Beaufort long after those owners are gone. Like the oldtimers, happy to talk with you in their down-home Carolina accent about the fish-town days, those homes have survived hurricanes, floods, and now an influx of newcomers, who recognize the town's deep-rooted, slow-moving charms.

Beaufort's harbor

Far from the roar of traffic and similar travails, Beaufort wakes up to the sounds of garden birds twittering and gulls cawing out along the creek edge. The streets are still quiet at nine o'clock, though a few old men might be gathered on porch steps or at storefronts to talk over the issues of the day—the fishing season, sports, the like. Morning is a good time to head for the **Old Burying Ground,** to wake the prominent dead. Nestled beneath lordly live oaks and lush resurrection ferns, most of the tombstones in the walled, crowded space face east toward the rising sun. Since the early 1700s, this was the coveted place to end your days, and such town fathers as Josiah Bell rest in peace here, along with the dead of the Revolutionary and Civil Wars.

But the town's roots go far back beyond them. The Coree Indians had their own village—Cwarioc (Fish Town)—on these banks long before Europeans arrived. In 1713 the earliest settlers carefully laid out the streets of the old village, declared it a seaport, and named it for the Duke of Beaufort. As Mamre Wilson proudly proclaims in *A Brief History of Beaufort and Carteret County, North Carolina,* "The families that had a part in the establishment of Beaufort as a seaport town and center of government and business continue to live here today through their descendants. It is not unusual to find that nearly everyone who was born and bred here is related."

That robust pride in roots is most obvious at **Beaufort Historic Site,** a clutch of buildings in the heart of town. Docents decked out in colonial mop caps and flocked skirts take great pleasure in leading tours through the six collected historic structures, a few still standing where they were built, several moved to the site. The docents narrate more than the usual litany of Canton china and wainscoting wonders. They tell you in detail the grisly doctoring techniques of a hundred years ago, how houses were built to withstand hurricanes, how the town has changed over time. If you want to keep more company with the docents (most in fact were born and bred here and sprinkle their historic narrative with pithy facts from the town's more recent past), then take the narrated bus tour of the town in an English double-decker that gingerly navigates the small streets.

Another big draw in this little town is the **North Carolina Maritime Museum,** which traces the coastal commerce of the state from the modern fish and shellfish industries to the shore whaling that went on in these waters in the past. (Beaufort was one of two places on the East Coast where whalers could put out in small boats, take whales, and return to shore—all in a day's work.) Probably the museum's most romantic

Fury from Hell

Edward Teach eschewed his English name and became Blackbeard, one of the most notorious pirates on the East Coast. Chased from Virginia's waters, Teach headed south to harass ships off North Carolina in the early 1700s. He went into battle with "lighted matches stuck under his hat...his eyes naturally fierce and wild...a Fury from Hell." The fury met his match in Virginia's Governor Spotswood, who sent two sloops out to hunt him down. Blackbeard withstood 25 wounds before succumbing to bounty hunters, who skewered his head to a pole and presented it to the governor.

Edward Barnwell House, Beaufort

exhibit is the one on Blackbeard, privateer extraordinaire. When pirates were driven out of the West Indies in the early 1700s, many of them relocated their operations to the filigreed inlets along the Carolina coast. In 1774, Spanish brigands pillaged Beaufort itself. The pirating legacy has a romantically swashbuckling appeal to the modern mind, drawing archaeologists to an underwater site not far off the coast where they think they've located Black-beard's ship, *Queen Anne's Revenge.*

When you have exhausted the town museums, the beaches are waiting. Pick up a sandwich at one of the many cafés overlooking Taylor's Creek along Front Street, then choose one of the local "water-taxi men" who dock along Front Street, at the foot of Orange Street. They'll ferry you across the creek and back again at whatever time you want. So, you can spend a few lovely, lonely windswept hours on **Carrot Island** and **Shackleford Banks,** walking the wide beaches and picnicking in utter peace.

The ferry will get you back in town in time to catch the sunset over gener-ous dinners of seafood, lamb, or beef at the **Spouter Inn,** right on the water-front. Or, if you prefer something a little more unusual, try a local favorite, the **Beaufort Grocery Store Company,** where the food is fresh and innovative and the setting is as welcoming as an old general store.   *K.M. Kostyal*

Travelwise

GETTING THERE

Beaufort is in eastern North Carolina, off US 70 and N.C. 101, at the Outer Banks' southern end. There are no public transportation services. The closest commercial airport is in New Bern, about 30 miles away.

GENERAL INFORMATION

With its coastal location, Beaufort is always humid, making for warm summers and damp but mild winters. Spring and fall are the most comfortable seasons. The best source of information on the town itself is the **Beaufort Historical Association** *(138 Turner St. 252-728-5225 or 800-575-7483. www.historicbeaufort.com).* For regional information, contact the **Carteret Chamber of Commerce** *(801 Arendell St., P.O. Box 3605, Morehead City 28557. 252-726-6350. www.sunnync.com).*

THINGS TO SEE AND DO

Beaches From resort-oriented **Atlantic Beach** on the mainland to the pristine beaches of **Cape Lookout National Seashore,** beaches abound in the surrounding area. Shelling, birding, horseback riding, and surf-fishing are popular along all of them.

Beaufort Historic Site *(100 Block Turner St. 252-728-5225 or 800-575-7483. April-Oct.,*

adm. fee. By guided tour only) Six restored buildings occupy this 2-acre complex in the heart of town. Tours begin at the visitor center, then take in a 1767 town house, a Victorian home, a 1778 cottage, the 1829 county jail, and an apothecary shop. An art gallery devoted to the works of local artists is housed in a 1730s house.

North Carolina Maritime Museum *(315 Front St. 252-728-7317)* The cultural, historical, and natural riches of coastal North Carolina are celebrated in dioramas and natural history exhibits. Across Front Street is the museum's

Watercraft Center, where visitors can watch historic small craft being restored.

Old Burying Ground (*Ann St. bet. Turner and Craven Sts.*) This site has been a town burying ground ever since it was deeded in 1731. Among its headstones are ones for Josiah Bell and men who served in the Revolutionary and Civil Wars. Self-guided tours and a brochure describing the graves are available at the Beaufort Historic Site.

ANNUAL EVENTS
Beaufort Old Homes and Garden Tour & Antiques Show and Sale (*Last weekend in June. Contact Beaufort Historical Assoc. 252-728-5225 or 800-575-7483. Adm. fee*) Visit the town's fine old private houses and purchase equally fine old antiques.

North Carolina International Choral Fest (*Early May. Crystal Coast Amphitheater. 252-247-5036 or 800-622-6278*) For several hours, the voices of choirs from across the U.S. and Europe fill the amphitheater.

North Carolina Yacht Racing Association Championship Series (*Mem. Day weekend. 252-726-6350*) Stand on the Beaufort waterfront and watch sails fill Beaufort Inlet.

WHERE TO EAT
Beaufort Grocery Store Company (*117 Queen St. 252-728-3899. $$*) This upscale-casual restaurant, housed in an old grocery store, features fresh and innovative offerings of local seafood, meats, and poultry.

Spouter Inn (*218 Front St. 252-728-5190. $$*) The water views here and the bountiful portions of lamb, shrimp, and chicken, seasoned with Mediterranean herbs and sauces, make this a pleasant dinner spot.

WHERE TO STAY
Carteret County Home B&B (*299 Hwy. 101. 252-728-4611. $$*) This former poor farm just outside town has been converted into a whimsical B&B.

Cedars Inn (*305 Front St. 252-728-7036. $$*) The elegant but intimate old southern inn has a long green yard sloping toward Front Street.

Pecan Tree Inn (*116 Queen St. 252-728-6733. $$*) This comfortable Victorian home has verandas for rocking and a welcoming atmosphere; the owners offer lots of information on touring the area.

NEARBY PLACES
Cape Lookout National Seashore (*Accessible via ferry from Harkers Island. 252-728-2250. www.nps.gov/calo*) The 56-mile-long national seashore protects sweeping stretches of barrier islands and marshlands. A great way to spend the day is to take a ferry to the island's southern tip and go beachcombing or picnicking. See the black-and-white-diamond, 1859 **Cape Lookout**

Old Burying Ground

Lighthouse and **Portsmouth Village**—a few preserved houses and a church.

Fort Macon State Park (*E. Fort Macon Rd., Atlantic Beach. 252-726-3775. Adm. fee*) Built as a coastal fortification in the 1820s and '30s, this casemated brick fort was used in almost every major U.S. war through World War II. It overlooks broad, windswept Atlantic Beach and Beaufort Inlet.

Beaufort

At what point and in what season does discovery of a community by the tourist troupes threaten the quiet enjoyment of the charms and laid-back lifeways that give the town a unique sense of place ? Beautiful Beaufort (say bew-fit), cocooned on Port Royal Island deep in "Gullah-land," bathed in warm ocean breezes that stir the live oaks, and bubbling with beguiling southern architecture and wide-smile attitudes, is a case in point. While not yet "overdiscovered," it's definitely getting there. So, go, but go soon.

Gullah-Land

African Americans in this part of South Carolina speak their very own language— Gullah or Geechee. Thought to have its origins in West Africa's Benta language, it's delivered with resonant rhythms and sing-song "shout" syntax. Along with ancient skills from the "rice coast culture" of Africa, the Gullah heritage is still alive and well. It's celebrated annually at the Penn Center on St. Helena Island, 9 miles southeast of town on US 21, at the Heritage Days celebration in November, and during the popular Gullah Festival held in Beaufort each May.

Not too long ago, beautiful Beaufort by the sea was a Shangri-la dream town, a languorous, semitropical hideaway for people in the know. But then came Hollywood and all the hysteria following the success of such box office hits as *The Big Chill*, Pat Conroy's (and Barbra Streisand's) *Prince of Tides, Forrest Gump,* Disney's *Jungle Book,* and Demi Moore's *G. I. Jane.* There's even a rumor that a sequel to *Gone With the Wind* (with a script by Conroy) may be filmed in this evocative place of Tara-type mansions and abundant Rhett-wannabes.

Imagine this scene on an early morning in spring in **Old Point** (the town's historic district): The blossom trees are glorious, the air is warm but without summer's oatmeal-thick humidity, and a dog barks lazily near the exquisitely furnished 1790 **John Mark Verdier House Museum** on Bay Street, one of the few stately homes in the historic district open to the public. Dozens of other homes here, some partly constructed of tabby (a lime, sand, and oyster shell cement) and limestone blocks, display the south-facing Beaufort style of raised basements and expansive verandas designed to capture every scintilla of ocean air and magnolia-perfumed breezes. Best known is **Tidal Holm** (the Edgar Fripp House on Laurens Street), which was featured prominently in *The Big Chill.* Equally photogenic and sketch worthy are the 1720 **Elizabeth Hext House** (Riverview), the **Cuthbert House** (one of many lovely old hostelries) on Bay Street, the 1813 **Milton Maxey House** (Secession House) on Craven Street, and the 1853 **Edward Means House** on Pinckney Street, noted particularly for its outstanding woodwork and "floating" spiral staircase.

Visitors on a horse-drawn carriage tour of Beaufort

It's usually quiet in the hallowed moments of early morning. Only a few visitors are out; horse-drawn carriage tours and boat trips are not being hawked on the waterfront walks; and there is no sign of Marines from the nearby **Parris Island** training center. The air, however, is filled with the aroma of cinnamon buns and country ham with coffee-laced redeye gravy.

Bay Street, the waterside commercial heart of town, is quiet, too, at this time. Until recently a rather faded enclave, the old banks and false-front stores are being transformed into galleries, boutiques, and small antique malls.

At the waterfront park just beyond **Blackstone's Café,** "where Beaufort meets for breakfast," seagulls wheel in expectation of discarded delicacies. The water is wobbly with silver-crested wavelets, and the last of the dawn haze floats over the marshy infinities of this complex cluster of islands, creeks, and rivers until the first heat of the sun strikes.

You can almost imagine how the place must have felt at the height of the King Cotton era in the early 1800s, when this was one of the most fashionable venues on the East Coast. That golden era began after the Revolution when Sea Island cotton, soft and silky and considered to be the world's finest, was grown in vast hinterland plantations. Wealth proliferated. Dozens of "snoblesse oblige" mansions, built primarily for the opulent entertainment of the mon-eyed clans, fully justified Beaufort's title as the Newport of the South; until the Civil War, there was much ship-shuttling between the two towns. In fact, despite the destruction of other southern communities during this period, Beaufort remained in pristine condition. Almost all its residents fled following a timely tip at the first sign of invasion in 1861, leaving the Unionists to protect it from 10,000 angry and hungry slaves left behind by the aristocratic families. For the rest of the war it was a hospital town and a regional headquarters.

If you really need seclusion, all you have to do is wander the local roads and you'll quickly find yourself amid vast stretches of marshland, serpentine estuaries, and dense swaths of vegetation (ideal apparently for the Vietnam scenes in *Forrest Gump*). Things have changed little here since the Archaic Indians roamed these rivers and gorged on the natural bounties of sea and land more than 4,000 years ago. And if the first Spanish explorers could be magically transported from 1521 they, too, would agree that these remote islets, marshes, mangroves, and dense tideland forests look very familiar— an enduring land veiled in time and timbre.

Guided pontoon trips through the 12,000-acre **ACE Basin National Wildlife Refuge** to the north of Beaufort, part of the 350,000-acre ACE Basin Project, reveal some of the secrets of this region, but the semitropical wilderness embraced by the Ashepoo, Combahee, and Edisto Rivers remains tantalizingly aloof. After such ramblings, nothing soothes the senses more than a mint julep on a shadowed veranda of a Beaufort inn.　　　　*David Yeadon*

Travelwise

GETTING THERE

Beaufort is on the Atlantic coast in southern South Carolina, on US 21. Major airlines serve Savannah, Georgia (45 miles south) and Charleston, South Carolina (70 miles north).

GENERAL INFORMATION

Summer's heat and humidity can be overbearing, so aim for a spring or fall visit. Abundant information and walking tour maps can be obtained from the **Greater Beaufort Chamber of Commerce** *(Carteret St., Beaufort 29901. 843-524-3163).*

THINGS TO SEE AND DO

Beaufort Arsenal Museum *(713 Craven St. 843-525-7077. Closed Wed. and Sun.; adm. fee)* See Indian artifacts, Civil War memorabilia, and exhibits on local lore, art, and textiles.

Beaufort Little Theatre *(Location varies; call ahead. 843-522-2000)* Famous for its spring and fall plays and musical productions, the theater is also known for its reasonable prices.

John Mark Verdier House Museum *(801 Bay St. 843-524-6334. Mon.-Fri.; adm. fee)* The restored federal-style home reflects the lifestyle of a 19th-century merchant planter.

North Street Public Aquarium *(608 North St. 843-524-1550. Thurs.-Sat.; adm. fee)* Ask about the riverwalk and aquarium tour.

Touring For boat tours of the ACE Basin, call the Islander *(843-671-5000).* Bus tours are available through Beaufort Tour Service *(843-525-1300).* Carriage Tours of Beaufort *(843-521-1651)* offers horse-drawn carriages. For walking tours, contact the Spirit of Old Beaufort *(103 West St. 803-525-0459).*

Taking in a Beaufort Harbor sunset

ANNUAL EVENTS

Gullah Festival *(Late May. Waterfront Park. 843-524-3163)* A Sea Island celebration of the West African Gullah heritage features music, plays, dancing, arts, crafts, and unusual cuisine.

Penn Center Heritage Days *(Mid-Nov. 843-524-3163)* Another Gullah festival, this one has parades, Gullah crafts, gospel singing.

Shrimp Festival *(Mid-Oct. 843-524-3163)* Sample shrimp dishes and watch the blessing of the fleet.

Spring and Fall Festival Home Tours *(Mid-March and late Oct. 843-524-3163)* See historic houses.

WHERE TO EAT

Bank Grill and Bar *(926 Bay St. 843-522-8831. $$)* The typical grill menu features seafood, steaks, and pasta in an old waterfront bank with a casual atmosphere.

Bistro de Jong *(205 West St. 843-524-4994. $$)* New Southern cuisine.

Plums *(904 Bay St. 843-525-1946. $$)* Enjoy eclectic cuisine, gourmet sandwiches, and homemade soups on the waterfront.

WHERE TO STAY

Beaufort Inn *(809 Port Republic St. 843-521-9000. $$)* A fabulous re-creation of a traditional Beaufort mansion, the inn has

13 luxury guest rooms and a celebrated restaurant, featuring seafood galore.

Craven Inn *(1103 Craven St. 843-522-1668. $)* The 1870 Victorian features double porches and elegant southern furnishings.

Cuthbert House *(1203 Bay St. 843-521-1314. $$)* A plantation-style beauty with 19th-century furnishings and gourmet breakfasts.

Rhett House Inn *(1009 Craven St. 843-524-9030. $$$)* The white-columned mansion has been praised for its southern hospitality.

NEARBY PLACES

ACE Basin NWR *(45 miles NE via US 21 and 17, on Willtown Rd. 843-889-3084)* See the wilderness from a pontoon boat. Call ACE Basin Tours *(888-814-3129)* for guided tours.

Hunting Island State Park *(16 miles E via US 21. 843-838-2011)* This popular park features a 4-mile beach, a lighthouse, nature trails, and camping.

Douglas Visitor Center at Parris Island *(Free bus tours Sat.-Wed. 1 p.m. 843-525-3650)* Learn about the island's history and the famous Marine base established in 1891.

Penn Center *(Martin Luther King Jr. Dr. on St. Helena Island. 843-838-2432. Adm. fee)* Discover Sea Island black history and the Gullah heritage.

Dahlonega

Set in forested foothills near the start of the 2,000-plus-mile-long Appalachian National Scenic Trail, Dahlonega was "America's first major gold rush city." Redolent with gold lore and rich in historic sites, the town is an ideal base for panning (oldtimers say there's still plenty of gold around here) or for exploring the vast wilderness of the Chattahoochee National Forest. It's perfect country for hiking, horseback riding, mountain biking, fishing, and kayaking.

The 729-foot-high Amicalola Falls, highest east of the Mississippi, is a favorite local attraction, but that's merely the beginning.

At first glance, Dahlonega seems typically small town in spirit. Its tree-shaded main square is dominated by the columned 1836 **Lumpkin County Courthouse** (now the Dahlonega Gold Museum); old inns and B&Bs are rich in 19th-century Victorian charm; a small college campus adds youthful energy to the place; and a huddle of antique galleries, Appalachian craft shops, and bric-à-brac stores around the square maintain a commercial heart of sorts despite the typical fringe-of-town strip outlets.

Dig deeper, though, and you'll literally strike gold. In fact the whole place is a gold mine, site of the first major U.S. gold rush in 1828. The courthouse is said to sit on an unexcavated, mini-mother lode: Traces of gold were found in 1966 when bricks were assayed during restoration. A mile or so away, on the outskirts of town, are two refurbished gold mines, and deep in the woods below the town is a "placer camp" where you can pan your days away in search of elusive riches.

This was a hotbed of mining a couple of decades before California's Sierra camps achieved renown. Legend has it that Benjamin Parks found the first nugget while hunting deer in the forest and was staggered by the sudden impact of his find: "It seemed, within a few days, as if the whole world must have heard of it; for men came from every state I ever heard of. They came afoot, on horseback, and in wagons, acting more like crazy men than anything else," he said. Their craziness was apparently amply rewarded. Claims vary but local historians believe that well over six million dollars worth of "official gold" was extracted between 1838 and 1861. The output

Smith House

Daily for over 70 years, the 1884 Smith House has offered gargantuan spreads on a first-come, first-served basis. Guests sit at long trestle tables where the fun of eating great food with as many as 260 friendly strangers is a big draw. Using family recipes dating back over a century, the current owners, Fred and Shirley Welch, continue the time-honored traditions of excellence and abundance with a range of culinary delights that can daunt the most dedicated diners. And if it's all been a tad too much, rooms are available at the adjoining Smith House inn.

One of Dahlonega's proud old buildings, occupied by craft shops

actually became so lucrative that in 1837 the government established the first of three branch mints on a hill overlooking the town. It is possible to see and tour the old mint's foundation, now under the Price Memorial building (housing the offices for North Georgia College and State University).

"Those were real wild, gold-fever days" says Robert Jenkins, who spends most days teaching panning techniques at the **Old Gold Miners Camp,** a forested enclave by a stream just below the town's other claim-to-fame, the beloved 1884 **Smith House,** an exquisitely restored Victorian home where family-style, all-you-can-eat dinners are served daily (see sidebar p. 132). Robert's tales of the old days make great listening, but he emphasizes the bad times, too. "Some weeks you hardly made a dollar. It was always feast or famine. Lots of people suffered."

Panning for gold

At the **Dahlonega Gold Museum,** exhibits include a five-ounce gold nugget and gold coins. While the museum focuses on the gold rush, it also displays an evocative painting on the forced removal of the Cherokee from this area in 1838. For more information on the Trail of Tears, visit the **Newechota State Historical Site** (*1211 Chatsworth Hwy. 706-624-1321*) in Calhoun.

"Once they got the smell of gold, you couldn't stop them" said Bryan Whitfield, owner of the **Consolidated Gold Mine.** Tours of the mine's old tunnel system and panning sessions led by world-class instructors are offered daily. "These mountains are riddled with tunnels, some a thousand feet deep and more. But first came the water cannons washin' away whole hillsides, the big stamp mills to crush the ore, and the mercury-coated sluices…a crazy place in the mid-1800s."

Riches of another kind can also be found here: 19th-century houses still stand on Hawkins Street in the heart of the historic district; the **Old Jail** on East Main is now a place for the historical society's small museum; the Eastern Tribe of Cherokee dwell here; and Dahlonega's original inn, the 1845 **Worley Homestead** on West Main, is a beautifully furnished B&B renowned for its "southern-vittles" breakfasts.

"This place could've faded away like so many other old gold-mining towns," said Dana LaChance, a co-owner of the **Appalachian Outfitters Trading Company.** "But we're doing fine. We have festivals galore throughout the year and local folks who care about protecting the town's historical integrity." Dana leads adventure hikes and canoeing and kayaking trips on the Chestatee and Etowah Rivers. She's a skiing instructor, songwriter, guitarist, and ecological land developer, too. "I just hope to make a difference by helping people reach into themselves and dig out their own riches. You don't need a gold mine to do that—just a nice thick vein of soul." *David Yeadon*

Travelwise

GETTING THERE

Dahlonega is 70 miles northeast of Atlanta via US 19. There are airports at Atlanta and Chattanooga, Tennessee. The closest Amtrak station is 25 miles away in Gainesville.

GENERAL INFORMATION

Late spring through fall is the best time to visit the town and the nearby Chattahoochee National Forest. Free information on the region can be obtained from the **Dahlonega-Lumpkin County Chamber of Commerce** (13 S. Park St., Dahlonega 30533. 706-864-3711. www.dahlonega.org).

THINGS TO SEE AND DO

Consolidated Gold Mine (185 Consolidated Gold Mine Rd. 706-864-8473. Adm. fee) Among an array of delights are underground tours, panning, and a store.

Crisson Gold Mine (2736 Morrison Moore Pkwy. E. 706-864-6363. Adm. fee) The 1847 mine offers a well-preserved 116-year-old stamp mill and gold/gemstone panning.

Dahlonega General Store (On Public Sq. 706-864-2005) This old-time country store sells a huge array of gifts, regional foods, and even 5-cent coffee.

Dahlonega Gold Museum (On Public Sq. 706-864-2257. Adm. fee) Get a fascinating overview of local history and the town's gold era (including film) in the ca 1836 courthouse.

Old Gold Miners Camp (Off Chestatee St., below the Smith House. 706-864-6373. Hours vary; adm. fee) The camp is not as well organized as the two mines, but it is fun for a little panning in a pleasant woodland setting.

Old Jail and Museum (Off Public Sq. 706-864-3711) The ca 1884 old county jail contains a small but interesting collection of historic artifacts and a Trail of Tears exhibit.

Outdoor Activities Contact Appalachian Outfitters (24 N. Park St. 706-867-6677) for help in organizing a wide range of activities, including canoeing, kayaking, and tubing on the Chestatee and Etowah Rivers. For information on hiking, climbing, fishing, etc. see Nearby Places.

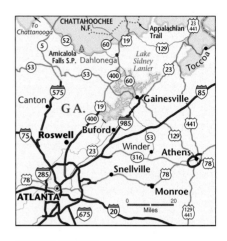

ANNUAL EVENTS

Dahlonega's festivities invariably feature mountain music, folk art, and unique regional traditions. Best known is the **Bear on the Square Mountain Festival** (3rd weekend in April. 706-864-6244), featuring all the above plus a World Championship Gold Panning competition.

WHERE TO EAT

Smith House (84 S. Chestatee St. 706-867-7000. Call for hours. $$) Without doubt, this eatery is the most popular place in town if not the whole region, for its southern country cooking. 16 guest rooms.

WHERE TO STAY

Worley Homestead Inn (168 Main St. W. 706-864-7002. $$) A beautifully restored home dating from 1845, the Worley Inn is filled with antiques and the aromas of fine country cooking.

NEARBY PLACES

Amicalola Falls State Park (18 miles W of town, off Ga. 52. 706-265-4703) A lovely woodland area is the setting for the highest waterfall in the eastern United States.

Chattahoochee National Forest (W of Dahlonega via Ga. 52. 770-297-3000) This vast and diverse 750,000-acre forest extends from the piedmont to the Blue Ridge. It features campsites, trails, wilderness areas, waterfalls, lakes, and the Appalachian Trail.

Madison

An early 19th-century issue of *White's Statistics of Georgia* described Madison as the "most cultured and aristocratic town on the stagecoach route from Charleston to New Orleans." And indeed, at first glance, the place still seems almost too perfect today. Plantation-era mansions sit proudly beside Victorian "grande- dame" mini-palaces and crisp, white colonial houses set in boxwood gardens and broad lawns. The streets are lined with enormous live oaks dripping, as one would expect, with ghost-gray Spanish moss, and the town square is so traditional it could have been modeled on a Currier and Ives print. Excellent museums, elegant B&Bs, and courteous locals will make you wonder why you'd ever think of moving on.

Antebellum Trail

Georgia's Antebellum Trail meanders more than 100 miles along Lake Oconee's west shore, on US 441, Ga. 22, and US 129. Driving slowly south from Athens—a 19th-century university city famous for its architecture, botanical gardens, and art museum—you can pause at Watkinsville's Eagle Tavern or covered bridge; at Eatonton, home of the Uncle Remus Museum; at Milledgeville, Georgia's antebellum capital; at Old Clinton, almost annihilated in the Civil War; and at Macon, a dream town of historic treasures. Call 800-709-7406 for information.

So, how did all this happen? How could such a community maintain its historical and aesthetic characteristics when its Dixie location put it right in destruction's path during the Civil War? Well, according to people who study the minutiae of the war, Madison is the "town Sherman refused to burn" on his march to the sea.

Apparently in November 1864, immediately after the burning of Atlanta, a 10,000-strong detachment of soldiers under General Henry Slocum arrived at the outskirts of town. At that time, one of Madison's most notable antisecession residents, Senator Joshua Hill, rushed out with a hastily assembled delegation of dignitaries to plead for the town's preservation, emphasizing his close friendship with General Sherman's brother in Washington. A hasty gentleman's agreement was made with Sherman, and Slocum modified his plans for Madison, thus sparing it from the destruction that befell other towns along the route of the Great March; instead, the soldiers burned only commercial and business properties. The decision was also doubtlessly influenced by the kindness of a local plantation owner, Col. John Bynne Walker. Despite the fact that three of his sons were Confederate officers, Walker offered his palatial home as a field hospital to the Northern troops.

Of course most residents, while recognizing the truth of the tale, also insist

Queen Anne-style Hunter House, dating from 1884

that "we Madisonians have long been a proud and caring people and we've always treasured our little town." These sentiments were expressed by an elderly lady as she walked her poodle past the 1905 **Morgan County Courthouse** *(149 E. Jefferson St.)*, with its beaux arts portico and dome, and then down to the **visitors bureau.** The bureau is housed in the 1887 fire station and topped by an elegant cupola complete with original fire bell.

This caring is apparent nearly everywhere you go in Madison. As with many towns, though, there are also enduring pockets of poverty. So, pause for a while and soak up the gentility and fascinating history—a history encompassed by four very different museums. Most notable, at least in terms of size and ambition, is the **Madison-Morgan Cultural Center** on South Main, housed in an 1895 school somewhat resembling the Smithsonian Castle in Washington, D.C. Opened in 1976 as a center for the visual, decorative, and performing arts, the center also contains a restored original schoolroom, a piedmont history museum, and a gallery of Arts and Crafts furnishings. It is the site of local juried art shows and festivals: There is even a Cow Day to celebrate the region's agricultural heritage.

Stroll over to the unique **African-American Museum** on Academy Street, where awareness-raising exhibits and changing art shows are crammed into a

Baldwin's Drugstore

tiny 1895 clapboard house. Be prepared: Docents can occasionally be stern, seeming to prefer visitors who come to conduct serious research among the impressive array of black culture books. But come here anyway, because it's not often you get to see the other side of the southern heritage.

The other museums are in town homes. The 1835 Greek Revival **Heritage Hall** on South Main is richly adorned in period furnishings (ask to hear the eerie tale about the ghost in the bedroom). The elegant 1810 **Rogers House** and diminutive 1891 **Rose Cottage** next to the courthouse are furnished in mid-19th-century style and set in period gardens. Not much is known of Adalene Rose except that she apparently made a good living taking in the laundry of the nearby Hardy Boarding Home, which was owned by the mother of comedian Oliver Hardy.

After admiring the dozens of antebellum Victorian houses here—from enormous porticoed Revival mansions to far more modest carpenter-Gothic trimmed cottages—you'll inevitably return to the focal point of the town around the square, with its brick sidewalks, gas lamps, art galleries, gift shops, and antique stores galore (Madison is a highlight of Georgia's Antique Trail). And, of course, there are restaurants here, most notably the **Madison Chop House Grille** for pub-grub and **Ye Olde Colonial Restaurant,** serving inexpensive buffets in a converted bank (take a peek at the "vault room").

If a little diversion is what you're seeking in the square, stroll into Charles and Joann Stewart's **Attic Treasures,** where curious collectibles of almost every kind can be found. Rusty swords, fishing rods, vintage jewelry, Indian artifacts, engraved thimbles, and Civil War regalia are watched over by lanky, always-laughing Charles; if you have the time, he'll tell you fascinating tales about anything that captures your fancy here.

Of course, it may be the privately owned antebellum houses here that are your real fancy. So, if you're really curious to see inside some of these carefully restored masterpieces, you could try smiling nicely at the owners from the sidewalk and take encouragement from this fragment of a 1930 poem written, quite obviously, by an ardent Madisonian. It's a little on the gushy side, but it's nonetheless true:

And of all endearing folks one will find
The people of Madison will prove most sweet and kind.   David Yeadon

Travelwise

GETTING THERE

Madison is 60 miles east of Atlanta, at the US 441 exit off I-20. The closest major airport is at Atlanta; bus services are from Atlanta and Athens (30 miles north).

GENERAL INFORMATION

Madison is delightful any time of year, but if your journey includes Georgia's Antebellum Trail and Lake Oconee, then late spring and late summer are best. Walking tour leaflets and other information are available from the **Madison and Morgan County Chamber of Commerce and Convention and Visitors Bureau** (*115 E. Jefferson St. Madison 30650. 706-342-4454 or 800-709-7406. www.madisonga.org*).

THINGS TO SEE AND DO

African-American Museum (*156 Academy St. 706-342-9191. Closed Sun.; adm. fee*) Located in the recently moved **Horace Moore House** (1895), the museum celebrates African-American heritage.

Guided Tours Call Regal Tours (*706-342-1612. Fee*) for customized tours; included are visits to restored historic houses.

Heritage Hall (*277 S. Main St. 706-342-9627. Closed a.m.; adm. fee*) The 1833 Greek Revival home offers intriguing glimpses of affluent 19th-century life in the South.

Madison-Morgan Cultural Center (*434 S. Main St. 706-342-4743. Closed Mon.; adm. fee*) Housed in an 1895 school building, the center offers historic collections, art exhibitions, room re-creations, and theatrical performances.

Rogers House and the Rose Cottage (*179 E. Jefferson St. 706-343-0190. Adm. fee*) Two delightful 19th-century homes just off the square are furnished to reflect the character of the times.

SHOPPING

Southern Antiques and Primitive Antique Mall (*1291 Eatonton Hwy.,* 706-342-0018) This antique nexus of 50 dealers offers a wide range of collectibles.

ANNUAL EVENTS

Madison Festival (*One day in late July. 706-342-1251, ext. 6*) This small town celebration of quality arts and crafts from regional artisans is often held in conjunction with the popular **Madison Theatre Festival** (*706-342-4743*).

Madison Home Tours (*Early May and early Dec. 800-709-7406*) See historic houses.

WHERE TO EAT

Madison Chop House Grille (*202 S. Main St. 706-342-0910. $$*) The woody-decor tavern on the square offers a typical but excellent menu.

Ye Olde Colonial Restaurant (*108 E. Washington St. 706-342-2211. $*) Basic but tasty southern buffets are served in an old bank building overlooking the square.

WHERE TO STAY

Burnett Place (*317 Old Post Rd. 706-342-4034. $$*) This restored 1830 federal home in the historic district offers 19th-century ambience with 20th-century comforts.

Farmhouse Inn (*1051 Meadow Ln. 706-342-7933. $$*) An enchanting farmhouse inn about 5 miles north of town is set on a 100-acre working farm with spacious rooms.

Southern Cross Ranch (*1670 Bethany Church Rd. 706-342-8027. $$/$$$*) A few miles south of Madison, this Dallas-style B&B offers large rooms, horseback riding, and explorations of the nearby 5,800-acre **Hard Labor Creek State Park** (*706-557-3001*).

NEARBY PLACE

Lake Oconee (*706-485-8704. Some fees*) The 19,000-acre lake boasts almost 375 miles of shoreline, with fine beaches, picnic spots, marinas, fishing, hiking, and camping.

Apalachicola

Try to imagine what Florida's Gulf Coast must have looked like before time shares, condo villages, and endless commercial and junk food strips appeared. Well, here at Apalachicola you'll discover all the charms of a so-called forgotten coast along with some splendid wildlife conservation areas. It's an irresistible, sweetly snoozing combination.

Apalachicola is best known for its oysters—Apalachicola Bay oysters are famous throughout the world for their delectable taste. A lesser known fact is that Apalachicola is also a first-rate producer of scallops. Every four or five years, commercial fishermen take in an extra bountiful harvest, a time when excitement sweeps through town as millions and millions of small gulf scallops cosseted in their fan-shape shells are unloaded and piled high on town docks.

The best way to experience Apalachicola's oysters and scallops is at one of the many dining spots in this faded fishing community, centerpiece of a stretch of Gulf affectionately known as Florida's Forgotten Coast. The few tourists who find their way here will dine in style at the 1907 **Gibson Inn,** a glowingly restored Victorian masterpiece that greets you like a fashionably attired dowager duchess as you enter the town from the east across the seemingly endless bridge from Eastpoint (rather an eerie drive in early morning or late evening mist).

Not far from two more magnificent Victorian houses, collectively known as the **Coombs House Inn,** is one of Florida's most notable small restaurants, **Chef Eddie's Magnolia Grill,** run by Eddie Cass, a genial and creative New Englander. He loves to cook with fresh-shucked oysters and scallops as do Susan and Cassie Gary, the mother-daughter owners and comfort-food creators at the **Owl Cafe,** and Jerry Hall at the **Apalachicola Seafood Grill and Steakhouse** (*100 Market St.*), which boasts the "world's largest fried fish sandwich" (it's true).

Long before Apalachicola's official founding in 1831, it was home to more than 40,000 Native Americans, who named the place "land of the friendly people." Then came the Spanish Franciscans who, in a fit of optimistic zeal, opened up a string of 11 missions along the coast. But finally its economic potential was recognized, and the town grew rapidly into one of the South's major cotton ports, third largest on the Gulf by the 1850s. Huge brick and

St. George Island

Across the bridge from Eastpoint, you enter a Robinson Crusoe-like paradise where water skitters over a plethora of seashells; the sand is soft and white; and the dunes are unmolested. Barely 700 people live year-round on St. George Island, but the population grows in summer. Most visitors come to enjoy one of the nation's top ten state parks, which offers 9 miles of gorgeous beach. If you're seeking complete solitude, you might consider a boat trip to **St. Vincent,** but the sambar deer and feral pigs there don't take kindly to strangers.

Weathered dock framing an idle outboard at Apalachicola

stone cotton warehouses were lined up cheek-to-cheek along the riverfront until the great fire of May 1900 wiped out most of them. The meticulously refurbished **Grady Building** *(76 Water St.)* survived the fire and today contains vacation rental suites and a fascinating antiques and collectibles emporium. Even after the decline of the cotton industry, the town found fame as a center for lumber and as a lucrative seafood nexus.

Today, you can sense that Apalachicola is on the cusp of a new era. While its rather remote location is likely to keep the tourist hordes at bay, the little town is becoming an increasingly popular place for the types who hunt for hidden corners. These souls have discovered Apalachicola's low-key charm and the lovely white-sand beaches offshore. And just offshore shimmer barrier islands, including **St. George** (see sidebar p. 141) and **St. Vincent**—with its huge wildlife reserve, home to sambar deer, feral pigs, bald eagles, and loggerhead turtles. Then there are the splendid 246,000 acres of the **Apalachicola National Estuarine Research Reserve,** which encompasses much of the river sloughs and channels surrounding the town and preserves more than 180 species of fish, 300 types of birds, and hundreds of different plants. Boat trips organized by the **Maritime Museum** and other groups run regularly in the summer and offer informed ecological tours. "It's like visiting another planet," commented one boat passenger. Of course, some people feel the same way about the town itself, where lanes lined with live oaks lead past 19th-century mansions to such oddities as the one-room **John Gorrie State Museum,** where the "inventor of the icemaking machine" is honored.

After you've had a chance to browse through Apalachicola's random scattering of galleries and boutiques, to attend a repertory performance at the **Dixie Theatre,** and to join in the happy hour madness on Friday evenings at the **Gibson Inn,** you may never want to leave this place.   *David Yeadon*

Travelwise

GETTING THERE

Apalachicola lies on US 98, 65 miles southwest of Tallahassee and 60 miles southeast of Panama City. The closest major airport is at Tallahassee (also served by Amtrak).

GENERAL INFORMATION

Apalachicola's location on the Gulf of Mexico causes its summers to be hot and humid, but other seasons offer a more moderate climate. Information on the town and region, including a walking tour map, is available from the **Apalachicola Bay Chamber of Commerce** *(99 Market St. Apalachicola 32320. 850-653-9419. Mon.-Fri. www.baynavigator.com).*

THINGS TO SEE AND DO

Apalachicola National Estuarine Research Reserve *(Visitor center, 261 7th St. 850-653-8063. Mon.-Fri.)* More than 246,000 acres of land, marsh, islands, and water offer

abundant opportunities for education, research, and resource management experiments. The reserve has an interpretation center and organizes a wide variety of estuarine walks, water tours, and related activities.

Dixie Theatre (21 Ave. E. 850-653-3200) This delightfully restored theater is famous for its professional summer repertory.

John Gorrie State Museum (46 6th St. 850-653-9347. Closed Tues.-Wed.; adm. fee) View an odd potpourri of regional exhibits, with emphasis on Dr. John Gorrie and his "first icemaking machine."

Maritime Museum (71 Market St. 850-653-8700. Mon.-Fri.; fare for schooner trips) Get an interesting overview of Apalachicola's history as one of the largest shipping ports on the Gulf of Mexico. See artifacts galore and enjoy a schooner trip on an 1877 wooden vessel.

Water Activities For information on area boat trips and boating, kayaking, snorkeling, fishing, dolphin-watching, and other activities, call the chamber (850-653-9419). Among the many resources available are Boss Charters (850-653-8055), Captain Black's Dive Trips (850-229-6330), Jeanni's Journeys (850-927-3259), and Estuary Tours (850-653-2593).

SHOPPING

In addition to a remarkable array of art and antique stores scattered around town, one of the most intriguing bazaar-like emporiums is the **Grady Market** (Water St. 850-653-4099).

ANNUAL EVENTS

Florida Seafood Festival (lst Sat. in Nov. 850-653-9419. Adm. fee) This day is a wild splurge of parades, oyster shucking, and eating. Browse among 100 arts and crafts booths, watch the blessing of the fleet, and see live entertainment.

Historic Tour of Homes (lst Sat. in May. 850-653-9419. Adm. fee) The tour showcases more than 20 historic private houses.

WHERE TO EAT

Chef Eddie's Magnolia Grill (133 Ave. E. 850-653-8000. $$) Eddie Cass's top-rated little hideaway is famous for innovative seafood, rack of lamb, and award-winning beef Wellington. A true find!

Owl Cafe (15 Ave. D. 850-653-9888. $$) This local favorite features rich soups and chowders, real crab cakes, pan-seared grouper, and pastas in large portions.

WHERE TO STAY

The Consulate (Grady Bldg., 76 Water St. 850-653-3333 or 800-624-3964. $$$) Four self-contained luxury suites on the waterfront.

Coombs House Inn (80 6th St. 850-653-9199. $$) Made up of two beautifully restored Victorian houses, the inn offers 19th-century indulgence.

Try the oysters!

Gibson Inn (51 Ave. C. 850-653-2191. $$) This well-restored Victorian offers period rooms and an excellent restaurant and bar.

NEARBY PLACES

St. George Island (E on US 98 to Eastpoint, then over the bridge to the island. See sidebar p. 141)

St. Joseph Peninsula State Park (25 miles W of Apalachicola, off US 98. Cape San Blas Rd. 850-227-1327. Adm. fee) Enjoy bird-watching, hiking, and camping on the park's 2,500 acres.

St. Vincent National Wildlife Refuge (Boat access and daylight use only. 850-653-8088) Large sambar deer, red wolves, and sea turtles reside on this pristine island, which has over 14 miles of beaches and 80 miles of sand roads.

Mentone

Mentone is thought to be French for "musical mountain spring." Another kind of spring—the season, that is—is certainly one of the best times to visit this coy little community of antique stores, art and boutique shops, a curious "tea room," and a superbly restored 1884 Queen Anne-style Victorian home, now a charming inn and craft center set atop Lookout Mountain with magnificent Appalachian vistas all around. Spring is also the time for wild azaleas and huge bloom-clouds of rhododendrons that edge the deep forests in this wilderness region known for its waterfalls and lakes, strange rock formations, shadowy canyons, and caves (some were home to Archaic Indians for more than 9,000 years). John Mason, who founded Mentone in 1870, declared his little mountain-top aerie to be the "most wonderful place in the world to live." Most visitors here heartily endorse his sentiment.

Remember that old chestnut: "If you blink, you'll miss it"? Well, in the case of Mentone, a diminutive, road-junction hamlet in the northeastern corner of Alabama, it's a most appropriate phrase. "No one seems to know what our resident population is here, but it's sure small, maybe four or five hundred. Maybe less," said Joe Hines, owner of the delightful **Dish-Mentone Tea Room Cafe,** whose walls are decorated with dozens of colorful dinner plates (located in the **Crow's Nest** antique store in the center of town). "Of course in the summer, with the camps and all that river rafting, hiking, mountain biking round here—you name it—it gets a tad more crowded. Still, it never really changes. We're just a little stop sign on a beautiful backcountry drive."

Sock Capital of the World

Settlers in the mid-1800s quickly began to develop valley agriculture, coal, and iron mining, and in 1889 they established the rail town of Fort Payne. The coal would play out, but the town would become the Sock Capital of the World. The region held over 150 hosiery mills, some of which are still in business and producing over 10 million dozen pairs a week! Both the tube sock and the cushion-sole sock were invented here. From those days, the 1889 Opera House continues to flourish, an old sock mill is now an antique mall, and the 1891 railroad depot is a museum.

But what magnificent backcountry. This is a region fat with time where you can appreciate just how richly endowed America's southern Appalachia region is in leisurely fashion. And there's a surprise in Mentone itself that sets the mood for all your subsequent ramblings. Follow the narrow road to the left of the sprawling **Mentone Springs Hotel,** elegantly restored to something approaching its original glory by a California

DeSoto Falls

couple, and you'll climb up high to a small clearing with a couple of benches. Here the thick forest has been cut away and a gasp-worthy, 40-mile panorama suddenly opens up, revealing rippled mountain ridges furred with forest and cut by deeply shadowed valleys all wrapped in silvery haze.

"Views like this were among the reasons we decided to relocate just a few years back," said Dave Wasson. He and his wife Claudia own the hotel here. The original builder, Dr. J. Frank Caldwell of Pennsylvania, claimed his health had been restored after drinking the local mineral spring water so he sold everything and settled here. By 1916 the structure had expanded to an 83-room complex, including the Sunset Hotel (now part of the **White Elephant Gallery**); it had hot and cold running water and carbide lights. Norville Hall bought the place after its near demise during the Depression and World War eras. He was a famous organist who brought his enormous contraption here, complete with scores of pipes that reached from the first floor into the attic. His late-night recitals, strictly for himself, were initially considered charming by the villagers, but they became a considerable annoyance throughout his 33-year residence. "It's a wee bit quieter now," grinned Claudia, "although our dining rooms see some pretty wild local weddings and whatnots." There's an even more stately grande-dame inn, the 1831 plantation-style **Winston Place**, down in Valley Head just below Mentone.

Once an ancient Creek/Cherokee settlement, this compact little town became a prosperous cotton-mill and lumbering center around the turn of the 20th century. One of the mills still stands, with all its machinery and spindles in place. The community itself has a slumbering spirit despite its proximity to the magnificent **Lookout Mountain Parkway**—a popular route winding through high plateaus that once were part of a vast seafloor. The sedimentary rock formations dating from that time are now part of a wonderland of state parks and preserves, including the Little River Canyon National Preserve, DeSoto State Park *(8 miles from Mentone),* and Sequoyah Caverns *(20 miles from Mentone).*

Within the **Little River Canyon National Preserve** you'll discover the nation's only river that flows almost its entire length along the top of a mountain. Although most visitors tend to admire the canyon's majesty from overlooks along the 22-mile **Canyon Rim Drive,** a few prefer to descend to its shadowy depths, where they enjoy rock climbing, white-water kayaking, or having a secluded picnic by the river beneath towering white cliffs.

Little River Canyon

The adjoining **DeSoto State Park,** while less dramatic in nature, offers a range of accommodations and excellent woodland trails radiating out from the nature center. It's probably most famous for its 100-foot-high falls and cliffside Indian fortifications.

A few miles farther north along the broad valley between the long Appalachian plateaus of Lookout Mountain and Sand Mountain are the **Sequoyah Caverns,** considered by many travelers to be one of the most outstanding show-caves in the United States. These caverns contain hundreds of remarkable formations and a series of reflecting pools known as the "looking glass pools." Indians used the extensive network of caverns as shelter for thousands of years, but gold-hungry settlers arrived and eventually ousted them during the notorious Trail of Tears era. It was a sad time, when the Cherokee nation was forcibly evicted and marched westward in the late 1830s to the new territory of Oklahoma.

"Too much hype, too much traffic, too much sad history down there in the valley," said a laughing Claudia (she always seems to be laughing). "And then, on top of it all, they've got all those weekly 'Trade Day' flea markets at almost every town down there. They're real crazy times!" Outside the hotel a breeze rising up from the lowlands stirred the uppermost leaves of the oaks and pines that surround this mountaintop haven. The aroma of fresh-baked breakfast muffins wafted out from Claudia's kitchen. "Mentone's just like founder John Mason once described it: 'The most wonderful place in the world to live,'" she said.

No one's arguing, Claudia.

David Yeadon

Cash Lake, DeSoto State Park

Travelwise

GETTING THERE

Tiny Mentone is hidden away in the northeast corner of Alabama, 50 miles west of Chattanooga, Tennessee, and 72 miles east of Huntsville. Take the Valley Head exit off I-59, then go east on Ala. 117 about 5 miles to the village (don't sneeze, or you'll miss it!). A more scenic alternative is the Lookout Mountain Parkway from Gadsden. There are airports at Birmingham and Chattanooga, and Amtrak serves Birmingham and Atlanta.

GENERAL INFORMATION

Just about any season is fine here, and fall drives are becoming increasingly popular. Abundant free information on the region can be obtained from local stores and inns, or you can contact the **Alabama Mountain Lakes Tourist Area** (25062 North St., Morresville 35649. 800-648-5381), the **DeKalb County Tourist Association** (1503 Glenn Blvd. S.W., Fort Payne 35968. 256-845-3957), or the **Fort Payne Chamber of Commerce** (300 Gault Ave. N., Fort Payne 35967. 256-845-2741). For a helpful website, go to www.mentone.com/tourist.

THINGS TO SEE AND DO

Mentone is a modest haven of antique and craft stores, and it is best used as a base for exploring this superb region of mountains, canyons, and caves. See Nearby Places.

ANNUAL EVENTS

Although it is a small place, Mentone offers quite an interesting selection of celebrations, including the following:

450-Mile Yard Sale (Aug. 256-845-3957) Indeed it is! For just a few days in August, find plenty of what some people would call junk—and others, cheap collectibles—on sale for 450 miles along the Lookout Mountain Parkway and beyond.

DeKalb County Artist Guild Art Show (Weekend after July 4. Mentone Springs Hotel. 256-634-4245) A regional arts and crafts event attracts a remarkable array of talent.

Mentone Colorfest (3rd week in Oct. 256-845-3957 or 888-340-3381) This true small town ritual is made up of country music and dancing, craft demonstrations, storytelling, and other such activities.

Rhododendron Festival (3rd week of May. 256-845-3957 or 888-340-3381) This colorful festival pays homage to the great mountain-spring blooming of these magnificent flowers.

WHERE TO EAT

Cragsmere Manna Restaurant (Cty. Rd. 89. 256-634-4677. Fri.-Sat. dinner only. $$) Occupying a 1920s farmhouse, this upscale restaurant offers a country gourmet menu.

Dessie's Kountry Chef (5951 Ala. 117. 256-634-4232. $) Renowned for country cooking, especially the fresh southern-style catfish. The home-breaded okra is also excellent.

Dish-Mentone Tea Room Cafe (6081 Ala. 117. 256-634-3669. $) Part of an antique shop, with dozens of parasols hanging from the lofty ceiling, this local favorite's menu changes every day but always features homemade bread.

WHERE TO STAY

Mentone Springs Hotel (6114 Ala. 117. 256-634-4040 or 800-404-0100. $) An 1884 Victorian mountain inn, this excellent hotel is full of home comforts and is always being restored by its owners, Dave and Claudia Wasson. It was placed on the National Register of Historic Places in June 1983. The Mentone Springs is also famous for its huge Sunday buffets.

Winston Place (353 Railroad Ave., Valley Head. 256-635-6381. $$) This sumptuous 1831 neoclassic mansion is located in a small village at the base of Lookout Mountain. Winston Place is very southern and quite charming. In March 1987, the inn was placed on the National Register of Historic Places.

Winston Place

NEARBY PLACES

Alabama Fan Club and Museum
(101 Glenn Blvd. S., Fort Payne. 256-845-1646. Adm. fee) Even if you are not familiar with the music of this famous country group, this is still a fascinating exhibit on local-boys-made-good and the glitter-and-guitars life.

Depot Museum *(105 5th St. N.E., Fort Payne. 256-845-5714)* View an excellent regional collection of Indian artifacts, see interesting dioramas, learn about Fort Payne history, and discover railroad memorabilia in a splendid Richardsonian Romanesque railroad depot.

Little River Canyon National
Preserve *(Off Ala. 35, 8 miles E of Fort Payne. 256-845-9605)* At the heart of this 14,000-acre mountaintop preserve is the magnificent Little River Canyon, one of the East's deepest gorge, sometimes referred to as the Grand Canyon of the East. Enjoy great vistas from the **Canyon Rim Drive,** which dips and twists for 22 miles along the gorge's western rim. The preserve's gem is **DeSoto State Park** *(7 miles S of Mentone on Ala. 89. 256-*

845-0051), which occupies 2,500 acres within the preserve in partnership with the federal government. The state park features several waterfalls, including the 100-foot-high **DeSoto Falls.** Hiking is great, especially in May and June when the rhododendron and mountain laurel burst into bloom.

Lookout Mountain Parkway The entire parkway runs through three states: Alabama, Tennessee, and Georgia. It shoots straight through Mentone into a wonderworld of vistas, caves, waterfalls, and rock formations. An especially pretty section meanders between the town of Fort Payne and DeSoto State Park.

Sequoyah Caverns *(NW of Valley Head off US 11 or via I-59. 256-635-0024. Daily March-Nov., weekends only Dec.-Feb.; adm. fee)* Attractions include fascinating stalactite formations and "looking glass pools," plus a bison herd and white fallow deer—all named in honor of the great Indian who taught the Cherokee nation to read and write. Sequoyah died shortly after the infamous 1837 Trail of Tears exodus of local tribes.

Oxford

Part Old South, part college town, part literary mecca, Oxford resists the stereotype of the sleepy, down-home southern community. Set in the gently rolling hills of northern Mississippi, it's friendly, yet sophisticated; historic, yet hip. A small town, yes—but few places loom as large in the world of the 20th-century novel.

First thing, you might as well get acquainted with Oxford's most famous resident. You can do it, in a manner of speaking, on the northeast corner of the picturesque **Courthouse Square** downtown, where William Faulkner sits on a bench watching the world go by—doing in bronze what he did so often in the flesh before his death in 1962. Faulkner made Oxford (renamed Jefferson and made the seat of fictional Yoknapatawpha County) the centerpiece of many of the novels that won him worldwide praise and, in 1949, the Nobel Prize. Such monumental books as *The Sound and the Fury* and *Absalom, Absalom!* were set in his "little postage stamp of native soil"—a place limited in area, but big enough for Faulkner to explore the farthest dimensions of the human condition.

Just across the street from the sculpture, the water oaks that Faulkner wrote about in *Sanctuary* still stand beside the white-columned **Lafayette County Courthouse,** which dates from 1873. Union troops burned the original courthouse in 1864, along with more than half the town. Stop at the **Oxford Tourism Council** on the east side of the square to pick up a walking tour guide to the downtown area, and to check out what's going on around town. Next door to the center, the **J.E. Neilson Co.** is the oldest continuously operating department store in the South, begun in 1839 in a log cabin on the north side of the square; its present home was built in 1897.

On the south side of the courthouse, a Confederate soldier atop a Civil War memorial looks toward **Square Books,** one of the nation's most famous independent bookstores and the scene of frequent readings and signing parties by visiting authors. (And local ones, too. Oxford is home to several prominent writers, including nationally known authors Barry Hannah, Larry Brown, and Cynthia Shearer.) The bookstore's 1860s building, originally a dry-goods store, was among the first structures built on the square after the devastation of the war. A few doors down, the balcony of the upstairs bar at **City Grocery** makes a great place to have a glass of wine and look down on activity in the square. The restaurant downstairs is one of Oxford's best and most popular establishments.

There's more to see and do around the square, but Faulkner fans will be eager to head a few blocks southwest to **Rowan Oak,** the novelist's home for the 32 years before his death. Built in the 1840s by an Irish immigrant, the two-story frame house was little changed from its original form when Faulkner bought it in 1930 for $6,000. The house had no plumbing or electricity; Faulkner did the wiring himself. He named his home for the rowan tree, which ancient Celts believed possessed magical powers of protection—

Faulkner's Rowan Oak

an apt image for a place where he undertook what he called the "solitary job" of writing his books.

Tall cedars line the drive leading to Rowan Oak, which appears to a very great extent just as it was when Faulkner died. His outline for *A Fable*, written on the wall of a downstairs room, can still be seen, along with many of his personal items. For the legions of Faulkner devotees who visit, the house and grounds remain a serene place to contemplate one of the 20th-century's greatest literary figures.

When three businessmen set out in 1837 to found a town on the site of today's square, they chose the name of the famed English university city in hopes that a college might be established here. Their dream came true in 1848 with the chartering of the **University of Mississippi,** more familiarly known to generations of alumni as Ole Miss. The university's 10,000 students keep Oxford's spirit young and active—especially on fall football weekends, when the tree-shaded section of campus known as the Grove is transformed into an enormous tailgate party. It's a heck of a celebration, and as much a part of Oxford as Faulkner's legacy—but don't even think about trying to get a bed-and-breakfast reservation on a game date. They're booked years in advance.

What's in a name? For Oxford, Faulkner means tourists.

You can visit the **University Museums** anytime, though, and what you'll find is just as stimulating, if far less frenzied. The collection of Greek and Roman antiquities is world-renowned, featuring sculpture, pottery, coins, and other objects dating from 800 B.C. to A.D. 300. You'll be fascinated, too, by the museums' array of 19th-century scientific instruments. The designs of all sorts of wonderfully complicated gadgets seem as much art as science. The University Museums are known for their excellent collection of southern folk art, as well as Roman surgical instruments that will make anyone glad for subsequent advances in medical technology.

Elsewhere on campus, **Barnard Observatory** was completed in 1859 and stands as one of the few Oxford antebellum structures to survive the Union Army's burning of the town. (During the war it served as hospital and morgue.) The observatory was built to house what was at the time the world's largest telescope, though the war prevented the instrument's delivery. Today the observatory is home to the Center for the Study of Southern Culture, which among many other activities hosts the annual Faulkner and Yoknapatawpha Conference each July, where scholars (and just plain fans) meet to discuss and debate Faulkner's works. And speaking of Faulkner, you can see his Nobel Prize, his National Book Award, and his French Legion of Honor on the third floor of the university's **J.D. Williams Library.**

Whether you're a dedicated Faulkner fan, or just someone who appreciates the charms of the South, Oxford makes a rewarding getaway. Walk its shady streets, stop in at some of the businesses around the square, and you'll find a place that in many ways is the best of both worlds: the slow pace and friendliness of a small town, with the urbane outlook of a community thoroughly imbued with the spirit of art and creativity. *Mel White*

Travelwise

GETTING THERE

Oxford is in northern Mississippi, 25 miles east of I-55 on Miss. 6. Many airlines serve Memphis, Tennessee, 75 miles north; Amtrak's *City of New Orleans* stops in Memphis.

GENERAL INFORMATION

Oxford can be visited all year, though the town is more sedate in summer, when most college students are gone. For information contact the **Oxford Tourism Council** *(S. Lamar St., at 111 Courthouse Square, Oxford 38655. 662-234-4680 or 800-758-9177).* Ask for the brochure or audiotape guide to the historic buildings of downtown Oxford.

THINGS TO SEE AND DO

Blues Archive *(Farley Hall, University of Mississippi campus. 662-232-7753. Mon.-Fri., by appt. on weekends)* One of the world's largest collections of blues recordings and related material, the archive includes the personal collection of singer-guitarist B.B. King. Though only a small amount of material is on display, visitors are welcome.

Rowan Oak *(Old Taylor Rd., 2 blocks W of S. Lamar St. 662-234-3284. Closed Mon.; donation)* The Greek Revival house that was William Faulkner's home remains essentially unchanged since his time. Tours emphasize its influence on his life and writing.

University Museums *(University Ave. and 5th St. 662-232-7073. Closed Mon.)* The museums of the University of Mississippi are known for Greek and Roman antiquities and for southern folk art. A walking trail leads from the museums to Rowan Oak.

SHOPPING

Southside Gallery *(150 Courthouse Sq. 662-234-9090)* This gallery specializes in southern photography, southern folk art, and Cuban art.

Square Books *(160 Courthouse Sq. 662-236-2262)* This nationally famous bookshop has a great selection of regional literature. A few doors west, **Off Square Books** sells used and rare books and hosts a weekly community radio show.

ANNUAL EVENTS

Double Decker Arts Festival *(Last Sat. in April. Courthouse Sq. 662-234-4680 or 800-758-9177)* Enjoy arts, crafts, food, and music that is performed on stages set up on the square. The **Children's Square Fair,** held nearby, offers activities for kids.

Faulkner and Yoknapatawpha Conference *(Last week in July. University of Mississippi. 662-232-7282. Adm. fee)* This important annual meeting features writers, critics, and scholars discussing Faulkner's work and influence on modern literature.

Oxford Conference for the Book *(April. University of Mississippi. 662-232-5993)* This annual conference examines issues concerning writing and literature, with lectures and panel discussions.

WHERE TO EAT

Bottletree Bakery *(923 Van Buren Ave. 662-236-5000. Closed Mon. $)* It's a popular spot for bagels, pastries, coffee, and deli sandwiches.

City Grocery *(152 Courthouse Sq. 662-232-8080. $$)* "New southern cuisine" is served in an old brick-walled livery; the upstairs bar has a balcony overlooking the square.

Yocona River Inn *(842 Miss. 334, 8 miles SE of town. 662-234-2464. Closed Mon.-Tues. $$)* Enjoy seafood, steaks, and other dishes in a converted gas station.

WHERE TO STAY

Oliver-Britt House Inn *(512 Van Buren Ave. 662-234-8043. $)* The inn occupies a circa 1905 house near Ole Miss and offers five rooms with private baths.

St. Francisville

For those who know Louisiana's French heritage, the idea that there's an off-the-beaten-track region called English Louisiana might be incentive enough to pay a visit to the green hills north of Baton Rouge. Even more tempting is the area's centerpiece: the lovely little town of St. Francisville, perched on a bluff above the Mississippi River, surrounded by historic houses and colorful gardens.

St. Francisville's location on a narrow ridge has often caused the town to be described as "two miles long and two yards wide." There's an element of truth in the hyperbole, because the historic old section of town, small enough to be seen easily on foot, is mostly set along two parallel streets.

Ready-to-eat crawfish

The road leading up from the Mississippi River becomes Ferdinand Street, and on it you'll find the **West Feliciana Historical Society Museum.** Inside this former hardware store, exhibits recall 19th-century days when a thriving river port called Bayou Sara was the main local settlement. Repeated floods and a lessening of riverboat traffic caused citizens to move the short distance eastward to higher ground at St. Francisville around the turn of the 20th century.

Long before then, this region was a territory called West Florida, ruled first by England and later by Spain. In the late 18th century, many English and Scottish immigrants received Spanish land grants to settle here, and as a result, English Louisiana has a character quite unlike the predominantly French land west of the Mississippi.

The redbrick Gothic-style **Grace Episcopal Church,** down the street from the museum, was completed in 1860, and just three years later it was severely damaged when Union gunboats shelled the town during the Civil War. Tradition says that the red-and-white Bohemian glass panels at the back of the church were bought with a hundred dollars sent after the war by a Union soldier who felt guilty about his part in the bombardment.

Make a loop by walking down Ferdinand Street and returning on Royal, enjoying the varied 19th-century houses and buildings. Some of the fine structures you see began as small cabins and were enlarged over the years to their present elegance. (A walking guide available at the museum will increase your enjoyment of this route.) The **United Methodist Church** was built in 1899, but the bell tower dates from a half century earlier; it was taken from the original 1844 church down in Bayou Sara. Take note of **Audubon Hall** at the east end of Royal: Built in 1819 as a public market, it features arched entryways large enough that wagons could be driven through.

While there's much to see in St. Francisville, an array of rewarding destinations lie just outside town, where historic plantation houses stand

Greenwood Plantation, authentic reconstruction of an 1830 home

as reminders of the antebellum days when more than half of America's millionaires lived along the river between New Orleans and Natchez.

The first stop for many people is **Rosedown,** a mansion built by wealthy planter Daniel Turnbull. A splendid avenue of live oaks fronts the house, built "after the most modern stile" in 1835. Turnbull and his wife, Martha, toured Europe after their 1828 wedding and were inspired by the great gardens they saw to create something of similar magnificence at their new home. The 28-acre garden at Rosedown ranks with the finest in America, with azaleas, camellias, roses, gardenias, and other plants creating a stunning display.

Far different, though equally fascinating, is **Oakley,** the house at the **Audubon State Historic Site.** Dating from the early 1800s, it shows evidence of West Indies influence and is much less elaborate than the grand Rosedown. John James Audubon lived here for a short time in 1821, tutoring the owners' daughter in drawing, dance, French, and Latin for $60 a month plus room and board. Half his time was left free to work on his paintings of birds.

On a hill north of St. Francisville stands the **Greenwood Plantation,** with its 28 white columns looking every bit the image of the Greek Revival mansion. What visitors see today, though, is a painstakingly authentic reconstruction of the 1830 original house, which burned in 1960 after being struck by lightning. Many movies have been filmed here.

Azaleas and live oaks gracing a plantation road

Closer to town, **Catalpa Plantation** has been in the same family since the late 1700s. The original house burned shortly after the Civil War, but most of the furnishings were saved, so that the present home is a treasure trove of historically significant items. Nearby is **The Myrtles Plantation,** which greets visitors with a long front gallery featuring fine decorative wrought iron. Several people met violent ends in the home, and ghosts are said to appear with regularity. A short distance down the road stood Afton Villa, an ornate mid-19th-century home that burned in 1963. The site is still worth a visit for **Afton Villa Gardens,** a showplace of plantings dating from 1849.

The rolling terrain around St. Francisville holds many treasures: History and beauty combine to make the serene hills of English Louisiana one of the South's most rewarding destinations. *Mel White*

Travelwise

GETTING THERE

St. Francisville lies on the east bank of the Mississippi River, about 20 miles northwest of Baton Rouge via US 61. Airlines service Baton Rouge; Amtrak stops in Hammond, Louisiana, about 60 miles east, and in New Orleans, 95 miles southeast.

GENERAL INFORMATION

Spring is the best time to see azaleas, camellias, and other flora. Visits can be made year-round, though summers are hot and humid; temperatures rarely dip to freezing even in midwinter. The **West Feliciana Parish Tourist Commission** is in the

Historical Society Museum *(11757 Ferdinand St., P.O. Box 1548, St. Francisville 70775. 225-635-6330 or 800-789-4221).*

THINGS TO SEE AND DO

Afton Villa Gardens *(4 miles N of town, on US 61. 225-635-6773. Daily March-June and Oct.-Nov., closed July-Sept. and Dec.-Feb.; adm. fee)* See well-tended plantings on the site of a 19th-century mansion that burned in 1963.

Audubon State Historic Site *(5 miles N of town on La. 965. 225-635-3739. Adm. fee)* Painter-naturalist John James Audubon lived and worked in the Oakley house; gardens, slave cabins, and a nature trail are on the grounds.

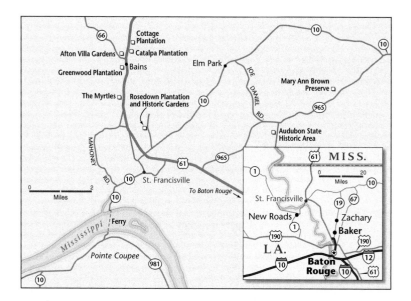

Catalpa Plantation *(4.5 miles N of town on US 61. 225-635-3372. Open p.m. only, closed Dec.-Jan. except by appt.. Adm. fee)* The 1880s plantation house holds wonderfully historic family possessions.

Grace Episcopal Church *(11621 Ferdinand St. 225-635-4065)* Begun in 1858, this Gothic-style building has an attractive interior and a cemetery shaded by live oaks.

Greenwood Plantation *(12 miles N of town via US 61 and La. 66, at 6838 Highland Rd. Adm. fee)* See a meticulous reconstruction of an 1830s Greek Revival mansion that burned in 1960.

Mary Ann Brown Preserve *(8 miles E of town on La. 965. 225-338-1040)* Hiking trails wind through this 109-acre Nature Conservancy area in the biologically distinctive Tunica Hills.

The Myrtles Plantation *(1 mile N of town at 7747 US 61. 225-635-6277 or 800-809-0565. Adm. fee)* Ghost tales abound at this 1796 house, with ornate wrought iron on the front porch.

Rosedown Plantation and Historic Gardens *(Just E of US 61 on La. 10. 225-635-3332. Adm. fee. House tours by appt. only)* The 1835 plantation mansion boasts beautiful gardens and many original family furnishings.

West Feliciana Historical Society Museum *(11757 Ferdinand St. 225-635-6330)* See exhibits on regional history, architecture, and the local exploits of John James Audubon.

ANNUAL EVENT

Audubon Pilgrimage *(3rd weekend in March at various sites. 225-635-6330 or 800-789-4221. Adm. fee)* Tour plantations and gardens.

WHERE TO EAT

Kean's Carriage House Restaurant *(1 mile N of town at 7747 US 61. 225-635-6276. $$)* A cozy venue on the grounds of The Myrtles Plantation, Kean's offers elegant dining.

Magnolia Cafe *(5687 E. Commerce St. 225-635-6528. $)* This popular and informal local hangout is in an old gas station.

WHERE TO STAY

Barrow House Inn *(9779 Royal St. 225-635-4791. $$)* Two guest houses date from around the start of the 19th century.

Several tour homes, including the **Cottage Plantation** *(5 miles N of town on US 61. 225-635-3674. $$)*, offer overnight accommodations in period settings.

Shadetree Inn *(Royal and Ferdinand Sts. 225-635-6116. $$$)* The inn has three rooms on a hilltop at the historic district's west end.

Natchitoches

In northwestern Louisiana, where the broad Red River Valley divides the rolling pinewoods, you'll find a town that proudly lays claim to being the oldest permanent European settlement in the Louisiana Purchase. Charming houses and inns line the shady streets of Natchitoches, set on the banks of picturesque Cane River Lake, where visitors experience a history as fascinating as it is long.

Founded in 1714, Natchitoches began as a French trading post on the Red River, just a few miles from the border separating French and Spanish claims in North America. Its name comes from a Caddo Indian word that means "place of the chinkapin" (a tree related to the chestnut); locals ignore the complicated spelling and pronounce it as NACK-uh-tish.

You can relive the early years at **Fort St. Jean Baptiste State Historic Area,** a replica of the 1730s-era military post charged with keeping an eye on a nearby Spanish garrison. French explorer Louis Juchereau de St. Denis established the post that became Natchitoches, and he later was named first commandant of the fort.

The little settlement quickly grew into an important trading center, but in the mid-1800s the Red River changed course, thus cutting off the town from its main channel and leaving an increasingly unnavigable subsidiary channel. Early in the 20th century earthen bridges were built at both ends of this channel to separate **Cane River Lake,** a waterway 32 miles long and only about 250 feet wide, from the river. Now lined with trees, lawns, and houses, the attractive lake has evolved into the symbolic center of Natchitoches.

Downtown's brick-paved **Front Street** parallels Cane River Lake, and there's a hint of the New Orleans French Quarter in its 18th- and 19th-century buildings. Drop in at **Kaffie-Frederick General Mercantile,** an old-fashioned hardware store established in 1863. Nearby, on the lakefront Rue Beau Port, stands historic **Roque House,** relocated here from its original site about 15 miles downstream. Built about 1797 by a freed slave, this small cottage is an important example of early French Creole architecture.

The adjacent **Natchitoches Parish Tourist Information Center** offers a variety of help for visitors, including a walking tour brochure covering the

Historical Park

South of Natchitoches on La. 119, the National Park Service is presently developing Cane River Creole National Historical Park at two plantations: **Oakland,** an 1821 structure, and **Magnolia,** where the emphasis is on 19th-century outbuildings. About 50 buildings are included in the park, which will focus on agricultural and social practices from antebellum plantation days into the era of tenant farmers. Because of the park's early stage of development, visits are by guided tour and reservation only. For information about this excellent historic site, call 318-352-0383.

Christmastime in Natchitoches

historic downtown area. Movie buffs should pick up a *Steel Magnolias* tour guide, as well; based on a play by Natchitoches native Robert Harling, the movie was filmed at sites in and around town, and fans will recognize several locations.

On Second Street have lunch at **Lasyone's Meat Pie Kitchen,** one of the most famous restaurants in Louisiana. Using a secret recipe, James Lasyone has been making meat-filled pastries here since 1967. Afterward, drop in at the **Old Courthouse Museum** next door. A branch of the Louisiana State Museum, it displays regional history exhibits in an imposing 1896 Richardsonian Romanesque building. Across the street stands the 1856 **Immaculate Conception Catholic Church,** and a block south is the 1857 **Trinity Episcopal Church.** Both are grandly towered and have beautiful interiors.

A few blocks south on Second Street you'll find the venerable **American Cemetery,** an evocative place where oaks and cedars shade gravestones weathered by the decades—or in some cases, the centuries. Continue south on Second Street to the campus of Northwestern State University and visit the **Williamson Museum,** which displays artifacts of several Native American cultures, concentrating on the local Caddo Indians.

Now it's time to head back downtown for an afternoon ramble along the waterside. The fickle Red River may have passed Natchitoches by, but it left behind one of the most historic towns in the South.   *Mel White*

Travelwise

GETTING THERE

Natchitoches is in northwestern Louisiana off I-49, 70 miles southeast of Shreveport, which has air service. The nearest Amtrak station is Marshall, Texas, 94 miles northwest.

GENERAL INFORMATION

Fall through spring is the best time to visit; summers are hot and humid, and while winters can be cold, they're rarely severe. For information contact the **Natchitoches Parish Tourist Information Center** (781 Front St., Natchitoches 71457. 318-352-8072 or 800-259-1714. www.natchitoches.net).

THINGS TO SEE AND DO

American Cemetery (2nd St., S of Rue Demeziere) This is a fascinating place to study old headstones from the town's early days.

Fort St. Jean Baptiste State Historic Area (130 Moreau St. 318-357-3101. Adm. fee) A replica of the 1730s-era fort that stood nearby is based on original plans.

Kaffie-Frederick General Mercantile (758 Front St. 318-352-2525. Closed Sun.) In operation since 1863, this hardware store offers a bit of everything.

Old Courthouse Museum (600 2nd St. 318-357-2270. Tues.-Sat.; adm. fee) The 1896 building holds revolving exhibits on aspects of state and regional history and culture.

Williamson Museum (2nd floor of Kyser Hall at Northwestern State University, College St. 318-357-4364. Mon.-Fri.) Exhibits focus on Native American culture.

SHOPPING

George Olivier and Company (117 2nd St. 318-352-1427. Mon.-Sat., Sun. by appt.) Handmade cypress furniture, beautifully detailed, is available in traditional Louisiana styles, from elaborate beds to chests and chairs.

ANNUAL EVENTS

Natchitoches Christmas Festival (1st Sat. in Dec. Front St. 800-259-1714. Fee) A very popular celebration, the festival includes fireworks, spectacular lighting, music, and food; lights remain up into January.

Natchitoches Jazz/R&B Festival (1st Sat. in April on Front St. 800-259-1714. Fee) Music lovers come to hear jazz, rhythm and blues, Cajun, and zydeco music on stages along Cane River Lake.

Pilgrimage of Historic Homes and Plantations (2nd weekend in Oct. at various sites. 800-259-1714. Tour fee) Tours of town homes and nearby plantation houses are available.

WHERE TO EAT

The Landing (530 Front St. 318-352-1579. Closed Mon. $$) Louisiana-style cooking.

Lasyone's Meat Pie Kitchen and Restaurant (622 2nd St. 318-352-3353. Closed Sun. $) Famous for meat-filled pastries, it also offers catfish and other regional dishes.

WHERE TO STAY

Judge Porter House (321 2nd St. 318-352-9206 or 800-441-8343. $$) The elegant 1912 house has four rooms and a guest house.

Levy-East House (358 Jefferson St. 318-352-0662 or 800-840-0662. $$) Built in the late 1830s.

NEARBY PLACES

Bayou Pierre Alligator Park (8 miles N of town, off La. 1. 318-354-0001. Mid-April–Oct.; adm. fee) The well-run alligator exhibition includes feeding shows and conservation displays.

Longleaf Trail Scenic Byway (Off La. 119, S of Derry) Drive 17 miles through Kisatchie National Forest, with overlooks, hiking trails, and magnificent longleaf pines.

Melrose (16 miles S on La. 119. 318-379-0055. Adm. fee) Don't miss a visit to this historic plantation house; its complex dates from the 1700s. On display are paintings by Clementine Hunter, a noted local artist.

GREAT LAKES

Mackinac Island

It's only a 20-minute ferry ride away, but that short, bracing ride across the Straits of Mackinac takes you back about a century in time. Mackinac (pronounced mackinaw) Island has lured generations of vacationers with its well-preserved air of Victoriana, its outdoor enticements, and its undeniable beauty. Whether you stay for a day or a month, you'll likely find yourself vowing to come back to this enchanted isle of horse-drawn carriages, splendid old cottages, and scenic pine-scented trails.

On the approach to Mackinac across the waters of Lake Huron, you can see its humped back rising higher than other islands in the straits. For good reason, then, the Ojibwa called it Michilimackinac, "Great Turtle." The wooded bluffs, highlighted by the spanking white colonnade of the **Grand Hotel,** yield on the island's south corner to a throng of turreted Victorian buildings gaily crowding the harbor. Here you disembark into the bustle of liveried porters, bicycle bells, the keen of gulls, and the striking lack of modern transportation.

Though you've probably been told, the first thing you notice on Mackinac is the absence of cars. There are no car noises, no car smells, no rush-hour traffic. Instead, you hear the clip-clop of horse hooves echoing along shady lanes and the whir of bicycles here and there. Since 1898 motor vehicles have been banned on the island, and the islanders like it just fine. Boats and planes deliver groceries, mail, supplies, and tourists to the docks. Carriages take things from there.

Sooner or later you'll end up on **Main Street** (officially called Huron Street), just off the ferry docks. In fact, many people get no farther than a stroll along Main, with its charming little shops and dozen or so fudge places. The smell of fudge is so pervasive that it's hard to resist stopping in for at least a sample, or two. Though no one appears to know exactly when fudge first appeared on Mackinac, the selling of "confections" is a tradition dating back to the 1880s. **Murdick's** and **Ryba's** are two of the older veterans in the fudge trade, the latter having gone into high gear in the 1960s with fans to waft the odors into the street. Stop in and watch chocolate being poured from copper kettles onto cool marble slabs. Among the more exotic flavors are strawberry, rum black walnut, and pistachio pecan.

Enchanting Winter

Come January, ferry lines stop running and the island, blanketed by snow, reverts to a more pristine state. Food, fuel, and necessities are stockpiled for the winter. With cold enough weather, ice bridges the distance between Mackinac and the mainland, 3.5 miles away. Christmas trees, placed every 100 yards, mark the trail for skiers and snowmobilers, who can feel the ice shifting deep down in the lake. The few visitors to the island discover an enchanted world, even more removed from the 21st century.

Grand Hotel, Mackinac Island

Continuing on foot east on Main and then up Fort Street soon brings you to the blinding white **Fort Mackinac,** the island's historical heavyweight. A long ramp leads up to the 150-foot-high South Sally Port entrance (or take a carriage around to the other side). Originally constructed during the American Revolution, the British fort finally became the property of the United States in 1796. But during the War of 1812, the British recaptured the seemingly invincible bastion by attacking from the high woods to the north. The Americans failed to regain the fort in a skirmish two years later, but with the end of the war the Stars and Stripes again waved in 1815. The U.S. War Department closed the fort in 1895. In summer, costumed reenactors lend an authentic feel with rifle and cannon firings and musical presentations.

Not to be missed at Fort Mackinac are the **Officers' Stone Quarters** and the **Soldiers' Barracks.** The former, the island's oldest building, dates from 1780 and contains a children's discovery room where the little ones can see, hear, and feel the sights and sounds of Mackinac's past. They might even try on a soldier's uniform or Victorian outfit. Also check out the extensive island history exhibits in the Soldiers' Barracks; especially fun are photographs from the Victorian era, when proper ladies biked in hats and long dresses. Before leaving the fort, take a look from the gun ports down on the village, the harbor, and the lake, and you can appreciate that what makes for a great view now made for a coveted strategic position 200 years ago.

On the way down from the fort, peek into the **Missionary Bark Chapel,** a dome-shaped re-creation of the hut used by Jesuit missionary Claude Dablon in 1670. Just across Marquette Park stands the three-story **Indian Dormitory,** which is furnished to illustrate the life of Native Americans here in the 1840s as they made the difficult transition to American culture.

To explore more on foot, continue down Main past old island inns and churches, or turn back and stroll Market Street, a relatively quiet lane of lilacs, lamp posts, and old houses with hanging flower baskets. In the early 1800s, this was the main thoroughfare, the headquarters of John Jacob Astor's American Fur Company. Imagine the street in those long-ago summers as Native Americans, traders, and trappers from the Northwest tramped through here by the thousands. In the 1830s fur trading declined, while tourism began its rise. Exhibits at the **Stuart House Museum** explore this fascinating history. Other buildings along here worth a look are the French-Canadian **McGulpin House,** one of the oldest on the island, from about 1780, and the **Benjamin Blacksmith Shop,** with live demonstrations. The **Dr. Beaumont Museum** is a new museum on the corner of Market and Fort with interactive displays and exhibits on medical history, including the work of Dr. William Beaumont, who made medical history here in the 1820s studying the digestive process of a patient whose stomach wound refused to close.

For the weary of foot, carriages are lined up in front of **Marquette Park,** waiting to tour you around the island. Another option is to rent a bike at one of the many stands on Main and pedal off into the interior or around the flat perimeter. It's only 8 miles around the island, and a circumnavigation gives you a wonderful natural history tour, with nature trails and picnic spots galore. Wherever you go, you're likely to be in **Mackinac Island State Park**—that's

Trinity Church as seen from Fort Mackinac, Mackinac Island

because the park occupies 81 percent of the island. In 1875, Congress declared the fort a national park (second after Yellowstone), but 20 years later it was turned over to the state. From the road on the east side, you can see the island's most prominent natural landmark, **Arch Rock.** There's a trail up to the 146-foot-tall limestone span, but it looks just as spectacular from below.

With all the bicycles and horses around, you might wonder just how many there are. Answer: nearly 2,000 bikes and 600 horses. They serve a year-round population of 500 that can swell fifteen times on a summer's day. Just think what a different place Mackinac Island would be if all those bikes were cars…. On second thought, don't. *John M. Thompson*

Travelwise

GETTING THERE

Mackinac Island is located in Lake Huron, a few miles east of St. Ignace, at the divide between Michigan's upper and lower peninsulas. A small airport at St. Ignace serves the island, though most people travel by ferry from St. Ignace or Mackinaw City (served by buses). Three ferry lines run May–Nov.: Arnold Transit Co. (906-847-3351), Shepler's Mackinac Island Ferry (906-643-9440), and Star Line Mackinac Island Ferry (906-643-7635).

GENERAL INFORMATION

Summer is the island's high season, when all attractions, shops, and lodgings are up and running. The cooler days of fall are also excellent for a visit, when crowds are down and autumn colors on the mainland are brilliant (less so on the island with its predominance of evergreens). For information contact the **Mackinac Island Chamber of Commerce** (P.O. Box 451, Mackinac Island 49757. 906-847-3783 or 800-454-5227).

THINGS TO SEE AND DO

Benjamin Blacksmith Shop (Market St. Early May–late Oct.; adm. with fort ticket) Using 19th- and 20th-century tools, a smith demonstrates a profession in high demand on the island.

Bicycling A number of shops on Main Street rent bikes, which you can take over some 40 miles of roads and trails.

Biddle House (Market St. Early May–late Oct.; adm. with fort ticket) Parts of this building date from the 1780s.

Carriage Rides Horse-drawn carriages are used as taxis, dray service, and tourist rides. You can rent drive-yourself carriages (Jack's Livery Stable, Mahoney St. 906-847-3391), hire a private tour with the carriages along Main (most economical with four people), or take a group jaunt over the eastern part of the island with Mackinac Island Carriage Tours (906-847-3307. Tickets available on Main St. across from Arnold Ferry Dock).

Dr. Beaumont Museum (Fort and Market Sts. Early May–late Oct.; adm. with fort ticket) Exhibits here detail the fascinating experiments conducted in the 1820s by Dr. William Beaumont on his willing, if not always happy, patient, Alexis St. Martin.

Fort Mackinac (Fort St. 906-847-3328. Early May–mid-Oct.; adm. fee) Prominent on the bluff above Main Street, the 18th- and 19th-century fort changed hands from America to Britain and back during the War of 1812. Admission to the fort includes entry to the Dr. Beaumont Museum, Benjamin Blacksmith Shop, Biddle House, Indian Dormitory, and McGulpin House.

Grand Hotel (906-847-3331. Adm. fee for non-guests, deductible from lunch buffet) The name says it all. The island's most impressive hotel, built in 1887, beckons with a 660-foot porch (over two football fields) decked with rockers and thousands of geraniums. On tap are high tea, croquet, and chamber music.

Indian Dormitory (Marquette Park, below Fort Mackinac. Early May–late Oct.; adm. with fort ticket) This building was erected in 1838 to house local Indians who ceded their claim on the island.

McGulpin House (Fort and Market Sts. Early May–late Oct.; adm. with fort ticket) Dating

Cadotte Avenue as viewed from the Grand Hotel, Mackinac Island

from 1780 or before, this ranks among the island's oldest structures, along with early sections of the fort.

Missionary Bark Chapel *(Marquette Park, Fort St. Early May–late Oct.)* The life-size diorama in this little re-created chapel gives a sense of what it was like for the French missionaries in Indian territory in the 1600s.

ANNUAL EVENTS

Lilac Festival *(10 days in early June. 907-847-3783 or 800-454-5227)* The island's big event celebrates the blossoming of trees introduced by French missionaries in the 17th century. Featured are concerts, performances, a parade, and more.

Yacht Races *(Mid-July. 313-822-9771)* The Port Huron-to-Mackinac and Chicago-to-Mackinac races are 75 and 100 years old, respectively, each drawing 250 to 300 sailboats.

WHERE TO EAT

Grand Hotel *(906-847-3331. May-Oct. $$$)* The elegant hotel restaurant serves classic American cuisine, with some local seafood specialties. Jackets and ties are required for men, a skirt or dress for women.

Horn's Gaslight Bar *(Huron St. 906-847-6154. $)* Where islanders, summer help, and tourists mingle, dance, and sing with live music. Mexican eats and traditional bar fare.

WHERE TO STAY

Grand Hotel *(Grand Ave. 906-847-3331. May-Oct. $$$)* The stately old summer hotel has been compared to a cruise ship that doesn't go anywhere. Enjoy a sunset from the cupola bar and see why.

Island House *(Huron St. 906-847-3347. May-Oct. $$$)* This turreted and columned beacon has been an island tradition since 1852.

NEARBY PLACES

Mackinaw City *(Chamber of Commerce 231-436-5574)* The gateway to the Upper Peninsula and Mackinac Island was a French trading post in the early 1700s. Here you can visit **Colonial Michilimackinac** *(S end of Mackinaw Bridge. 231-436-5563. Mid-May–mid-Oct.; adm. fee)*, a complex of 18th-century barracks, blockhouses, and workshops first occupied by the French and then the British, who were vying for control over the local fur trade. Costumed interpreters dressed as British redcoats show what life was like. The nearby **Historic Mill Creek** *(9001 US 23. 616-436-7301. Mid-May–mid-Oct.; adm. fee)* is where a single water-powered sawmill supplied much of the lumber for building Mackinac Island during the fur trade's boom in the 19th century; the site was rediscovered in the 1970s and the sawmill has since been rebuilt.

Petoskey

If there were no Petoskey, people would have invented one. Toeing the south shore of Lake Michigan's Little Traverse Bay, this friendly town of waterfront parks, 19th-century brick buildings, and to-die-for sunsets has small-town heart and year-round appeal. With water sports in summer, color touring in fall, and skiing in winter and early spring, Petoskey covers all the bases and presents a serious case for life without skyscrapers.

Freshwater Coral

How can you find coral along a freshwater lake? Michigan's state stone, the Petoskey stone is actually a fossilized coral that lived in this area 350 million years ago, when a warm sea covered northern Michigan. Some are smooth, others rough and porous, but what distinguishes them all is the hexagonal patterns covering them—the footprint of the coral colonies. Each little hexagon contains a dark "eye" where the polyp once resided. Look for them along the shores during spring ice thaw, or after a wind storm in summer.

Not that Bear River was a bad name for the Native American village the French missionaries and voyagers discovered in the 1850s, but in 1873 officials decided to rename the town in honor of local Ottawa chief Pe-to-se-ga ("Rising Sun") and the closest they could get was "Petoskey," pronounced pet-AH-ski. By now the little town was up and running, channeling lumber from the surrounding big woods into Great Lakes freighters. Trains and steamships soon began bringing summer visitors from Chicago, Cincinnati, and Detroit, drawn by the salubrious climate and resort atmosphere. Many wealthy families put up grand houses across the bay in Harbor Springs, which maintains a tony, yachty flavor, while Petoskey boasts a solidly middle-class, family-oriented feel and a vital downtown core that puts many larger cities to shame.

Pick up a walking tour brochure at the Chamber of Commerce at Mitchell and Howard Streets and take a look at how Petoskey was wisely built with brick to avoid the fires that plagued many other lumber towns. Known as the **Gaslight District,** the Victorian buildings between Bay, Lake, Division, and Howard Streets contain wall-to-wall shops and businesses. The elaborate cornices and pilasters of the 1880s **Cook Building** on Mitchell provide one example of the stalwart architecture downtown. The alley between Lake and Bay gives an interesting, alternate perspective on some of these old buildings—exterior staircases and fading block letters provide a glimpse at the history behind the facades.

Shopping has long been a big attraction in this resort town. If you're in the mood for browsing and buying, drop by **Grandpa Shorter's Gifts** (301 E. Lake St.), which in 1878 was a souvenir shop owned by the son of

Holy Childhood Church in nearby Harbor Springs

Chief Pe-to-se-ga. Or look in the 1879 **Symons General Store** *(401 E. Lake St.)*, filled with wonderful smells, classical music, and big glass jars of candies.

Ernest Hemingway spent his early summers in the area, including a stint in the winter of 1919-20 at a rooming house in Petoskey. The 20-year-old future Nobel laureate had just returned from the war in Italy, and to get away from his parents and do some serious writing he set up his typewriter in the frame house on the southeast corner of State and Woodland Streets. The stories he wrote here were apparently pretty awful, but he did establish some work habits. Local legend points out a couple of his haunts, including the Noggin Room of the **Stafford's Perry Hotel** *(Bay and Lewis Sts.)*, an elegant 1899 hostelry.

The nearby **City Park Grill** *(432 E. Lake St.)* no longer has pool tables as it did when Hemingway dropped by, but you can eat a local whitefish or a stylish sandwich in this classy, dark wood interior, its pressed tin ceiling and ornately carved bar adding nostalgic ambience. Bare-knuckles boxing matches were held here, and a speakeasy was located in the basement; history does not record whether Hemingway partook of either. Just around the corner spreads the lovely greensward of **Pennsylvania Park,** accented by a gazebo and crossed by a now defunct railroad. If Hemingway were in town now, he'd probably enjoy the salty, convivial, working-man's atmosphere of the **Mitchell St. Pub** *(926 E. Mitchell St.),* where you can bend an elbow with the locals and see how many weird ceiling decorations you can spot—a motel vacancy sign and a rubber chicken are two.

The waterfront is a natural magnet for visitors and locals, and **Bayfront Park** enhances the location. Children frolic in the playground; fishermen cast from the docks; a clock tower chimes the hours; bikers and joggers churn along a path that runs all the way to **Bay View,** 3 miles east, and beyond. The park is also the spot to watch the town's magnificent sunsets.

The **Little Traverse History Museum,** located in the park, occupies an 1892 railroad depot that served passengers until the 1960s; it presents exhibits on Indians, tourists, Hemingway, and Civil War author Bruce Catton, another homegrown writer. For a deeper look at the area's nautical history and a view of Petoskey and Harbor Springs from the lake, head out to the dock for a 45-minute tour aboard the *Bay Pride.* In cushioned comfort, you cruise by the dunes and rolling hills of **Petoskey State Park** and the eye-popping cottages of well-heeled summer people. Up on the deck, the fresh breeze keeps a perpetual smile on your face. As one enthusiastic skipper says, "Every day on the Great Lakes is a beautiful day." And in Petoskey every day is a Great Lakes day. — *John M. Thompson*

Travelwise

GETTING THERE

Petoskey is situated 38 miles southwest of Mackinaw City and 23 miles west of I-75, at the junction of US 31 and US 131. There is an airport in Pellston, 22 miles northeast. Rental cars are available there and in Petoskey.

GENERAL INFORMATION

Peak season is summer, with July highs averaging 78°F; fall also makes a delightful time to visit with sugar maple, oak, ash, and birch trees coloring the roadsides. Plentiful winter activities include skiing and ice fishing; February lows average 5°F. For additional information contact the **Petoskey-Harbor Springs-Boine County Visitors Bureau** *(401 E. Mitchell St., Petoskey 49770. 231-348-2755 or 800-845-2828. www.boinecountry.com).*

THINGS TO SEE AND DO

Bay Water Ferry & Tours *(Bayfront Park. 231-347-5550. Late May–mid-Oct.; fare)* Nautical history tours of Little Traverse Bay provide scenic panoramas.

Biking Call the visitors bureau for bike and in-line skate rentals. You can bike along the bay, or take off on other trails.

Boating Among the options are skiing on the bay or navigating the 38-mile inland waterway all the way to Lake Huron. Rentals are available at numerous area marinas. For canoe rentals in Petoskey, try Bear River Canoe Livery (*2517 McDougall Rd. 231-347-9038*).

Fishing In addition to the bay, lakes and rivers offer plenty of sport—catches include bass, trout, panfish, and walleye. Check with the visitors bureau for charter information.

Little Traverse History Museum (*100 Depot Ct., Bayfront Park. 231-347-2620. Mem. Day–Labor Day Mon.-Sat., call for hours after Labor Day; adm. fee*) This spruced-up old railroad depot houses exhibits on the Ottawa, pioneers, and local industries and writers.

Northern Michigan Hardwoods, Inc. (*5151 Manthei Rd. 231-347-4575. Mon., Tues., Thurs., and Fri.*) A good rainy day activity for children, these tours show the entire milling process, from de-barking to creation of boards and mulch.

Petoskey State Park (*5 miles NE via US 31 and Mich. 119. 231-347-2311. Beach closed in winter; adm. fee*) These 305 bayside acres offer hiking, fishing, swimming, and camping.

Scenic Driving Several roads in the area offer possibilities, particularly in fall. A 30-mile loop around Walloon Lake includes forest and bay views: Take US 131 and Mich. 75 south, then County Road 56 north and US 31 east back to Petoskey. A fall colors brochure is available at the visitors bureau.

ENTERTAINMENT

Crooked Tree Arts Center (*461 E. Mitchell St. 231-347-4337*) Concerts, plays, films, and exhibits are held in this 1890 Victorian Methodist church building.

Gaslight Cinema (*302 Petoskey St. 231-347-9696*) Watch a film in this multiplex created from the 1913 Temple Theatre.

SHOPPING

Some 60 shops in the Gaslight District sell clothing, jewelry, ceramics, and Petoskey stones.

Grain Train (*421 Howard St. 231-347-2381*) This natural foods co-op is your stop for wholesome goodies, elixirs, and homeopathic remedies. The bakery/deli makes avocado club sandwiches, organic grain breads, and so on.

McLean & Eakin Booksellers (*307 E. Lake St. 231-347-1180*) Two floors hold some

70,000 titles, including a whole section devoted to Hemingway.

ANNUAL EVENT

Art in the Park (*3rd Sat. in July. Pennsylvania Park*) More than 100 artists bring their work to this juried show.

WHERE TO EAT

Roast & Toast Cafe (*309 E. Lake St. 231-347-7767. $*) Young and old collect in this relaxed bistro for great salads and sandwiches, light entrées, coffee, and conversation.

Great Lakes sunset

WHERE TO STAY

Stafford's Perry Hotel (*Bay and Lewis Sts. 231-347-4000 or 800-456-1917. $$$*) Situated in the Gaslight District, this attractive turn-of-the-20th-century boutique hotel is the only remaining hotel downtown.

NEARBY PLACES

Bay View Take a walking tour of this national historic landmark community of nearly 500 Victorian buildings.

Harbor Springs (*Chamber of Commerce, 365 E. Main St. 231-526-7999*) About 12 miles around the bay, this charming town of 1,500 year-round residents showcases the summer mansions of both the pioneering and newly rich; the harbor buzzes with activity in summer.

Kelleys Island

A speck of dust in the eye of Lake Erie, the quiet family-oriented resort of Kelleys Island is actually the largest U.S. island in the lake. Its 17 miles of shoreline encompass 2,800 acres of low-lying woods with a south-facing cottage-lined cove for a front door and a state park for a back. Board a ferry at Marblehead for a brisk 25-minute ride across the choppy lake waters and step off on Kelleys, your low-key island get-away for fishing, swimming, bird-watching, and doing nothing.

Island Business

Entrepreneurs Datus and Irad Kelley, brothers from Cleveland, bought up the entire island in the 1830s and began exploiting its riches, investing particularly in quarrying and wine production. With the growth of big cities not far away, later inhabitants were content to use Kelleys for vacations, buying into its beauty instead of its resources. That trend continues today, with tourism as the island's main moneymaker.

The first sight to greet you upon arrival on Kelleys is the handful of salty saloons and charming Victorian cottages along Lakeshore Drive. Many of the latter are B&Bs. Drop your bags and breathe in the fresh air. When you feel like exploring, pick up a map at the information station on Division Street just north of Lakeshore. Finding your bearings on this small island is easy, and once you've done so drive north on Division all the way to the top end of the island. Division more or less divides the island into east and west halves. If you left your car on the mainland, you can rent a bike or golf cart—it's only 2.5 miles to the north end.

On this end of the island spreads 660-acre **Kelleys Island State Park,** site of one of the country's finest examples of glacial grooves. Some 25,000 years ago the Wisconsin glacier flowed down across this area, scouring everything in its path. The grooves it carved into Kelleys' limestone bedrock look as if a giant train has rolled through. You can take a short loop around the trough and marvel at the polished stone highway left by that long-ago glacier.

Elsewhere in the park are picnic tables and campsites with lake views, a stone pier for fishing, and a free boat ramp. You can fish for perch, catfish, and smallmouth bass, or wander a wooded trail and maybe see a white-tailed deer. The **North Pond State Nature Reserve,** opened in fall 1999 off Ward Road, boasts a mile-long boardwalk made of recycled plastic that curves back into a bird-rich wetland. From an observation deck you can watch herons and egrets dipping among the bulrushes and pond lilies.

Back down in the village, you will find a dozen or so shops and restaurants—just enough to keep you from needing to cross back to the mainland. But, really, commercialism is almost nonexistent. As innkeeper Caroline Jorski puts it, "There's no bank here, or pharmacy, no McDonald's, no stop-

Victoriana on Kelleys Island

Sunrise over Lake Erie

light, no crime. It's a different, slower way of life." What's here, you can see practically all of by standing at the corner of Lakeshore and Division. Down Division there's a small museum in a mid-19th-century **German Reformed Church building** *(224 Division St.)* with a few historical displays. Then view the bulky stone **City Hall,** from 1861, and a pleasant little lakefront park.

Across the street you can pick up groceries, play a game of putt-putt, and buy souvenirs. Along Lakeshore you have a choice of about five restaurant/bars that vary in their emphasis on drink or food, from the rollicking, pool-hall atmosphere of **Bag the Moon Saloon** *(109 W. Lakeshore Dr.)* to the more upscale **Water Street Cafe** *(101 W. Lakeshore Dr.).*

Take a spin along Lakeshore Drive along the island's south and west sides. From the road you get the best water views—views shared by smart Victorian cottages with turrets, big porches, and trim lawns. These handsome dwellings, several of which are now B&Bs, date from the turn of the 20th century, when quarrying, winemaking, logging, fruit-growing, and fishing were at their heyday.

On the south side of Lakeshore at Addison, take a look at the tremendous limestone slab called **Inscription Rock.** Erie Indians more than 300 years ago etched figures of men, birds, and animals; a wooden pavilion now protects the faint petroglyphs from further erosion. In 1665, some time after the rock was carved, Iroquois destroyed two Erie villages on the island; white settlement did not occur here for another 150 years. Life on the island then, even for the wealthy, was fairly primitive, as it still is in the winter. The population in winter drops from 2,000 to less than 200. When the lake freezes over, residents depend upon small airplanes for mail and groceries, and a particularly bad spell can mean days of isolation. Driving around the island will take you past the airstrip (Morgan and Lincoln Roads), where a sign warns you to look both ways and proceed with caution. Not to worry—planes on laid-back Kelleys, if you hadn't already guessed, are few and far between. *John M. Thompson*

Travelwise

GETTING THERE

Kelleys Island is situated in Lake Erie 4 miles north of Marblehead, which sits on the tip of the Sandusky Bay peninsula. The Kelleys Island Ferry Boat Line provides daily passage between Marblehead *(510 W. Main St., opposite police dept.)* and Kelleys Island, with departures every half hour during peak times. The trip lasts about 25 minutes; late night boats run in high season. Marblehead lies 55 miles east of Toledo (served by trains, planes, and buses): Take I-80/90 east to Ohio 53; at Port Clinton take Ohio 163 east to Marblehead.

GENERAL INFORMATION

May through September are the best times for a visit. Midsummer is the peak time for water activities, particularly sailing and jet-skiing, with crisp lake breezes and steady wavelets. Monarch butterflies return to the island every September on their way to Mexico. In winter, ice rimes the streets, and many businesses close. For information contact the **Kelleys Island Chamber of Commerce** *(P.O. Box 783-F, Kelleys Island 43438. 419-746-2360. www.kelleyschamber.com).*

THINGS TO SEE AND DO

Bicycling Rent bicycles, with or without motors, at several locations in the "downtown" area, along Division and Lakeshore Streets. Island streets are uncrowded and flat.

Hiking Kelleys Island State Park (see below) claims 6 miles of trails, and the island itself has plenty of quiet roads to wander.

Inscription Rock *(Lakeshore Dr. and Addison Rd.)* Though faded over the centuries, the 300-year-old petroglyphs on this waterfront boulder are worth a look.

Kelleys Island State Park *(Division St. and Titus Rd. 419-746-2546. Camping fee)* Don't miss the glacial grooves laid down 25,000 years ago and embedded with coral fossils. Overlooks along a short loop include one with an excellent view west to the vast canyonlike quarry that was the hub of island commerce in the 1910s. You can also camp, fish, and hike in this woodsy, lakeside park. The **North Pond State Nature Reserve** *(Off Ward Rd.)* features an interpretive mile-long boardwalk nature trail.

SHOPPING

Several stores on Division Street, just north of Lakeshore, are housed in 19th-century buildings that offer a nostalgic atmosphere, along with resort wear, T-shirts, souvenirs, fudge, and ice cream.

ANNUAL EVENT

Islandfest *(End of July. 419-746-2360)* This street party includes a parade, dancing, a crafts market, and fireworks.

WHERE TO EAT

Village Pump *(103 W. Lakeshore Dr. 419-746-2281. Closed Jan.–Feb. $)* A relaxed atmosphere prevails at this lakeside hangout. Try the walleye or Lake Erie yellow perch; Brandy Alexanders and onion rings are also specialties.

WHERE TO STAY

Cricket Lodge *(111 E. Lakeshore Dr. 419-746-2263. $$)* Enjoy homemade muffins and fresh coffee with a view of Lake Erie in this cozy 1905 cottage. Three rooms.

The Inn on Kelleys Island *(317 W. Lakeshore Dr. 419-746-2258. $$)* A quaint 1876 Victorian inn offers four rooms with reasonable rates and a private beach.

NEARBY PLACES

Put-in-Bay *(South Bass Island, 7 miles NW of Kelleys Island via ferry)* More of a party scene than Kelleys, Put-in-Bay nonetheless boasts the **Perry's Victory and International Peace Memorial** *(419-285-2184. Adm. fee)* honoring Commodore Perry's defeat of the British near here in 1813. The 352-foot memorial has an observation deck with bold lake views.

Berlin

Surrounded by peaceful rolling farmland, tiny Berlin hearkens to a slower, simpler time, a time when the horse-drawn buggy was the only way to travel and sitting on the front porch with a friend was the best form of entertainment. In Berlin, heart of the world's largest Amish community, you can see how the Amish of eastern Ohio have preserved their uncluttered way of life and you can sample their wares in craft stores, antique shops, and good home-style restaurants.

The history of the Plain People in the area goes all the way back to 1809, when an Amish settler named Jonas Stutzman built a small cabin a few miles east of Berlin (pronounced BUR-lun) in what is now Walnut Creek. Another pioneer platted the town of Berlin seven years later; other settlers followed, mostly from Pennsylvania, and the settlement grew. By the middle of the century, most of the state's rural Amish and Mennonite communities had been established. Today about 50 percent of Holmes County's 38,000 residents are of Amish background; the Amish country, which includes several adjacent counties, counts a total of about 80,000 Amish.

If you want to delve farther back in Amish history, and learn more about how their religion and history play an integral part in their daily lives, stop by the **Mennonite Information Center.** The key attraction here is a 10-by-265-foot circular mural called Behalt ("to remember") that vividly depicts the history of the Amish and Mennonites from their Swiss origins in 1525 up to the present. Guides tour you around the mural, which begins with gruesome scenes of martyrs being burned, beheaded, drowned, and tortured; farther along you come to more peaceful activities—a barn raising, an Amish wedding, and so on. In short, the Anabaptist movement, from which the Amish and Mennonites sprang, believed in adult rather than infant baptism, and for holding fast to this principle they were put to death by the thousands. Throughout the centuries, the Amish have cherished their martyrs and kept copious records and letters about them so as to challenge people to live as the martyrs did.

As you drive the county back roads and stroll the village sidewalks, you'll see buggies clipping smartly along, driven by men with long beards and traditional straw hats and dark clothes. And you'll see groups of women in their monochromatic aprons and bonnets shopping and conversing in Pennsylvania Dutch, a mix of German and English. Those driving buggies and wearing old-fashioned clothes are Amish, while many Mennonites are indistinguishable from outsiders. As a rule of thumb, the Amish are more conservative; the Mennonites in this area are often former Amish who have opted for a modern lifestyle. Most Amish don't drive cars, use electricity, keep telephones in their homes, or buy insurance. But they will ride in cars and use gasoline motors: The idea is that they take care of their own, without reliance upon the outside world.

Country lane outside Berlin

At **Schrock's Amish Farm** you can gain more insight into Amish ways. The 150-year-old farmhouse is furnished to reflect both Old Order and New Order Amish lifestyles. Throughout, you'll notice how the furnishings embody the Amish people's concern for peace, family solidarity, and humility ("the most beautiful virtue"). There is no television, no electric lights, no clutter; pictures are limited to scenic scenes, and mirrors are found only in bathrooms. Out back you can pet goats and sheep and ramble through a barn redolent with the odors of horses and hay. Visitors tempted to try the Amish life should think hard—very few outsiders have permanently converted unless they married into an Amish family. Giving up modern conveniences is not easy, and the Amish, though friendly, are almost exclusively clannish—missionaries they are not.

Take a walk down Berlin's Main Street to see the kinds of businesses that locals are turning to as available farmland shrinks and tourism grows. The three or four blocks of Ohio 39 clustered with shops and eateries are sometimes busy with traffic, but you can park and wander. Emporiums such as the **Berlin Country Market** and **Sommers' General Store,** both at the intersection of US 62 and Ohio 39, are chockablock with pottery, kitchenware, cookbooks, oil lamps, and old-fashioned candy. Other shops along the way specialize in woodwork, leather, quilts, candles, and more.

Amish gathering in Berlin

Warm aromas from **Der Bake Oven** *(4766 Ohio 39)* can easily tempt you to take a break from shopping and settle into some of the pies, breads, and cookies for which the Amish country is famous. Continuing west on Main offers you more chances to savor area cooking. Locals gather at **Boyd & Wurthman Restaurant** *(4819 E. Main St.)* for heaping plates of sausages, Swiss steak, pork chops, mashed potatoes, and green beans; about a dozen different kinds of pies are offered every day. Tables at area restaurants are usually supplied with apple butter and a sauce made of peanut butter, marshmallow cream, and karo syrup—it's pretty tasty on bread. The **Berlin Cafe** *(4860 E. Main St.)* across the street caters to slightly more refined palates—their homemade soups, sandwiches, and salads make for a healthy lunch; on weekend evenings you can sip cappuccino or latte while listening to live music. Shop for wholesome natural foods and vitamins at the adjacent **Nature's Food Market.** Another fun store nearby with a distinct local flavor, **Berlin Bulk Food** *(2 N. Market St.)* is a great place to pick up locally made meats, cheeses, and spices, as well as friendly conversation.

Don't leave without taking a drive out into the countryside. If you're staying at one of the area's many bed-and-breakfasts you'll likely be heading at least a few miles off Main Street. One nice little excursion, **Wendell August Forge** lies just a few miles north. Visitors are encouraged to wander through the back of the cavernous store to watch workers turning out decorative pieces of aluminum, bronze, and pewter. Or just drive at random along the country roads, lovely in all four seasons, and take in the long fields of grain and soybeans, the light of late afternoons on white farm buildings, and the measured pace of peaceful living.   *John M. Thompson*

Travelwise

GETTING THERE

Berlin is located 90 miles south of Cleveland, off I-77. Airplanes, trains, and buses service Cleveland; airplanes and buses also service Columbus, to the southwest. Rental cars are available in both cities.

GENERAL INFORMATION

Each season in Holmes County is distinct, with its own charms. Autumn makes for especially nice touring, when the air is crisp and leaves are at peak color. Contact the **Amish Country Visitors Bureau** (P.O. Box 177, Berlin 44610. 330-893-3467) or the **Mennonite Information Center** (P.O. Box 324, Berlin 44610. 330-893-3192).

THINGS TO SEE AND DO

Farmers' Auctions (Mon. and Fri. Sugarcreek, 330-852-2832. Tues. Farmerstown, 330-897-6081. Wed. Mt. Hope, 330-674-6188. Thurs. Kidron, 330-857-2641) At these spirited markets, watch Amish farmers buying and selling livestock, grain, straw, and hay.

Mennonite Information Center (1.2 miles N of town on Cty. Rd. 77. 330-893-3192. Closed Sun.) Half-hour tours (fee) of the "Behalt" cyclorama detail the history of the Amish and Mennonites. Exhibits, 15-minute video on the area, and bookshop.

Schrock's Amish Farm (1 mile E of Berlin on Ohio. 39. 330-893-3232. April-Oct. Mon.-Sat.; adm. fee) A 20-minute film and a house tour show what Amish life is like behind the curtains. Freshly baked cookies and breads are for sale at the end of the tour.

Wendell August Forge (3 miles N of town on US 62. 330-893-3713. Closed Sun.) Self-guided tours of the production workshop.

SHOPPING

Berlin and the nearby villages in Amish country are celebrated for their fine selections of well-made crafts, including wooden toys, baskets, and furniture. Other area specialties include cheeses, popcorn, and jams.

Bunker Hill Hardware (1 mile N of town, off US 62. Closed Sun.) This is where the Amish purchase non-electric appliances like stoves, grinders, waffle irons, oil lamps, and pumps.

Heini's Cheese Chalet and Country Mall (6005 Cty. Rd. 77, Millersburg. 330-893-2131) More than 50 kinds of cheeses (free samples), hand-dipped ice cream, fudge, and more.

ANNUAL EVENTS

Christmas in Berlin (Weekends bet. Thanksgiving and Christmas. Main St. 330-893-3467) A festive series of events including a Nativity parade and candle-lighting ceremony.

Singing on the Amish Farm (Early July. Schrock's Amish Farm. 330-852-3230. Adm. fee) Top-notch Southern gospel concerts fill the air.

WHERE TO EAT

Der Dutchman (4 miles E in Walnut Creek, at 4967 Walnut St./Ohio 515. 330-893-2981. Closed Sun. $) One of the area's best Amish kitchens, the Dutchman serves family-style dinners and has a huge in-house bakery.

Dutch Harvest Restaurant (1 mile W on Ohio 39, at 5324 Cty. Rd. 201. 330-893-3333. $) Owned and operated by a former Old Order Amish family, this place knows how to deliver Amish cooking. Don't miss the bag apple pie.

WHERE TO STAY

Main Street Bed & Breakfast (W. Main St. 330-893-1300. $$) A small establishment with Amish furniture and quilts, as well as Jacuzzis.

Rose Arbor Inn (W. Main St. 330-893-4167. $) A cozy, two-bedroom inn in Victorian cottage style.

Columbus

Graceful modern buildings by the likes of I.M. Pei and Eliel
Saarinen, a golf course designed by Robert Trent Jones, Sr., a
lively downtown with 19th-century shopfronts. What major city
is this? With 37,000 people, Columbus in southern Indiana is
barely a city at all. Yet the American Institute of Architects puts
only a handful of U.S. cities above Columbus in innovation and
architectural design. Like a living lab for architecture, this town
embraces aesthetics and boasts a self-
assured sense of purpose and direction.

Old-time Respite

When you need
a break from the
modern, come back
down to 329 Washing-
ton Street and step
into Zaharako's. Dating
from 1900, this charm-
ing ice-cream parlor
has a working pipe
organ, marble counters,
an onyx soda fountain
(purchased in 1905 at
the St. Louis World's
Fair), and stained-glass
accents—proof that
Columbus has pre-
served the best of
its past. Locals gather
here for homemade
chili, Braunschweiger
sandwiches, and grilled
cheese sandwiches
with meat sauce—
not to mention the real
milkshakes and floats.

If you arrive from the southwest corner of
town, you'll immediately be struck by the twin-
ribbed steel arch bridge at the I-65 overpass, and
the soaring red and white suspension bridge on
Second Street. These city landmarks are symbols
of the aesthetic values you'll witness in town. As
you enter Columbus, the main commercial drag
of Washington Street may not impress you as
particularly contemporary with its solid row of
handsome turn-of-the-20th-century office and
shop buildings. That's because city leaders wisely
decided not to tear down all the old to make way
for the new.

But things are different on Fifth Street,
"avenue of architects," where the plaza outside
the public library was designed by I.M. Pei. In
the plaza stands sculptor Henry Moore's monumental "Large Arch." Across the street rises Eliel
Saarinen's serene **First Christian Church.** Three
major works of art in one view—and that's just
for starters.

Columbus looked not unlike other prosperous
midwestern county seats in the early 1940s. It was
a growing trade and transportation center sporting a palatial old courthouse and several elegant
Queen Anne-style houses. Then, in 1942, the First
Christian Church, looking for an architect for a
new church building, decided to head into uncharted waters. They chose
renowned Finnish-born Eliel Saarinen. His boxy, steeple-less sanctuary and
adjacent monolith were the result. A lot of locals were flummoxed, and in fact
nothing else changed for 15 more years. But in the late '50s the Cummins
Engine Company, the town's top employer, offered to donate architects' fees
for the creation of new schools if the architects were chosen from a list made

Cummins Engine Company, designed by Kevin Roche and John Dinkeloo and Associates

up by the company CEO, whose friends included Eero Saarinen, son of Eliel. The program expanded over the years to include other public buildings. Private businesses and churches have also commissioned top designers, and now the number of significant buildings totals more than 50.

The best way to see the architecture is to drop by the **visitor center** and sign up for one of their excellent bus tours, or pick up a self-guided walking or driving tour map. The film and exhibits here offer a good primer on the structures outside. And you can't miss Dale Chihuly's "Yellow Neon Chandelier," with 900 pieces of hand-blown glass. The corner of Fifth and Franklin, just outside the visitor center, is a natural magnet for architecture students, architects, and other lovers of design. People stand around sketching, gazing, and discussing the buildings.

Regular tours will take you inside a couple of buildings, including the First Christian, with its mysterious long narrow nave, and **St. Peter's Lutheran Church,** designed in 1988 by Gunnar Birkerts—a huge circular sanctuary with a skylight from which hang two interlocked disks. The effect of both interiors is strange, almost otherworldly, but elegantly simple. As is the sci-fi-like **North Christian Church.** Eero Saarinen's final completed design, the church consists of a pencil-thin spire surmounting a concrete, six-sided building. The interior has the close feel of a planetarium—pews on two levels surround 12 dark wood communion tables. Symbolic details are everywhere, from the center oculus to the sunken baptismal font with a suspended metal dove.

Your tour will pass the **Veterans' Memorial** *(Washington at 2nd Sts.)* next to the courthouse. Even so, come back and take a closer look. Here 25 columns of local limestone are engraved with letters from the 171 area people who died in 20th-century wars. Reading these letters home, now inscribed for the ages, is a moving experience. "When I get home it will be summer," reads Marvin Monroe's letter to his mother in 1968. "I really shouldn't plan so far ahead, but I do anyway."

Is Columbus the perfect small town? Well, it thrives largely because of its industrial muscle—companies like Cummins and Arvin Industries produce diesel engines, catalytic converters, and other pieces of machinery. And while they pump money directly into civic projects such as architecture, they add to the traffic and population. But on a nice day, when you're strolling the town's parks or sidewalks, you tend to forget the big-city part of Columbus and to think of it more as a small town that got lucky. *John M. Thompson*

Travelwise

GETTING THERE

Columbus is located just east of I-65 in southern Indiana. It is 45 miles south of Indianapolis, which is served by planes, buses, and trains. Columbus has bus and taxi service.

GENERAL INFORMATION

Autumn and spring are the best times to visit; foliage and flowers are complemented by moderate weather. Winters are generally cold; summers are hot and humid. Bear in mind that Indiana stays on eastern standard time year-round. For information and architecture tours, contact the **Columbus Area Visitors Center** *(506 5th St., Columbus 47201. 812-378-2622 or 800-468-6564. http://columbus.in.us).*

THINGS TO SEE AND DO

Columbus Area Visitors Center *(506 5th St. 812-378-2622. Closed Sun. Dec.-Feb.)* The video, models, and hands-on exhibits on Columbus architecture are a good place to start. Bus tours *(fee)* begin from here.

First Christian Church *(5th St. and Lafayette Ave. Mon.-Fri. Contact visitor center for tour)* A landmark of modern architecture that fits well in its small town setting, this church and 166-foot tower were designed by Eliel Saarinen.

Fishing Cast for bluegill, channel catfish, and red ear sunfish at the 5,000-acre **Atterbury Fish and Wildlife Area** *(10 miles N via US 31. 812-526-2051).*

Hiking Trails lace the **Anderson Falls** area *(8.5 mile E of town off Ind. 46).*

Indianapolis Museum of Art–Columbus Gallery *(The Commons, 3rd and Washington Sts. 812-376-2597. Closed Mon.; donation)* This small satellite gallery of the Indianapolis Museum of Art holds 3,000 square feet of space for traveling exhibits.

Irwin Gardens *(5th St. and Lafayette Ave. April-Sept. Sat.-Sun.)* These lovely formal gardens adjoin an Italianate home built in 1864 by local banker William Irwin.

Main Street parade, Columbus

Mill Race Park *(5th and Lindsey Sts., along the White River)* Concerts and other big events take place in this popular downtown park, featuring an 84-foot viewing tower, an amphitheater, and the oldest single-lane covered bridge in Indiana.

North Christian Church *(850 Tipton Ln. Mon.-Sat. Contact visitor center for tour)* The hexagonal base and spire form a unified whole, creating, in effect, a church within a steeple.

St. Peter's Lutheran Church *(719 5th St. 812-372-1571. Mon.-Fri.)* Bush-hammered concrete slabs and a tall gray steeple contrast with the rounded interior in this striking house of worship.

ENTERTAINMENT

Columbus Area Arts Council *(812-376-2535)* Call for information on area performances of dance, music, and theater.

SHOPPING

In addition to the shops along Washington Street, there are several antique stores scattered about town. Among malls, the **Commons** stands out for its downtown location *(3rd and Washington Sts.)*, its hands-on children's museum, restaurants, movie theaters, and art gallery—not to mention the fact that it was designed by prominent architect Cesar Pelli.

ANNUAL EVENT

Ethnic Expo *(2nd weekend in Oct. Downtown. 812-376-2502)* A parade, fireworks, international bazaar, and exotic foods are featured to celebrate the town's Asian and other ethnic groups.

WHERE TO EAT

Peter's Bay *(The Commons. 812-372-2270. $$)* The best place for fine dining downtown, this unstuffy bistro serves fresh seafood.

WHERE TO STAY

Columbus Inn *(445 5th St. 812-378-4289. $$)* Originally the 1895 city hall, this attractive 34-room inn offers buffet breakfasts and high teas. High-ceilinged rooms are on the first floor.

Ruddick-Nugent House Bed and Breakfast *(1210 16th St. 812-379-1354 or 800-814-7478. $$)* This grand colonial revival-style mansion dates from 1884 and has four rooms, each with different, luxurious appointments. Candlelight breakfasts are sumptuous feasts.

Madison

Nestled along the banks of the Ohio River in southeastern Indiana, this attractive small town presents the state's best collection of 19th-century architecture. Only an hour southeast of contemporary Columbus (see pp. 180-183), Madison has remained decidedly in the past—devotedly preserving more than 133 blocks of old houses and buildings, including two national historic landmarks and eight historic museums. Wineries, antique and craft shops, a state park, and a delightful riverside setting add to Madison's many charms.

Paddle wheeler on the Ohio

You can tell as you amble along Main Street that this was once an important town and that locals have remained proud of their heritage. The proper rows of 19th-century office buildings, painted in strong reds, yellows, and blues and showing off decorative rooflines and wrought iron, shoulder the street like respectable Victorians on parade. Madison was well on its way to greatness in the mid-1800s as a midwestern river port and supply town for pioneers heading west. Steamboats and trains chugged through, bringing a stir of activity and plenty of money, much of it going into the federal, Italianate, and classical revival architecture you see today. Then, as the better positioned towns of Louisville and Cincinnati rose in prominence, Madison slipped into quiet obscurity. But with the boom in tourism in recent decades, the town has reaffirmed its position on the map.

Its vigor is apparent in Main Street's potpourri of shops, antique stores, nice restaurants, soda fountains, and that index of small town vitality, an operating movie theater. Fanning out from Main lies a national register district of some 1,500 structures. Pick up a walking tour brochure at the visitor center; the core of the historic area is easily covered on foot.

The grande dame of Madison houses, the ocher-colored **Lanier Mansion State Historic Site** owns gracious views of gardens and the river from its high-ceilinged rooms. Francis Costigan, whose name is on several Madison houses, designed and built this Greek Revival manse in the 1840s. A couple of blocks away stands another Costigan creation, the **Shrewsbury-Windle House.** Built for a riverboat captain, it claims an awesome freestanding spiral staircase and massive 12-foot-tall doors. Be sure during your perambulations to pass by the **Broadway Fountain,** a double-tiered cast bronze work that forms a bubbly, flower-decked oasis at Broadway and Main. The trickle of

Lanier Mansion State Historic Site

water and the leafy streets along here almost make you feel as if you're in Savannah or some equally lush southern town.

If you want to feel what it's like to live in one of Madison's architectural gems, you can choose from about ten B&Bs. In fact, if you're staying downtown, you don't have much other choice—there's not a motel in sight. Canopy beds, fine china, hearty morning meals, and river views are some of the offerings. And at some point in your stay, take a walk along the riverfront. May through October, the *Mississippi Queen* and other paddle wheelers dock here as they did more than a century ago. There's also a floating restaurant and frequent musical events along the grassy banks. If things are quiet, just soak up the calmness of the wide Ohio—what was once the lifeblood of Madison now makes a lovely backdrop to a town that time forgot.   *John M. Thompson*

Travelwise

GETTING THERE

Madison is located on the Ohio River 55 miles northeast of Louisville and 65 miles southwest of Cincinnati. Both cities are accessible by plane and bus; trains serve Cincinnati.

GENERAL INFORMATION

Most house museums are open mid-April through October. Riverside musical events take place in the summer; fall weather in this part of the state is particularly pleasant with warm days and cool evenings. Indiana remains on eastern standard time year-round. For information contact the **Madison Area Convention & Visitors Bureau** *(301 E. Main St., Madison 47250. 812-265-2956 or 800-559-2956).*

THINGS TO SEE AND DO

Canoeing The gentle Ohio makes for an easy paddle and a good way to spot wildlife. Call Kate's Canoe Rental Adventures *(812-273-5915).*

Clifty Falls State Park *(1 mile W of town on Ind. 56. 812-273-8885. Open year-round; adm. fee April–Oct.)* This woodsy 1,400-acre park features rugged gorges, four waterfalls up to 83 feet high, 14 miles of trails, and a lodge.

Dr. William Hutchings' Office *(120 W. 3rd St. 812-265-2967. Mid-April–Oct.; adm. fee)* All the instruments and furnishings are original, providing a look at early medical practice.

Francis Costigan House *(408 W. 3rd St. 812-265-2967. Mid-April–Oct. Sat.-Mon.; adm. fee)* Take a look at the small but masterly 1851 home of the architect who designed the Lanier Mansion.

Jeremiah Sullivan House *(304 W. 2nd St. 812-265-2967. Mid-April–Oct.; adm. fee)* Madison's first mansion is a federal-style house built in 1818 by a distinguished lawyer and legislator.

Lanier Mansion State Historic Site *(511 W. 1st St. 812-265-3526. Wed.-Sun. mid-Dec.–mid-March, Tues.-Sun. rest of year; donation)* This meticulously restored showplace was built for financier J.F.D. Lanier, who loaned enough money to equip six Indiana regiments during the Civil War.

Shrewsbury-Windle House *(301 W. 1st St. 812-265-4481. April-Oct. by appt. only; adm. fee)* This opulent 1849 Regency home is, like the Lanier place, a national historic landmark.

SHOPPING

In addition to antiques and traditional gifts, Madison has a growing reputation as an arts and crafts colony. Main Street alone holds six antique stores and more than 20 specialty shops, with items ranging from woodcarvings and tinware to paintings and pottery.

ANNUAL FESTIVALS AND EVENTS

Madison Chautauqua *(4th weekend in Sept. Riverfront Park. 800-559-2956)* The state's top juried fine arts and crafts show features 270 booths, live music, kids' activities, and lots of food.

Madison in Bloom *(Last weekend in April and 1st weekend in May. 800-559-2956)* See the gardens of houses not normally open to the public.

WHERE TO EAT

Mundt's JWI Confectionery *(207 W. Main St. 812-265-6171. $)* This fun confectionery and soda fountain has been an in spot since 1917; choose from a menu of ice cream and luncheon specials.

WHERE TO STAY

Historic Broadway Hotel & Tavern *(313 Broadway. 812-273-6467. $$)* Built in 1834, this redoubtable old landmark one block from the river has Victorian antiques and a courtyard for breakfast service.

Vintage Views Inn *(411 W. 1st St. 812-265-6856. $$)* Located in the historic district, this Victorian B&B boasts original parquet floors and oak woodwork.

ILLINOIS

Nauvoo

You won't just stumble upon the peaceful little Mississippi River town of Nauvoo. You have to seek it out. Hidden in a bend of the river, this charming footnote to American history preserves more than 40 houses and shops built by the Mormons in the early 1840s. Walking the wide shady streets along parklike blocks when the sun is out and a river breeze freshens the air, you can understand why the town was called Nauvoo, "beautiful place."

Driven out of Missouri in 1839, Joseph Smith and his followers of the Church of Jesus Christ of Latter-day Saints crossed the river and settled at a nearly abandoned fur-trading village. Within three years the industrious Mormons had built a thriving town, its 12,000 citizens making it one of the largest in the state. But all was not well in the Saints' new Jerusalem. Mayor of Nauvoo, Smith was planning a run for the office of the President of the United

Nauvoo House, built in 1842

Inside the historic post office, Nauvoo

States in order to address the issue of religious freedom. His militia, land deals, and suspected polygamy began making neighbors nervous. Some Mormons themselves began having misgivings, but when they tried to publish a dissenting newspaper, Smith's city council destroyed the press. Soon thereafter Smith and his brother were put in jail, where a mob assassinated them.

Most of the Mormons picked up with Brigham Young and in two years began trekking with him out to Utah. Others stayed and eventually took up with Smith's son, Joseph Smith III, and formed the Reorganized Church of Jesus Christ of Latter-day Saints, one of more than 150 factions of the organized church in existence today. Their story is what you'll hear at the **Joseph Smith Historic Center.** The **Nauvoo Restoration, Inc., Visitors Center,** just north, is run by the mainstream Mormon church, which owns most of the historic district. The Smith Center presents a somewhat more balanced view of history, but it's all interesting, partly because this is not the typical state-sanctioned history lesson. Furthermore, all of the historic sites are free and free of touristy glitz.

If you start at the Smith Center, you'll see the **Homestead,** an 1824 log cabin that Smith bought in 1839. The small adjoining cemetery contains the graves of the elder Smith and various family members. Nearby stands one of Smith's money-making enterprises, the 1842 **Red Brick Store,** and cater-corner at Water and Main Streets is the white-frame **Mansion House,** where members of the Smith family lived until 1890.

While the exhibit hall up at the church's visitor center is more one-sided, the film is better. Costumed reenactors and a script made entirely from early journal entries lend veracity to a re-creation of the pioneer period of Nauvoo. The two dozen outlying historical buildings have been carefully restored, though some of the tours end with a zealous spin that may make non-believers a tad uncomfortable. But the houses, bakery, drugstore, printing office, mercantile, and others are well worth a look.

The **Browning Home and Gun Shop** does a good job detailing the work of gunsmith Jonathan Browning, who invented the repeating rifle and began a gun company here in 1845. The restored **Brigham Young Home** and the federal-style **Wilford Woodruff Home** are other highlights. Drive north on Main, then left after Hubbard toward the river for an overlook of the now partially submerged limestone quarry used for building the **Nauvoo Temple.** The unfinished temple was abandoned after the Mormons left and burned in 1848, but you can see the ruins up at Well and Mulholland Streets. Recent plans for the construction of a new temple have made some locals, now 90 percent non-Mormon, fear a sudden growth spurt in their quiet town.

Temple Square stands on the bluff above the flats. While the flats hold the historic area, the bluff is where you'll find Nauvoo's commercial district: the four blocks of Mulholland from Bluff to Wilcox Streets. A few restaurants, two antique stores, the old **Hotel Nauvoo,** a bookshop, and a few other establishments vie for your money. Take a walk at sundown into the neighborhoods just off the main stem, and the only thing you'll hear is your own footsteps. The seren-

Sunstone from the original Nauvoo Temple

ity is hard to believe. The smell of dinners cooking and a few stray sounds from birds and children are the only signs that life goes on in this hamlet, once the hub of such earnest intentions.   *John M. Thompson*

Travelwise

GETTING THERE
Nauvoo is located on Ill. 96 in western Illinois, 12 miles north of Hamilton and 14 miles south of Fort Madison, Iowa. The nearest airport is 30 miles northeast in Burlington, Iowa, which is also served by bus and train.

GENERAL INFORMATION
Nauvoo is basically a three-season destination, with some attractions shutting down in winter. For information contact the **Nauvoo Chamber of Commerce** *(1295 Mulholland St., P.O. Box 41, Nauvoo 62353. 217-453-6648 or 877-628-8661).*

THINGS TO SEE AND DO

Bar Y Horses and Trail Rides *(Mulholland and Winchester Sts. 217-453-2091. Fee)* Guided horseback rides through scenic woods.

Brigham Young Home *(Kimball and Granger Sts. 217-453-2237)* The house served as LDS church headquarters after Joseph Smith's death in 1844.

Browning Home and Gun Shop *(Main and Munson Sts. 217-453-2237)* Learn about gunsmithing in this two-story brick reconstruction.

French Icarian Living History Museum
*(2205 Parley St. 217-453-2281. April–Oct.
Tues.-Sat.)* Not long after the Mormons left
Nauvoo, another group of idealists arrived.
Calling themselves Icarians, a band of 500
French settlers practiced communal life
here until the late 1850s. Some stayed and,
with arriving Swiss and Germans, began to
cultivate grapes for wine production. Not
much is left from the Icarian days, though
there are a couple of surviving wineries
and the restored 1850s home housing the
French Icarian Living History Museum. Here, a
genealogy corner and exhibits tell the story
of the mid-19th-century utopian society.

Joseph Smith Historic Center *(Water
and Partridge Sts. 217-453-2246. Closed late
Dec.–Jan.)* Exhibits include letters, paintings, and
artifacts of Mormon pioneers. From the center,
guided tours start with a film, then proceed to
the **Homestead** and the **Mansion House.**
You can only visit these on a tour.

**Nauvoo Restoration Inc., Visitors
Center** *(Main and Young Sts. 217-453-2237 or
888-453-6934)* Displays outline the Mormon
settlement and its religion. The "Monument
to Women" sculpture garden outside has
heroic bronzes of the Smiths and tableaus of
the life stages of a woman, including "Woman
Learning" and "Companionship for Eternity."

Nauvoo State Park *(Ill. 96, S edge of
Nauvoo. 217-453-2512)* This 148-acre park
holds a lake for fishing and boating, and a
museum *(May–mid-Oct.)* features four rooms
depicting periods in Nauvoo history—Indian,
Mormon, French, and pioneer.

Red Brick Store *(Water and Granger Sts. 217-
453-2246)* Smith's office was on the second
floor of the original store; this reconstruction
sells copies of typical pioneer items such as
tinware and hand-dipped candles.

Scenic Driving Follow Ill. 96 south of
Nauvoo for 10 miles to Hamilton—an
extremely scenic portion of the Great River
Road. Tracing the Mississippi River, it passes
shady groves and river bluffs, with turnouts
to enjoy the views. Bald eagles like to
congregate around Keokuk Dam, especially
on January mornings.

Wilford Woodruff Home *(Ill. 96 and
Hotchkiss St. 217-453-2716)* This eight-room
home was built by the fourth LDS president.

ENTERTAINMENT

Historic Musicals *(Summer evenings except
Sun., in the visitor center and the Cultural Hall)*
Musical dramas re-create scenes from
old Nauvoo.

SHOPPING

Nauvoo is known for its blue cheese,
produced at the Nauvoo Cheese Company
and available at shops in town. Antiques and
gifts are available in several stores.

ANNUAL EVENTS

"City of Joseph" *(Late July–early Aug. Adj. to
visitor center. 800-453-0022, ext. 324)* More
than 300 actors, singers, and dancers perform
in this award-winning outdoor musical.

Nauvoo Grape Festival *(Labor Day
weekend. Nauvoo S.P. 217-453-6648)* Parades,
an outdoor pageant, a car show, and music
celebrate the annual grape harvest.

WHERE TO EAT

Grandpa John's Cafe *(1250 Mulholland St.
217-453-2310. $)* This old-fashioned cafeteria
and grill serves breakfast and lunch. Try the
homemade ice cream.

Hotel Nauvoo *(1290 Mulholland St. 217-
453-2211. Mid-March–mid-Nov. $)* Order from
the menu or dig into the bountiful buffet.

WHERE TO STAY

1850s Guest House *(1550 E. Ill. 96, Dallas
City, 15 minutes NE of Nauvoo. 217-852-3652.
$)* Stone and stucco mansion with a 70-foot
covered porch. 10 rooms.

Ancient Pines B&B *(2015 Parley St. 217-
453-2767. $)* Turn-of-the-20th-century home
with stained-glass windows, pressed metal
ceilings, carved woodwork, and a claw-foot
tub, set amid 150-year-old evergreens.

Hotel Nauvoo *(1290 Mulholland St. 217-
453-2211. Mid-March–mid-Nov. $)* This 1840s
hostelry, graced with an upper veranda and
cupola, started life as a private home. Rooms
are a bit small, but fully modernized.

NEARBY PLACES

Carthage The county seat of Hancock
County, here is where Joseph Smith and his
brother were jailed and murdered. The visitor
center *(Ill. 136. 217-357-2989)* is located in the
Old Carthage Jail.

WISCONSIN

Ephraim

Summer people, who inflate its permanent population of about 270 roughly tenfold during the season, consider Ephraim—pronounced E-from—the most desirable among a dozen charming hamlets decorating Wisconsin's Door Peninsula, a 75-mile-long limestone finger pointing northeast across Lake Michigan toward Canada. It holds its harbor in a more protective embrace than do most others on the Door, just as its heritage-conscious citizens do its oldest buildings, relics of the Norwegians who settled here to farm, log, quarry, and fish. Today Ephraim is a place to relax—to swim, sail, row, paddle, walk and hike, jog and bike, play tennis, hit golf balls, browse in homey shops, and watch sunsets flare above the emerald expanse of Green Bay. It's the kind of town that reminds grown-ups of carefree childhood summers decades ago, where kids can play safely and taste the calmer freedom of those simpler times.

Eagle Harbor and the town of Ephraim

No one knows how many generations the Potawatomi and the Winnebago scuffled for control of the peninsula. Both tribes were in retreat from the European exodus to North America when Ephraim's pioneer history commenced in 1853. That spring, some 40 Moravians—reformist-minded mainstream Protestants—staked out farmsteads on Eagle Harbor and optimistically christened their new community Ephraim, a biblical term meaning "doubly fruitful." Within 40 years, tourists were striding down the gangways of Lake Michigan steamers onto **Anderson Dock,** where visitors still embark from sailboats and cruisers, or stroll out from the shoreline to shop for art in the **Hardy Gallery** *(920-854-5535)* and watch sunsets that look like spilled paint. Like their pious predecessors, Ephraim's Victorian-era

Ephraim Moravian Church

sojourners sought spiritual rejuvenation here, in the pleasures of the peninsula's serene beauty and unusual geography. (Nearly surrounded by water, Door County has more miles of shoreline—about 250—and more state parks—five—than any other county in the U.S.) The Gilded Age folks who established Ephraim's reputation as a summer resort trouped up to the **Anderson Store** and bought what they needed, then checked into gracious harborfront hostels like the **Evergreen Beach Waterfront Resort** and the **Hillside Hotel.** It's likely that at least a few of them worshiped downtown at the **Bethany Lutheran Church** or the **Ephraim Moravian Church.** Summer folks still do all that, although the Anderson family's store, like the 1880 **Anderson Barn,** the **Pioneer Schoolhouse,** and the **Goodletson Cabin,** built of logs circa 1850 by one of the town's founders, is one of the **Ephraim Foundation Museum** sites now.

Today, Ephraim welcomes people from all over the United States, many of them from the Chicago, Milwaukee, and St. Louis areas. The first European known to set foot on the peninsula was French adventurer Jean Nicolet, sent in early 1634 by the governor of New France (today's Quebec Province) to find a water route across North America to Asia. Nicolet's exploration of the Door led him eventually to Horseshoe Island off Ephraim, then inhabited by friendly Winnebago. Believing they were Asians, Nicolet donned Oriental robes brought along for the occasion. Winnebago hospitality and the region's hitherto unknown natural wealth—most of all in fur—solaced him in his disappointment.

The only Winnebago hereabouts today are the rubber-tired kind that ease into **Peninsula State Park** campsites for the same views of Horseshoe Island and Green Bay that Nicolet saw from these bluffs. Wedged between Ephraim and the town of Fish Creek, the 3,776-acre park is one of Wisconsin's finest

Old fishing building, Ephraim

all-around outdoor recreation spots and its second oldest, established in 1909. The landscapes tend toward the rugged—trails through stony woods can be steep and challenging, particularly in winter when cross-country skiers replace hikers and mountain bikers—but typically lead to lofty overlooks. A few miles farther in, on a high wooded bluff, the Civil War-era **Eagle Bluff Lighthouse** beacon still flashes its beacon to mariners on Green Bay. In 1926 automation replaced its resident light-keepers, but the family quarters below the tower are kept as they were three generations ago and open for your inspection. When days are warm and calm, take your bathing suit and towel to the sandy beach of **Nicolet Bay,** a peaceful, family-oriented swimming and sunbathing spot with lifeguards, refreshments, and boat and bicycle rentals. If you feel like pedaling, check out posted park maps and find the **Sunset Trail,** a popular bike path through marshes and hardwood forest.

   Come evening, you'll probably find yourself most happily situated with a view of Green Bay. A beach, a bluff, a dining room table—anywhere; it doesn't matter as long as there's nothing between you and the moment when the sun dips beneath the horizon. Come morning, you can pedal, drive (or walk—it's only 4 miles) east on County Road Q to North Bay on Lake Michigan and watch it rise. In these northern latitudes, summer days are long, and mornings come early, but never too soon for Ephraim's summer people.

Mark Miller

Travelwise

GETTING THERE

Ephraim is 65 miles northeast of Green Bay on Eagle Harbor, and a five-hour drive from Chicago. Public transportation and taxi service are limited on the Door; a bicycle will get you around town—be careful on Wis. 42, the main thoroughfare—but you'll need a vehicle to roam more widely.

GENERAL INFORMATION

The "season" commences in spring, when peninsula wildflowers bloom, and continues until autumn colors fade in October. Lake Michigan's breezy embrace moderates summer heat. On arriving, stop at the **Ephraim Visitors Information Center** (*Wis. 42 and Spruce St., Ephraim 54211. 920-854-4989. May–mid-Oct.*). See Ephraim's web page at www.co.door.wi.us/ephpage.htm. The Ephraim Business Council's annually updated brochure/map "Ephraim" identifies historic structures, and is an excellent guide for a self-guided walking or driving tour.

THINGS TO SEE AND DO

Ephraim Foundation Museum A cluster of historic buildings has been preserved to tell Ephraim's history; among them the **Anderson Store** (*Wis. 42 and Anderson Dock*), the **Pioneer Schoolhouse,** and the **Goodletson Cabin** (*9998 Moravia St. Closed Sun.*).

Peninsula State Park (*Entrances off Wis. 42 in Ephraim and in Fish Creek. 920-868-3258. Adm. fee*) Over 3,000 acres of forest and beaches on Green Bay's emerald expanse, with trails, camping, and an 18-hole golf course. Tours of the **Eagle Bluff Lighthouse,** offered from early June to mid-Oct., require an additional fee.

ANNUAL FESTIVALS AND EVENTS

Ephraim Regatta (*1st weekend in Aug. Ephraim Yacht Club. 920-854-4989*)

Fyr Bal Festival (*Waterfront. 920-854-4989. Mid-June*) Concerts, sing-alongs, bonfires, fish boils, and walking tours reflect traditional Scandinavian celebrations to welcome summer, brought here by Norwegian settlers.

Midsummer's Music Festival (*Mid-June. 920-854-7088. Adm. fee*) A dozen chamber music concerts by a professional chamber ensemble.

WHERE TO EAT

Inn at Cedar Crossing (*336 Louisiana St., Sturgeon Bay. 920-743-4249. $$. Inn: 920-743-4200. $$*) Some rate this century-old establishment the county's best, with regional fare served in a genuine Victorian setting. The inn offers nine comfortable rooms.

Leroys Coffee Bar (*9922 Water St. 920-854-4044. $*) A clean, well-lighted café with a Bohemian flair in Shorewood Village, a warren of appealing little shops off Wis. 42.

White Gull Inn (*4225 Main St., Fish Creek. 920-868-3517. $$*) This homey restaurant within a pretty, New England-style inn attracts diners from all around. Traditional fish boil, by reservation, Wed., Fri., Sat., and Sun. from May through Oct.; Fri. only in winter. Nine rooms and four cottages for overnight guests (*$$$*).

WHERE TO STAY

Evergreen Beach Waterfront Resort (*9944 Water St. 920-854-2831 or 800-420-8130. $$*) All rooms of this handsome three-story century-old retreat overlook its expansive front lawn and private beach.

Hillside Hotel (*9980 Water St. 920-854-2417 or 800-423-7023. $$$*) A stately resort overlooking the harbor, this 1890 European-style inn holds restored original furnishings. Private beach.

Waterbury Inn (*10321 Water St. 920-854-2821 or 800-720-1624. $$$*) A handsome contemporary retreat catering to families.

Red Wing

Spend any time at all in Minnesota and you'll be encouraged at least once to tour the bucolic Bluff Country along the Mississippi River in the state's southeastern corner. Named for the high wooded limestone brows overlooking one of the most scenic northerly stretches of the serpentine Father of Waters, this is a region of picturesque farms, emerald pastures, and shady rural hamlets, and of stolid port towns "put together," as Mark Twain said of St. Paul, "in solid blocks of honest brick and stone" and with "the air of intending to stay." None stayed more successfully than Red Wing, which got what it needed many years ago and aged with dignity, resisting cuteness in favor of simply keeping up its vintage architecture and commodious parks, a policy that consistently places the city of 16,000 high on lists of "best small towns" for residents and sojourners alike.

This part of the glacier-sculptured Mississippi River Valley was once the homeland of the Mdewakanton Dakota, who farmed here, and whose chiefs

Riverfront Center, Red Wing

Red Wing from Barn Bluff

carried as a symbol of authority a swan's wing dyed red. Stroll and browse the shops along Red Wing's vintage red brick **Main Street** and you're walking where their summer village—some 30 bark and pole lodges and tepees—stood until the mid-19th century, when treaties opened this region for settlement. Red Wing prospered from the river trade, shipping grain from inland farms away from where **Levee Park** sprawls today, on paddle wheel steamers piloted by the likes of young Sam Clemens, then still years from reinventing himself as Mark Twain. The town's advantageous location—a placid river bend and natural harbor convenient to the region's abundant farming plains—paid off; by 1873 it was the largest primary wheat market in the world, a title eventually won by Minneapolis-St. Paul.

The wheat shipping business, followed by regional manufacturing—stoneware, shoes, barrels, lime works, and linseed oil particularly—were Red Wing's economic mainstays and financed its Victorian building boom. Railcars still load local harvests along the quay where tall grain elevators cast shadows across Red Wing's handsome **Old Milwaukee Depot.** Opened in 1904, the squat brick and limestone terminal still welcomes visitors arriving aboard Amtrak's Chicago-to-Seattle *Empire Builder.*

The town's historical pageant is recounted on a bluff overlooking the city's old neighborhoods at the **Goodhue County Historical Society,** one of Minnesota's best-regarded small museums. Another fine viewpoint is **Sorin's Bluff,** a limestone outcropping reached by driving up East Seventh Street, turning into Memorial Park opposite the **Notebaart House,** a Tudor cottage-style limestone block home at 620 East Seventh. While at the Society, consider purchasing *The Houses of Red Wing,* an illustrated guide to the town's architectural gems that will add considerable interest to your walking (or driving) tour of its older neighborhoods. A good many Victorian residences are grouped one block east of US 61/Main Street; bounded by Cedar, West Third, and West Fourth Streets; and West Avenue. Another collection decorates West Seventh and West Eighth between East Avenue and Bush. Don't miss splendid examples of American four-square (especially the 1916 **Louis Bach House** at 318 East Seventh) and the prairie school, of which the 1913 **Hoyt House** at 300 Hill Street is a perfect expression. The crown jewel of downtown is the **Sheldon Theatre,** nationally acclaimed on its debut in 1904 for being America's first municipally-funded performing arts showcase. When the house isn't hosting top-ranked headliners, tours explore its fancy Gilded

Desirable City

Inspired by the thoughtfully planned White City at the 1893 World's Columbia Exposition in Chicago—source of the City Beautiful movement that swept America until World War I—Red Wing boosters sought to beautify their town by promoting classical architecture. The self-styled Desirable City financed parks and cut carriage roads to scenic overlooks. Business owners were urged to adopt the classical revival style, creating the elegant mercantile blocks that make Red Wing among the handsomest old river towns on the Upper Mississippi.

Age interior, lavishly decorated with gold leaf and hand-painted murals.

One of Red Wing's best-known industries—pottery—bloomed in the 1870s when widespread rural settlement created a market for utilitarian stoneware, particularly crocks, jars, and churns. Rich local clay deposits and transportation links made Red Wing's pottery ubiquitous in the Mississippi River Valley. Two early-day producers, **Red Wing Stoneware** and **Red Wing Pottery,** are again in business at the west end of town, their artisans still using traditional methods to throw copies of old-time designs.

How to get the most from your Red Wing sojourn? Bring your bicycle, if you can, your walking shoes, and, if the bluffs beckon, your hiking boots. Bring a good book, too—there's nothing like a day beside the Mississippi under a shade tree in **Bay Point Park** off Levee Road. Time moves at an early-century pace here, in keeping with the flavor of the town, and so should you.

Mark Miller

Travelwise

GETTING THERE

Red Wing is located on the west bank of the Mississippi River about 50 miles southeast of the Minneapolis-St. Paul International Airport. Take I-35 and US 61 south. Amtrak's *Empire Builder* stops twice daily at the Old Milwaukee Depot in Levee Park with service to and from the Twin Cities (*800-872-7245. No tickets sold at station*). Greyhound (*800-231-2222*) provides bus service from Minneapolis and St. Paul. Regional airlines use Red Wing Airport, 5 miles away in Bay City, Wisconsin. The RIDE, passenger vans (*651-388-0332*), shuttles throughout town.

GENERAL INFORMATION

April-May and September-October are the best times to visit, when temperatures are typically moderate. Autumn brings beautiful colors and roadside apple stands, but expect occasional rain showers. The **Red Wing Visitors and Convention Bureau** (*418 Levee St., Red Wing 55066. 651-385-5934 or 800-498-3444. www.redwing.org*) and the Chamber of Commerce share the Old Milwaukee Depot in Levee Park beside the Mississippi River. The free brochure "Footsteps through Historic Red Wing" outlines three walking tours showcasing the town's vintage architecture.

THINGS TO SEE AND DO

Bicycling The paved 19.7-mile **Cannon Valley Trail** (*Trail Office 507-263-0508. User fee April-Nov.*) between Red Wing and Cannon Falls follows an old railroad bed along the

Cannon River, over low hills, passing marshland, pastures, and rocky cliffs. Bicycle rentals in Red Wing at the Outdoor Store (*651-388-5358*).

Goodhue County Historical Society (*1166 Oak St. 651-388-6024. Closed Mon.; adm. fee*) Exhibits on regional and local history include its Dakota Indian heritage. It displays the largest publicly owned collection of Red Wing pottery.

Red Wing Visitors Center/Old Milwaukee Depot (*420 Levee St. 651-385-5934 or 800-498-3444*) A handsome brick station completed in 1904, its waiting room displays railroad company emblems and memorabilia.

Walking Barn Bluff overlooks Red Wing and the river, rewarding strollers with a river panorama. Marked paths and stairways ascend from the end of East Fifth Street.

ENTERTAINMENT

Sheldon Theatre *(443 W. 3rd St. 651-385-3667 or 800-899-5759. Wheelchair accessible)* Restored to its original Victorian splendor, it mounts a year-round schedule of live, often top-billed entertainment. Call about tours, which focus on its fancy Victorian decor and Red Wing history.

SHOPPING

Red Wing is regionally known for its glazed stoneware and has a lively trade in antiques. Outlets for both range from large long-established firms to small shops located throughout the town. Ask the Visitors and Convention Bureau about antique festivals.

Red Wing Antique Emporium *(420 W. 3rd St. 651-267-0689 or 888-407-0371)* Minnesota's largest antique mall, featuring many dealers under one roof, is housed in Red Wing's early 20th-century Farmers Store.

Red Wing Pottery Salesroom *(1920 W. Main St. 651-388-3562 or 800-228-0174)* Potters here make old-fashioned salt-glazed stoneware. Showrooms offer a broad selection of dinnerware, flatware, glassware, and pottery. Similar activity and a showroom are found at nearby **Red Wing Stoneware** *(4909 Moundsview Dr. 651-388-4610 or 800-352-4877. Factory tours Mon.-Fri. at 1 p.m.).*

ANNUAL EVENTS

Fall Festival of the Arts *(2nd weekend in Oct. 651-388-7569)* A juried outdoor fine arts fair in the downtown historical district includes children's activities, food vendors, and music.

River City Days *(1st full weekend in Aug. 651-385-5934 or 800-762-9516. Some fees)* A busy 3-day festival of music, crafts, and boat racing capped by a parade, fireworks, and an eclectic car show.

WHERE TO EAT

Port of Red Wing *(St. James Hotel. 651-388-2846. $$)* Traditional American lunch *(June-Dec.)* and dinner *(year-round)*, prepared with haute cuisine flourishes and served in the hotel's cozy limestone-block cellar.

Staghead *(219 Bush St. 651-388-6581. Closed Sun. $$)* Exposed brick walls, antique paintings, and vintage maps evoke old Red Wing. The fare, however, is contemporary American.

WHERE TO STAY

Candlelight Inn *(818 W. 3rd St. 651-388-8034 or 800-254-9194. $$)* A five-room, three-story Victorian B&B in one of Red Wing's older neighborhoods, with period furnishings and fireplaces in all bedrooms.

Pratt-Taber Inn *(706 W. 4th St. 651-388-5945. $$)* There are five guest rooms in this 13-room, 1875 brick Italianate residence, all with private bath and period furnishings.

St. James Hotel *(406 Main St. 651-388-2846 or 800-252-1875. $$)* Completed in 1875 and on the National Register of Historic Places, many of the 60 rooms in this nicely refurbished downtown four-story brick Italianate edifice feature antique Victorian furnishings and handmade quilts.

NEARBY PLACES

Alma, Wisconsin *(City Hall, 314 N. Main St., Alma 54610. 608-685-3330)* Winding along the bluffs above the Mississippi River in Wisconsin, this picturesque little river town has only two streets, each lined with charming 19th-century structures. **Pepin,** north of Alma, was the childhood hometown of Laura Ingalls Wilder, who grew up to write the popular *Little House* series. You can visit a reconstruction of the 1867 Ingalls log cabin on County Road CC, 7 miles north of town. Her first book, *Little House in the Big Woods,* is full of tales about her life here—the Christmas that she received her ragdoll, Charlotte, eating molasses-on-snow candy, making bullets, and weaving straw hats. No visit is complete without a picnic on the shore of **Lake Pepin,** picking up pebbles as Laura did so long ago. The small **Pepin Historical Museum** *(306 3rd St., Alma. 715-442-3161. Closed mid-Nov.–mid-May; donation)* has exhibits on local history, with special emphasis on Laura Ingalls.

Richard J. Dorer Memorial Hardwood State Forest *(Hay Creek Management Unit. 651-345-3216)* A serene and leafy retreat about 6 miles south of Red Wing off Minn. 58, this state forest is a popular destination for hikers, horseback riders, bicyclists, and trout-seeking flycasters.

Grand Marais

Grand Marais on Lake Superior has always been as much a jumping-off place as a sojourner's idyll, although many come to this hamlet of 1,800 with no intention of wandering far from the sheltered little bay for which it was named—not "great swamp" as some literal types suppose but "good harbor," at least in the colloquial French of the 18th-century French-Canadian voyageurs who came here to gather furs for European buyers.

Today people come for the town's friendly cafés, unpretentious galleries and gift shops, pebbly beaches, and wave-splashed rocky points. They come to beachcomb for agate beside the world's largest body of freshwater, set up easels and dab paintbrushes, and hike through birch and aspen, maple and pine, and canoe on mirrory lakes seeming as pristine as they must have been when only the Ojibwa knew them. They come to add new sightings to bird-

Walking along Lake Superior near Grand Marais

watching ledgers, contemplate the great lake from the more comfortable immersion of a hot tub, recline on deck chairs and let Lake Superior's blue horizon roil unnoticed beyond the pages of a good book. Grand Marais, despite what its literal name implies, is a gentle harbor not only for the moored sailboats whose lines slap musically against their metal masts, but for the senses as well.

Walk out past the old Coast Guard Station and have a picnic on the rugged little wooded peninsula known as **Artist's Point,** which inspired some of the paintings of Lake Superior displayed at the **Johnson Heritage Post Art Gallery** and the **Kah-Nee-Tah Gallery** in the nearby town of Lutsen. The Cook County Historical Society maintains the Post, along with the **Lighthouse Keeper's House** at 8 South Broadway, which dates from 1896.

Peacefulness is public policy here; a city ordinance bans idling automobile engines between 10 p.m. and 7 a.m. Though high season crowds make parking scarce at times, few summer folk complain because many are headed out of town anyway. A short drive up the **Gunflint Trail** into **Superior National Forest** and you'll find yourself on the edge of the **Boundary Waters Canoe Area Wilderness,**

Artist's Point in winter

the world's largest preserve devoted to backcountry paddling. Today's Kevlar canoes and kayaks fare better than the voyageurs' birchbark craft did against the sharp rocks of these glacier-gouged lakes, and unlike early trappers, some contemporary adventurers trek in the company of a guide. Grand Marais and other North Shore communities are chockablock with experienced outfitters able to acquaint you with everything from a kayak to a sailboat, show you how to orient using a topographic map and compass, and how to properly cast flies into a trout stream. Come winter, you'll find yourself quickly accustomed to the pleasant rhythmic exertion of cross-country skiing through silent forests, or perhaps becoming proficient with snowshoes as you tramp across white fields stitched with the tracks of deer, moose, and wolf.

But other seasons are just as nice. Wild berries ripen along the Gunflint Trail in summer—strawberries in June, blueberries in July, followed by chokecherries, pin cherries, raspberries, and thimbleberries in August. Just find a pail, ask your hosts to point you in the right direction, and search out the sweet harvest. Come October, when the crowds are gone and streams are sailed by yellow armadas of fallen leaves, you won't need F. Scott Fitzgerald to tell you, as he once wrote, that a Northern autumn is "something gorgeous."

If you're sojourning, consider spending time—a half-day, a day, a week or more if you like—at the **North House Folk School,** at the foot of the Gunflint Trail back in town, where craftspeople pass along skills this region's Scandinavian settlers brought from the Old World, like beeswax candlemaking, birchbark weaving, and knifemaking. You can learn to cut a quill pen, spin wool, make soap, tap a sugar maple, and carve a wooden spoon. If you have more time, the North House folks will help you build a birchbark canoe or cast a bronze ship's bell. You can even build your own casket, which in the big-windowed, sawdust-fragrant harborfront workshop seems not at all macabre but rather a transcendent expression of clear-headed self-sufficiency. (Meanwhile they make excellent bookcases.)

And one last thing, particularly in summer and fall: Don't fail to take in a moonrise. Sometimes alabaster, sometimes made yellow or red by the atmospherics left over from a hot day, a full Lake Superior moon can be so theatrically luminous it elicits applause from summer folk chatting in the dark on the decks of lakeshore inns. Take a seat among them and see for yourself.   *Mark Miller*

Travelwise

GETTING THERE
Grand Marais is located 110 miles northeast of Duluth on Minnesota's North Shore of Lake Superior. Trains and planes service Duluth; however, most visitors who fly in arrive via Minneapolis-St. Paul International, rent a car, and take I-35 north past Duluth to Minn. 61, a scenic lakeside route to Grand Marais, a drive of about 270 miles.

GENERAL INFORMATION
Summer is the North Shore's high season; June and July are Lake Superior's calmest months, October and November its stormiest. A 40°F average water temperature and cool lake breezes moderate summer heat and humidity. Fall colors peak mid-Sept. to mid-Oct. The "Fall Colors" brochure, available at the **Grand Marais Visitor Center** *(13 N. Broadway, P.O. Box 1048, 55604. 218-387-2524 or 888-922-5000. www .grandmaraismn.com)* proposes walking and auto leaf tours. (The Lutsen-Tofte Tourism Association's "Fall Color Tour" brochure suggests additional nearby routes.)

THINGS TO SEE AND DO
Canoeing, Kayaking, and Hiking The Boundary Waters Canoe Area Wilderness holds over 1,000 lakes and 1,500 miles of routes through diverse terrain. Bear Track Outfitting Co. *(2011 W. Hwy. 61. 218-387-1162 or 800-795-8068. www.bear-track.com)* will arrange and guide individual and family canoe, sea kayak, and backpacking trips. Located on East Bay in Grand Marais, Cascade Kayaks *(218-387-2360 or 800-720-2809. www.cascadekayaks.com)* offers instructional day tours, and longer guided trips throughout the North Shore region. Shop outfitters online *(www.gunflint-trail .com/canoetrips/outfitters.html).*

Johnson Heritage Post Art Gallery *(115 W. Wisconsin St.. 218-387-2314. Daily May-Oct., Tues.-Sun. p.m. Nov.-April; donation)* Revolving exhibits of regional and national artists, plus a permanent collection of paintings by pioneer Anna Johnson.

Lighthouse Keeper's House *(8 S. Broadway. 218-387-2883. May-Oct.)* Nineteenth-century furnishings evoke the genteel isolation of earlier times.

North House Folk School *(On the harbor, 500 W. Minn. 61. 218-387-9762)* Year-round hands-on instruction is offered in over 70 traditional skills.

SHOPPING
Kah-Nee-Tah Gallery *(4210 W. Minn. 61, Lutsen. 218-387-2585 or 800-216-2585)* Fine arts and crafts by Minnesotans— paintings, pottery, jewelry, baskets, photography, stained glass, sculpture, carvings, cards, forged bronze, and turned wood and bentwood vessels.

ANNUAL EVENTS

Fisherman's Picnic *(1st weekend in Aug. Downtown. 800-622-5380)* Fishing contests, "fishburger" stand, ball tournaments, handicrafts, a parade, dance, and trail run end with fireworks.

Grand Marais Arts Festival *(2nd weekend in July. 218-387-2585 or 218-387-1284)* The two-day waterfront event features fine arts and crafts, musical performances, and special events.

Grand Marais Classic Car Show *(1st weekend in June. Artist's Point. 218-387-2524)*

Birchbark canoe at Grand Portage NM

Antique automobile buffs arrive in force for viewing, entertainment, and social events.

Gunflint Trail Boreal Birding Days *(Weekend after Mem. Day. 218-387-2870 or 800-338-6932. Registration fee)* A three-day festival during spring migrations, including presentations on forest birds, hikes, seminars, and field trips.

WHERE TO EAT

Angry Trout Cafe *(Grand Marais harbor. 218-387-1265. May-Sept. $$)* Often crowded in summer, for good reason: Its renditions of local favorites like grilled walleye and shiitake-shingled lake trout are skillful.

Blue Water Cafe *(101 Wisconsin St. 218-387-1597. $)* This popular summer and fall hangout serves comfort food at reasonable prices, including a hearty breakfast all day long.

WHERE TO STAY

Clearwater Canoe Outfitters and Lodge *(774 Clearwater Rd. 218-388-2254 or 800-527-2254. Mid-May–Sept. $$)* A historic log lodge on Clearwater Lake by the

BWCAW, 28 miles north of town on the Gunflint Trail, with 6 log cabins. Canoe and kayak excursions.

MacArthur House Bed & Breakfast *(520 W. 2nd St. 218- 387-1840 or 800-792-1840. $$)* This tall, contemporary yellow clapboard holds five guest rooms.

Naniboujou Lodge and Restaurant *(20 Naniboujou Trail, 15 miles E of town. 218-387-2688. Mid-May–mid-Oct. and Christmas–New Year's, then weekends through mid-March. $$)* A rustic shingled retreat built in 1929 as a private sportsman's club, its charter members included Babe Ruth, Jack Dempsey, and Ring Lardner. Two dozen guest rooms and a spacious sunroom overlook Lake Superior. The 80-foot-long Great Hall dining room holds Minnesota's largest native rock fireplace. High tea and formal dining.

NEARBY PLACES

Grand Portage National Monument *(218-387-2788 or 218-475-2202. 36 miles N of Grand Marais off Minn. 61, in Grand Portage. Mid-May–mid-Oct.; grounds, portage trail year-round; adm. fee)* The partially reconstructed old fur-trading outpost displays historical artifacts and living history demonstrations. The 8.5-mile "Grand Portage" between Lake Superior and the Pigeon River is preserved for hikers, snowshoers, and skiers.

Gunflint Trail *(Gunflint Trail Assoc., P.O. Box 205, Grand Marais 55604. 218-387-2870 or 800-338-6932. www.gunflint-trail.com)* Beginning at Grand Marais, 63-mile paved County Rd. 12 winds through Superior NF to the edge of the buffer zone of the Boundary Waters Canoe Area Wilderness.

North Shore Commercial Fishing Museum *(Minn. 61 and Cty. Rd. 2, Tofte. 218-663-7804. Adm. fee)* It chronicles a once vital local industry that peaked with some 400 fishing operations before depleted stocks killed it in the early 1940s.

Split Rock Lighthouse Historic Site *(3713 Split Rock Lighthouse Rd., Two Harbors. 218-226-6372. Daily mid-May–mid-Oct., Fri.-Sun. rest of year, closed Dec.; adm. fee)* Located 63 miles southwest of Grand Marais on Minn. 61, the lighthouse, fog signal building, and keeper's home are preserved as they were in 1910. Exhibits and a short historical film recount its life-saving career.

THE PLAINS

Medora

Driving west across the rolling pastures and fields of North Dakota, you suddenly find yourself in a strange, yet strangely beautiful, country of colorful bluffs, rugged canyons, and eroded hills. You've entered the famed badlands, where countless visitors before you have paused in awe at the scene around them. At the heart of this landscape lies Medora, the gateway to Theodore Roosevelt National Park and a town with a history as extraordinary as the terrain around it.

Badlands Beauty?

From a saddle on a trail ride, or from an air-conditioned vehicle, the badlands unquestionably possess great magnificence—even if it is a kind of "desolate, grim beauty," as Theodore Roosevelt once wrote. Not all badlands visitors have been so taken with the place, though. U.S. Army Gen. Alfred Sully, who passed through the area in 1863, had a slightly different opinion: He described the Dakota badlands as "hell with the fires out."

Medora began as the dream of an aristocratic Frenchman named Antoine de Vallombrosa, the Marquis de Mores. The marquis not only wanted to be rich, he wanted to be the "richest financier in the world"—and part of his plan was to found a cattle empire in the American West. He would own the cattle, the land they grazed, the slaughterhouse where they were processed, and the railcars that would ship meat to eastern markets, controlling the entire operation and enjoying what he thought would be substantial rewards.

The marquis arrived in Dakota Territory in 1883, and the next year he brought his wife, Medora, daughter of the wealthy von Hoffman family of New York. The family moved into a fancy home the marquis had built on a hill overlooking the Little Missouri River. Soon he had established his meat-packing plant, founded a stage line, and built a brickyard, a church, and several businesses. The new town he named for his wife quickly became a thriving community. Unfortunately, the marquis's dream couldn't face the harsh light of reality. As his enterprises foundered, he seemed more interested in socializing, traveling, and hunting than in looking after them. In 1886 the marquis shut down his businesses and left Medora (the town, not his wife). The boom had gone bust. Medora slept quietly until the 1947 establishment of Theodore Roosevelt National Memorial (now National Park) and later restoration efforts transformed the settlement into the modern community it is today.

On the outskirts of Medora, beneath the buff badlands cliffs, stands a tall brick chimney and a few building foundations—all that remains of the marquis's slaughterhouse. These relics are part of the **Chateau de Mores State Historic Site,** which includes the de Mores's impressive, 26-room house. Full of original furnishings and de Mores possessions, the chateau is an evocative symbol of wealth on the frontier.

Riding in the badlands near Little Missouri National Grassland

One of the many guests visiting the de Mores's hilltop home was a young New York politician named Theodore Roosevelt, who had his own western dreams. T.R. came to Dakota Territory in 1883 to hunt and quickly decided to become a cattleman. He bought one ranch and part of another in the Medora area, and organized and served as head of a local Stockman's Association. But in truth he was more interested in the idea of the cowboy life than in the business of cattle; he hired a manager to run the ranch in 1887. But he had formed a deep attachment to the region and so visited often until he sold the ranch in 1898. He

Bison

saw first-hand the disappearance of wildlife from the badlands—bison, elk, pronghorn, wolves—and when he became President in 1901 his experiences here inspired him to establish the U.S. Forest Service and to designate many new national parks, monuments, and wildlife refuges.

Theodore Roosevelt National Park honors this dedicated conservationist,

Chateau de Mores State Historic Site

protecting more than 70,000 acres of splendid badlands terrain. The park's
Painted Canyon Visitor Center, 7 miles east of Medora off I-94, offers broad
views of hills and canyons striped with multicolored rock. For a closer look,
take the 36-mile scenic loop drive through the park's south unit, beginning on
the western edge of Medora. A museum in the **Medora Visitor Center** intro-
duces the park's natural history and describes T.R.'s connection to the region.
Out back stands his **Maltese Cross cabin,** restored and moved from his ranch
7 miles south of town.

The town of Medora has undergone a complete transformation in recent
decades. In the 1960s, North Dakota businessman Harold Schafer began
investing in Medora, hoping to preserve its heritage and western character.
Several buildings were restored, including the 1884 **Rough Rider Hotel** and
the **Ferris Store,** once owned by T.R.'s friend Joe Ferris. Today, the nonprofit
Theodore Roosevelt Medora Foundation, begun by Schafer, owns many local
businesses and attractions, maintaining the western theme and keeping alive
the memory of T.R., the Marquis de Mores, and their frontier era. Perhaps
most notable among the foundation's efforts is the **Medora Musical,** an elaborate stage show paying tribute to Roosevelt and the American West in an
outdoor amphitheater just outside town.

Back in town, it's easy to walk to Medora's favorite sights, scattered around
its compact downtown area. Exhibits at the **Museum of the Badlands** cover
Native American artifacts, wildlife displays, and mementos of T.R. The
Medora Doll House contains a fascinating collection of historical dolls and
toys from around the world; the buff-brick house in which they're located was
built in 1884 by the Marquis de Mores for Medora's parents, the von Hoff-
mans. The nearby **Billings County Courthouse Museum** is full of local items
from ranching gear and tools to guns and old photos. The courthouse building was originally used as a residence and only became the courthouse in
1913; it has a restored courtroom upstairs, and some of the exhibits are set in
cells of the old county jail.

Whether you're marveling at badlands scenery or reliving pioneer ranching days, Medora makes a fine base for exploration. T.R. enjoyed what he
called the "perfect freedom" of the cowboy life here, and as you drive, hike,
or ride through this rugged country, you may find that his frontier spirit
endures even today.   *Mel White*

Travelwise

GETTING THERE

Medora is located in southwestern North Dakota, just off I-94, 130 miles west of Bismarck and 30 miles east of the Montana state line. Airlines serve Bismarck, and Amtrak stops at Williston, 126 miles north.

GENERAL INFORMATION

Spring through fall is the best time to visit; the town can be crowded at the height of summer vacation. Many attractions are closed in winter. For information, write or call the **Medora Chamber of Commerce** *(P.O. Box 186, Medora 58645. 701-623-4910).* More information is available from the **Theodore Roosevelt Medora Foundation** *(P.O. Box 198, Medora 58645. 701-623-4444 or 800-633-6721).* Medora is in the Mountain, not Central, time zone.

THINGS TO SEE AND DO

Billings County Courthouse Museum *(4th St. 701-623-4829. Adm. fee)* Local historical memorabilia in a early 1900s courthouse.

Bully! *(Medora Community Center, 465 Pacific Ave. 701-623-4444 or 800-633-6721. Mem. Day–Labor Day p.m.; adm. fee)* A one-act play on the life of T.R.

Chateau de Mores State Historic Site *(W of town, S off N. Dak. 10. 701-623-4355. Mid-May–mid-Sept. or by appt.; adm. fee)* The Marquis de Mores's elaborate home, furnished with original family possessions. The historic site also includes the old slaughterhouse location and **de Mores Memorial Park** in downtown Medora.

Horseback Riding Trail rides offered both inside and outside the national park. Contact Peaceful Valley Ranch *(701-623-4568)* or Medora Riding Stables *(701-623-4444, ext. 133).*

Medora Doll House *(Broadway and 5th St. 701-623-4444. Summer only; adm. fee)* An excellent collection of historical dolls.

Medora Musical *(W of town, S off N. Dak. 10. 701-623-4444 or 800-633-6721. Mem. Day–Labor Day; adm. fee)* An outdoor production recalling the days of T.R.

Mountain Biking The 120-mile **Maah Daah Hey Trail** offers excellent biking, winding north through the **Little Missouri**

National Grassland. Shorter rides near Medora range from easy to challenging. For rentals contact Dakota Cyclery *(3rd Ave. 701-623-4808).*

Museum of the Badlands *(Main St. and 3rd Ave. 701-623-4444. Mem. Day–Labor Day; adm. fee)* A varied collection of Native American items, Roosevelt exhibits, and more.

Theodore Roosevelt National Park South Unit *(N of town off N. Dak. 10. 701-623-4466. Adm. fee)* The park's South Unit encompasses two visitor centers, a 36-mile scenic drive through the badlands, hiking trails, a campground, and the chance to see bison, elk, prairie dogs, and wild horses.

WHERE TO STAY

Dahkotah Lodge Guest Ranch *(17 miles S of town, via W. River Rd. 701-623-4897 or 800-508-4897. $$)* A working ranch on the Little Missouri River.

Rough Rider Hotel *(3rd St. and 3rd Ave. 701-623-4444 or 800-633-6721. $$)* Nine rooms in a reconstructed 1884 hotel. Its elegant restaurant *($$)* serves western fare including North Dakotan buffalo steaks.

NEARBY PLACES

Theodore Roosevelt National Park North Unit *(70 miles N of town. 701-623-4466. Adm. fee)* A 14-mile, one-way scenic drive winds through picturesque badlands panoramas in this separate section of the national park. Watch for bison, deer, and bighorn sheep.

De Smet

More than a century ago, a little girl named Laura Ingalls moved with her family to the brand-new town of De Smet, in eastern Dakota Territory, to make a home on the vast prairie. Today, thousands of people from around the world visit this charming South Dakota community each year, drawn to see the Little Town on the Prairie of Laura Ingalls Wilder's *Little House* books, stories of pioneer life that have become modern classics.

Little House in Missouri

Almanzo and Laura Ingalls Wilder moved to Mansfield, Missouri, in 1894, when Laura was 27, and spent the rest of their lives on a farm there. Though Laura wrote many newspaper and magazine articles, she didn't write the first of her *Little House* books until she was in her sixties. Since *Little House in the Big Woods*, the story of the Ingalls family's early years in Wisconsin, was published in 1932, more than 60 million *Little House* books have been sold around the world.

It was in 1879 that Charles Ingalls— Pa in the *Little House* books—came to De Smet to work for the Dakota Central Railway, which had recently opened the area to settlement. With him were his wife, Caroline, and his four daughters, Mary, Laura, Carrie, and Grace. An illness had left Mary blind, so 12-year-old Laura took on many household responsibilities, from caring for her sisters to helping Pa with his animals and crops after the family moved to a homestead a mile from De Smet. From the Ingallses' experiences—challenges and adventures, happy times and hardships—the grown-up Laura wrote such novels as *By the Shores of Silver Lake, The Long Winter,* and *Little Town on the Prairie,* books that have entranced children and adults since they began appearing in the 1930s.

Many things have changed in De Smet, of course, since those late 19th-century times, but some things have stayed the same. The railroad still runs along the north side of town, but the empty expanse about which Laura wrote, "Here on the Dakota prairies there was not a single tree…not a bit of shade anywhere," is now the setting for a town of tree-lined streets and neat houses, where 1,300 folks live amid great fields of corn, wheat, soybeans, and alfalfa.

The friendly feeling of pioneer days endures in De Smet: It's the kind of place where downtown businesspeople are never so hurried that they can't stop and chat on the sidewalk; where kids ride their bikes from one end of town to the other and parents never worry; where the talk at the cafés is of the local basketball teams, how the walleye are biting, or perhaps who's going to have the lead roles in the *Little House* pageant out by the Wilder homestead.

De Smet's original railroad depot, where Laura went to one of her first parties, burned down in 1905. Its 1906 replacement is now the **Depot Museum,**

Reenacting *Little House on the Prairie*

a storehouse of historical items and local memorabilia, from an old dentist's office to railroad gear to vintage clothing. Outside, a brick sidewalk laid in 1906 still borders the street beside the old city fire bell.

Running south from the depot, Calumet Avenue, De Smet's main street, is still as wide as it was in *The Long Winter*, when snowstorms made it impossible to see from one side to the other. Few who've read that book can forget how the lights of the stores meant safety for the schoolchildren who came so close to losing their way during one particularly terrifying blizzard. Among the redbrick buildings now housing shops, restaurants, and offices stands the **Loftus Store** *(205 Calumet Ave. S.W.),* where Laura and Carrie bought Pa a colorful pair of suspenders that hard Christmas season.

If you're a fan of the *Little House* books, you'll enjoy visiting a number of sites in and around town. After checking in at the headquarters of the **Laura Ingalls Wilder Memorial Society** on Olivet Avenue, walk next door to see the **Surveyor's House,** where the Ingalls family lived during the winter of 1879-80. Moved here from Silver Lake, a mile east of town, the small frame structure has been restored to its original appearance and contains a few Ingalls family possessions. In back stands a reproduction of the one-room **Brewster School,** where Laura taught for a brief (and unhappy) period after she won her teaching certificate at the age of fifteen.

A few blocks west you'll find the 1887 **Ingalls Home and Museum** *(210 3rd*

St. S.W.). Pa built this frame structure as a three-room house and expanded it to its present two-story form by 1889. Laura never lived here (she was married to Almanzo Wilder by then), but the house displays Ingalls family items, as well as mementos of Rose Wilder Lane, Laura's only child, who was a successful journalist in her own right before her mother began the *Little House* series.

A short distance southeast of De Smet, as you pass through the marshy Big Slough where Laura and Carrie got lost returning from town one afternoon, you'll note five large cottonwood trees in the distance. Planted by Pa Ingalls in honor of Ma and the four daughters, they stand at the edge of the homestead where the family lived from 1880 until 1887. A stone marker memorializes the

Calumet Avenue, De Smet's main street

homesite. Just across the road, local actors present a pageant on three weekends each summer, with costumed performers re-creating scenes from the *Little House* books.

Nearby, the **Ingalls Homestead** complex, located on the family's original farm site, encompasses a number of buildings from the time of Laura's childhood. Among them are an 1878 "half-house," like the tiny shanty where the Ingallses lived before they moved to town in *The Long Winter*, and an 1888 school where a costumed interpreter shows kids what education was like a century ago. Areas of native grass give visitors a glimpse of the days when unbroken prairie stretched to the horizon in every direction. The homestead emphasizes hands-on activities for children, from pony rides to pettable farm animals, as well as trails for hiking and biking.

With a map available from the De Smet Chamber of Commerce, or at local businesses, you can explore several other local attractions, including **Lake Thompson State Recreation Area** (known for excellent fishing), and the historic **cemetery** where Pa, Ma, Mary, Carrie, and Grace rest. Don't miss a stroll through pretty **Washington Park,** dominated by a statue of Father Pierre-Jean De Smet, the Belgian priest who spent his life as a missionary to Indians in the American West. Father De Smet never visited the De Smet area; railroad executives named the town to commemorate the life of this brave, influential, and intensely honorable man. The impressive statue was in part a gift from the citizens of Dendermonde, the priest's home town in Belgium.

The United States has changed much from Laura Ingalls Wilder's pioneer days, but a visit to De Smet, with its beautiful courthouse square, quiet streets, and unhurried air, seems a return to a simpler era. Take your time here, and you'll be rewarded with a relaxing sojourn in a town filled with the congenial spirit that shines through the pages of the *Little House* stories.   *Mel White*

Travelwise

GETTING THERE

De Smet is in eastern South Dakota, on US 14, 42 miles west of I-29 at Brookings. Airlines serve Sioux Falls, 80 miles southeast. The closest Amtrak station is St. Cloud, Minnesota, 190 miles east.

GENERAL INFORMATION

Late spring through fall is the best time to visit De Smet. Winters can be very cold with occasional periods of heavy snow. For information, contact the **Chamber of Commerce** (127 Calumet Ave., P.O. Box 105, De Smet 57231. 605-854-3688).

THINGS TO SEE AND DO

Christian Alliance Church (2nd St. and Locust Ave.) Charles, Caroline, and Mary Ingalls were among the first eight charter members of the First Congregational Church, which was organized in 1880 but didn't hold its meetings in a church until this one was built in 1881.

De Smet Cemetery (1.5 miles SW of town via Prairie Ave.) The graves of Pa and Ma Ingalls and daughters Mary, Carrie, and Grace are here, along with several other people mentioned in the Little House books.

Depot Museum (Calumet Ave. and 1st St. 605-854-3991. Closed Sun. and Sept.-May) Local historical items, including Indian artifacts, pioneer household furnishings, and a re-created general store, are located in a 1906 railroad depot; also wildlife exhibits and antique printing equipment.

Hazel L. Meyer Memorial Library (102 1st St. N.E. 605-854-3842) Original paintings by South Dakota artist Harvey Dunn, plus a display of Laura Ingalls Wilder memorabilia.

Ingalls Homestead (20812 Homestead Rd., 1 mile E of De Smet. 605-854-3984 or 800-776-3594. Closed Oct.–April; adm. fee) Reproductions of Ingalls family buildings, along with an authentic claim shanty and an 1888 schoolhouse, are located on the original plot of land where the Ingalls homesteaded. Farm animals, covered-wagon rides, camping, and other activities.

Lake Thompson State Recreation Area (8 miles SE of town via US 14. 605-847-4893. Adm. fee) A swimming beach, camping, and cabins beside 16,000-acre Lake Thompson, South Dakota's largest natural lake. The lake is known for its excellent fishing for walleye, northern pike, and perch.

Laura Ingalls Wilder Memorial Society (105 Olivet Ave. 605-854-3383 or 800-880-3383. Closed Sun. April, May, and Oct.; and Sat.-Sun. Dec.-March; adm. fee) The society offers guided tours of the Ingalls family's 1879 **Surveyor's House** and the 1887 **Ingalls Home,** plus information on visiting the cemetery and the homestead memorial site southeast of town. The ticket office includes a gift shop where Little House books and other items are sold.

ANNUAL EVENT

Laura Ingalls Wilder Pageant (Last weekend in June and 1st 2 weeks in July. Homestead Rd., S of US 14. 605-692-2108 or 800-880-3383. Adm fee) Local actors portray characters and scenes from the Little House books in a prairie setting near the Big Slough. Free horse-drawn wagon rides for kids before the show.

WHERE TO EAT

Oxbow Restaurant (US 14 and Calumet Ave. 605-854-9988. $) An informal spot where locals meet for coffee and meals.

WHERE TO STAY

Heritage House (126 Calumet Ave. 605-854-9370. $) Three rooms with private baths in an 1889 building that was once a land and loan office; restaurant on the ground floor.

Prairie House Manor (Poinsett Ave. and 3rd St. 605-854-9131 or 800-297-2416. Closed Dec.-April. $) Six rooms with private baths in an 1894 house once owned by "banker Ruth," a character in The Long Winter. A tea room serves homemade breads, meat pies, and pasta salads in June, July, and August.

Valentine

The tree-lined streets and pretty parks of Valentine create a welcoming enticement for travelers crossing the vast, wide-open spaces of north-central Nebraska. Set between the Niobrara River and Minnechaduza Creek, just 9 miles from South Dakota, Valentine serves as a gateway to some of the most outstanding natural areas in the Midwest, encompassing superb river scenery and abundant wildlife.

Nebraska's Sandhills may not be as well known as the nearby Black Hills of South Dakota, but in their own way they're just as fascinating. Covering more than 19,000 square miles, this region of rolling, wind-deposited dunes was formed about 5,000 years ago. The largest dunes can be 400 feet tall and 20 miles long, giving shape to a landscape unique in North America.

But this is no sandy desert: Native grasses cover the dunes, creating highly productive cattle country. Herds of Hereford and Angus help make Nebraska the second leading cattle state in the country. Ranches are huge here, and towns are scarce. Cherry County, of which Valentine is the seat, is larger than Connecticut, yet it has fewer than 7,000 inhabitants.

Real-life cowboys still walk the streets of Valentine, on business or to escape the toil of ranch life at country-music bars. Many still sport cowboy boots, stetsons, and drive mostly pick-ups, though it's not unheard of for today's cowboy to be driving a fancy sport-utility vehicle and to be keeping track of his herd on a computer.

At Valentine's annual fall Old West Days, the town fills up with people celebrating America's Western heritage, from trail rides to music to a popular Cowboy Poetry Gathering, where writers swap rhymes about horses, campfires, and solitary nights under the stars. With a new hat and some boots from one of Valentine's ranch-supply stores, you can play the part of a cowboy or cowgirl yourself, even if you don't know a steer from a heifer. Everyone is welcome.

You'll want walking shoes, though, to enjoy one of Valentine's most rewarding attractions. **Trailhead Park,** at First and Main Streets, provides access to the **Cowboy Trail,** a rails-to-trails conversion that eventually will cover 321 miles across northern Nebraska. Scattered divisions of the trail are

From Valentine, With Love

When February rolls around, the Valentine post office gets quite a bit busier than usual, as people across the country send Valentine's Day cards to be postmarked "Valentine" and remailed to their sweeties. The Heart City even offers special romance-themed cachets for the envelopes. Send your stamped, addressed cards (in a separate envelope, of course) to Cupid's Mailbox, P.O. Box 201, Valentine, NE 69201, far enough in advance to travel to Valentine and back to the recipient by February 14.

At Smith Falls State Park, near Valentine

complete, including a 5-mile section traveling southeast from Valentine on the old Chicago Northwestern line. About 2 miles along this segment, you'll reach a refurbished railroad bridge over the beautiful **Niobrara River**—a great destination for a relaxing stroll or bike ride.

Valentine got its start in the early 1880s as a railroad town and was named for a popular Nebraska congressman of the time. You can learn about the town's beginnings, Sandhills history, Native Americans, and cattle ranching at the **Cherry County Historical Society Museum,** on Main Street in the heart of town, and at **Centennial Hall,** just a few blocks away. The latter museum occupies an 1897 brick-and-stone structure that's the oldest still-standing high-school building in the state. From either museum it's just a few blocks to **City Park** on Minnechaduza Creek, where tall oaks and cottonwoods shade picnickers, romping kids, and anglers hoping to pull a trout from the stream.

In 1879 conflicts between early settlers and the Sioux who still hunted in the Sandhills caused the Army to establish Fort Niobrara a few miles east of today's town site. The fort was abandoned in 1911, and the land it occupied eventually became **Fort Niobrara National Wildlife Refuge,** a popular spot for wildlife observation just minutes from Valentine. A visit to the grasslands here may bring sightings of bison, elk, prairie dogs, and a wide variety of birds, as well as Texas longhorn cattle. From the refuge picnic area, a trail leads to **Fort Falls,** a scenic cascade that's the state's second highest waterfall.

The refuge is set along the Niobrara River. Designated a national scenic

Bull elk at Fort Niobrara National Wildlife Refuge, near Valentine

river in 1991, the Niobrara winds along low bluffs with a gentle current that makes it an excellent float for beginning canoeists—or for those who just want to laze along on an oversized inner tube. A number of outfitters in the Valentine area will set up trips of varying lengths along the river, taking care of everything from the canoes to shuttle service.

About 15 miles downstream from Valentine, **Smith Falls State Park** protects the site of Nebraska's highest waterfall, a 70-foot drop accessible by a footbridge over the Niobrara. The park's surroundings here in the forested Niobrara Valley, as anyone can see, are superbly beautiful. Ecologists, though, note something more: The Niobrara represents the meeting place of several of North America's natural divisions. The ponderosa pines on the dry north bank of the river exemplify the West; black walnut, basswood, oaks, and other hardwoods on the south bank are typical of eastern forests; and birch and aspen are characteristic of northern woodland.

For another viewpoint of the lovely Niobrara, drive south a short distance from town on US 20/83, watching for a turn to reach an overlook of the historic 1931 **Bryan Bridge,** an arched cantilever span over the river that many believe is the most graceful bridge in the state. And while you're out this direction, continue south on US 83 for 16 miles and turn west on Nebr. S16B to reach one of Nebraska's finest spots for wildlife observation.

Valentine National Wildlife Refuge preserves 71,516 acres of Sandhills prairie habitat, including numerous shallow lakes and marshy areas. In spring and fall migration, more than 100,000 ducks of various species stop to rest and feed at the refuge. In spring, the refuge provides observation blinds from which visitors can watch the amazing "dance" of courting male grouse and prairie chickens, a foot-stamping display that inspired ceremonial dances of some Plains Indian tribes.

Simply driving through the Sandhills and admiring the scenery is a revelation for people who've thought of Nebraska as flat cropland. But taking time to explore the country around Valentine brings a new appreciation for a little known part of the Midwest, revealing this rolling grassland as a paradise for nature-lovers of all varieties.   *Mel White*

Travelwise

GETTING THERE

Valentine lies in north-central Nebraska, at the junction of US 83 and US 20, 235 miles west of Sioux City, Iowa. Airlines serve North Platte, Nebraska, 130 miles south. The Amtrak *California Zephyr* stops in McCook, Nebraska, 198 miles south.

GENERAL INFORMATION

Late spring through early fall is the best time to visit Valentine; winters can be very cold, and occasional storms can make the isolated roads hazardous for the inexperienced. Ice-fishing and hunting are popular winter activities, though. For information contact the **Valentine Visitor Center** (239 S. Main St., P.O. Box 201, Valentine 69201. 402-376-2969 or 800-658-4024).

THINGS TO SEE AND DO

Centennial Hall (3rd and Macomb Sts. 402-376-2418. May–Labor Day Thurs.-Sat.; adm. fee) Exhibits on local history and a collection of more than 1,700 bells are housed in an 1897 high-school building.

Cherry County Historical Society Museum (Main St. and US 20. 402-376-2195. Mem. Day–Labor Day Wed.-Sun.; adm. fee) Artifacts recall Fort Niobrara, Native Americans, and early homesteaders in the Sandhills.

Cowboy Trail (Trailhead Park, 1st and Main Sts. 402-370-3374 or 402-471-0641. Adm. fee) Five miles of the old Chicago and Northwestern rail line have been converted to a hiking-biking trail; ask at the visitor center for names of local bike-rental companies.

Fort Niobrara National Wildlife Refuge (4 miles E of town off Nebr. 12. 402-376-3789) The refuge includes a wildlife drive with wildlife viewing; a trail leads to Fort Falls, the state's second highest waterfall.

Niobrara National Scenic River (402-336-3970) A 76-mile stretch of the Niobrara has been designated a scenic river; the 30 miles east of Valentine comprise one of the Midwest's favorite canoe journeys. Many local outfitters can arrange one-day or overnight float trips.

Smith Falls State Park (15 miles E of town, off Nebr. 12. 402-376-1306. Closed mid-Nov.–April; adm. fee) Located on the Niobrara River, this park boasts the state's highest waterfall; hiking trails and picnic grounds.

Valentine National Wildlife Refuge (20 miles S of town, on US 83. 402-376-3789) Lakes (popular for fishing) and marshland attract an excellent variety of birds and other wildlife.

ANNUAL EVENTS

Old West Days (1st weekend in Oct. Various sites. 402-376-2969 or 800-658-4024. Adm. fee) A mountain-man rendezvous, a Native American powwow, music, and a renowned cowboy poetry gathering are among the activities at this annual event.

Valentine's Day (Feb. 14. 402-376-2969 or 800-658-4024) Coronation of a Valentine king and queen, a masquerade ball, and other romantic activities involve the whole town.

WHERE TO EAT

Jordan's (Nebr. 20 E. 402-376-1255. $) Steaks, seafood, and pasta are featured at this popular gathering place.

WHERE TO STAY

Heartland Elk Guest Ranch (17 miles E of town on Nebr. 12 to Sparks, then 2.5 miles S on Brewer's Bridge. 402-376-1124. $$) Fully furnished log cabins overlook the Niobrara River Valley; trail rides and a trout pond.

Lovejoy Ranch (17 miles S of town, off US 83. 402-376-2668 or 800-672-5098. $$) Two rooms and a suite, all with private baths, on a working ranch near Valentine NWR.

Niobrara Inn (525 N. Main St. 402-376-1779 or 877-376-1779. $$) Six rooms in an antique-filled 1912 Arts and Crafts-style house.

Amana Colonies

In a natural amphitheater of gentle hills carved by the Iowa River lies a ring of seven villages built nearly 150 years ago by a group of German religious refugees. Their successful experiment in deliberate, peaceful living continues to this day amid the bucolic splendor of eastern Iowa, and visitors are welcome to stroll the quiet streets past sturdy redbrick and cedar-sided houses and post-and-beam barns and to visit the workshops, wineries, museum buildings, and restaurants of this utopian enclave lying a mere half-dozen miles off the interstate.

Hobo Stopover

Throughout Amana history, hoboes often drifted though looking for food and a few dollars. The hobo grapevine considered the Amanas an "easy touch" for handouts. One famous tramp, Franz Loibel was feared for his looks, his slouch hat shading a scraggly beard and bloodshot eyes. Sometimes, in exchange for food and wine, he played haunting songs on his zither that he had learned as a child in Vienna. Instead of accepting community housing, he kept to himself in the woods. He died one winter in a hollow tree trunk, holding tight to his zither.

When Buffalo, New York, grew too crowded for Christian Metz and his Community of True Inspiration, he led them west into the new state of Iowa in 1855. They had come from Germany 13 years earlier seeking a place to live and worship in peace. They found what they were looking for in the Iowa River Valley, and in time the community of 1,200 souls bought a 26,000-acre parcel of farmland and began putting up houses, mills, shops, and churches. In addition to the Bible and belief in quiet, inward devotion, the Inspirationists believed that God spoke to them through chosen "instruments." Christian Metz was one; Barbara Heinemann, the last, died in 1883. Scribes followed these instruments around so that nothing would be missed when the spirit moved them. The recorded testimonies remain a key part of the community faith.

Each village was laid out along orderly, Old World lines, with barns at one end, workshops at the other, and orchards and vineyards on the edge of town. A 16-mile driving loop connects the seven villages, which were spaced about an hour's ox-car drive apart. The main village of **Amana** is a good place to start a tour. It was the first to be established (in 1853) and is now the site of the **Museum of Amana History,** housed in an 1864 home and adjacent 1870 schoolhouse. A beautiful audio-visual presentation answers a lot of questions about the Amana Colonies, and the wealth of exhibits—handmade toys, textiles, gardening tools, and so on—begins to create a picture of the early life of the community. One thing you learn is how well documented the Amanas are—reams of papers and books have been written by graduate students and historians in an

Communal kitchen in Middle Amana

attempt to preserve the oral history of an intact religious colony. Quotations about every facet of life adorn the exhibits, a testament to the hospitality of the colonists and to their permanence here—descendants of original colonists still outnumber outsiders.

The Amana Colonies were a communal society, with housing, medical care, food, jobs, and education supplied by the community. But hard times hit the area, along with a level of dissatisfaction within the community—and in 1932 the people voted to separate economic activity from the church; members were given shares of stock. Many old-timers still vividly remember the Great Change (or simply the Change) and though some "didn't think much of it," it enabled the community to adapt to modern life—many bought cars and started their own businesses. One enterprising villager started the company that grew into Amana Appliances, based in Middle Amana and now a national manufacturer of appliances, including refrigerators and air conditioners. Though people sometimes confuse Amana people with the Amish, they actually have nothing to do with each other except that both groups came from Germany. Technology is fine with Amana—think refrigerators, not people in buggies.

Though not very commercial by today's standards, the village of Amana possesses the highest concentration of shops and restaurants and thus the most touristy feel of the seven villages. But you can easily drive or walk the unhurried streets and visit shops that sell handcrafted furniture, sweet wines, smoked meats, and colorful woolens. One place where you can see and talk to

Amana meat shop

people involved in the craft is the **Amana Woolen Mill.** Walk through the weaving room, thumping with the sound of machine looms, and you'll quickly realize that Amana is not stuck in the past. The mill dates from 1857, though part of the original building burned in a 1923 fire. The oldest looms here date from the 1940s, but the newer ones can turn out a 6-foot blanket in under four minutes.

Only a few minutes down the road from Amana is **Middle Amana,** where the **Communal Kitchen and Coopershop Museum** is the last surviving of the 50 communal kitchen houses in the Amanas. Furnished as it was in 1932, this kitchen once served three meals a day to 40 people. The dry sink, the 1860s hearth, and the long table where villagers ate in silence speak eloquently of days gone by, but even more eloquent are the village residents who staff these museums, who will happily tell you about life in the Amanas past and present. Next door, you can indulge your palate with butter streusel, cinnamon coffee cake, or whole wheat bread made the old-fashioned way in the 100-year-old oven at **Hahn's Hearth Oven Bakery.**

If you wander around this tiny town, you'll see lush gardens with trellises, children playing behind old brick and sandstone houses, and grown-ups taking easy strolls. The pace is decidedly calm. At the west end of town lies the calmest place of all, the village cemetery. Each village has its own little graveyard, the neat rows of small, uniform headstones like a separate, even more peaceful village of ancestors. Symbolizing the belief that all are equal in God's eyes, graves are not grouped by family, but simply in order of death.

Stones are inscribed only with the name, age, and date of death. For the oldest ones—from the mid-1800s—look in the far left corner.

Continue around the village circuit, admiring the scenery and stopping where your fancy dictates, passing thru **High Amana, West Amana, South Amana,** and **Homestead.** Each village is worth several hours of exploration. Perhaps the most interesting stop is the **Community Church** in Homestead. Now a museum, the 1865 redbrick structure is typical of the long, plain buildings that continue to serve as village churches in the Amana Colonies. Churchgoers sit on pegged white pine benches made in the mid-19th century, when the community was in New York. Large windows let in natural light; unadorned walls have a light blue tint. There are no icons, not even a cross to distract worshipers. Singing is a cappella, and if you're lucky enough to be here on Sunday, you may attend a service at one of the churches. Men sit on the right side, women on the left. Visitors are asked to do similarly.

In the 1960s, church services in English were added to the traditional German. But despite this and other changes, much remains the same in the Amanas. As one villager says, "We're a little like *Fiddler on the Roof.* We use the word 'tradition' a lot."

John M. Thompson

Travelwise

GETTING THERE

The Amana Colonies are located in central Iowa, 18 miles southwest of Cedar Rapids and 18 miles northwest of Iowa City. The Eastern Iowa Airport lies about halfway between Amana and Cedar Rapids. The seven towns are linked by a 16-mile auto loop.

GENERAL INFORMATION

The peak season runs from May through September, though most shops and B&Bs stay open year-round. Some restaurants have limited winter hours. Special events and festivities occur throughout the year. October makes a delightful time to visit—most museums are still open, days are usually warm, and autumn light falls crisply on harvested fields. For information contact the **Amana Colonies Convention and Visitors Bureau** *(The Visitor Center, 39 38th Ave., Ste. 100, Amana 52203. 319-622-7622 or 800-579-2294).*

THINGS TO SEE AND DO

Amana Arts Guild Center *(1210 G St., High Amana. 319-622-3678. May-Sept. Wed.-Sun., Oct. weekends)* The 1858 former church houses quilts, baskets, rugs, pottery, needlework, brooms, and other traditional Amana crafts for display and sale.

Amana Woolen Mill *(800 48th Ave., Amana. 319-622-3432 or 800-222-6430)* Watch how quality wool, acrylic, and cotton blankets and apparel are made. In the early 1980s, the looms operated non-stop for two years, turning out 380,000 blankets for a U.S. Army contract.

Communal Kitchen and Coopershop Museum *(1003 26th Ave., Middle Amana. 319-622- 3567. May-Oct.; adm. fee)* One of the original community kitchens displays early cookware and utensils; barrels were fashioned in the separate cooper shop.

Community Church Museum *(4210 V St., Homestead. 319-622-3567. May-Oct.; adm. fee)* Amana's community values and history merge in this serenely simple building.

Hahn's Hearth Oven Bakery *(Adj. to Communal Kitchen, at 2510 J St., Middle Amana. 319-622-3439. April-Oct. Tues.-Sat.; March, Nov.-Dec. Wed., Sat.; Jan.-Feb. Sat.)* Scrumptious baked goods will tempt you as soon as you open the door.

Hiking and Biking The 3.1-mile hard-surface **Kolonieweg Recreational Trail**

Period clothing at Amana

circles Lily Lake and is perfect for walking and biking; it connects with other low traffic roads. Or try the **Amana Colonies Nature Trail** *(US 151 and US 6)*, which has loops up to 3.2 miles through a hickory and maple forest. There is some highway noise, but you pass 1,000-year-old Indian mounds and an overlook of the Iowa River.

Museum of Amana History *(Just E of US 151 in Amana, at 4310 220 Trail. 319-622-3567. Daily April-Oct., Sat. only Feb.-March and Nov.-Dec., closed Jan.; adm. fee)* The award-winning 20-minute slide presentation and thorough exhibits in 19th-century buildings are plenty to get you started.

ENTERTAINMENT

Old Creamery Theatre Company *(The Visitor Center, 39 38th Ave., W of Amana. 319-622-6194 or 800-352-6262. May-Dec.)* A professional troupe stages bedroom farces and other light fare.

SHOPPING

The Amana Colonies have a longstanding tradition of excellent craftsmanship—brooms, baskets, quilts, and woodwork are specialties. Also highly regarded are hickory-smoked hams and sausages, fresh pastries,

and homemade wines. **Ehrle Brothers Winery** *(V St., Homestead. 319-622-3241)* is the oldest—the 1934 establishment vends dandelion, blackberry, and other sweet wines.

High Amana Store *(G St., High Amana. 319-622-3797)* For a real time-warping experience, step into this 1857 general store. Family operated since the early part of the century, the old-fashioned store features wide plank floors, a patterned tin ceiling, and big glass display cases. Purchases are totaled on an old adding machine or by hand.

ANNUAL EVENTS

Maifest *(Early May. Amana. Call visitors bureau for information)* Maypole dancers, a parade, local foods, and more herald the arrival of spring.

Oktoberfest *(1st weekend in Oct. Amana. Call the visitors bureau for information)* This traditional event features German food and folk entertainment. A crowd favorite is a cannon that shoots pumpkins into a field.

WHERE TO EAT

Colony Inn *(741 47th St., Amana. 319-622-6270 or 800-227-3471. $$)* Traditional Colony favorites, including bratwurst, Swiss steak, fried chicken, sauerbraten, and jager schnitzel.

Ox Yoke Inn *(4420 220 Trail, Amana. 319-622-3441 or 800-233-3441. $$)* One of the oldest and best restaurants around, the Ox Yoke serves heaping platters of German and American food family-style, with refillable bowls of sauerkraut, corn, slaw, cottage cheese, bread, and various potato dishes.

Ronneburg Restaurant *(4408 220 Trail, Amana. 319-622-3641 or 888-348-4686. $$)* German and American meals served family style, including sauerbraten with potato dumplings and wiener schnitzel.

WHERE TO STAY

Die Heimat Country Inn *(4430 V St., Homestead. 319-622-3937 or 888-613-5463. $)* An 1854 stage stop, this unique 19-room inn has canopy beds and a full buffet breakfast.

Rose's Place B&B *(1007 26th Ave., Middle Amana. 319-622-6097. $)* Rose-patterned wallpaper and sheets are among the quaint touches at this comfortable lodging in an 1870 Sunday school building. The full breakfast includes local meats, coffee cakes, and rolls from Hahn's Bakery next door.

Ste. Genevieve

Sometime around 1750, a small band of French settlers crossed the Mississippi River from the town of Kaskaskia, in present-day Illinois, to establish a new community on the river's western shore. The town they founded, which they named for the patron saint of Paris, still exists two and a half centuries later: Ste. Genevieve, Missouri's oldest settlement and one of the most historic and architecturally significant sites in America.

The pretty little midwestern town you'll find today, set among the rolling pastures and cropland of eastern Missouri, occupies a slightly different location from the original. Those first settlers built along the Mississippi near an opening in the woods they called *le grand champ*—"the big field"—and time and again they were plagued by flooding. After a 1785 flood so severe that boats were tied to house chimneys, the citizens began moving to higher terrain just a short distance westward.

On your visit to Ste. Genevieve, your first stop should be the **Great River Road Interpretive Center** on Main Street, where exhibits and a video presentation will ground you in the town's long history. From here it's just a short walk to the **Bolduc House,** considered the most authentically restored French

Bolduc House's gallery, in French West Indies style

The French colonial-era Bolduc House, Ste. Genevieve

colonial-era house in America. Built by wealthy merchant and planter Louis Bolduc in 1770 at the old town site, and moved and expanded about 1784, it shows a notable blend of styles: The roof above its two large rooms is supported by heavy trusses taken from medieval Norman French construction techniques; the gallery (porch) shows French West Indies influence; and the tall stockade reflects the pioneer American need for protection against Indian attack. The house contains a few original Bolduc family pieces and many authentic period items. Next door, the **Bolduc-LeMeilleur House,** a mix of French and American architectural styles, was built about 1820 by the grandson-in-law of Louis Bolduc.

Two blocks away, the **Felix Vallé House State Historic Site** is named for a member of Ste. Genevieve's most prominent early family. Two earlier Vallés were civil commandants of the town, and Felix, born in 1800, oversaw the family's extensive business interests in mining and trading. The 1818 federal-style house that is the centerpiece of the site was acquired in 1824 by Felix's father; the son later bought it and lived in it for more than 50 years, until his death in 1877. The present restoration reflects its use as both a store and residence in the 1830s.

Also part of the state historic site, the **St. Gemme Beauvais-Amoureux House** sits on a rise overlooking the "big field" of the first settlers. It was built about 1792 using *poteaux-en-terre,* or "posts-in-ground," construction, a style common in the early years at Ste. Genevieve. Heavy cedar timbers were set vertically into the ground to form the wall structure, and the spaces between were filled with stone rubble or a mixture of clay and animal hair. Only five such structures are known to have survived in the United States, and three of them are in Ste. Genevieve. Displays in the Beauvais-Amoureux House show the varied construction techniques used here and in other houses around town.

You'll find a quite different scene from these modest early houses at the **Maison de Guibourd-Vallé,** on Merchant near the massive 1880 Gothic Revival-style Catholic church. Built on a Spanish land grant in 1806, this home was owned for a time by a prosperous Vallé descendant and is filled with European and Asian antiques. Climb the narrow stairs to the attic to see the massive, hand-hewn original timbers of the Norman trusses, the tops of the vertical-post walls, and the mortise-and-tenon construction.

Walk west on Merchant to visit **Memorial Cemetery,** where gravestones with French inscriptions date back to the late 1700s, memorializing Vallés, Guibourds, Roziers, and other early families. One marker honors a man born in 1746 who fought under George Washington in the Revolutionary War.

The French were by no means the only group to leave their mark on Ste. Genevieve. Beginning in the 1840s, German immigrants began settling here, and the gabled

Candlelight tour of a historic house

redbrick buildings that line many streets are evidence of their architectural tastes. In fact, by the beginning of the 20th century the town's French influence had essentially diminished to the names of families living there (by then thoroughly Americanized) and to a few street names, as the town took on a predominantly German flavor. Stop in at the **Ste. Genevieve Museum** on Dubourg Square for an overview of the town's development and to browse through all sorts of quirky local items. Among other facts, you'll learn here that the great painter-naturalist John James Audubon spent six weeks in Ste. Genevieve in 1811, operating a store with a business partner before the two parted ways.

If all this history makes Ste. Genevieve sound like one big museum, that's hardly the case. Its melting pot of cultures has matured into a genuine American small town, with shops, restaurants, and inns coexisting with private houses and historic sites. The old downtown area is small enough to see easily on foot, and on summer evenings you'll especially enjoy a stroll along the quiet streets, admiring the old houses and businesses.

For more than fifty years, it's been a Ste. Genevieve tradition to head down to the high school, just north of Dubourg Square, for the municipal band concerts held every Thursday night in summer. Get an ice-cream cone, take a seat, and enjoy the music: It's a good way to meet some of the friendly residents of Ste. Genevieve, and a happy and relaxing way to end a day spent exploring one of the most fascinating small towns in America.   *Mel White*

Travelwise

GETTING THERE

Ste. Genevieve is in eastern Missouri, about 50 miles south of St. Louis, on US 61 just east of I-55. Airlines and Amtrak serve St. Louis.

GENERAL INFORMATION

The best time to visit is spring through fall; some of the sites close in winter. Information is available at the **Great River Road Interpretive Center** (66 S. Main St., Ste. Genevieve 63670. 573-883-7097 or 800-373-7007).

THINGS TO SEE AND DO

Bolduc House (125 S. Main St. 573-883-3105. Closed Nov.-March; adm. fee) One of the most architecturally important buildings in America, this is an excellent example of a French colonial-style house. Next door stands the ca 1820 **Bolduc-LeMeilleur House** (Daily July-Aug., weekends only April-June and Oct., closed Sept.-March; adm. fee), illustrating a later era of Ste. Genevieve development.

Felix Vallé House State Historic Site (Merchant and 2nd Sts. 573-883-7102. Adm. fee) A limestone federal-style structure built in 1818 and restored to its 1830s appearance as part business, part wealthy family's home. Also included in the SHS is the **St. Gemme Beauvais-Amoureux House** (May-Sept.; adm. fee) on St. Mary's Road, a ca 1792 house featuring rare posts-in-ground construction.

Maison de Guibourd-Vallé (Merchant and 4th Sts. 573-883-7544. Closed Jan.-March; adm. fee) This 1806 house, renovated in the 1930s, still shows early construction methods and displays a splendid collection of antiques.

Ste. Genevieve-Modoc Ferry (1.5 miles N of interpretive center on Main St. 573-883-7097 or 800-373-7007. Fare) Take a ride across the Mississippi into Illinois, and then drive north along Levee Rd. to reach **Fort de Chartres State Historic Site** (618-284-7230), a partially reconstructed French fort dating from the 1750s that served as regional headquarters for the French colonial administration.

Ste. Genevieve Museum (Merchant St. at Dubourg Sq. 573-883-3461. Adm. fee) Indian artifacts and birds mounted by Audubon are displayed in a 1935 stone building.

SHOPPING

Al Agnew Gallery (10 S. Main St. 573-883-5397) One of the country's foremost wildlife artists has a gallery offering prints and original paintings.

Ste. Genevieve Winery (245 Merchant St. 573-883-2800) Red and white wines (try the semi-sweet Vallé Rhine), plus a selection of traditional fruit wines.

ANNUAL EVENTS

Country Christmas Walk (2nd weekend in Dec. Downtown. 573-883-7097 or 800-373-7007) A parade, a tree-lighting ceremony, and caroling are part of this holiday fest.

Jour de Fête (2nd full weekend in Aug. Downtown. 573-883-7097 or 800-373-7007) A hugely popular celebration of the town's French heritage, with music, food, and arts and crafts.

WHERE TO EAT

Bogy House (163 Merchant St. 573-883-5647. $$) An eclectic assortment of Italian, Southwestern, and Cajun dishes are served in a home dating from 1810.

WHERE TO STAY

Inn St. Gemme Beauvais (78 N. Main St. 573-883-5744 or 800-818-5744. $$$) Nine antique-furnished rooms with private baths are in an 1848 house.

Main Street Inn (221 N. Main St. 573-883-9199 or 800-918-9199. $$) Eight spacious rooms with private baths in an 1882 building that was once the Hotel Meyer.

Southern Hotel (146 S. 3rd St. 573-883-3493 or 800-275-1412. $$) Eight rooms with Victorian antiques in a building that began operating as a hotel in 1805.

Hermann

The Germans settled Hermann on lush, rolling hills along the green, smooth-flowing Missouri River, a scene more European than American. A century and a half later, this handsome town 70 miles west of St. Louis offers a sampling of Old World traditions in the heart of mid-America, from the oompah music of Octoberfest to the taste of award-winning wines.

In 1836 a group of Germans in Philadelphia, fearful that their heritage was disappearing, dreamed of a new home where they could keep their customs alive in the isolation of the American frontier. The town they founded in Missouri in 1838 was named for Hermann, a legendary German warrior, and it began with appropriately heroic ambitions: Today's broad Market Street is said to reflect the planners' vision that Hermann would one day surpass Philadelphia in population, a metropolis at the heart of a new German state.

Hermann never grew to become the city its founders foresaw, but it was in the vanguard of a flood of Germans who settled in Missouri throughout the mid-19th century. So significant was this immigration that today, more than half of all Missourians have at least one grandparent of German ancestry.

You'll learn about this aspect of Missouri's past at the **Deutschheim State**

An oompah band celebrating Octoberfest

Historic Site, a collection of historic buildings at the top of Market Street, just a couple of blocks from the river. Deutschheim means "home of the Germans," the name settlers used for their adopted region; tours and exhibits here interpret the years from 1830 to 1900, when German influence in the state was at its height.

The brick **Pommer-Gentner House** *(108 Market St. 573-486-2200)* was built in 1840 in the German *Klassizismus,* or neoclassic, style. The home's furnishings, representing the 1830s and 1840s, include a Biedermeier sofa and chairs, silver, and porcelain, proclaiming the well-to-do status of its owners, but the overall aspect of the house shows typical German restraint. Like many of the early buildings in Hermann, the Pommer-Gentner House was built close to the street, creating extra room in back for gardens and domestic animals—German practicality at work. Behind the house today you'll see a barn built around 1880 in the Old World half-timbered style, beehives, and a garden with typical plantings of the 1840s, including herbs, vegetables, and flowers.

A short walk west on Second Street, **Deutschheim's Strehly House** *(130 W. 2nd. St. 573-486-2200)* and its adjacent winery illustrate the life of an immigrant family of modest means. Dating from 1842-69, the house is decorated in the bright colors typical of its era, and rooms are mostly filled with furnishings from the 1880s and the personal possessions of the Strehly family. Taking center stage in the 1857 winery is the only remaining 19th-century carved wine cask in the Midwest, its design depicting Bacchus holding a drinking bowl. Nearby, an exhibit displays wooden shoes of the type used by German families in Missouri well into this century. Behind the Strehly complex, in a yard circumscribed by a traditional double-heart picket fence, vines planted in the 1850s still produce grapes.

The Germans who came to Hermann brought with them a love of wine, though, since most were from non-wine regions in Germany, they had to learn how to make it, which they did. Local wines were winning awards as early as the 1850s, and by the turn of the 20th century Missouri was the nation's second largest wine-producing state. Hermann boasted dozens of wineries—and then, in 1919, Prohibition came to Missouri, shutting down the industry and severely harming the town's economy.

Several wineries have since revived the traditional art, foremost among them **Stone Hill Winery,** which offers daily tours at its headquarters on a high point just southwest of downtown Hermann. (Even if you don't know beans

Fighting Old Men

When Confederate Gen. John S. Marmaduke approached Hermann during the Civil War in 1864, he expected no resistance, since the town's men had left to fight for the Union. He was surprised, therefore, when shots from three different locations indicated substantial opposition. Investigation quickly revealed that a few elderly men had been carrying one small cannon from place to place, trying to delay Rebel movement. Marmaduke threw the cannon into the river. Citizens later recovered it, and today it sits on the lawn of Hermann's Gasconade County Courthouse.

In Hermann's German-style historic district

about grapes, you should make the drive up to Stone Hill to enjoy the view of Hermann's tree-covered hills, punctuated by church steeples, with the silver-domed, 1896 **Gasconade County Courthouse** in the distance.) Visitors walk through vaulted cellars (used for growing mushrooms during Prohibition) and sample Stone Hill's award-winning wines in the firm's 1869 main building. The dry red Norton is Stone Hill's best, though several other reds and whites have won medals in various competitions.

True oenophiles will want to try the products of some of Hermann's other wineries as well, including **Hermannhof Winery,** in a redbrick 1852 building on First Street near Frene Creek, and **Adam Puchta Winery** *(573-486-5596),* 2 miles southwest of town, established in 1855 and still operated by descendants of the founder. Both have won their share of awards, and both offer tours.

You'll find memorabilia of early-day local wineries, and lots of other entertaining stuff, too, at the **Historic Hermann Museum,** located in an 1871 schoolhouse on Schiller Street. (Hermann's founders named streets for German heroes Schiller, Gutenberg, Goethe, and Mozart, as well as American founding fathers Washington and Jefferson.) Climb stairs worn by generations of schoolchildren to visit the museum's River Room, full of relics of Hermann's days as a riverboat-building town. Hermann natives have served as captains on the Missouri and the Mississippi from steamboat days to today's diesel-engine era. You can pretend you're guiding a riverboat when you take the wheel of the *Pin Oak,* a steamer owned by the Hermann Ferry & Packet Company in the late 19th century; the great wooden wheel now rests in a re-created pilot house in the museum. Down the hall, take a peek at the works for the town clock, set in a tower atop the school; it's been running continuously since 1891.

Downstairs, the **Hermann Visitor Information Center** offers maps, brochures, and advice. Staff members can help you choose from the more than three dozen bed-and-breakfast inns in the Hermann area, and they'll tell you about some of the town's many special events. Like every German community, Hermann welcomes visitors to Octoberfest with music and food, and the local wineries host sundry celebrations throughout the year (Stone Hill's August Grape Stomp is a favorite). Hermann's most historic event, though, is its Maifest. What began as an end-of-school picnic for kids expanded in the 1950s to encompass the traditional German celebration of spring—even including the ancient ritual of the dance around the Maypole.

Hermann's various festivals are fine times to make the town's acquaintance, but it's also fun to visit during quieter moments—to stroll the streets and admire the architecture of venerable buildings, many of which look as though they belong on a *Strasse* in Bavaria. Look up to see the rooster on the steeple of the **St. Paul Church of Christ** (another reminder of Germany), and walk to its north side for a great view of the Missouri River.

Hermann's founders intended to create a city "characteristically German in every particular." While over the years the "particulars" have inevitably become a bit less Germanic and a bit more midwestern, Hermann remains a historic and charming place with a strong European heritage. Sit back, order a bratwurst and a glass of Hermannsberger red wine, and enjoy the atmosphere.   *Mel White*

Travelwise

GETTING THERE

Hermann sits at the junction of Mo. 100 and Mo. 19 in central Missouri, about 70 miles west of St. Louis. Major airlines serve St. Louis, and Hermann has an Amtrak station.

GENERAL INFORMATION

Hermann can be visited year-round, though there are occasional periods of snow in winter when driving can be difficult. The town can be crowded during Maifest and Octoberfest. The **Hermann Visitor Information Center** is in the 1871 German schoolhouse *(312 Schiller St., Hermann 65041. 573-486-2744 or 800-932-8687. www.hermannmo.com)*.

THINGS TO SEE AND DO

1894 and More Museum *(129 E. 3rd St. 573-486-1894. Adm. fee)* A collection of guns is the main attraction here, along with varied local memorabilia.

Deutschheim State Historic Site *(109 W. 2nd St. 573-486-2200. Adm. fee)* Exhibits on Missouri's German heritage, with tours through historic buildings.

Hermannhof Vineyards and Winery *(330 E. 1st St. 573-486-5959 or 800-393-0100. June-Aug.; fee for tours)* See wine cellars and sample wines in an 1852 building; a deli offers sausage, cheese, and other foods.

Historic Hermann Museum *(312 Schiller St. 573-486-2017. Closed Thurs. and Nov.–mid-March; adm. fee)* Upstairs in the 1871 school house, you'll find local items ranging from toys to guns to riverboat relics.

Katy Trail State Park *(Trailhead 2 miles N of town, off Mo. 19 in McKittrick. 660-882-8196)* Cross the Missouri River bridge to reach this hiking-biking trail, which follows the former route of the Missouri-Kansas-Texas rail line; excellent for a relaxing stroll (or a vigorous hike). Check at the Hermann Visitor Information Center about local bicycle rentals.

Stone Hill Winery *(1100 Stone Hill Hwy. 573-486-2221 or 800-909-9463)* Once the world's third largest winery, this newly thriving enterprise offers tours *(adm. fee)* of its cellars, tastings, and an extensive gift shop in a restored 1869 building. The winery's **Great Stone Hill Grape Stomp** *(2nd Sat. in Aug. Adm. fee)* is a lively and messy celebration.

SHOPPING

Swiss Meat & Sausage Company *(12 miles S of town on Mo 19. 573-486-2086 or 800-793-7947)* Award-winning ham, bacon, and sausage offered by a family-run business.

ANNUAL EVENTS

Maifest *(2nd weekend in May. Various sites. 573-486-2744 or 800-932-8687)* This traditional German gala salutes spring, with Maypole dances, carnival rides, specialty foods, arts and crafts, and music.

Octoberfest *(Oct. weekends. Various sites. 573-486-2744 or 800-932-8687)* Food, music, arts and crafts honor Hermann's German heritage.

Wurstfest *(4th weekend in March. Various sites. 573-486-2744 or 800-932-8687)* A celebration of sausagemaking, with contests, demonstrations, and music.

WHERE TO EAT

Vintage Restaurant *(1100 Stone Hill Hwy. 573-486-2221 or 800-909-9463. $$)* Part of the Stone Hill Winery, this excellent restaurant is located in the winery's original stable and carriage house.

WHERE TO STAY

Birk's Gasthaus *(700 Goethe St. 573-486-2911 or 888-701-2495. $$)* Nine rooms in an 1886 mansion with fanciful architectural details.

Market Street Bed and Breakfast *(210 Market St. 573-486-5597. $$)* Three rooms in a turn-of-the-20th-century house with beautiful original woodwork.

Pelze Nichol Haus *(179 Mo. 100 E. 573-486-3886. $$)* Set on 8 acres, this mid-1800s house is full of eclectic antiques.

Abilene

Amid the wheatfields and rangeland of central Kansas sits one of the legendary towns of the Old West: Abilene, where lawman Wild Bill Hickok once kept an eye on rowdy cowboys spending their trail-ride wages on whiskey and women. Abilene's a quieter place now, of course, but history is still alive here, from the echoes of gunslingers' six-shooters to cherished memories of native son Dwight D. Eisenhower, World War II general and one of America's most popular presidents.

Arts Scene Success

From March through December, Abilene's Great Plains Theatre Festival offers visitors a special cultural experience: a highly acclaimed professional theater company performing comedies, musicals, and dramas in the Tietjens Center for the Performing Arts, a renovated 1880s church at W. Third and Mulberry Streets. Started on a shoestring in 1995, the GPTF has grown into one of the success stories on the Kansas arts scene. For information about upcoming productions and tickets, call 785-263-4574 or 888-222-4574.

Nineteenth-century America had a number of famous cowtowns—places like Wichita, Dodge City, and Fort Worth, celebrated in Western novels, movies, and television shows. Abilene still fits the original mold.

In 1867 businessman Joseph G. McCoy conceived the notion of bringing cattle north from Texas to the Union Pacific Railway, where they could be sent to eastern markets by boxcar. He built shipping yards at Abilene, and over the next four years millions of cattle were driven up along the Chisholm Trail to this once-quiet village, now transformed into a booming and unruly place full of saloons, cowboys, gamblers, and women of dubious virtue. The cattle-drive days lasted only a short time here, as the railhead moved southwest to towns closer to Texas. By 1872, Abilene's streets were said to be "growing up with grass," and farming took over as the main local source of income. The tall grain elevators rising beside N.E. Third Street show that agriculture is still important here on the prairie.

Abilene's colorful past is on display at the **Heritage Center,** which includes the **Dickinson County Historical Museum.** Here you'll learn about the first city marshal, Tom Smith, who enforced a "no-guns" policy, and about James B. "Wild Bill" Hickok, marshal in 1871, who shot a gambler in front of the notorious Alamo Saloon.

But of course there's much more to Abilene than its cowtown days: You can read excerpts from the diary of George Freeman, who settled in Dickinson County in 1855, and who wrote of hunting bison and of grasshopper plagues that darkened the sky. You'll see Native American artifacts, tools used by Swiss and German immigrants, and exhibits on the railroads that opened the Great Plains to pioneers. Out in back stands a beautiful and historic turn-of-the-20th-century carousel built in Abilene by C.W. Parker, the nation's "amuse-

Eisenhower's boyhood home, Abilene

ment king" of the early 1900s, complete with 24 prancing horses, 4 chariots, and a Wurlitzer band organ.

Also part of the Heritage Center is the **Museum of Independent Telephony,** dedicated to the non-Bell System telephone companies that have served so much of rural America. (One of those companies, founded by C.L. Brown in Abilene, evolved into today's Sprint Corporation.) On display are all kinds of telephones and related equipment, dating back to the days when a journalist wrote that the telephone, while interesting, "can never be a practical necessity."

In the years just after the turn of the 20th century, when telephones were gaining acceptance in American life, a young man named Dwight David Eisenhower was growing up in Abilene, one of six sons of a working-class family. He was an avid athlete, and when he went to West Point his goals had less to do with the military than simply with playing football and getting a free college education. Later, of course, Gen. Dwight D. Eisenhower faced the awesome responsibility of commanding the Allied D-Day invasion of France, a massive operation that assured victory in World War II. So popular was this humble yet strong and decisive career soldier that he easily won election to the presidency in 1952 and 1956, his supporters proclaiming, "I Like Ike."

A visit to Abilene's **Eisenhower Center** can quite profitably take up several hours, as you learn about the President's remarkable life. Watch the fine short film at the visitor center for an introduction to his career, and then walk to the family home, which looks just as it did when Eisenhower's mother, Ida, died in 1946. (The newest thing in the house is a radio that Dwight's brothers

Historic Lebold-Vahsholtz House, Abilene

bought their mother so she could listen to World War II news.) Afterward, continue to the museum, which displays Eisenhower personal items, photographs, and wartime memorabilia, as well as a superb array of gifts from foreign heads of state. As you walk outside to see the statue of Ike, or visit the Place of Meditation, the chapel where Eisenhower is interred, it's impossible not to have a renewed respect for the man who led Allied forces through one of the darkest times in human history.

For a change of pace, cross Buckeye to see the **Greyhound Hall of Fame,** which claims to be the world's only museum devoted to a single breed of dog. You'll see exhibits on the history of this speedy animal, on the sport of greyhound racing, and on programs to promote adoption of retired racers. Greyhounds were brought to Kansas in the 1800s to help control jackrabbits, and today the Abilene area is a renowned breeding center for the dogs.

They may not be quite as fleet as greyhounds, but many of the athletes enshrined in the **Kansas Sports Hall of Fame** in downtown Abilene moved with considerable rapidity themselves. Consider Glenn Cunningham, the Kansas Flyer, and Jim Ryun, both champion runners, or Gale Sayers, the outstanding NFL running back. Among the other athletes honored here are basketball great Wilt Chamberlain, baseball pitcher Walter Johnson, and legendary Kansas basketball coach Forrest "Phog" Allen.

Walk south a couple of block to the **Abilene Visitor Information Center,** where you can pick up guides to walking and driving tours of the town. With the walking guide in hand you can stroll along shady Buckeye, N.W. Third, and Olive Streets, enjoying wonderful old structures such as the **Lebold-Vahsholtz House** at First and Vine. This five-level, Italianate-style house was built in 1880 on the site of town founder Timothy Hersey's 1857 dugout cabin, which also served as a stop on the Butterfield Overland Stage line.

North Buckeye owns some impressive 19th-century dwellings as well, the most notable of which is the white-columned Georgian home built in 1905 by A.B. Seelye, who made his fortune selling patent medicines such as Wasa-Tusa (the "great healer"), Fro-Zona, Ner-Vena, and Oriental Ointment. Tours of the **Seelye Mansion** prove that, whatever the medical worth of Seelye's cure-alls, they were definitely good for his bank balance. From the top-floor ballroom to the bowling alley in the basement, the home's 25 rooms, full of original family possessions including a Tiffany-designed fireplace and gilded furniture, are an amazing showcase of early 20th-century wealth. The Seelye's gave dinner parties to which the Eisenhowers, who lived on the wrong side of the tracks, were not invited—though future president Dwight is said to have delivered ice here in one of his teenage jobs.

Using the driving-tour guide you can visit other significant spots around town, including the northern terminus of the **Chisholm Trail,** the site of the shipping yards, the old Butterfield stage route, and the grave of murdered lawman Tom Smith. Rowdy cowtown no more, Abilene these days is a peaceful community far removed from the saloons of old Texas Street. But the spirit of history is ever present here, and the town's attractions offer entertainment and education enough to keep anyone as happily busy as a cowboy celebrating the end of a cattle drive.   *Mel White*

Travelwise

GETTING THERE

Abilene is on I-70 in central Kansas, 89 miles west of Topeka. Airlines serve Kansas City, Missouri, 150 miles east, and Wichita, 94 miles south. Amtrak stops in Topeka.

GENERAL INFORMATION

Spring through fall is the best time to visit Abilene. Some attractions are closed in winter, and there are spells of frigid and windy conditions. The **Abilene Visitor Information Center** is in the old Union Pacific depot *(201 N.W. 2nd St., P.O. Box 146, Abilene 67410. 785-263-2231 or 800-569-5915).*

THINGS TO SEE AND DO

Abilene and Smoky Valley Railroad Association *(417 S. Buckeye. 785-263-1077 or 888-426-6687. May-Oct.; fare)* An 11-mile ride on antique rail equipment heads east across the Smoky Hill River on old Chicago–Rock Island line track.

Eisenhower Center *(200 S.E. 4th St. 785-263-4751 or 800-746-4453)* This tribute to President Dwight D. Eisenhower's military and political careers includes his boyhood home, a museum *(adm. fee)*, a statue, the chapel where he and wife Mamie are interred, and his presidential library.

Greyhound Hall of Fame *(407 S. Buckeye. 785-263-3000)* Exhibits on the history of »the breed, as well as on the dogs' breeding and racing.

Heritage Center *(412 S. Campbell St. 785-263-2681. Adm. fee)* This complex includes the **Dickinson County Historical Museum,** with displays on local history and a marvelous 1901 carousel, and the **Museum of Independent Telephony,** with antique and modern telephones and a reproduction of an old-time telephone office.

Kansas Sports Hall of Fame *(213 N. Broadway. 785-263-7403. Adm. fee)* Dozens of professional and amateur athletes with links to Kansas are honored.

Seelye Mansion *(1105 N. Buckeye. 785-263-1084. Fee for tour)* The nicely restored home of a patent-medicine maker.

SHOPPING

American Indian Art Center *(206 S. Buckeye. 785-263-0090)* Arts and crafts by Native Americans, including pottery, dolls, paintings, and leather paintings.

Bow Studio and Gallery *(921 S. Buckeye. 785-263-7166)* Decorative tiles, plates, and sculpture made from local clay and often using native plants in designs.

ANNUAL EVENTS

Chisholm Trail Day Festival *(Oct. Heritage Center. 785-263-2681)* Arts and crafts, music, and more celebrate the historic cattle trail.

Wild Bill Hickok Rodeo *(Aug. Eisenhower Park. 785-263-7838. Adm. fee)* Ridin' and ropin' at a rodeo considered one of the nation's best.

WHERE TO EAT

Kirby House *(205 N.E. 3rd St. 785-263-7336. $$)* A fine restaurant with a varied menu, in a nicely restored 1885 Victorian-style house.

WHERE TO STAY

Balfours' House *(940 1900 Ave. 785-263-4262. $$)* One suite with private bath in a contemporary house, plus a separate bungalow; indoor swimming pool and spa.

Ehrsam Place *(103 S. Grant St., Enterprise. 785-263-8747. $$)* Four rooms with private baths in an 1879 Victorian house are furnished with eclectic antiques and art. Nature trails meander through 15-odd acres on the Smoky Hill River.

NEARBY PLACES

Tallgrass Prairie National Preserve *(40 miles SW of town via Kans. 177. 316-273-8494. Donation)* This area protects nearly 11,000 acres of tallgrass prairie, an ecosystem that's nearly disappeared from the American landscape. The visitor center is in an 1881 French Second Empire-style mansion. Hiking trail.

Guthrie

The streets of downtown Guthrie, lined with handsome redbrick and sandstone buildings, hummed in the late 1880s with the commerce and political dealmaking befitting Oklahoma's new state capital. Though it's no longer the Sooner State's major metropolis, this community just north of Oklahoma City stands proudly today as a veritable time capsule of turn-of-the-20th-century architecture—a lively town full of inns and shops in one of the Midwest's most historically significant settings.

On April 22, 1889, the city that would become Guthrie exploded into life on a site that had been nearly uninhabited prairie the day before. In the first of several land runs into the area then called Indian Territory, newly arrived settlers staked claims in a frenzy of scouting and bargaining, and within hours the freshly minted town had a population of more than 10,000. While several communities were born that day, Guthrie, with its land office and rail depot,

Annual 89er Day Parade, Guthrie

quickly became predominant in the region. When Oklahoma Territory was established the following year, Guthrie became the first capital, and it kept that status when statehood arrived in 1907.

Just three years later, though, political and economic intrigue culminated in the designation of Oklahoma City as the new capital. Guthrie's splendid commercial center, bypassed by development, remained intact through the succeeding decades. As a result, Guthrie today encompasses the largest contiguous urban district on the National Register of Historic Places, including more than 400 city blocks and more than 2,100 buildings.

If it's your first visit to Guthrie, you'll enjoy simply strolling the sidewalks, admiring the facades along Oklahoma Avenue and Harrison Street. Most of the buildings were constructed of red brick, but here and there native sandstone adds variety, as do colorfully painted trim and ornate Victorian details on roofs and windows. Several of Guthrie's most attractive structures were designed by French architect Joseph Foucart, including the 1890 **DeFord Building** on Second Street, with its fancy turret, and the imposing **Victor Building** at First and Harrison, with graceful arched windows and intricate cornices.

Oklahoma's pre-statehood years were a rough-and-ready era of "boomers" (those pushing for development of Indian Territory), "sooners" (people who slipped across the border before the official land rush to stake illegal claims), speculators, con artists, and roving outlaw gangs, as well as honest, hardworking settlers. The **Oklahoma Territorial Museum** interprets this pioneer period with exhibits on the Native American tribes that were forced to move here, historic land runs, early homesteaders, the first territorial towns, and bad guys like the Dalton and Doolin gangs. While you're visiting the museum, be sure to drop in next door at the 1902 **Carnegie Library,** which boasts impressive woodwork and a striking silver dome in the Second Empire Revival style.

Be sure, too, not to miss the **State Capital Publishing Museum,** which preserves in astounding detail what was once the largest printing plant west of the Mississippi. Housed in a 1902 brick building (also designed by Foucart) are an array of still-operational presses, Linotype machines, and a wonderful sales office that looks as though it was sealed decades ago and has slept untouched ever since. At the turn of the 20th century the *State Capital* newspaper, printed here, was one of the most influential periodicals in Oklahoma; in fact, a rivalry between the publisher and the first state governor was a factor in Guthrie's loss of the statehouse to Oklahoma City.

Completed in 1929 after nine years of construction, the **Guthrie Scottish Rite Masonic Center** sits on a plot of land east of downtown where the State Capitol was to be built—before it slipped away from town to Oklahoma City in 1910. As monumental as any governmental building, this columned edifice comprises 268,000 square feet (more than 6 acres) of marble, limestone, stained glass, murals, chandeliers, elaborate woodwork, and fascinating architectural details. On a tour through this huge space you'll admire the workmanship that went into its construction during the high-flying Roaring Twenties, right before the Depression put a damper on such ambitious projects.

Not nearly so big, but nearly as entertaining, the **Oklahoma Frontier Drugstore Museum** is set in the 1890 Gaffney Building downtown, next door to Guthrie's visitors bureau. Old-time remedies from heroin to witch-hazel bark fill antique cabinets and display cases, and posters advertise cure-alls in brands long vanished from modern pharmacies. It's lots of fun to browse the shelves here, and as you do you can't help but wonder how many people were actually helped, and how many made worse, by the strange concoctions on the market a century ago.

Right now you might enjoy a little refreshment yourself, so head a block south to the **Blue Belle Saloon,** a friendly local hangout with a tile floor, a tin ceiling, and a superb wood back bar. It's a fine place to have a drink and a sandwich and to meet some local folks. If you'd dropped in at the Blue Belle in 1902, you could have chatted with a bartender named Tom Mix, who later moved to Hollywood and became a famous cowboy-movie star during the silent era.

Restoration of Guthrie's venerable buildings has seen them converted into art galleries, antique shops, cafés, and a host of other uses. Today's city center increasingly is coming to replicate the scene in the early 20th century. In addition, more and more people have been moving into converted apartments above downtown businesses, adding liveliness to what is, despite its tourist attractions, a genuine Oklahoma town.

The growth and bustle of a contemporary state capital may have passed Guthrie by, but left behind was a true treasure of architectural heritage, a place where visitors can relive the heady spirit of one of America's most historic frontier boomtowns.

Mel White

Travelwise

GETTING THERE

Guthrie lies just west of I-35 in central Oklahoma, 30 miles north of Oklahoma City and 90 miles southwest of Tulsa. Major airlines serve Oklahoma City and Tulsa; Amtrak's *Heartland Flyer* stops in Oklahoma City.

GENERAL INFORMATION

Guthrie can be visited year-round; summers are often extremely hot, and the winter's north wind off the Great Plains is pretty chilly at times. The **Guthrie Convention and Visitors Bureau** is located in the historic Gaffney Building (*212 W. Oklahoma Ave., P.O. Box 995, Guthrie 73044. 405-282-1947 or 800-299-1889. www.guthrieok.com*).

THINGS TO SEE AND DO

Double Stop Fiddle Shop and Music Hall (*121. E. Oklahoma Ave. 405-282-6646. Closed Sun.; fee for concerts*) Former national fiddle champion Byron Berline, who's played and recorded with groups from Bill Monroe's Bluegrass Boys to the Rolling Stones, runs this music store with a concert hall upstairs; call for upcoming events, including combined barbecue dinners and concerts.

First Capital Trolley (*405-282-6000. Fare*) For an easy introduction to Guthrie's early days, hop aboard the First Capital Trolley, which takes on passengers at various stops for a 45-minute ride through downtown and residential neighborhoods. Narration points out entertaining historical and architectural highlights; after your ride you'll have a better idea which attractions you'd like to investigate further. Trolley rides begin on the corner of 2nd St. and W. Harrison Ave., in front of the State Capital Publishing Museum.

Guthrie Scottish Rite Masonic Center (900 E. Oklahoma Ave. 405-282-1281. Closed Sun. Adm. fee for tour) A huge classical-style structure with ornate furnishings and rooms in a wide variety of designs, well worth a visit.

Oklahoma Frontier Drugstore Museum (214 W. Oklahoma Ave. 405-282-1895. Closed Mon.) Old-time remedies, advertising materials, and antique drugstore furnishings are on display in an 1890 building.

Oklahoma Sports Museum (315 W. Oklahoma Ave. 405-260-1342. Closed Sun.; adm. fee) Displays and memorabilia honor Sooner State sports heroes, from baseball stars Mickey Mantle and Johnny Bench to Olympic decathalete, pro footballer, and baseball player Jim Thorpe to Olympic gymnast Shannon Miller to rodeo legend Jim Shoulders.

Oklahoma Territorial Museum (406 E. Oklahoma Ave. 405-282-1889. Closed Mon.; donation) Fine historical exhibits on the pre-statehood era of 1889 to 1907. Also part of the museum is the restored 1902 **Carnegie Library**, which stands next door.

Pollard Theatre (120 W. Harrison Ave. 405-282-2800) Oklahoma's only full-time professional theater group stages dramas, comedies, and musicals throughout the year in a restored vaudeville hall.

State Capital Publishing Museum (301 W. Harrison Ave. 405-282-4123. Closed Mon.) An excellent showplace of early printing equipment includes foot-powered presses and complex typesetting machines.

Walking Tours Guided visits of the town's historic, turn-of-the-20th-century neighborhoods are conducted by the Guthrie Chamber of Commerce (212 W. Oklahoma Ave. 405-282-1947 or 800-299-1889).

SHOPPING

Bah-Kho-Je Gallery (103 S. 2nd St.) Authentic Native American crafts, jewelry, paintings, and other art, much of it from Oklahoma's Iowa tribe.

Sorrell Custom Boots (306 W. Industrial Rd. 405-282-5464) Lisa Sorrell makes elaborate and beautiful cowboy boots in an amazing variety of styles, and welcomes visitors to her shop to see some of her designs.

ANNUAL EVENTS

89er Day Parade (Sat. in mid-April. 405-282-1947) Guthrie's largest parade showcases floats, music, and costumes galore.

International Bluegrass Festival (Early Oct. Various locations. 405-282-4446. Adm. fee) Music stars highlight this three-day event featuring bluegrass tunes at indoor and outdoor venues around town.

Territorial Christmas Celebration (Late Nov.–Christmas. Various locations. 405-282-1947 or 800-299-1889) A parade, home tours, and a Victorian Christmas Walk, with carolers and decorated store windows, are among the festivities during this holiday happening. There are also candle-lit trolley tours, theater productions, and other events on specific days throughout the holiday season.

WHERE TO EAT

Blue Belle Saloon (224 W. Harrison Ave. 405-260-2355. $$) Sandwiches and steaks in a longtime local favorite downtown, billed as "Oklahoma's oldest saloon."

Granny Had One (111 W. Harrison Ave. 405-282-4482. $$) An eclectic menu, fresh-baked bread, and fine desserts make this one of Guthrie's most popular restaurants.

WHERE TO STAY

Gold Penny Inn (1421 W. Noble St. 405-282-0678 or 877-837-4667. $$) Three rooms with private baths in a 1937 Williamsburg-style house in a residential neighborhood; notably fine breakfasts. Its Cowboy Tearoom serves "lots of vittles, not much tea."

Red Stone Country Inn (206 S. 2nd St. 405-282-2667. $$) Five suites with private baths in a downtown 1890s red sandstone building that was originally a wholesale grocer.

Victorian Garden Inn (324 S. Broad St. 405-282-8211 or 888-792-1092. $$) Four rooms with private baths in a 1908 colonial revival-style house furnished with fine antiques.

Eureka Springs

Driving to Eureka Springs along winding roads though the Arkansas Ozarks, and marveling at its setting in a steep, narrow valley, a traveler naturally might wonder, "Who decided to put a town here?" To learn of Eureka Springs's birth is to understand how this picturesque village full of Victorian houses came to be preserved—and how it became a lively, colorful haven for artists, mystics, and eccentrics of all persuasions.

In the mid-1800s, settlers in the remote Ozark mountains heard stories from Native Americans of "medicine springs" back in the hills. Occasionally an intrepid traveler would visit and come away claiming to have found relief from an illness or infirmity. Before long, a makeshift little settlement had grown up around the springs, and in 1879 it became an official town.

Flatiron Flats building, in downtown Eureka Springs

As it happened, Eureka Springs appeared on the map during a rampant American fad for "taking the waters," with a general belief in the power of "healing" springs. Eureka Springs quickly became a popular spa: Six trains a day brought eager bathers, and fancy hotels and bathhouses sprang up to accommodate them. Eureka Springs was a boomtown, boasting gas streetlights in 1894 and electric streetcars in 1898. "Where is there another health resort which has so much to offer the invalid as Eureka Springs?" asked city publicity in 1890.

But what booms often busts, and so went Eureka Springs, as modern medicine cast doubt on the power of spring water to cure disease. The "city that water built" sank into obscurity—and while other towns were tearing down their old buildings in the name of progress, Eureka Springs's endured.

Through the years, Eureka Springs's beautiful setting attracted people longing for a peaceful retreat, including painters, writers, and craftspeople. In the countercultural sixties, back-to-the-landers found Eureka Springs an open-minded spot to drop out of one life and start another. "You could dream here and make it happen," one such immigrant recalls.

The legacy of all this is today's Eureka Springs: a town where streets lined with restored 19th-century houses wind along tree-covered hillsides, where quaint limestone buildings downtown are home to art galleries, shops, and restaurants, and where you're likely to see almost anyone walking down the sidewalk, from straitlaced businesspeople to aging flower children to successful artists to out-there spiritualists—sometimes all the same person.

The **Eureka Springs Historical Museum,** downtown on Main Street, recounts the town's early days, when more than 50 hotels welcomed thousands of travelers annually. The 1889 limestone building houses historic photos, maps, and varied local memorabilia among its exhibits. After a visit here, walk north along Main Street and swing left on Spring Street. Here at **Basin Spring,** Osage Indians hollowed out a rock basin for bathing long before Europeans arrived on the scene. Today, the spring is at the center of a pretty park where special events are held throughout the year.

Pea Ridge

Travel 25 miles west of Eureka Springs on US 62 to visit the site of one of the largest Civil War battles west of the Mississippi at Pea Ridge National Military Park (501-451-8122). The "battle that saved Missouri for the Union" took place on March 7-8, 1862, when Confederate troops intending to capture St. Louis were intercepted by Union soldiers. The bloody battle ended when the Southerners, far from supply lines and low on ammunition, were forced to retreat. A self-guided, 7-mile auto loop leads past battle sites.

Stroll up Spring past stores, restaurants, art galleries, and antique shops; take time to drop in here and there to chat with the owners, who often have interesting stories to tell. If you're feeling energetic, continue as the street winds uphill to see some of the other springs that built the city. Several, such as **Harding Spring,** have been turned into miniature botanical gardens, with

Victorian splendor in Eureka Springs

colorful flowers, shrubs, and trees beneath striking limestone bluffs.

Here and there you'll notice stairways, some stone and some wooden, heading uphill from the street. These lead to a network of walking paths and alleys interlaced along the hill, skirting old rock walls shaded by oaks and maples. Exploring these paths is by far the best way to enjoy Eureka Springs's quirky architecture, with houses perched at odd angles on precipitous hillsides. At the same time, you'll leave behind the crowds of shoppers downtown. Don't worry about getting lost: Heading downhill will always return you to Spring Street eventually.

From many viewpoints, the dominant structure in Eureka Springs is the **Crescent Hotel** *(75 Prospect St. 501-253-9766),* a massive French Gothic stone building completed in 1886. Set castlelike atop a hill north of downtown, the Crescent has undergone a graceful restoration, and it's well worth a visit to see its old-fashioned lobby and, especially, to have a drink in the fourth-floor lounge and enjoy the evening view of Eureka Springs's tree-covered hills. Next door, stop in at **St. Elizabeth's Catholic Church.** While the turn-of-the-20th-century chapel and church feature lovely stained glass, they're best known for an aspect once described in *Ripley's Believe It Or Not:* Thanks to the hillside setting, visitors enter through the chapel bell tower.

Rambling around downtown's Main, Center, and Spring Streets, as well as walking the lanes above, can easily occupy a couple of days in Eureka Springs. To make your explorations more enjoyable, be sure to pick up the illustrated booklet describing six walking tours, available at the historical museum and from area merchants. With it you'll discover some of Eureka Springs's historic curiosities that you might otherwise miss. For example: Carry Nation, the renowned prohibitionist who used a hatchet to smash up midwestern saloons in the late 19th century, ran a girls' school here in 1910; and John Phillip Sousa, the march composer, conducted a concert to open the city auditorium in 1929.

South of downtown, motels and fast-food restaurants line US 62, but the highway leads to several worthwhile attractions. One of the finest rises in the woods a few miles west: **Thorncrown Chapel's** innovative design of glass and interlaced wood beams has earned some of the world's most prestigious architectural awards since its completion in 1980. This ethereal chapel was created by E. Fay Jones of nearby Fayetteville, winner of the Gold Medal of the American Institute of Architects.

Farther west, a side road off US 62 leads to **Eureka Springs Gardens** *(501-253-9244),* offering fine views of the White River Valley along the way. The gardens themselves, in a quiet hillside setting, center on Blue Spring, whose discharge powered a series of earlier mills dating back to pre-Civil War times. Paths wind through informal plantings covering 33 acres, and from spring through fall the woods and fields are filled with blooms, birds, and butterflies.

Though it's been overtaken in part by modern tourism, Eureka Springs remains an authentically historic small town, appealing both to those who simply want to gawk and shop and to those willing to dig deeper—to get to know the place and its people. Put yourself in the second group and you'll find a fascinating getaway here at the "city that water built," hidden in the hills of the Arkansas Ozarks. *Mel White*

Travelwise

GETTING THERE

Eureka Springs is in northwestern Arkansas, on US 62 between Rogers and Harrison; it's about 65 miles southwest of Springfield, Missouri. Several airlines fly to Springfield and to the Northwest Arkansas Regional Airport in Bentonville, about 55 miles west.

GENERAL INFORMATION

Spring and fall are the best times to visit. Summer is fine, though the town is usually crowded; fall weekends are also extremely popular. Walking is the best way to see the historic district, since traffic and parking both can be difficult. An alternative is to take the trolley; five color-coded routes pass nearly all local attractions. For more information, contact the **Eureka Springs Chamber of Commerce** *(Information Center, 137 W. Van Buren St./US 62, P.O. Box 551, Eureka Springs 72632. 501-253-8737. www.eurekasprings.org).*

THINGS TO SEE AND DO

Eureka Springs & North Arkansas Railway *(299 N. Main St. 501-253-9623. Closed Nov.-March; adm. fee)* Restored steam locomotives and passenger cars take riders on a short journey through wooded valleys.

Eureka Springs Historical Museum *(95 S. Main St. 501-253-9417. Adm. fee)* Local household items and other artifacts in an 1889 former grocery store and residence.

Kings River *(8 miles E of town on US 62. 501-253-8737)* A typically clear, beautiful Ozark stream with gorgeous scenery and good fishing for channel catfish and smallmouth bass. Kings River Outfitters *(501-253-8954)* can provide canoes and guides.

Lake Leatherwood City Park *(2 miles W on US 62. 501-253-8624. Boating and fishing fees)* A 1,600-acre park with hiking, biking, boating.

Last Precinct *(4 miles W of town on US 62. 501-253-4948. Closed Sun.-Mon.; adm. fee)* A collection of law enforcement gear.

Queen Anne Mansion *(Just W of Ark. 23 on US 62. 501-253-8825. Adm. fee)* An 1891 house with intricate woodwork.

Thorncrown Chapel *(1 mile W of town on US 62. 501-253-7401. Closed Jan.-Feb.; donation)* An award-winning wood-and-glass building.

ANNUAL EVENTS

Blues Festival *(1st weekend after Mem. Day. Downtown. 501-253-5366. Adm. fee)* Nationally known blues artists perform.

Ozark Folk Festival *(Fall. Downtown. 501-253-5366. Adm. fee)* Begun in 1947, this renowned festival is the oldest of its type west of the Mississippi.

WHERE TO EAT

Autumn Breeze *(0.5 mile S of town off US 62, via Ark. 23 S. 501-253-7734. Closed Sun. Dinner only. $$)* Upscale Continental food (try the rack of lamb), steaks; excellent wine list.

Center Street South *(10 Center St. 501-253-8102. Closed Tues.-Wed. $$)* Mexican and Caribbean food in a friendly, informal local hangout downtown.

Cottage Inn *(US 62 W. 501-253-5282. Closed Sun.-Mon. Dinner only. $$)* Greek, Italian, and French cooking at a long-time local favorite.

WHERE TO STAY

Ellis House *(1 Wheeler St. 501-253-8218 or 800-243-8218. $$)* Five rooms in a secluded, 1933 English Tudor-style house.

Enchanted Cottages *(18 Nut St. 800-862-2788. $$)* Three cottages on a quiet street.

Heartstone Inn and Cottages *(35 Kingshighway. 501-253-8916 or 800-494-4921. $$)* Ten rooms with private baths and two separate cottages.

Rock Cottage Gardens *(10 Eugenia St. 501-253-8659 or 800-624-6646. $$)* Five nicely decorated cottages.

Fredericksburg

Travel west from Austin into the rolling woods and fields of the Texas Hill Country and you'll find Fredericksburg, a town that preserves a fascinating chapter of the Lone Star State's history. Here, the legacy of German immigrants has endured for more than 150 years, as authentic as the taste of homemade apple strudel.

Fredericksburg was founded in 1846 by a small group of German settlers fleeing religious oppression and economic hardships in their homeland. These 120 or so original pioneers brought the food, architecture, and traditions of the Old World to their new community on the American frontier. Living in relative isolation for decades, they and their descendants maintained German customs even as they adapted to their Texas environment: German was spoken commonly on the streets of Fredericksburg well into the 20th century, and events such as the *Schuetzenfest* (shooting competition) and the *Saengerfest* (singing festival) were, and still are, part of the town's lifestyle.

Today's Fredericksburg is probably more Texas than Deutschland, but evidence of the town's heritage is everywhere. German names on businesses, *fachwerk* (half-timbered) buildings, and German restaurants and bakeries coexist with cowboy hats, pickup trucks, and barbecue and fajitas.

Take a walk past the limestone storefronts on Main Street and note the width of this thoroughfare: The first settlers made it broad enough that an ox-drawn wagon could turn around. At the **Marktplatz,** the town's Market Square, visit the distinctively shaped **Vereins Kirche** (Community Church), which houses a small museum recalling the founding and early days of Fredericksburg. The original Vereins Kirche was constructed in 1847 and served as a church, school, and meeting hall; torn down in 1897, it was reconstructed by the local historical society in 1936. Its unusual eight-sided design inspired the nickname die Kaffee Mühle Kirche: the coffee-mill church.

From here it's just a couple of blocks west to the **Pioneer Museum Complex,** a fine collection of structures interpreting local history. Enter through an 1849 general store displaying fachwerk construction, and continue out back to a smokehouse and barn typical of a German pioneer homestead. An 1880s log cabin and a 1920s one-room school are among the other buildings here, but the most distinctive is an example of a unique bit of Fredericksburg history called a "Sunday house." From about 1890 to 1920, families living in the country often built tiny second houses in town, where they stayed overnight between Saturday shopping and Sunday church. Several of these quaint houses remain standing; the museum's **Weber Sunday House** dates from about 1904, and its size and simplicity, though surprising to modern eyes, are standard for its type.

Head back east now on Main. (If you're feeling hungry you'll find no shortage of possibilities along the way, from good restaurants to a brew pub to authentic German-style bakeries.) At Washington Street, you can't miss the elaborate facade of the **Admiral Nimitz Museum,** located in a restored 1850s

Strolling down Fredericksburg's Main Street

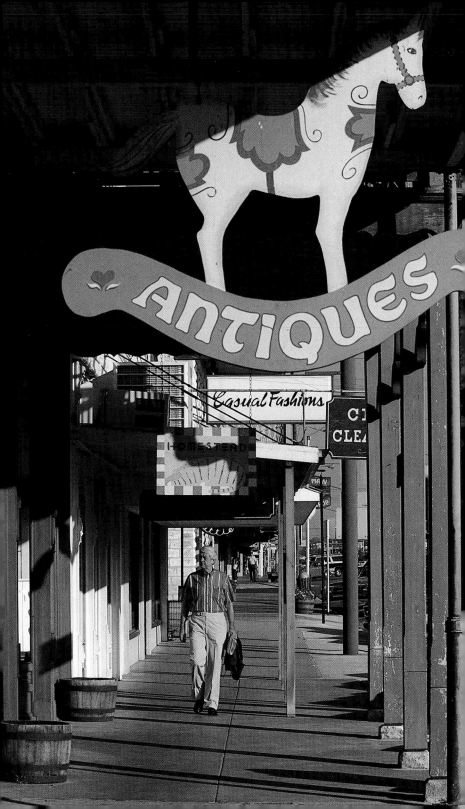

Admiral Nimitz Museum, shaped like a ship's helm

hotel once owned by the grandfather of Fleet Admiral Chester W. Nimitz, commander of the U.S. Pacific naval forces in World War II. The museum's excellent exhibits tell the story not just of Nimitz but of all the men and women who served in that long and bloody campaign. For many people, a visit to this superb museum is the highlight of a trip to Fredericksburg.

In its early days, the Nimitz Hotel was the only proper inn between San Antonio and San Diego, and guests included Robert E. Lee, Rutherford B. Hayes, and O. Henry. Today it's dedicated to the life of Admiral Nimitz, who grew up in Fredericksburg and went on to command a force of more than two million in World War II. Nimitz treated the Japanese people with respect after the conflict, and the **Japanese Garden of Peace** behind the hotel, created by Japanese gardeners in 1976 as a symbol of that country's appreciation, is a tranquil place to sit and consider the lessons of war.

Nearby, the **National Museum of the Pacific War George Bush Gallery** takes visitors through the course of the hostilities, from the first Japanese expansionist policies to surrender in September 1945. Photos, artifacts, and realistic environmental exhibits make this an educational and compelling experience. The gallery was dedicated in 1999 by former President George Bush, who served as a Navy pilot in World War II and earned the Distinguished Flying Cross. Two blocks away, the **History Walk of the Pacific War** displays tanks, warplanes, artillery, and other equipment on more than three acres of grounds.

Two attractions outside of Fredericksburg might at first seem to appeal mostly to nature-lovers, but in fact both are so spectacular that no one should miss them. First, drive north 18 miles on Ranch Rd. 965 to **Enchanted Rock State Natural Area,** home of one of the most amazing sights in all of Texas. At the center of the park is a gigantic dome of pink granite, rising 400 feet above the surrounding terrain and covering about 70 acres—the second largest single mass of exposed granite in the country, after Georgia's Stone Mountain. Just to gaze at this massive monolith is astonishing. Better yet, put on sturdy shoes and walk to the top. While the climb is more than a gentle stroll, it's not too difficult, and the summit panorama is well worth the effort. Enchanted Rock is a small and very popular park, and when visitation reaches capacity it closes until late afternoon; visit on a weekday if possible.

To reach the other nature site, drive a mile east from Fredericksburg on US 290, turn south on the Old San Antonio Road, and drive 11 miles to the **Old Tunnel Wildlife Management Area.** Here, in an abandoned tunnel of the defunct Fredericksburg & Northern Railway, more than one million Mexican free-tailed bats roost from late spring to fall. Around dusk each day, the bats emerge for their nightly hunting flights in a dramatic whirl of tiny winged bodies. A free viewing deck allows good looks at this phenomenon, while on Thursday and Saturday nights from June to October wildlife officials lead special tours (for a fee) to a lower level for closer observation.

On either of these drives, or any other route out of Fredericksburg, you'll experience one of the major pleasures of a visit here: the landscape of the Hill Country itself. It's easy to see why this region has long been so popular for vacations and retirement. There's something especially appealing about the oak-covered hills and clear rivers, a terrain with just the right blend of ruggedness and peaceful, parklike vistas. Combine Hill Country scenery with the attractions of a friendly small town like Fredericksburg and you have a near-perfect respite from big-city pressure—a spot where echoes of a simpler time are as pervasive as sunshine on a summer afternoon. *Mel White*

Travelwise

GETTING THERE

Fredericksburg is in central Texas, at the junction of US 290 and US 87, about 70 miles northwest of San Antonio and 80 miles west of Austin. Major airlines serve both those cities, as does Amtrak.

GENERAL INFORMATION

Fredericksburg can be visited year-round, though spring and fall are most pleasant; summer can bring spells of very hot temperatures. The town can be extremely crowded during festivals such as Oktoberfest. For information contact the **Fredericksburg Visitor Information Center** (*106 N. Adams St., Fredericksburg 78624. 830-997-6523 or 888-997-3600*).

THINGS TO SEE AND DO

Admiral Nimitz Historical Center (*340 E. Main St. 830-997-4379. Adm. fee*) An excellent assemblage of historical sites

honoring native son Chester W. Nimitz and recounting the story of the war in the Pacific. The center's scattered sites include the Admiral Nimitz Museum, Japanese Garden of

Peace, National Museum of the Pacific War George Bush Gallery, and History Walk of the Pacific War.

Fort Martin Scott Historic Site *(1606 E. Main St. 830-997-9895. Closed Mon.-Thurs.; adm. fee)* Reconstructed buildings of Texas' first frontier military post, active from 1848 to 1853.

Pioneer Museum Complex *(309 W. Main St. 830-997-2835. Adm. fee)* An 1849 general store, an 1880s barn, a fire department museum, and a 1904 "Sunday house" are among the structures at this historical complex.

Vereins Kirche *(W. Main St. bet. Adams and Crockett Sts. 830-997-2835. Adm. fee)* This reconstruction of the 1847 community church features displays on Fredericksburg's early days.

SHOPPING

Wildseed Farms Market Center *(7 miles E of town on US 290. 830-990-1393)* A working wildflower farm with expansive fields of brilliant color, especially in spring. Many varieties of seeds are for sale.

Wineries Several wineries in the Fredericksburg area produce an array of vintages and offer tastings. Ask for directions at the information center.

ANNUAL EVENTS

Easter Fires Pageant *(Sat. before Easter. Gillespie Cty. Fairgrounds, Tex. 16 S. 830-997-2359. Adm. fee)* Local actors reenact a story from the town's early days, in which a mother comforted her children when they were frightened by Indian signal fires on nearby hilltops.

Food and Wine Fest *(4th weekend in Oct. Market Sq. 830-997-8515)* A celebration of Texas wine and food; entertainment and cooking demonstrations.

Oktoberfest *(1st weekend in Oct. Market Sq. 830-997-4810. Adm. fee)* A popular traditional German festival, with polka music, German food, arts and crafts, and children's activities.

WHERE TO EAT

Der Lindenbaum *(312 E. Main St. 830-997-9126. $$)* Authentic German schnitzels, sausages, and pastries.

Hill Top Cafe *(10 miles N of town on US 87. 830-997-8922. Closed Mon.-Tues. $)* A lively, informal spot well worth the drive; Cajun and Greek specialties and live music on weekends.

Navajo Grill *(209 E. Main St. 830-990-8289. Closed Sun.-Mon. $$)* An excellent selection of dishes combine Southwestern, Louisiana, and Caribbean cooking; fine desserts.

The Nest *(607 S. Washington St. 830-990-8383. Closed Tues.-Wed. Dinner only. $$)* Well-prepared seafood, pasta, and steaks.

WHERE TO STAY

Fredericksburg has a remarkable abundance of B&Bs and guest houses. The information center can provide a list; there are also several reservation services that offer advice and bookings.

Das Garten Haus *(604 S. Washington St. 830-990-8408 or 800-416-4287. $$)* Two spacious suites and a separate cottage, all with private baths and access to a nicely landscaped courtyard garden.

Hoffman Haus *(608 E. Creek Rd. 830-997-6739 or 800-899-1672. $$)* A secluded compound with 11 rooms, all with private baths and each decorated with a distinctive theme.

Schandua Suite *(205 E. Main St. 830-990-1415 or 888-990-1415. $$$)* A very large upstairs suite in an 1897 limestone building.

NEARBY PLACES

Enchanted Rock State Natural Area *(18 miles N of town on RR 965. 915-247-3903. Adm. fee)* Don't miss a visit to this huge mass of pink granite, thought to be one billion years old; hiking trails, primitive camping.

Lyndon B. Johnson National Historical Park *(16 miles E of town on US 290, near Stonewall. 830-868-7128)* The park includes bus tours of the LBJ Ranch and visits to the boyhood home of the former President in Johnson City, 15 miles farther east. Adjacent in Stonewall is the **Lyndon B. Johnson State Historical Park** *(830-644-2252)*, with a visitor center, nature trail, longhorn cattle, and a living-history farm.

Old Tunnel Wildlife Management Area *(11 miles S of town via Old San Antonio Rd. 830-644-2478)* Nightly from June to October, there's viewing of the emergence of thousands of Mexican free-tailed bats from their daytime roost in an old train tunnel.

Rockport

Set at the midpoint of the Texas Gulf Coast's nearly 400-mile arc of beach and bay, Rockport offers in microcosm much of what makes this region such an appealing destination. From nature and history to deep-sea fishing to just lazing on the sand, the pleasures of a gulfside getaway await in this friendly community amid the live oaks on Aransas Bay.

The shrimp boats in the harbor, the barges on the Intracoastal Waterway, and the tractors on the surrounding cotton fields show that Rockport is a working town, not just a seaside resort. You can enjoy the fruits of some of this labor by going down to **Rockport Harbor** during the day, when the fishing boats come in, and buying shrimp, croaker, flounder, and other seafood delights right off the piers. Many of the boatmen enjoy talking with visitors, so don't hesitate to ask questions if you're curious about the boats or their catch.

Rockport sunrise

If you'd like to try your hand at harvesting some of the Gulf's bounty, walk the short distance to the **Rockport-Fulton Area Chamber of Commerce Visitor Center** and pick up a list of charter fishing boats and professional guides. These services can arrange everything from license to gear, and before you know it you could be reeling in a redfish or spotted speckled trout.

If, on the other hand, you're a staunch landlubber, the visitor center can provide all sorts of information about Rockport's attractions on terra firma. Take a stroll down adjacent Austin Street with the downtown walking-tour brochure and learn which of the buildings survived the massive hurricane that flattened much of Rockport in 1919. You'll find interesting shops and galleries all along this one-mile route.

On your return to the visitor center, it's just a few steps to the **Texas Maritime Museum,** full of fascinating displays showing the growth of the Texas Gulf Coast and relating Texas' maritime history, beginning with the first French and Spanish explorers and continuing to modern fishing fleets and oil platforms. Climb up to the mock-up of a ship's bridge, from which you can look out on Rockport Harbor and Aransas Bay and see the interaction of people and sea right before your eyes. A collection of watercolors of Texas lighthouses recalls the days when navigation aids were less certain than today's high-tech devices. Outside, admire the "scow sloop" replica, a specialized type of fishing boat used locally from the mid-1800s to the 1950s.

Over the years Rockport has attracted an active and accomplished arts community, and samples of the resulting work are displayed at the **Rockport Center for the Arts.** Set on the harbor in a restored Victorian-era house, the center features—as you might expect—many works depicting seashores, boats, and waterbirds, and much of it is of very good quality.

Right next to the arts center you'll find the entrance to **Rockport Beach Park,** a neat, mile-long strip of sandy beach and picnic shelters perfect for sunning and swimming on a hot summer day. The waves are relatively gentle here, since Rockport is sheltered from the main Gulf of Mexico by St. Joseph Island, a barrier island a few miles from the mainland.

Don't miss a visit to **Fulton Mansion State Historical Park,** on the bayfront just north of Rockport. Built in the late 1870s by George Fulton, who'd made a fortune in the cattle business, this elegant and ornate French Second Empire-style house features a remarkable array of innovative construction techniques and conveniences, including central heat, gas lighting, and modern plumbing. The house was one of the few local structures to survive the 1919 hurricane, which won't seem surprising when you see how it was constructed: Its extra-thick walls and floors use "enough wood to build a small subdivision today," as one park interpreter put it.

Definitely on the list of memorable local sights: Drive north across the Copano Bay causeway to **Goose Island State Park,** famed as the home of the **Big Tree,** a spectacular coastal live oak estimated to be over 1,000 years old. The largest of its type in Texas, this venerable tree has a crown spread of 89 feet, and is said to have been a meeting spot for the Native Americans who lived along the coast before the arrival of Europeans.

Rockport has long been especially renowned among one specialized group

Fulton Mansion State Historical Park

of visitors. Bird-watchers enjoy the great variety of species attracted to the area's waters, beaches, and woodland, and a guide to local birding "hot spots" is available at the visitor center. The most famous feathered resident (at least from mid-October through March) is the very rare whooping crane, which numbers fewer than 300 individuals in the wild. The largest wild flock (183 members) nests in the Northwest Territories and winters in or near **Aransas National Wildlife Refuge,** 35 miles north of Rockport. The best way to see this tall, white bird with black-tipped wings is to take a guided boat tour from one of the docks in the Rockport area (the visitor center can provide a list). Although much of the refuge is off-limits to protect this critically endangered species, a pair of cranes can frequently be spotted from the observation tower there.

Even if you're not a birder when you come to Rockport, the odds are you'll be at least a little bit converted by the time you leave. Birds are so abundant and conspicuous here that you're bound to notice, and to wonder, "What is that?" From huge brown pelicans to tall, stately herons to the ubiquitous gulls to the colorful roseate spoonbill, birds are ever present. Rockport salutes them with its annual **Hummer/Bird Celebration** in September, a festival recognizing the great number of hummingbirds that throng the town in fall migration, along with other varieties present throughout the year.

Whether you enjoy the solitude of a nature trail or the lively dinner scene at a local seafood restaurant, Rockport is almost certain to offer something you'll savor. It might well be that, after your first visit, you'll become a regular migrant yourself.   *Mel White*

Travelwise

GETTING THERE

Rockport is located on Tex. 35 in southern Texas. Major airlines fly to Corpus Christi, 30 miles north.

GENERAL INFORMATION

Rockport's subtropical climate makes it a year-round destination, though spring and fall are best. Summers are hot and very humid, but the beach is most appealing then; winters are mild. For information contact the **Rockport-Fulton Area Chamber of Commerce Visitor Center** at Rockport Harbor (404 Broadway, Rockport 78382. 361-729-6445 or 800-242-0071).

THINGS TO SEE AND DO

Aransas National Wildlife Refuge (35 miles N of town via Tex. 35 and RR 774 and 2040. 361-286-3559. Adm. fee) Walking nature trails and driving the 16-mile auto loop will likely turn up deer, alligators, turkeys, and more.

Birding The Texas Gulf Coast rates among the country's best bird-watching areas. Ask at the visitor center for a guide to nearby birding spots. From mid-Oct. through March, guided boat trips take visitors across Aransas Bay to see the rare whooping crane.

Fishing Rockport is celebrated for its varied fishing, both inshore and deep-sea. The visitor center has a list of charter boats and guides, or cast a line from one of the public piers.

Fulton Mansion State Historical Park (317 Fulton Beach Rd. 361-729-0386. Closed Mon.-Tues.; adm. fee) Guided tours through an 1877 house noted for innovative construction.

Goose Island State Park (10 miles N of town via Tex. 35 and Park Rd. 13. Adm. fee) Nature trails, fishing, and the Big Tree.

Rockport Center for the Arts (902 Navigation Circle. 361-729-5519. Closed Mon.) Changing exhibits, many featuring local artists.

Texas Maritime Museum (1202 Navigation Circle. 361-729-1271. Closed Mon.; adm. fee) Exhibits focus on the influence of the Gulf on Texas maritime history.

ANNUAL EVENTS

Fulton Oysterfest (1st weekend in March. Fulton Navigation Park. 361-729-2388. Adm.

fee) This popular celebration salutes the local oyster industry.

Hummer/Bird Celebration (Mid-Sept. Various sites. 361-729-6445 or 800-242-0071. Adm. fee) Programs and field trips center on the migration of ruby-throated hummingbirds and other species through the Rockport area.

Rockport Seafair (2nd weekend in Oct. Festival grounds. 361-729-3312. Adm. fee) Fresh seafood, music, arts and crafts, and crab races.

WHERE TO EAT

Boiling Pot (201 S. Fulton Beach Rd. 361-729-6972. $$) A popular, informal spot featuring Cajun-style seafood and other ocean treats.

Charlotte Plummer's Seafare (202 N. Fulton Beach Rd. 361-729-1185. $) Seafood and steaks. Its deck overlooks Fulton Harbor.

WHERE TO STAY

Blue Heron Inn (801 Patton St. 361-729-7526. $$) Four rooms in an 1890 federal-style house just across from Little Bay.

Chandler House (801 S. Church St. 361-729-2285 or 800-843-1808. $$) Three rooms in an 1874 house in a residential area.

Hoopes' House (417 N. Broadway. 361-729-8424 or 800-924-1008. $$) Eight rooms in a beautiful 1890s Queen Anne-style house.

Fort Davis

Out in the West Texas territory known as the Trans-Pecos, the Davis Mountains rise majestically from the vast surrounding Chihuahuan Desert grassland. In this dramatic setting of rugged volcanic spires, the town of Fort Davis invites travelers to explore its Wild West history, enjoy its natural beauty—and even to venture into the far reaches of the universe itself.

As its name implies, Fort Davis began as a military outpost. In 1854, when Mescalero Apache and Comanche warriors dominated much of the Southwest, the U.S. Army established a garrison to try to protect transportation on the increasingly well-traveled route between San Antonio and El Paso. Set beside cottonwoods just south of Limpia Creek, the fort was named for Secretary of War Jefferson Davis, who seven years later would assume the presidency of the Confederacy during the Civil War.

Fort Davis National Historic Site preserves the remains, not of the original fort (which was abandoned during the Civil War and destroyed by Indians), but of a second fort built on the same plot of land beginning in 1867, with construction continuing into the 1880s. Of the more than 50 buildings here, some exist only as rock foundations or ghostly ruins, while others have

The historic fort

Old barracks at Fort Davis National Historic Site

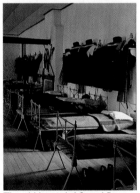

The old barracks' Squad Room

been restored much as they were 120 years ago. Bunks ready for inspection line the enlisted men's barracks, and family furnishings and personal items bring the commanding officer's house to life. At regular intervals during the day, bugle calls ring out across the parade ground as they did when the notes regulated the lives of the soldiers here.

Westward-bound immigrants, merchants, and the Butterfield Overland Mail traveled that early road past Fort Davis, and eventually a town grew up near the post, beside the rock formations of Sleeping Lion Mountain—a town that survived after the fort was abandoned in 1891. With the threat of Indian attack gone, the Davis Mountains region became cattle country; settlers established sprawling ranches in the foothills, stocking them with herds of Herefords. You'll find memorabilia of those early ranching days at Fort Davis's **Overland Trail Museum,** along with other local historical items and photos filling the rooms of a restored 1883 structure.

Some of the most interesting buildings in Fort Davis's diminutive town center date from the early years of the 20th century. The **Jeff Davis County Courthouse** *(State St. and Court Ave.),* with its silvery clock dome, was erected in 1911, and the picturesque **Fort Davis State Bank** across the street was built two years later (be sure to drop in to see the old-time teller's window in the nicely restored interior). Just across the square, the 1906 **Union Mercantile Building,** for decades the major business in Fort Davis, has been converted for use as the county library.

In the days before air-conditioning, Fort Davis's 5,050-foot elevation attracted vacationing Texans eager to escape the heat and humidity of the eastern part of the state. Locals called these migratory visitors "summer swallows." Many of them stayed at the **Hotel Limpia,** which was established in 1884 but moved into a new stone building in 1913. The Limpia still welcomes travelers today at its location on the town square, and its restaurant still serves tasty home-style cooking.

After you've looked around town a bit, follow Tex. 118 up Limpia Creek to **Davis Mountains State Park,** just 4 miles away. Admire the superb scenery from viewpoints along Skyline Drive, and then visit the park's **Indian Lodge,** an inn built in the 1930s in the pueblo style, with adobe walls 18 inches thick. While you're in the park, a morning or evening hike through grassland studded with juniper and yucca might reward you with views of javelina (a piglike mammal), mule deer, a road-runner, or even the shy, colorful Montezuma quail.

Beyond the park, Tex. 118 winds up 13 miles to **McDonald Observatory,** where massive telescope domes sit atop 6,792-foot Mount Locke. Some of the world's most important astronomical research is carried out here; tours of the facility let visitors see some of what goes on, and regularly scheduled "star parties" allow viewing of the moon, planets, and other celestial bodies.

For views that are more down-to-earth, but beautiful in their own right, keep driving on Tex. 118 to its junction with Tex. 166; turn southwest to make a 74-mile circle back to Fort Davis. This loop winds uphill past slopes covered in oak, juniper, and pine before heading back down into rolling grassland. Craggy mountain peaks and striking rock formations make this one of Texas' most scenic drives.

Nearly all the land along this drive is private, so if you want to venture out on foot you'll need to return to the state park, or drive south from Fort Davis a few miles on Tex. 118 to the **Chihuahuan Desert Research Institute,** a facility dedicated to studying the arid ecological region that stretches from the southwestern U.S. south into Mexico. Here you're welcome to stop in at the visitor center, enjoy the cactus greenhouse, or hike two trails meandering across high desert grassland.

Buffalo Soldiers

When the U.S. Army returned to Fort Davis in 1867, African-American troops (popularly known as Buffalo soldiers) took on the tasks of rebuilding the post, protecting traffic on the San Antonio-El Paso road, and fighting Apache and Comanche in the Trans-Pecos region. Among the first blacks to serve in the West, they compiled a distinguished record, which included a hard-fought campaign against Apache warrior Geronimo. By the time the Buffalo soldiers left Fort Davis in 1885, the Trans-Pecos was in large part a safe place for travelers and settlers alike.

With its Old West heritage and gorgeous mountain setting, Fort Davis amply repays the trip to reach it across the immense Trans-Pecos landscape. That you're tracing a path traveled by Army troops, gold-hungry immigrants bound for California, and stagecoach lines makes your visit even more evocative—a journey back in time to one of the small town gems of Texas.   *Mel White*

Travelwise

GETTING THERE

Fort Davis is located in West Texas, at the junction of Tex. 17 and Tex. 118, about 210 miles southeast of El Paso and 75 miles southwest of Pecos. Airlines serve Midland-Odessa, 160 miles northeast. Amtrak stops in Alpine, 26 miles southeast.

GENERAL INFORMATION

Fort Davis can be visited year-round; summers are made pleasant by its nearly mile-high elevation, and winters rarely see severe weather. For information contact the **Fort Davis Chamber of Commerce** *(Jct. of Tex. 17 and 118, at S end of town. P.O. Box 378, Fort Davis 79734. 915-426-3015 or 800-524-3015. www.fortdavis.com).*

THINGS TO SEE AND DO

Chihuahuan Desert Research Institute *(4 miles S on Tex. 118. 915-364-2499. Closed weekends Sept.-April; donation)* Greenhouse, arboretum, and hiking trails interpreting the ecology of the Chihuahuan Desert.

Davis Mountains State Park *(4 miles N on Tex. 118. 915-426-3337. Adm. fee)* Hiking trails allow exploration of the foothills grassland, and Skyline Drive offers good views of the surrounding mountains; **Indian Lodge** is a pueblo-style inn with a good restaurant.

Fort Davis National Historic Site *(Just N of town on Tex. 17/118. 915-426-3224. Adm. fee)* Restored buildings of a mid-19th-century Army post, along with a museum, picnic ground, and nature trails.

McDonald Observatory *(17 miles N of town on Tex. 118. 915-426-3640. Adm fee)* Tours of the world-famous astronomical research institute, and "star parties" with public viewing of celestial objects on Tuesday, Friday, and Saturday nights.

Overland Trail Museum *(3rd and Fort Sts. 915-426-3904. March-Sept. Tues., Fri., and Sat.; adm fee)* Local artifacts include early ranching gear, a saddle collection, antiques, old photos, and a restored kitchen and barbershop.

ANNUAL EVENTS

Friends of Fort Davis National Historic Site Festival *(Sat. before Columbus Day. 915-926-3224)* Enjoy reenactments of life in the 1880s

Hummingbird Round-up *(One midsummer weekend. In town and Davis Mountains SP. 915-426-3015 or 800-524-3015. Adm. fee)* A festival centered on hummingbirds, with feeder tours and bird-banding.

Old-fashioned Fourth of July *(915-426-3015 or 800-524-3015)* A popular traditional celebration with a parade, melodrama performance, street dance, bank "robbery," and arts and crafts on the courthouse lawn.

WHERE TO EAT

Cueva de Leon *(Main St. 915-426-3801. Closed Sun. $)* A local favorite for Mexican food.

The Drug Store *(Main St. 915-426-3118. $$)* Popular for breakfast and lunch, homemade burgers, and chicken-fried steak.

Hotel Limpia Dining Room *(Main St. 915-426-3241. $$)* Fine home-style food.

Pop's Grill *(Main St. 915-426-3195. $)* A popular diner known for its hamburgers.

WHERE TO STAY

Hotel Limpia *(Main St. 915-426-3237 or 800-662-5517. $$)* A restored 1913 inn with rooms in three downtown buildings, plus separate houses and cottages.

Prude Ranch *(6 miles N on Tex. 118. 915-426-3202 or 800-458-6232. $)* Horseback riding, hiking, birding, and chuckwagon cookouts are among the attractions at this famed 1,200-acre ranch, established by the Prude family in 1897.

Veranda Country Inn Bed and Breakfast *(1 block W of courthouse on Court St. 915-426-2233 or 888-383-2847. $$)* Built in 1883 as a hotel, this popular adobe-walled B&B offers 14 rooms and suites.

ROCKIES AND THE SOUTHWEST

McCall

McCall is a sure-fire antidote for anyone suffering from big-city blahs. Tucked away on the shore of a sapphire-blue lake in the sunny, forested uplands of north-central Idaho, it's a place to kick back, chill out, and savor the glories of the great outdoors.

McCall's sunny skies, crystalline air, and picture-postcard setting on Payette Lake have an invigorating allure that draws people back year after year. Poised on the edge of 3.5 million square miles of backcountry wilderness, it's the sort of place where people routinely ask, "Did you see any elk today?" If a bear is caught scavenging in a resident's backyard, the local paper dutifully reports on the attempts by "Fish and Game" to get rid of it.

Finnish Influences

McCall is one of several small towns in Long Valley, an area settled by Finnish immigrants in the 1890s. By 1905 Finns made up about 40 percent of the local population. They were noted for their building skills, and some of the earliest Finnish log houses, saunas, and farm buildings are still in use today.

Life is simpler here, and you notice it in little ways. When a local gives you a McCall phone number, it's always four digits. Why? Because the first three numbers are the same everywhere in town. There's a different aesthetic, too, one that is rustic, woodsy, and based on the log cabin and Western lodge. Don't be surprised if you come across elk antlers being used for the base of a lamp or the legs of a table.

Founded in 1901, McCall is not particularly old, but it does have a long history as a resort town. For decades it was a place where city-dwelling husbands (particularly from Boise) sent their wives and families for the summer, joining them on weekends. Much of the architecture reflects that not-so-distant but now bygone era. Comfy lakeside cabins are nestled in the beautiful ponderosa pine forest that surrounds Payette Lake. There are a couple of lakefront resorts and some expensive newer houses, but overall the town is as straightforward and unpretentious as a snapshot taken with a Kodak Brownie in the 1950s.

The center of the village, clustered around the **Hotel McCall** on the south side of the lake, has changed over the years. Now that the train is no longer running, the depot has been made over into a tiny retail-restaurant mall but still maintains its small town feel. There's a sandy public beach right across the street, and just down the road are the eight buildings that comprise the **Central Idaho Cultural Center.** Dating from the 1930s, these structures form a small "campus" built by and for the Southern Idaho Timber Protection Association (which later fell under the auspices of the U.S. Forestry Service). The dovetailed log construction used for some of the buildings was a characteristic style of the Finns who settled in the area. The **Fire Warden's House,** completed in 1937 by the Civilian Conservation Corps, is the gem of this collection: Completely intact, with different woods used for every interior

Quiet retreat on Payette Lake

surface, it reveals a level of craftsmanship (and a quality of lumber) that is rare today. All the furniture and contents are original.

In the summer, as families return to their lakeside cabins and nature-starved adventurers arrive to take advantage of the area's almost limitless recreational opportunities, the town's full-time population of 3,600 swells to about three times that number. But residents pride themselves on the year-round appeal of McCall, and the sense of community is never stronger than during preparations for Winter Carnival. That's when generations of families gather, as they've done for years, to create the splendid ice sculptures that people come from miles around to see. Under its blanket of snow, McCall becomes a stage for outdoor bonfires, barbecues, and every winter sport you can think of. Just outside of town, at the 7,640-foot **Brundage Mountain Resort,** downhill and cross-country skiers enjoy some of the best powder in the Northwest—and a spectacular vista that stretches from the Seven Devils Mountains in northwest Idaho west across Hells Canyon to the Wallowa Mountains in Oregon.

Frozen solid in the winter, the pristine waters of 7-mile-long **Payette Lake** remain briskly fresh through the hottest summer months. The breezy blue lake is used for every kind of water sport—sailing, swimming, canoeing, water-skiing, fishing, even scuba diving.

If you're looking for a secluded beach, a beautiful walk, or a special picnic spot, head for **Ponderosa State Park,** located on the peninsula that juts into the lake just northeast of town. Giant ponderosa pines reign supreme here, but you'll also see a mix of the other softwood trees—Engelmann spruce, black cottonwood, larch, lodgepole pine, and aspen—found throughout this rugged part of Idaho. The resiny scents of the forest, particularly on a hot summer's day, are intoxicating.

The people of McCall live with the knowledge that complete solitude is never far away. The town is located in the vast **Payette National Forest,** which abuts the 2.3-million-acre **Frank Church-River of No Return Wilderness,** the largest chunk of protected American wilderness outside Alaska. There are some 300 lakes within a 20-mile radius of McCall, some so remote that anglers hire planes to drop them off in the morning and pick them up at night. Elk, bear, mountain lions, moose, deer, and pronghorn roam through the grassy uplands and thickly forested alpine terrain.

That's the glory of the place. You can use McCall as a springboard for as much in-your-face nature as you can handle. But if your idea of a wilderness adventure is sipping a glass of wine while contemplating beautiful scenery from a lakeside resort or cabin, you don't have to leave town at all.

Donald S. Olson

Travelwise

GETTING THERE

McCall is located about 100 miles north of Boise on Idaho 55, in an area of north-central Idaho known as the Heartland. You really need to have a car or sport-utility vehicle to explore this area. Salmon Air Taxi *(800-448-3413)* provides air service to and from Boise.

GENERAL INFORMATION

Every season has its own beauty and recreational attractions. Summers are generally sunny and warm, winters brisk and snowy but rarely bitingly cold. You can pick up information about the town and surrounding region at the **McCall Area Chamber of Commerce** *(1001 State St., McCall 83638. 208-634-7631)* or at the **McCall Welcome Center** (In the McCall Mall, *317 E. Lake St. 208-634-6084*).

THINGS TO SEE AND DO

Central Idaho Cultural Center *(120 Lake St. 208-634-4497. Call for hours)* Built in the 1930s by master craftsmen, the eight historic buildings range from a perfectly preserved CCC-constructed Fire Warden's house to smaller outbuildings.

Mountain Sports For skiing, Brundage Mountain Resort *(8 miles NW of town off*

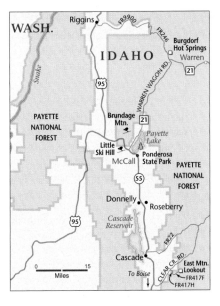

Idaho 55. 208-634-7462 or 800-888-7544) has a vertical rise of 1,800 feet and a day lodge with a restaurant; in the summer you can bring your mountain bike to the top and

McCall's Winter Carnival

ride down. Little Ski Hill *(2 miles N of McCall on Idaho 55. 208-634-5691)* has a T-bar to give skiers a lift up its 405 vertical feet; cross-country skiing, lodge, and snack bar.

Ponderosa State Park *(2 miles NE of McCall on Miles Standish Rd. 208-634-2164)* Occupying a 1,000-acre peninsula, the forested park on Payette Lake has scenic overlooks, hiking and cross-country ski trails, swimming beaches, and 84 popular campsites.

Water Sports For fun on Payette Lake, Cheap Thrills *(303 N. 3rd St. 208-634-7472 or 800-831-1025)* rents various watercraft. Canoes and kayaks are available seasonally at Silver Pig Enterprises *(Westside North Beach, Payette Lake. 208-634-4562)*. Brundage Mountain Adventures *(1410 Mill Rd. 208-634-4151 or 888-839-8320)* offers float and rafting trips on the Salmon River.

Wilderness Trips For access to remote lakes and the Frank Church-River of No Return Wilderness, call McCall Wilderness Air Taxi *(208-634-7137 or 800-992-6559)* or Salmon Air Taxi *(208-756-6211 or 800-448-3413)*.

ANNUAL EVENT

Winter Carnival *(Late Jan.–early Feb. Various locations in town. Call chamber for info.)* An annual event since 1964, this 10-day festival features giant ice sculptures, a torchlight parade, bonfires, and outdoor activities of all kinds.

WHERE TO EAT

Bear Creek Lodge *(Mile Marker 149, Idaho 55. 208-634-3551. Closed Mon.-Tues. $$)* This upscale lodge features exceptionally fine local and international cuisine.

McCall Brewing Company *(807 N. 3rd St. 208-634-2333. $)* If you're looking for fresh, pan-fried, locally caught trout, try this attractive, wood-filled restaurant and brew-pub.

WHERE TO STAY

Hotel McCall *(1101 N. 3rd St. 208-634-8105. $)* McCall's landmark hotel, with 22 guest rooms, has a warmth and graceful charm reminiscent of a small European inn.

NEARBY PLACES

Burgdorf Hot Springs *(32 miles N of McCall on Warren Wagon Rd. to junction with FR 21; go left for 2 miles. 208-636-3036. Adm. fee)* Relax in a large, outdoor, hot springs-fed pool in the middle of an alpine meadow.

East Mountain Lookout *(S of town on Idaho 55 to Clear Creek Rd.; go left to FR 417F, which branches right, to the lookout)* This handhewn log structure was used as a fire lookout from the 1930s to the 1990s; fabulous views and a great place for a picnic.

Warren *(37 miles N of McCall on Warren Wagon Rd.)* Ghost town dating from 1862, with a collection of tumbledown buildings.

Bigfork

On the shore of a mirror-smooth bay in the northeast corner of the West's largest natural freshwater lake, Bigfork is the sort of snug harbor voyagers search the world looking for. To the east is a rough wilderness, thick forest and grizzly bears and craggy peaks. To the north is the helter-skelter modern world of airports and ski resorts and shopping malls. But at the mouth of the Swan River, where Flathead Lake gentles the weather and cherry trees blossom, little Bigfork nestles among the pines.

Lake Monster

Flathead Lake has inspired tales of a lake monster. It's a huge lake, over 350 feet deep in places—plenty of room for a gargantuan being. Sightings date from 1898, when steamer passengers spotted a whalelike creature. More recent sightings have favored a dark, serpent-headed thing followed by a series of humps. Whether the monster has been affected by recent changes in the lake's biology—kokanee salmon and bull trout are all but gone—is uncertain, but it seems likely the monster will surface again.

If you grew up in the Bigfork area during the 1930s, old-timers say, the Great Depression bypassed you: Catching fish in the lake, shooting grouse in the woods, eating apples from the lakeside orchards, your life was full and prosperous. Still today, there is a sense in this faraway corner of Montana that modern worries are cordoned off, and if the rest of the world should fall away, Bigfork's streams and forests and neighbors will suffice.

Of course, the town now is wired like the rest of us to the outside world, and the world outside northern Montana is winding its way to Bigfork. It's beautiful country, after all, with craggy mountains, alpine lakes, deep curtains of forest, and a picture-book rustic town. There are times in the summer when the stream of visitors is more frothy than the Swan River during spring runoff—tourists in the art galleries, in the restaurants, on the lake tour boats, at the **Bigfork Summer Playhouse** humming along to *Oklahoma!* But there are also times when the crowds thin and Bigfork feels like a sturdy village of homesteaders clustered together in a remote wilderness—as it was, and as it still is for part of the year.

Some of the history is still writ in the landscape. Where the Flathead River flows into the lake, just north of town, behind Kehoe's Agate Shop, you'll find artifacts of the steamboats that carried passengers and freight around the lake around the turn of the 20th century. The shopowners are descendants of a lake ship captain and know the local history. That history began with the construction of a power plant on the Swan River in the early 1900s, and if you walk up Grand Avenue east of Bigfork's downtown area you'll find the plant works still there, now part of a delightful path for walking, biking, and horseback riding along the tumbling river, the **Swan River Nature Trail.**

Rustic architecture on Electric Avenue

Though there are summer crowds, downtown Bigfork is an unhurried place, on a walking scale, its streets twisting to accommodate old buildings, hills, and the river. Bookstores, gift shops, and restaurants encourage unhurried browsing. "I'm afraid Kalispell beat us out for the Wal-Marts," says one local with a chuckle, referring to a larger town to the north.

A century ago, this was a wisely chosen townsite, between the Flathead and Swan Rivers where they spill into the big lake, on a sheltered bay surrounded by forested hills. You could actually grow fruit here, because the lake buffered the killing freezes of higher elevations. The town was less prettified then, when the first power plant harnessed the Swan River's energy in the early 1900s, and loggers sent timber floating down the Swan River and across the lake in big booms.

Locals are proud of the way their hardy forebearers felled the big trees and built the old town, but these days any new timber sales cause a squabble: Many are equally proud of the way they've protected some of the timber and riparian areas loaded with wildlife, like the **Swan River Oxbow Preserve,** which adjoins the Swan River National Wildlife Refuge.

There is still some logging in the Mission Range, but Bigfork has made the transition to a resort town. It has the requisite fine dining, quaint inns, and over a dozen art galleries, mostly in the rustic, compact buildings on **Electric Avenue.** South along the lakeshore are cherry orchards, brilliantly blooming in the spring. There is a world-class golf course just to the west along the lake at Eagle Bend, a famous dude ranch just south of town that provides boat trips on the lake, and a growing ski area outside Whitefish to the northwest. Oh, yes, about an hour's drive north there's a national park called Glacier.

That's just one of the large natural wonders that surround this small town. There is **Flathead Lake,** of course, where you can sail and water-ski and fish for enormous mackinaw trout. There is the **Jewel Basin Hiking Area,** a tight package of alpine lakes where you can spend a day on the trail or several nights. There is **Swan Lake** and the **Swan River,** a fly-fishing favorite, twisting down toward the town from the Swan Valley, quickening in the spring to become the Class V **Wild Mile,** a kayaking challenge that draws paddlers from around the country. East and south stretches the enormous expanse of the **Bob Marshall Wilderness.** That wealth of easily accessible outdoor recreation raises the pulse rate; but at the end of the day, the payoff is the serenity of this enclave, the reflective moments walking by the bay or dabbing at a canvas, a quiet meal and conversation, the sunset on the lake. *Geoffrey O'Gara*

Travelwise

GETTING THERE

Bigfork sits at the inlet where the Swan River empties into the northeast corner of Flathead Lake, in northwestern Montana. There is no local air or ground transportation. Major airlines fly into Glacier International Airport, north of Kalispell, or into Missoula, south of the lake. From Kalispell drive south on US 93 to Somers, then east on Mont. 82 to Mont. 35, then south to Bigfork. From Missoula drive north on US 93 to the south end of Flathead Lake, then north along the lake on Mont. 35 to Bigfork.

GENERAL INFORMATION

Though spring can be wet, it's when the cherry trees bloom along the lake, and adventurous paddlers like the streams running high and fast. The high country east of Bigfork is often snowbound

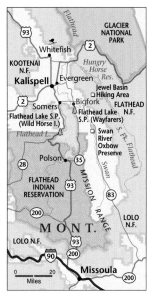

well into June; if you want to get into the high wilderness, plan on a trip in July and August. Fall is a quieter season, favored by anglers and hunters. For more information, contact the **Bigfork Area Chamber of Commerce** (*8155 Mont. 35, P.O. Box 237, Bigfork 59911. 406-837-5888. www.bigfork.org).*

THINGS TO SEE AND DO

Creston National Fish Hatchery (*10 miles N of Bigfork on Mont. 35, then 1 mile N on Creston Hatchery Rd. 406-758-6868. Adm. fee)* Fish of all ages raised to stock streams and lakes are in tanks here; osprey and eagles hang out nearby.

Flathead Lake State Park (*406-752-5501)* Six different units to this lakeshore park include **Wayfarers,** on the south side of the

Swan River inlet, a great place to camp and walk the beach during dramatic sunsets.

Hiking Backcountry enthusiasts can use Bigfork as a base while trekking into the Bob Marshall or Mission Mountains Wilderness areas. The **Jewel Basin Hiking Area** *(E of Mont. 83)* is crammed with good fishing lakes and scenery. The **Sprunger-Whitney Nature Trail** is a short loop hike at lower elevation, with interpretive stops that identify plants and wildlife in an old growth forest. The Swan Lake Ranger District *(200 Ranger Station Rd. 406-837-7500)* can provide information on these and other hiking trails. Following the Swan River from Grand Avenue in Bigfork, the **Swan River Nature Trail** is a wide jogging and biking path with great river views.

Lake Fishing Fishing charters on Flathead Lake are popular. A Able Fishing Charters & Tours *(Marina Cay Resort. 406-257-5214 or 800-231-5214)* offers half- and full-day trips, as well as customized tours and excursions.

River Floats The Swan River has both smooth paddling water (through the Swan River National Wildlife Refuge just south of Swan Lake) or white water, including the famed white-water run coming down to the city from the wooden bridge at South Ferndale Dr. For a guided trip, try Outlaw River Runners *(406-837-4337)*.

Sailing The *Questa* and the *Nor'easter* *(Averill's Flathead Lake Lodge. 406-837-5569. Fare)* are sleek 51-foot sloops that take two-hour excursions on the lake in the summer, including evening cruises.

Scenic Driving Coming or going from Bigfork, you have a Solomonic choice to make: Whether to drive the lakeside Mont. 35, with views of the lake and cherry orchards, or go overland through the beautiful Swan Valley on Mont. 83.

Swan River Oxbow Preserve *(S on Mont. 83 past Swan Lake, W on Porcupine Creek Rd. to parking area)* A trail winds through a marshy area set aside to protect rare plants.

SHOPPING

More than a dozen art galleries cluster downtown, mostly on Electric Avenue, many of them emphasizing landscapes and wildlife art, but there are some quirky alternatives, too.

Bigfork Art & Cultural Center *(525 Electric Ave. 406-837-6927)* A non-profit, community-run facility with exhibits and art workshops.

Electric Avenue Books *(490 Electric Ave. 406-837-6072)* A friendly shop with lots of Montana and Western books.

Kehoe's Agate Shop *(1020 Holt Dr., near Eagle Bend. 406-837-4467)* A big collection of Montana sapphires, agates, lapis lazuli, plus fossils, and gold jewelry, all for sale.

ENTERTAINMENT

Bigfork Summer Playhouse *(524 Electric Ave., in the Bigfork Center for the Performing Arts. 406-837-4886. Mid-May–Aug.; fee)* Quality productions of mainstream Broadway plays, mostly musicals.

Riverbend Concerts *(Everit L. Sliter Memorial Park. 406-837-4848. June-Aug. Sun. p.m.; fee)* An eclectic series of outdoor concerts.

ANNUAL EVENTS

Tamarack Time! *(Mid-Oct. Electric Ave. 406-837-4848. Fee)* A laid-back harvest celebration, with food tasting and entertainment.

Whitewater Festival *(Mem. Day weekend. 406-881-5202)* World-class kayakers compete on the Class V Wild Mile.

WHERE TO EAT

Bigfork Inn *(604 Electric Ave. 406-837-6680. $$)* Bigfork's oldest restaurant, with a big band dance combo on Friday and Saturday nights.

Showthyme *(548 Electric Ave. 406-837-0707. $$)* A fine restaurant housed in a 1908 bank building, serving scampi, penne carbonara, and other delicious dishes.

Swan River Cafe *(360 Grand Ave. 406-837-2220. $$)* A busy, gabby place with good food.

WHERE TO STAY

Averill's Flathead Lake Lodge *(1 mile S on Mont. 35. 406-837-5569. June-Sept. $2,063 per week)* An old-fashioned dude ranch where you can sail, fish, ride, and enjoy cookouts.

O'Duachain Country Inn *(675 Ferndale Dr. 406-837-6851 or 800-837-7460. $$)* Set back in the woods just outside town, this big, friendly house has a spacious hot tub, attractive landscaping, and peacocks.

Red Lodge

It takes a Yellowstone gateway road and a ski resort to keep a little Montana mountain town in business these days, but that's only the economic picture: The views that really define Red Lodge are its historic Main Street and the towering Beartooth Mountains nearby. A look backward, too, reveals a proudly remembered history of immigrant miners braving a remote and often harsh wilderness. The hard work and hard play tradition of those early Irish, Finn, and Italian settlers continues today, from the three-job waitress working the downtown bistro to the pig races—that's right, pig races—behind the bar in Bear Creek. Could it be the altitude?

Red Lodge entertainers

Take a quick winter trip to the recently expanded **Red Lodge Mountain resort** and you'll probably rave about the big, uncrowded ski runs and the small, unpretentious, packed-with-people restaurants. A sunny day schussing down the pine-lined runs off **Grizzly Peak,** a 2,400-foot vertical drop, is followed by a chummy evening eating gourmet pizza and downing microbrews at busy **Bogart's,** one of several eateries among the tightly packed old brick buildings downtown.

But don't mistake Red Lodge for a ski resort town—that's only the most obvious of its allures, and it has many more charms and seasons. You must visit in the spring, when the rivers run high, the wildflowers riot, and the kayaks fly; you could stop by in the fall, when the tourists thin, the elk bugle, and the fish are teeming in the streams; or come in the summer, a great time to explore the high country, by foot or saddle or car.

The town is situated in the foothills of the Rockies—foothills that would qualify as a mighty range in many parts of the country, but here are just milk-teeth, compared to the soaring Beartooth Mountains that rise south and west. We are on the edge here of the Yellowstone Plateau, in the outer layer of a wilderness deeper and richer in natural resources than any other in the lower 48 states. In **Custer National Forest** and the **Absaroka-Beartooth Wilderness** there are more than two dozen peaks over 10,000 feet, and rivers tumble down into trout-filled pools. You can wander extensive trails with a backpack, or ride in with one of numerous outfitters based around Red Lodge. Rafters and kayakers embark on the Stillwater and Yellowstone Rivers, which, depending on the time of year, can offer you white-water thrills or a placid scenic float (celebrity note: Mel Gibson has a ranch along the Stillwater).

A great many visitors to this area, though, take in the scenery from behind the steering wheel, and even diehard footsloggers will confess to the glories

Downtown Red Lodge

of a drive on the **Beartooth Highway.** It starts just south of Red Lodge, 68 miles of US 212 that challenge drivers to keep their eye on the twisting road as they rise among granite peaks, glaciers, forests, and creeks, crossing over 10,947-foot Beartooth Pass on the way to the northeast entrance to Yellowstone National Park (the pass closes in the winter, of course). You may perhaps spot a stately elk, a bighorn sheep with a big curl, or a golden eagle. You will certainly gaze down at crystal-clear alpine lakes, peaks etched by year-round snowfields, and deep valley bowls cradled by granite walls.

If this makes Red Lodge seem merely a portal to such beautiful, wild country, let's correct that impression. Admittedly, some gateway towns around Yellowstone are little more than faceless motels and fast-food joints thrown up to catch a few monetary feathers as the tourists fly by. Not Red Lodge. It has a history, which you can discover on an afternoon walk down its streets. Or street. This is not a big town, with only about 2,300 year-round residents, and its commercial district is concentrated along Broadway, the north-south axis.

Here you'll find some sturdy examples of the town's early 20th-century brick-and-stone glory, preserved as a **commercial historic district,** but fully alive with new shops, hotels, and restaurants. One three-block stretch, between Eleventh and Eighth Streets, has a particularly historic feel, and if you want to trade that feeling for fact, stop in at the **Peaks to Plains Museum.** Housed in a 1910 "Labor Temple," the museum is a work in progress—it's "on the grow," said one local. Back when it was built, there was no ski resort. Rather, there were coal mines, unearthing sub-bituminous coal for the railroads that were laying track all over the West. European immigrants provided the muscle—Irish, Italian, Scottish, and Finnish miners who comprised the largest ethnic group in town around the 20th-century's turn, most of them living in Finn Town just east of Broadway (you can still spot the old company boarding houses). The museum's basement simulates an underground coal mine, with exhibits about the labor movement and the dangers of mining.

Coal mining was risky but lucrative, so Red Lodge has a rich lode of sturdy buildings still standing a century after they were built. None is nicer than the **The Pollard Hotel,** which from the outside looks much as it did in 1897 when the Sundance Kid tried to rob the bank across the street. The hand-oiled oak woodwork and brass inside also suggests an earlier era, but the rooms are modern and comfortable.

Having assured you that Red Lodge is not a typical ski town, note that new lifts and runs on Red Lodge Mountain have raised the ski resort from a friendly neighborhood family tow to a serious contender for serious skiers. It is still uncrowded—there's just a lot more terrain to ski, and two high speed quad lifts. Whether that accelerates the transformation of Red Lodge into a resort like any other remains to be seen. The expansion of the new museum in the old Labor Temple indicates an untiring interest in history and local culture that, like the old buildings so full of life on Broadway, seems as sturdy and enduring as the mountains that loom above. *Geoffrey O'Gara*

Travelwise

GETTING THERE

Red Lodge is located in southwestern Montana, south of Billings and northeast of Yellowstone National Park in the upper Stillwater Valley. There is bus and plane service to Red Lodge, and no public transportation or taxi service in town. Commercial airlines serve Logan International Airport, in Billings, 60 miles north, and Yellowstone Regional Airport in Cody, Montana, 62 miles south.

GENERAL INFORMATION

Most visitors come in the summer so they can drive the Beartooth Highway to Yellowstone. That road is closed in the winter (times vary according to snow), when another crowd comes for the skiing on Red Lodge Mountain. Spring comes wet and late here, but you can see a great wildflower show in June. For more information, contact the **Red Lodge Area Chamber of Commerce** (601 N. Broadway, P.O. Box 998, Red Lodge 59068. 406-446-1718 or 888-281-0625. www.redlodge.com).

THINGS TO SEE AND DO

Bear Creek Downs Pig Races (7 miles E of Red Lodge on Mont. 308 at Bear Creek Saloon. 406-446-3481. Mem. Day–Labor Day Fri.-Sun.) It's fun, and it's not harmful to the porkers,

Skiing in the Beartooth Mountains

who ham it up as they race around an oval track to dishes of food.

Beartooth Highway *(68 miles on US 212 from Red Lodge to Yellowstone NP)* One of America's finest scenic drives.

Hiking or Horsepacking There are excellent trails in Custer NF and the Absaroka-Beartooth Wilderness *(406-446-2103 for both)*. The chamber has a list of outfitters leading wilderness day- and overnight trips out of Red Lodge.

Peaks to Plains Museum *(516 E. 8th Ave., in the Labor Temple building. 406-446-3667)* A fine and growing museum with exhibits on 19th-century Red Lodge, rodeos, and mining.

River Rafting Float trips on the Stillwater and Yellowstone Rivers—scenic or white-water rafting, plus some fun in open-top kayaks for experienced river runners. Contact Adventure Whitewater *(406-446-3061 or 800-897-3061)* or Beartooth Whitewater *(406-446-3142)* for rentals.

Skiing One of the best and least crowded mountains for skiing in the northern Rockies, Red Lodge Mountain *(West Fork Rd. off US 212. 406-446-2610)* offers seven chairlifts.

ANNUAL EVENTS

Festival of Nations *(Early Aug. 406-446-1718)* A week of ethnic food and dancing.

Mountain Man Rendezvous *(Last week in July. 406-446-1718. Adm. fee)* Traders and artisans hawk 19th-century wares and practice such arts as tomahawk throws.

Ski Joring *(Early March. 406-446-1718. Adm. fee)* The national finals in this hybrid sport—cowboys on horseback race through gates pulling a skier on a 250-yard course—are held at the Red Lodge Rodeo grounds.

WHERE TO EAT

Bogart's *(11 S. Broadway. 406-446-1784. $)* A lively, elbow-to-elbow bar and restaurant; hefty salads, Mexican dishes, gourmet pizza.

Greenlee's at the Pollard *(2 N. Broadway. 406-446-0001. $$)* A classy, quiet restaurant with fine food, from pistachio salmon in the evening to fine omelettes for breakfast.

WHERE TO STAY

The Pollard Hotel *(2 N. Broadway. 406-446-0001. $$/$$$)* Luxury and history within easy reach of the lively downtown night scene.

Red Lodging *(424 N. Broadway. 406-446-1272)* A wide range of vacation houses in the Red Lodge area rent through this agency.

Rock Creek Resort *(4 miles S of Red Lodge on US 212. 406-446-1111. $$)* Modern and comfortable, with airy and luxurious (and expensive) rooms.

Sheridan

From the finely preserved old buildings along Main Street to the historic ranches in the surrounding hills, Sheridan would be a museum of the West's most alluring era if it weren't so fully alive today. The alpine meadows of the Bighorn Mountains empty into wide, green valleys, where you'll find not just cattle drives and fly-fishing streams, but Mediterranean nouvelle cuisine and afternoon polo matches.

People today come to the Rocky Mountain West for its jagged mountains, its ski slopes, and the elk in its high mountain meadows. But more than a hundred years ago settlers sought cozier environs, valleys with good streams where they could raise cattle and children and put up a town. In 1882 a Civil War veteran named John Loucks looked around the Powder River country east of the Bighorn Mountains and saw wide, grassy valleys with all sorts of resources. Within a decade there were sugar beet fields, coal mines, and flourishing ranches, and within 20 years the town of Sheridan had two opera houses and ten times as many saloons.

Walking the streets of Sheridan today, there are fewer saloons and no opera houses, but there's a fine old theater, the **Wyo,** that brings in world-class theater, dance, and music. The Wyo embodies a cultural and historical richness here that is unusual in the relatively young towns of the West. You wouldn't think, either, that you were in a coal town: Main Street is an array of densely packed commerce, much of it in beautifully maintained buildings in the historic **Main Street District;** and on the outskirts of town there are no coal tipples or black-dusty rail cars, but rather ranches and pasturelands of the richest green, framed by the snow-capped mountains in the west. Nevertheless, coal is a big part of the area's prosperity, paying for fine schools and other amenities—but it's mined in big open pits far west and north, and hauled out of state directly from the mine mouth.

Some of these huge mines provide tours, but most visitors come to experience a soft-pillow version of ranch life hereabouts, bunking with outfits like the **Eaton Ranch,** one of the first in the country to realize you could make as much money herding dudes as cattle. The dude ranchers take their guests on horsepacking trips into the mountains

Gliding High

You may notice, as you descend from the Bighorns to the beautiful valley where Sheridan lies, some broad-winged birds far up in the sky. Those are hang gliders, and this is one of the country's finest hang-gliding areas. As US 14 descends the mountain, there's a pullout at Sand Turn where, on a nice day, you'll find a few fliers launching off a small concrete runway—after which, they can climb the thermals to extraordinary heights and spend an entire afternoon in the air. You can even try it yourself if you'll submit to a few lessons with Eagle Air (307-655-2562).

Mountains around Sheridan

rising to the west, which also attract backpackers and fishermen, particularly the **Cloud Peak Wilderness.**

The other attraction is Sheridan itself. It's the sort of human-scale, walking-distance town that has all but disappeared in most of mall-encrusted, strip-oriented America. Downtown bustles with restaurants, theaters, and shops, including true cowboy-country gems like **King Ropes and Saddlery** *(184 N. Main St.),* where you can learn all about the twists and fibers of a good lariat.

There are some interesting twists to the ranching lifestyle in these parts, too. A little south of town, outside the town of Big Horn, is a huge expanse of perfectly level, perfectly manicured grass half-encircled by mountains, and there a different sort of "cowboy" rides out with mallet in hand to play polo on Sundays at the **Big Horn Equestrian Center,** an outgrowth of a longstanding connection between Wyoming horse-breeders and British cavalry. Polo may be a game of aristocrats, but there is nothing snobby about the locals' easygoing social style.

That may be in part because they count themselves lucky to live here, and live as ranchers, though few could be said honestly to make a living solely on the hoof. This is actually one of the wealthiest corners of the world. First there is the old money, the scions of Eastern families who went native back in the 1930s after a taste of dude ranch life; then there is the new money, executives from corporations like Coca-Cola and Target stores, who needed a little country retreat of a few thousand acres. And, of course, the coal.

That wealth creates a few class tensions locally, but it has protected the ranches in this area from subdivision, and allowed the little satellite towns like Big Horn to survive. To most people in Wyoming, Sheridan, really, is not a small town at all, but the fourth largest city, with 16,900 people. On its outskirts are the kind of towns that qualify as "small" in the Cowboy State—towns like Ranchester and Story and Big Horn, with the requisite eccentrics and survivors who remained behind while the rest of us went urban. And Sheridan is the kind of "urban" that most of us can cherish—the small town virtues of unlocked doors and unpolluted skies, combined with the cosmopolitan benefits of string quartets and cappuccino. *Geoffrey O'Gara*

Travelwise

GETTING THERE

Sheridan sits in north-central Wyoming in the Big Goose Valley, adjacent to the plains of the Powder River Basin. Visitors who prefer jet service come in by way of Billings, Montana. There is daily commuter airline service into the Sheridan County Airport, just southwest of town, and there is regional bus service to Sheridan with Powder River Transportation *(307-674-6188)*.

GENERAL INFORMATION

When the mountain snows finally melt enough for trails to open (as late as June in the high country), Sheridan begins a frenetic outdoor season, both locals and visitors intent on cramming all the adventure they can into about four months of comfortable, mostly sunny weather. The chanciest time to visit if you want to be outdoors is spring, with its late snows and then rain and mud. In the fall you can enjoy fishing, hunting, and sunbursts of yellowing cottonwood and aspen, as well as fewer people. It's harder to get here in the winter, but the Bighorn Mountains are an attractive place to ski and snowmobile. Contact the **City of Sheridan Convention and Visitors Bureau** *(P.O. Box 7155, Sheridan 82801. 307-672-2485. www.visitsheridan.com)* or the **Sheridan County Chamber of Commerce** *(P.O. Box 707, Sheridan 82801.*

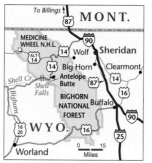

307-672-2485 or 800-453-3650. www.sheridan wyo.com).

THINGS TO SEE AND DO

Bradford-Brinton Memorial Ranch *(239 Brinton Rd., Big Horn. 307-672-3173. Adm. fee)* This cottonwood-shaded ranch has been here since 1892, with additions, but what makes it special is the historic Western art hanging on the walls, including Russells, Audubons, and Remingtons.

Hiking Several strenuous trails into **Cloud Peak Wilderness** have trailheads in Bighorn NF *(307-672-0751)*. More accessible day hikes include beautiful **Tongue River Canyon.**

Polo Bring your own horse and equipment, or just sit on the sidelines and watch, as locals carry on this longstanding tradition at the Big Horn Equestrian Center, in the little town of Big Horn just south of Sheridan. Contact the Chamber of Commerce.

Sheridan Inn *(856 Broadway. 307-674-5440. Adm. fee)* Buffalo Bill Cody used to sit on the long porch of this majestic hotel and audition performers for his Wild West Show. It's a museum and restaurant now, with hopes of opening some of its 62 rooms to guests.

Trail End State Historic Site *(400 Clarendon Ave. 307-674-4589. Adm. fee)* It took a ton of coal a day to heat the 20 rooms

At the Sheridan rodeo

of this Flemish Revival mansion-on-the-hill, elegant proof that nearly a hundred years ago you could actually make money raising cattle.

Winter Sports Cross-country skiing, downhill skiing (at Antelope Butte Ski Area), and snowmobiling lure snow enthusiasts into the Bighorns during the winter.

ENTERTAINMENT

Wyo Theater (42 N. Main St. 307-672-9084) This lovingly restored art deco relic hosts a wide range of live entertainment.

The Mint (151 N. Main St. 307-674-9696) There are many things besides liquor to appreciate in this bar, which has been around since 1907: the 8-foot rattlesnake skin above the bar, the brands on the twisted cedar walls, and the huge Charles Belden photographs.

WHERE TO EAT

Ciao Bistro (120 N. Main St. 307-672-2838. $$) Mediterranean fare is served in a small, intimate room with an excellent wine list.

Sanford's Grub (1 E. Alger St. at N. Main St. 307-674-1722. $) Inexpensive, abundant, and pretty tasty fare, and a

huge beer list, served among junkman's decorations.

WHERE TO STAY

Eaton Ranch (270 Eaton Ranch Rd., Wolf. 307-655-9285 or 800-210-1049. $$$) This working cattle ranch at the foot of the Bighorns has been hosting dudes for week-or-longer stays since 1904.

Spahn's Big Horn Mountain B&B (9 miles W, off Wyo. 335, in the Bighorn Mountains. 307-674-8150. $$) A towering house in the pines, with claw-foot tubs and a roaring fire.

Spear Ranch Bed and Breakfast (170 Brinton Rd., Big Horn. 307-673-0079) A stately old ranch home along a trout stream has luxurious, antique-stocked rooms, rambling grounds, and great views.

NEARBY PLACES

Buffalo About 30 miles down the road on I-90, this handsome old town of 4,000 could earn its own place in this book if neighbor Sheridan hadn't grabbed the slot. It's got the fine **Jim Gatchell Memorial Museum** (100 Fort St. 307-683-9331) and nearby historic sites like Fort Phil Kearney.

Saratoga

A sudden thrust of mountains breaks the high desert plain of southern Wyoming, sieving snow from the clouds, later to melt and flow down the canyons to Saratoga, a foothill town on the banks of one of Wyoming's finest trout streams. Indoors, over a beer in a century-old bar, folks are relaxed and hospitable; outdoors, floating beneath the tall cottonwoods or skimming across the snowfields in the high country, it's the same gorgeous wilderness that has dazzled and challenged visitors for two centuries.

There are still places in the world where at 2 a.m. doors remain unlocked and it is perfectly safe to be cruising the streets in search of, well, a good hot soak. There isn't much else going on here at that hour anyway, since many of the locals and visitors have retired at a sensible hour so they can rise at an insensible hour to go fishing. Insomniacs, though, can take comfort amid the cottonwoods along the bank of the North Platte River, where the steaming grotto of the **Saratoga Hot Springs** is open 24 hours a day.

There's no price of admission to the hot springs, a tradition dating back to the Depression years, though today's indolent soakers hop out of mini-vans and RVs, not rail cars. Visitors soak and converse quietly—no one wants to splash around in 117°F water—now and then climbing over the moss-faced cinderblock walls and tip-toeing down to the river for the milder temperatures in the pools formed by hand-built rock dams.

After an hour under the stars you will be thoroughly parboiled, and thankful that this is a genuinely small town, a throwback to the days when everyone knew everyone and work, school, and home were within walking distance. And so your flaccid muscles will not have to walk or drive far to a comfortable bed. You may have planned to climb **Medicine Bow Peak** the next morning, or play a few holes of golf, or tie a black wooly bugger on a 6-pound-test flyline…well, it's not so oldfangled that they don't have snooze buttons here.

But do save at least one morning for the river. The scenery easily justifies a float trip. The blue-ribbon stretches of the meandering **North Platte** are the area's big drawing card, along with the rolling ranch country that steepens into forested mountains. People who despaired that the decline of the mineral digs and sawmills in the latter half of the 20th century would mean the end of Saratoga didn't realize they could mine their recreation and open space. Now they watch the summer parade of anglers—pickup truck "greenies" from Colorado and corporate CEO's in Lear jets—with growing optimism.

Faith in a brighter future is what pioneers eat for breakfast, and Fenimore Chatterton was obviously thinking big in 1884 when he renamed the little settlement of Warm Springs after the posh Saratoga hot spring spa back east in New York. Though the hot spring had been decidedly unhelpful in curing Indians of the smallpox brought by white immigrants, word went out that it could heal arthritis, digestion problems, and "all diseases of the mucous mem-

An aspen-lined trail near Saratoga

brane." Though it attracted mendicants, what initially brought jobs and people to the Platte Valley back in the 1860s were the open ranges for cattle ranching and the railroads, which needed timber for ties. Copper mining at the turn of the 20th century in the Sierra Madre to the south also attracted people.

Even after the mining stopped, many people stayed—for the still open range, wildlife, fish, hot springs…. In an increasingly urban world, those are prize possessions, and they have not diminished four generations later. If anything, the area is a little less crowded and a little more beautiful than it was in the days when the ore and timber came down from the mountains. Take a spring white-water float down the **Encampment River,** through a steep canyon as densely wooded as when trappers first searched for beaver here; spend a night in the historic **Wolf Hotel;** walk down an autumn trail in "aspen alley" in **Medicine Bow National Forest;** explore the life of 19th-century miners at the **Grand Encampment Museum;** cast beneath the sandstone cliffs of the North Platte for a fat, 18-inch cutthroat trout—in this blue-ribbon trout stream, there are more than 2,500 trout per mile, all grown naturally without any stocking by wildlife agencies.

Strolling along the river, fourth generation Saratoga resident Teense Willford wasn't talking about trout when he said drolly: "We don't live in a cutthroat world. I had a terrible decision to make this morning: Whether to fish, golf, or sit in the hot springs…or talk to you. Well, we don't mind visitors, as long as they don't break too much stuff."

Geoffrey O'Gara

Travelwise

GETTING THERE

Saratoga is located in south-central Wyoming along the North Platte River. There is no rail, commercial plane, or bus connection to the town, and no taxi service. The nearest major airports are Casper, Wyoming (148 miles by car), and Denver, Colorado (207 miles by car).

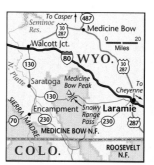

GENERAL INFORMATION

Though winter recreation—primarily snowmobiling—is on the rise in the Saratoga area, roads can be slick and dangerous, even I-80. Spring, which doesn't kick into high gear until May, attracts white-water rafters and wildflower fans; summer is a great time to hike in the mountains; and fall is the best time to fish the rivers. Contact the **Saratoga/Platte Valley Chamber of Commerce** (115 W. Bridge St., P.O. Box 1095, Saratoga 82331. 307-326-8855. www.trib.com/ SPVCC) or the **Carbon County Visitors**

Council (P.O. Box 856, Saratoga 82331. 307-326-5292 or 800-228-3547. www.wyoming carboncounty.com).

THINGS TO SEE AND DO

Floating Scenic floats and white-water rafting (spring only) are the things to do on the **North Platte** and **Encampment.** Contact the outfitters below.

Fly-fishing The **North Platte** is a blue-ribbon trout stream, and the **Encampment River** is a smaller, steeper delight. If you want a boat and a guide, try Medicine Bow Drifters (307-326-8002) or Great Rocky Mountain Outfitters (800-326-5390). Anglers can also wade these rivers, but be sure you're not trespassing to reach the river.

Hiking Wilderness hikes in the Sierra Madre to the south and west are one option;

hikes in the Snowy Range to the east are spectacular, particularly around the snow-draped cirque topped by Medicine Bow Peak. For maps and advice, contact Medicine Bow-Routt National Forest *(2468 Jackson St., Laramie. 307-745-2300)* or the Brush Creek/Hayden Ranger District Visitor Center *(307-326-5258)*, located south of Saratoga near the intersection of Wyo. 130 and Wyo. 230.

North Platte River *(Several bridge crossings and open shore in town; public fishing accesses N and S of town)* Whether you fish or not, it's a beautiful, meandering, cottonwood-lined river, swifter and more woodsy upstream. Though much of it is surrounded by private land, river access roads are marked on Wyo. 130.

Saratoga Hot Springs *(201 S. River St., behind public swimming pool)* It's open 24 hours a day, 365 days a year, with an average temperature of 117°F even when there's snow on the ground. There are changing rooms for men and women, with showers. Slip over the wall and down to a side channel of the North Platte River—only 20 feet away—to cool off.

Saratoga Museum *(104 Constitution Ave. 307-326-5511. Adm. fee)* Housed in the old Union Pacific Railroad depot, this museum has exhibits on the Indians who considered the hot springs a peaceful meeting place, and on the pioneer settlers who eventually took over the valley. There's also a collection of minerals and fossils.

Scenic Driving The 79-mile trip over the 10,847-foot Snowy Range Pass between Saratoga and Laramie is one of the country's most beautiful *(pass closed in winter)*. Another fine drive is to go south on Wyo. 70 through the Sierra Madre west to the ranch towns of Savery and Baggs.

ANNUAL EVENTS
Donald E. Erickson Memorial Chariot Races *(Presidents' Day weekend. 307-326-8855. Adm. fee)* Horse-pulled chariots race.

Official Wyoming State Microbrewery Competition *(Aug., call for dates. 307-326-8855. Fee for tasting)* Wacky floats and a lot of good Wyoming-brewed beer on Veterans Island in the North Platte River.

Woodchoppers Jamboree & Rodeo *(3rd weekend in June. 307-326-8855)* Just up the road in the one-time logging town of Encampment, a fun mix of log-rolling and other woodchopper skills and traditional rodeo.

WHERE TO EAT
The best restaurants in town are at the inns below—the Wolf has steaks and prime rib with an excellent salad bar in a crowded, convivial atmosphere; the Saratoga Inn's restaurant is quieter, with fine cuisine featuring seafood, steak, and the occasional game dish.

Lazy River Cantina *(134 Bridge St. 307-326-8472. $)* Decent Mexican food, huge margaritas, and a cheerful bar with occasional live music you can dance to.

Mom's Kitchen *(402 S. 1st St. 307-326-5136. $)* The place to get a bottomless cup of coffee, a big plate of breakfast, and local gossip if your ears are sharp.

WHERE TO STAY
Saratoga Inn Resort & Hot Springs Spa *(E. Pic Pike Rd. 307-326-5261. Limited hours Nov.-April. $$)* This fancy resort has its own hot spring pools, golf course, and river frontage. Pricey for these parts, but the combination of rustic resort luxury, poolside seclusion, and excellent cuisine is unique.

Wolf Hotel *(101 E. Bridge St. 307-326-5525. $)* This venerable, deep-porched, three-story brick hotel has been around since 1893, and it retains an Old West flavor (and low prices). A popular bar and good restaurant included.

NEARBY PLACES
Battle As Wyo. 70 twists up into the Sierra Madre, you'll come to this, one of several abandoned mining towns, with an odd sprinkling of vacation houses now interspersed.

Grand Encampment Museum *(817 Barnett Ave., Encampment. 307-327-5308. Daily Mem. Day–Labor Day, weekends only through Oct.)* A great little museum featuring mining artifacts and a two-story outhouse.

Medicine Bow Peak *(Off Wyo. 130 near Snowy Range Pass)* If you don't mind the dizzying elevation (12,013 feet), the 5-mile, very steep hike to the top of this granite hump is not bad, and the view is spectacular. The trailhead is at the west Lake Marie parking area. An easier option is to stroll along the lakeshore.

Georgetown

What better memorial to generations of volunteer firemen who kept Georgetown from falling victim to the fires that razed so many of Colorado's old mining towns, than the 200-plus Victorian houses, bungalows, and storefronts that have been designated a national historic landmark? Georgetown is distinguished by its resistance to the terminal cuteness that so many Old West hamlets hadn't. Indeed, many of its 950-odd residents are fervent preservationists whose sentiments rule here. Georgetown's first railroad still chuffs to neighboring Silver Plume. Sojourners who use Georgetown as a base camp for skiing, hiking, and mountain biking expeditions know that, at day's end, this lofty little burg offers something Colorado's famous upscale resort towns cannot: the peace and quiet that comes from sidewalks that roll up early, and the sound sleep engendered by crisp night air and starry skies.

Georgetown sprouted in 1858 after two brothers, George and David Griffith, struck gold. (David had to settle for having a main street named for him.) Silver strikes brought wealth and swelled the population to over 5,000. Even some miners could afford ornate Victorian cottages. Prospering merchants put up near-mansions, and Louis Dupuy, a French immigrant chef, built the luxurious **Hotel de Paris** to cater to the mining moguls and affluent travelers. His guest book opened in 1875, welcoming them to rooms with hot and cold taps (unheard of in a mining town), private baths, and piped-in glacial ice water. Chef Dupuy fussed over his restaurant's French cuisine and wine list. That mostly ended when the silver and gold petered out, but you can still visit the hotel, now a museum.

On any given night, you might have found Georgetown's preeminent silver baron, William Hamill, holding court in Dupuy's ornate dining room. More likely, however, the Englishman was hosting guests in his Gothic Revival-style home, completed in 1879 and now the **Hamill House Museum.** He spared no expense, importing Italian marble fireplaces and hand-painted wallpaper.

Since the entire town has been preserved as a national historic landmark,

Practical Art

Georgetown's elegant Victorians belie the dangerous and difficult labor of the miners whose modest cottages and bungalows also survive. Mining demanded skill and courage, fostering pride among the town's underground toilers. A symbol of their self-esteem is the metal candleholders they fashioned to light pitch-black tunnels. Powder Cache Antiques (*612 6th St.*) displays an amazing collection. Hand-wrought utilitarian tools rendered into art, the candleholders are reminders of the dignity possible from even the most humble work.

Old Georgetown Victorian

its streets still evoke a sense of a past. Pick up a self-guided tour brochure from the Downtown Information Center and stroll past some of the most beautiful structures, still clustering in its central core. Among them is the **Bowman-White House** *(Open by appt. only to groups of 10 or more)* on Rose Street, an impressive example of boomtown affluence. A more brawny look at the early 1900s can be found at the historic **Georgetown hydroelectric plant,** whose waterwheel-powered generators still supply some of the town's public electrictity. Be sure to stop by the energy museum if it's open.

When business called the town's early elite to nearby **Silver Plume,** another mining community, they rode along **Clear Creek,** where you can pedal a mountain bike or take a peaceful walk, or boarded the **Georgetown Loop Railroad,** once touted as the world's most complex rail route. Though Silver Plume

Georgetown's mountain setting

is only 2 miles away it lies 638 feet above Georgetown, requiring the railroad's engineers to lay a contorted, 4.5-mile-long track to gain the elevation slowly enough so trains could climb the grade. They spanned Clear Creek with a 95-foot-high, 300-foot-long steel trestle called the **Devil's Gate Viaduct,** a steel spiral that in the 1870s was such an engineering marvel it became a tourist attraction. Take the 40-minute ride to Silver Plume—the old bridge, scrapped in 1939, was replaced in 1984 by a reconstruction of the original, and the railroad is now a project of the Colorado Historical Society. Stroll **Main Street** to inspect Silver Plume's Victorian architecture. Peek at the historical photos and displays in the **George Rowe Museum,** then catch the train back to Georgetown. If you have two hours to spare, stop en route at the retired **Lebanon Silver Mine,** where guides lead tours through perfectly safe (if chilly) tunnels, whose veins once so rich, it was said, that ore spilled out in "silver plumes."

The gold and silver may be gone, but the beauty of this region is undiminished, and probably more appreciated than it was a century ago. One of the prettiest drives—or bicycle trips—you'll ever make in the Rockies could well be the 22-mile **Guanella Pass Scenic Byway** from Georgetown to Grant through the **Arapaho** and **Pike National Forests.** On your way to 11,669 feet you'll enter a sturdy natural garden of flowered meadows, gravelly glacial terraces, and dense lodgepole pine and spruce forests, a rough beauty so perfect no amount of treasure could create it.   *Mark Miller*

Travelwise

GETTING THERE

Georgetown is located in central Colorado, 47 miles west of Denver on I-70. Amtrak serves Denver, and Denver International Airport is a hub for many airlines.

GENERAL INFORMATION

Late spring, summer, and autumn are Georgetown's most comfortable seasons, although severe thunderstorms and winds with chilling temperatures can occur at any time at its 8,519-feet elevation. For information, contact the **Georgetown Community Center** *(P.O. Box 444, Georgetown 80444. 303-569-2888 or 800-472-8230)*. Pick up the "Georgetown Map and Walking Tour" brochure at the center's **Downtown Information Center,** open daily at Argentine and Sixth Sts., and the **Georgetown Gateway Visitor Center** *(1491 Argentine St. 303-569-2405)*. For museum information call **Historic Georgetown** *(303-569-2840. www.historic georgetown.org)*.

THINGS TO SEE AND DO

Georgetown Energy Museum

(600 Griffith St. 303-569-3557. Closed weekends Labor Day–Mem. Day; adm. fee) Historical displays adjoin working antique hydroelectric generators rarely seen today. The plant is Colorado's oldest operating hydroelectric facility.

Hamill House Museum *(305 Argentine St. 303-569-2840. Daily June-Sept., weekends only Oct.-Dec., closed Jan.-May; adm. fee)* Lovingly restored and maintained, this handsome residence is a genuine relic of genteel 19th-century life hereabouts, and the pride of the Historic Georgetown preservation movement.

Hiking The 2.4-mile **Notch Trail** from Georgetown to Silver Plume is rated from moderate to strenuous, however the reward is exceptionally pretty scenery. From the **Guanella Pass Scenic Byway**, a moderately difficult footpath leads to Silver Dollar Lake. A popular day hike is the walk up the old **Argentine-Central Railroad grade** to Waldorf mine. The railbed continues to the summit of Mount McClellan and splendid views of surrounding peaks.

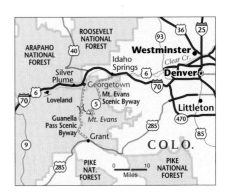

Hotel de Paris Historical Museum *(409 6th St. 303-569-2311. Daily Mem. Day–Labor Day, weekends only rest of year; adm. fee)* Painstaking, historically accurate restoration here faithfully re-creates the world of deluxe 19th-century travel.

Georgetown commercial district

The area bounded by Griffith, Seventh, Argentine, and Fifth Streets is rich in vintage architecture, museums, galleries, shops, restaurants, and cafés. Park your vehicle and let your eyes and interests guide you. Or obtain a self-guided walking tour brochure from the chamber.

Skiing and Snowboarding The 1,365-acre **Loveland Ski Area** *(12 miles W of Georgetown off I-70. 303-569-3203 or 800-736-3754)* straddles the Continental Divide in Arapaho National Forest. Runs range from beginner to advanced, and there's instruction for children and adults.

Vintage Railroading The **Georgetown Loop Railroad** *(Ticket office in Old Georgetown Station, 1106 Rose St.; departures at Devil's Gate Boarding Area, at the end of Loop Dr. 303-569-2403 or 800-691-4386 On-line reservations: www.georgetownloop.com)* departs 6 times daily on 70-minute round-trips between Georgetown and Silver Plume.

Wildflower Viewing In spring the Mount Evans and Guanella Pass summits are stippled with blooms, as is the **Herman Gulch Trail** *(Exit 218 off I-70 W of town; trailhead is on the N side of the interstate)*.

SHOPPING

Georgetown's products traditionally have been limited to those related to mining, although preservationist sentiment has encouraged the antique trade.

Georgetown Antique Emporium *(501 Rose St. 303-569-2727)* Features oak furniture and brass fixtures.

Georgetown Gallery *(612-B 6th St. 303-569-2218. Closed Tues. and Thurs. Jan.-April)* Colorado's second oldest cooperative space showcases the work of local artists and craftspeople.

Georgetown Rock Shop *(501 6th St. 303-569-2750)* Features minerals and crystals from Colorado and elsewhere, fossils, and ancient insects preserved in amber.

ANNUAL EVENTS

4th of July *(303-569-2888)* The traditional celebration includes a parade, a public barbecue in City Park, bucket brigade races, and fireworks.

Georgetown to Idaho Springs Half Marathon *(Aug., call for date. 303-694-2030. Entry fee)* More than 3,000 people make the run along the asphalt frontage road winding gently downhill through Clear Creek Valley, from about 8,500 to 7,500 feet elevation.

WHERE TO EAT

Depot Express *(1106 Rose St. 303-569-2403 or 800-691-4386. Closed Oct.-May. $)* Located in the Old Georgetown Station, this summer hangout with outdoor patio features baked goods and sandwiches, microbrewed beers, and Italian-style espresso coffee.

Happy Cooker *(412 6th St. 303-569-3166. $)* In the heart of Old Town, open year-round for breakfast and lunch, it's known locally for European waffles, homemade breads, and soups. In summer, the best tables are outdoors in the garden.

Red Ram Restaurant & Saloon *(606 6th St. 303-569-2300. $)* Located downtown in the historic district, this popular local hangout serves hearty casual fare and offers Western-flavored musical entertainment on Friday and Saturday nights.

WHERE TO STAY

Georgetown Motor Inn *(1100 Rose St. 308-569-3201 or 800-884-3201. $)* Well-run

and friendly, this 32-room hostel toward the center of town has a heated summer pool and a year-round hot tub. Two units have kitchenettes.

Hillside House Bed & Breakfast *(1034 Main St. 303-569-0912 or 800-490-9012. $$)* There are only two guest units in this old Victorian, but panoramic valley views, an outdoor hot tub, and a suite with a freestanding fireplace win local raves.

Silver Heels Guest Suites *(506 6th St. 303-569-0941 or 888-510-7628. $$/$$$)* Its pair of suites on the upper floor of the Buckskin Trading Company Building in downtown Georgetown are well suited to extended stays.

NEARBY PLACES

Guanella Pass Scenic Byway *(FR 38/Guanella Pass Rd., at S end of town)* About half of this 24-mile road from Georgetown to Grant is rough gravel, which means dust and vibration. Guanella Pass views of Mount Bierstadt and other "fourteeners"—peaks 14,000 feet high or more—are memorably photogenic.

Lebanon Silver Mine *(303-569-2403 or 800-691-4386. Mem. Day–Labor Day; adm. fee in addition to train fare. Reservations recommended)* Accessible only by the Georgetown Loop Railroad, the 80-minute tour of the old mine requires comfortable shoes. Bring a jacket or sweater, as the temperature underground is a constantly chilly 44°F.

Mount Evans Scenic Byway *(Vehicle fee above Echo Lake)* From Idaho Springs, the 27-mile route on Colo. 5—the nation's highest paved road—climbs through high country to the summit of 14,264-foot Mount Evans and panoramas of the Rockies' Front Range and the Continental Divide. The road is open year-round as far as Echo Lake; beyond it closes mid-September to Memorial Day.

Silver Plume A silver-mining hamlet like Georgetown, its key attractions are the **George Rowe Museum** *(905 Main St. 303-569-2562. Mem. Day–Labor Day; donation)* and Main Street's Victorian buildings, identified in the free "Silver Plume Walking Tour" brochure. Ask any merchant in town for a copy.

Ouray

Self styled the Switzerland of America, Ouray is simply too all-American to quite pull that one off, being a barrel-chested old mining town, named for a leader of the Tabequaghe Ute people who once summered here, and enjoying a comfortable retirement while doting proudly on its collection of vintage brick and stone mercantile buildings and Victorian houses. Mountains it has, however; situated at 7,760 feet in southwestern Colorado's magnificent San Juans, it's surrounded by scores of peaks rising above 13,000 feet.

People come to Ouray to savor its slow pace, friendly cafés, unassuming shops, and relaxed restaurants. But sooner or later, you won't be able to ignore the mountains' alluring call. Walk a few hundred yards from town, into the stony forests, and the loudest sounds you'll hear will be the creak of evergreens bending in the breeze, birdcalls, and falling water. Keep going and in an hour or two you can spread your picnic blanket out in an alpine meadow, a granite canyon, or the shade of a high spruce stand. Heavy winter snows turn Ouray into a staging area for skiers, snowshoers, and other winter sports enthusiasts, while spring through autumn it hosts day-hikers and backcountry trekkers,

Main Street, Ouray

mountain bikers, fly-fishing aficionados, and four-wheel-drive backroaders.

Old mining roads wander through the mountains, dotted with abandoned mining operations and ghost towns—providing a clue as to who first settled these wild lands. More information can be found back in town at the **Ouray County Museum,** with exhibits on local gold and silver mining, Ute culture, and ranching. The museum is site no. 4 on the historic walking tour mapped out in Ouray's free visitor's guide. The map identifies 16 significant sites within a five-by-six-block downtown area, but don't let that limit you. Many of its buildings were built between 1880 and 1900, and the entire town is designated a national historic district. Now serving as hotels, inns, shops, cafés, bookstores, restaurants, and bars, they once housed their Old West equivalents: hardware, clothing, mining supply stores, and dozens of saloons and brothels.

Without a doubt, some of their patrons ended up in front of a judge in the **Ouray County Courthouse.** And it's likely that the judge, being a prominent citizen, belonged to the **Elks Lodge No. 492,** an eclectic combination of architectural styles created in 1904 by an amateur architect, the town's grocer. Past is present at the **St. Elmo Hotel** on Main, which opened its rooms and restaurant in 1898. The Italian fare served in its restaurant is hearty, but there are always all those trails winding up into those glacial peaks and gorges that in fact do look rather like the Swiss Alps. *Mark Miller*

Travelwise

GETTING THERE

Ouray is located in southwestern Colorado on US 550, about 70 miles north of Durango and 34 miles south of Montrose. Airlines serve Montrose, Telluride, Grand Junction, and Durango. There is bus service through Ouray. The 300-mile drive from Denver requires 6-7 hours.

GENERAL INFORMATION

Ouray is a year-round destination, averaging 285 sunny days annually. Summer days are warm, evenings cool. Winter snowfall averages 140 inches. A typical winter day is clear and bright, though occasional snowstorms can be heavy, making driving difficult or impossible. Four-wheel drive vehicles, snow tires, or chains are advisable but not

necessary. For more information, and the "Ouray Chamber Resort Association Visitor's Guide," contact the **Ouray Visitor Center** *(1230 Main St., Ouray 81427. 970-325-4746 or 800-228-1876. www.ouray .colorado.com).*

THINGS TO SEE AND DO

Bachelor Syracuse Mine Tour *(2 miles E of Ouray at 1222 Cty. Rd. 14. 970-325-0220. Mid-May–mid-Sept.; adm. fee. Reservations recommended)* Hour-long mine tours deep in a mountain led by working miners.

Back Road Adventuring Guided jeep tours offered by Switzerland of America *(226 7th Ave. 970-325-4484 or 800-432-5337)* and Colorado West Jeep

Rentals & Tours (701 Main St. 970-325-4014 or 800-648-JEEP). Or rent a jeep and head out on your own.

Downhill Skiing Telluride, 50 miles away, is the San Juans' premier ski center. For information call 888-605-2573. Ask about the Ski Telluride Half Price program, offering discounts to guests of participating Ouray lodgings.

Elks Lodge No. 492 (421 Main St.) Original furnishings and local antiques are on display.

Hiking A few of the local favorite hikes include: the moderately strenuous **Portland/Cascade Falls Trail,** which departs from the Amphitheater Forest Service Campground and skirts the pretty falls and the rock formations of a bowl-like amphitheater formation. The **Bear Creek National Recreation Trail** is tougher; it follows an old mining trail along steep canyon ledges and switchbacks 4.2 miles to the Yellow Jacket mine; to find the trailhead, take US 550 south 2 miles from Ouray, passing through the tunnel. Park on the road's east side. The trail begins on the west side, crosses above the tunnel, and heads east. Another recommended day hike is along the **Horsethief Trail,** which leads to the Bridge of Heaven and its spectacular views of the Sneffels Range and the Uncompahgre Wilderness. Find the trailhead at the end of Dexter Creek Rd., 3 miles northeast of town. For more information on area hiking, call the Ouray Ranger District (970-240-5400).

Horseback Riding The Ouray Livery Barn (834 Main St. 970-325-4606. June-Sept.) has been outfitting mountain trail rides, pack trips, and elk hunts for 30 years.

Kayaking At the Ouray Kayak School (1805 Main St. 970-325-0344 or 800-432-4170. Spring and early summer), instruction ranges from beginning to advanced river running. All equipment is provided.

Ouray County Museum (620 6th Ave. 970-325-4576. Adm. fee) Housed in the 1887 Miners' Hospital, the collection focuses on mining, Ute heritage, and ranching, and displays vintage medical equipment.

Swimming The million-gallon Ouray Hot Springs Pool & Fitness Center (Hot Springs Park, 1200 Main St. 970-325-4638. Adm. fee) is open year-round.

Vintage Railroading The **Durango & Silverton Narrow Gauge Railroad** (479 Main Ave. 970-247-2733 or 888-872-4607. Late June–late Aug.; fare) travels the scenic backcountry between Silverton and Durango.

ENTERTAINMENT

Grounds Keeper Coffeehouse & Eatery (524 Main St. 970-325-0550. Summer) Local musicians play bluegrass, ballads, and guitar.

Suzanne's Broadway to Branson Show (Chipeta Emporium Theatre, 630 Main St. 970-325-0357. Mem. Day–Labor Day Tues.-Sun.) Two shows nightly, plus a Sunday matinee.

ANNUAL EVENT

Ouray County Fair & Rodeo (Labor Day weekend. Ridgway fairgrounds, US 550 and Colo. 62. 970-325-4746. Adm. fee) A true small town affair with a country-western flavor.

WHERE TO STAY

Box Canyon Lodge & Hot Springs (45 3rd Ave. 970-325-4981 or 800-327-5080. $/$$) A popular retreat with four redwood hot tubs on the hillside behind.

China Clipper Inn (525 2nd St. 970-325-0565 or 800-315-0565. $$) Designed for hospitality, this handsome three-story has 11 rooms and an enclosed garden.

Manor Bed and Breakfast (317 2nd St. 970-325-4574 or 800-628-6946. $$) A meticulously restored Georgian Victorian built in 1890 with period decor and down comforters.

WHERE TO EAT

Mountain Garden Restaurant (520 Main St. 970-325-7285. Mon.-Fri. in summer, daily in winter. $) Specializing in thoughtfully prepared homemade breakfasts, including vegetarian fare, it opens early and closes just before noon.

Ouray Coffeehouse (960 Main St. 970-325-0401. Closed Thurs. in winter. $) This pleasant two-roomer across from the hot springs opens early, serves breakfast and lunch all day, and will prepare sack lunches for hikers and day-trippers.

Piñon Restaurant and Tavern (737 Main St. 970-325-4334. May-Oct. $$) The menu includes duck, elk, and trout. A local standout.

Taos

Situated between a thousand-year-old Pueblo community and an 18th-century farming village, this 400-year-old Spanish colonial outpost in north-central New Mexico's Sangre de Cristo Mountains exudes a remarkable peacefulness even at the peak of its summer tourist invasion. Its styles have influenced fashion from Tokyo to Paris, yet the village is not chic in the way Santa Fe is seen to be. To many Taos is simply quaint, chockablock with shops, galleries, museums, and antique adobes. To others it is an exotic foray into American antiquity, where outsiders may observe feast days and festivals at the Tiwa-speaking village in the shadow of Taos Mountain. Those who know Taos best, however, cherish it for the reasons its original folk were determined to hold on to their homes here: its beauty and the pleasing sense of place engendered by its surrounding peaks, a strong painterly sunlight capable of boosting colors to a wonderful intensity, dramatic skies, distinct seasons, crisp air, and the luxury of living in a lofty remove far from the world's intrigues and follies.

Visiting the Pueblo

Visitors to the Pueblo de Taos—a sovereign nation—must respect its rules and customs. Don't photograph or sketch without a tribal government permit (obtainable upon request for a small fee). During dances and other ceremonies, refrain from applause or asking questions. Though public, these are religious observances, not performances.

Strictly speaking, Taos is the village christened Don Fernando de Taos by Spanish settlers in 1598. Popularly, however, it includes the separate but adjoining **Pueblo de Taos,** located on the Pueblo de Taos Indian Reservation and one of America's oldest communities, and **Ranchos de Taos,** the Pueblo's 18th-century farming annex at Taos's southern fringe. Its center is **Taos Plaza,** laid out three centuries ago for defense. Doors and windows are few, designed to be barricaded in the event of attack. (Spanish rule, which force-fed Christianity and demanded tribute, did not go down well with the Pueblo, which led other native communities in an 1680 revolt that kept Europeans at bay for a couple of decades.) The plaza's protective embrace creates a cloister for bookstores, shops, art galleries, offices, and cafés. The only reminder of Taos's growing pains is the **Governor Bent House.** Here in 1847, a mob enraged by the government's annexation of New Mexico killed the territorial governor in his home. The gloomy residence is a museum now, filled with furnishings and equipment from that tense era.

Early in the 20th century, enthralled by its sophisticated artists and their

Church of San Gerónimo

Fall foliage outside Taos

wealthy patrons, English writer D. H. Lawrence rhapsodized about the village. He also painted, and some of his artworks are displayed in the **Hotel La Fonda de Taos** on the plaza's south side. The nearby **Old County Courthouse** holds Depression-era murals by luminaries of the original Taos art colony. Upstairs in the courthouse, the **Taos County Historical Society** has an interesting library.

You'll find many galleries on nearby Ledoux Street, which leads to the **E.L. Blumenschein Home and Museum.** A co-founder of the Taos Society of Artists, Ernest Blumenschein, and his artist wife, Mary Shepherd Greene Blumenschein, filled it with paintings and handmade furniture displayed here. A few doors away, the **Harwood Foundation Library and Museum** (another art patron's residence) exhibits artworks that define the group, drawn to the area by its captivating light and supportive society. The collection includes many old wooden saints, or *santos,* by Spanish carvers.

Making utilitarian things artful is a Taos tradition born in the Pueblo. Inspired by it, Russian émigré Nicolai Fechin adorned his adobe home with woodwork reflecting his Slavic origins. It's now the **Fechin Institute/Museum,** where artworks and historical displays celebrate the painter.

Just east of Paseo del Pueblo Norte on Kit Carson Road (US 64) is the **Kit Carson Home and Museum,** originally an 1843 wedding present from the famed Army scout to his young bride, Josefa Jaramillo—she was 15, he 33. Their life together is evoked by historical documents, artifacts, and antiques. Kit and Josefa are buried a short stroll north in a cemetery adjoining 20-acre **Kit Carson Park,** also off Paseo del Pueblo Norte. The grave of Mabel Dodge

Luhan, Taos's most influential early-century art patron, is near the Dragoon Lane gate. Close by is a marker commemorating Padre Martinez, a significant figure in Willa Cather's novel *Death Comes for the Archbishop.*

A reminder that Taos was once New Mexico's most forlorn settlement lies 2 miles south of the plaza on Ranchitos Road, where the **Hacienda de los Martinez,** the Southwest's best-preserved Spanish colonial home, looks as it did in 1825. Filled with period furniture and decorations, it's a fortress, its massive walls without windows to bar marauding Apache, Navajo, and Ute who sought to push back the tide of settlers. Continue south on Ranchitos Road to Paseo del Pueblo Sur (N. Mex. 68) and the village of **Ranchos de Taos,** best known for its **Church of San Francisco de Asís.** If the squat adobe seems unimpressive, walk behind it. Chances are you've seen this west side view in paintings by Georgia O'Keeffe, or in Ansel Adams's famous black and white image.

While in Taos, don't fail to visit the **Pueblo de Taos,** a short drive from the plaza and yet centuries removed. Its multistory adobe "apartments," North House and South House, date from A.D. 1000 and 1450. About 200 of the tribe's 2,000-odd members live here, without electricity or running water other than the rocky creek splashing through the dirt plaza. If the Pueblo's **Church of San Gerónimo** is open, slip inside to view the painting of the Virgin Mary surrounded by a halo of golden corncobs, a powerful image reflecting the blend of native and European culture—an uneasy historical fusion that still generates heat throughout this region and symbolizes the peculiar overlap of new and old that gives Taos its unusual ambience of seeming to exist in a time and place parallel to the rest of the world.   *Mark Miller*

Travelwise

GETTING THERE

Taos is in north-central New Mexico, 75 miles northeast of Santa Fe and 135 miles from Albuquerque via I-25 and US 285 and N. Mex. 68. Albuquerque International is the closest major airport. Daily and weekend shuttle bus services operate between Albuquerque Airport, Santa Fe, and Taos *(Faust Transportation 505-758-3410).* Public Chile Line *(505-737-2606)* shuttles run on the half-hour, Mon.-Sat., between the Pueblo de Taos and the Ranchos de Taos Post Office, Faust Transportation also provides taxi service in Taos.

GENERAL INFORMATION

Taos summers are sunny, dry, and warm, with daytime highs in the 80s and overnight lows in the 50s. Afternoon thundershowers occur frequently from July through August. Winters are moderate; January temperatures range between 29°-64°F, however, snowfall at higher elevations can top 300 inches. Contact the **Taos County Chamber of**

Commerce Visitor's Center *(1139 Paseo del Pueblo Sur, P.O. Drawer I, Taos 87571. 505-758-3873 or 800-732-TAOS. www.taoschamber .com).* Ask about brochures suggesting walking tours of historic buildings and other points of interest.

THINGS TO SEE AND DO

Church of San Francisco de Asís
(Ranchos de Taos. 505-758-2754. Closed Sun.; adm. fee) Before you enter the circa 1815 church, visit the parish hall to watch a video about its history.

E.L. Blumenschein Home and Museum
(222 Ledoux St. 505-758-0505. Adm. fee) The home is exactly as it was when the artist lived here in the early 20th century.

Fechin Institute/Museum *(227 Paseo del Pueblo Norte. 505-758-1710. Wed.-Sun. Call to confirm hours; adm. fee)* The home, designed and built by Fechin, displays furnishings he carved by hand and some of his distinctive art.

Governor Bent House (*117A Bent St. 505-758-2376. Adm fee*) This stolid building is dramatic proof that, in the mid-19th century, even the well-positioned enjoyed few domestic comforts or refinements.

Hacienda de los Martinez (*Ranchitos Rd. 505-758-0505. Adm. fee*) One of the few original Spanish colonial haciendas open to public view. Living history demonstrations re-create the family's domestic life.

Harwood Foundation Library and Museum (*238 Ledoux St. 505-758-9826. Tues.-Sun.; adm. fee*) Many of Taos's most noted artists, from the founding art colony members to contemporary members, are shown along with 19th-century Hispanic artwork.

Hiking, Biking, and Rafting Taos-based Native Sons Adventures (*1033-A Paseo del Pueblo Sur. 505-758-9342 or 800-753-7559*) offers guided wilderness hiking, biking, and rafting tours in the Rio Grande Gorge and the Sangre de Cristos. June to mid-October, the Bavarian (*505-776-5301*), a small Taos Sky Valley lodge, organizes daily guided nature hikes into the neighboring wilderness area.

Hot Air Ballooning From June through October, the Pueblo Balloon Company (*505-751-9877*) launches 4-passenger sight-seeing flights, usually including a drift through part of the Rio Grande Gorge.

Hotel La Fonda de Taos (*108 S. Plaza. 505-758-2211 or 800-833-2211. $$*) Ask to see the Lawrence paintings, and expect to pay a small fee if you are not a guest.

Kit Carson Home and Museum (*Kit Carson Rd./US 64. 505-758-0505. Adm. fee*) Note the souvenirs of Carson's mountain man days. There is an impressive vintage gun collection, along with unusual Hispanic and Indian artifacts.

Literary Events Check the calendar at the Taos Public Library (*402 Camino de la Placita. 505-758-3063*) for readings and poetry recitals by Taos-area writers.

Pueblo de Taos (*505-758-1028. Adm. fees, plus permits for photography, sketching, filming, and videotaping*) Park on the plaza and look for signs identifying shops and bakeries. Permits are available at the admission kiosks.

Taos County Historical Society (*Old Taos County Courthouse, Taos Plaza. Mon., Wed., and*

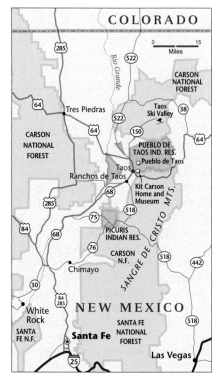

Fri. p.m.) Visitors are welcome to the History Room, a small archive located upstairs.

Van Vechten-Lineberry Taos Art Museum (*501 Paseo del Pueblo Norte. 505-758-2690. Wed.-Sun.; adm. fee*) For a comprehensive survey of works by virtually every member of the original Taos Society of Artists—about 130 works by more than 50 artists—this is the place to visit.

ENTERTAINMENT

Adobe Bar (*Historic Taos Inn, 125 Paseo del Pueblo Norte. 505-758-2233*) Long a favorite local watering hole, it features a bar menu and live music and entertainment (*Wed., Fri.-Sun.; fee*).

SHOPPING

Pueblo de Taos (*505-758-1028. Daily except during certain religious holidays or tribal events; call to confirm open hours*) Many residential ground rooms are used for selling authentic Native American jewelry, weavings, pottery, drums, paintings, sculptures, and more. (Enter only open doorways clearly marked as shops.)

Sandra Miller Studio (212 Paseo del Cañon, #C2. 505-758-0123. Tues.-Fri. p.m., Sat. by appt.) The noted Taos designer's handmade stone clocks, frames, and mirrors are produced here.

Taos Drums (5 miles S of Taos Plaza on N. Mex. 68, at N. Mex. 570. 505-758-3796 or 800-424-3786. Workshop tours Mon.-Fri. 11 a.m. and 2 p.m.) Craftspeople using traditional methods make and decorate Native American drums. Native American-made items sold here include pottery and ceramics.

ANNUAL EVENTS

Pueblo de Taos (505-758-1028) The Pueblo observes many feast days and religious holidays, most involving dances and other traditional activities to which the public is invited. (No photography permitted.) Among them, in June, the **Feast of San Antonio** and **Feast of San Juan;** in July, the **Feast of Santa Ana and Santiago** and the **Taos Pueblo Powwow;** in September, the **Feast of San Gerónimo.** Christmas holiday observances include several dances and a bonfire procession.

Taos Fall Art Festival (2 weeks in fall. Taos Civic Center. 505-776-2388 or 800-732-8267) The event includes two juried exhibitions of works by more than 200 Taos County artists.

Taos Poetry Circus (2nd week in June. 505-758-1800) The main event is the World Heavyweight Championship Poetry Bout, a competitive reading by poets of their work.

Taos Trade Fair (End of Sept. Hacienda de los Martinez. 505-758-0505. Adm. fee) Hispanic and Native American arts and crafts, food, dancing.

Wool Festival (1st weekend in Oct. Kit Carson Park. 505-751-0306) Celebrates the region's four-century history of wool producing. Demonstrations of sheep shearing, wool processing, spinning, and quilting.

WHERE TO EAT

Apple Tree Restaurant (123 Bent St. 505-758-1900. $$) A comfortable eatery serving hearty Southwestern food and tasty desserts.

Doc Martin's (505-758-1977. $$) The Historic Taos Inn's restaurant is cozy and intimate, the modern Southwestern cuisine creatively conceived and elegantly presented.

Lambert's of Taos (309 Paseo del Pueblo Sur. 505-758-1009. Dinner only. $$) Haute cuisine

and fine wines at reasonable prices in an elegant but informal setting. Ask about single-vineyard California Zinfandels, a house specialty.

WHERE TO STAY

Casa Benavides (137 Kit Carson Rd. 505-758-1772 or 800-552-1772. $$/$$$) This well-run B&B consists of a group of historic buildings housing huge rooms creatively decorated with handmade furniture, down comforters, and antiques.

Taos Trade Fair

Fechin Inn (227 Paseo del Pueblo Norte. 505-751-1000 or 800-811-2933. $$/$$$) A pueblo-style hotel with 85 rooms decorated in earthy colors and handmade furniture, on the secluded grounds of the Fechin Institute/Museum.

Historic Taos Inn (125 Paseo del Pueblo Norte. 505-758-2233 or 800-826-7466. $$/$$$) This 64-year-old inn incorporates some of the oldest houses in Taos. Its 36 rooms have Southwestern furnishings. Some are quite small; ask for one on the courtyard.

Inn on La Loma Plaza (315 Ranchitos Rd. 505-758-1717 or 800-530-3040. $$/$$$) A historic walled adobe, parts of which date from 1800, on a hill near the plaza.

Mesilla

It may be the best preserved old Spanish-Mexican settlement in the Southwest, so authentic that to some, upon first look, it is disconcertingly humble. It did not grow up in easy times. Its thick adobe walls were built to protect against Apache raiders, and many of its most historically significant buildings, put up by untrained settlers, are low, small, squat, or just terribly plain. Nearly every one has a history arising out of pioneer family sagas, tragedies, or a footnote to an Old West legend. Back when it was young, it welcomed visitors who survived the perils of the lonely roads leading here. Hospitality is still its forte.

Blue Windows, Blue Doors

Why are so many old Southwest doorways and window frames painted vivid blue or indigo? Mexican folklore holds that blue offers protection against the Evil Eye, and that turquoise brings good fortune. Sun-faded lighter hues were sometimes called "Virgin Mary" blues— referring to the traditional depictions of her robe in paintings.

Architecturally speaking, time stopped here in 1881. Until then Mesilla was this region's commercial and transportation center, hub of the southern New Mexico Territory's mining and cattle business, and the political and social center of Doña Ana County. In 1854 the flag-raising ceremony putting into effect the 1853 Gadsden Purchase of over 30,000 square miles from Mexico took place on the **Old Mesilla Plaza,** now a state historic district. Mesilla was designated territorial capital and seemed destined for prosperity and growth. But in 1881 the railroad, an essential link to distant markets, was diverted 4 miles northeast to Las Cruces, and Mesilla's fortunes nose-dived. It got by with her original adobe and redbrick buildings until the 1950s, when residents recognized Mesilla's architectural legacy as something to be cherished.

If, like most, you arrive from Las Cruces via N. Mex. 28 (here called Avenida de Mesilla), leave your vehicle in the public lot where the road meets Calle de Santiago. Old Mesilla is small and best explored on foot. Both sides of **Calle de Santiago** date from the 1850s, its buildings housing a clan from Mexico named Gallegos. Patriarch Manuel Valles, being the region's only carpenter and coffinmaker, traveled widely, framing windows and hanging doors and working out of the Valles Carpentry Shop near the intersection of Calle de Guadalupe, now a jewelry store. When the three bells of the double-spired **San Albino Church** chime, you're hearing the work of his descendants— ringing them is a family tradition. The Catholic chapel is a relative youngster, a 1907 replacement of the original 1855 adobe church that stood there.

When you exit the church, the long building on your right (on Calle de Principal) is the superbly restored **Barela-Reynolds Building,** built between 1850 and 1860 and once a general store. One of the shops in the

Ballet Folklorico at Mesilla's Cinco de Mayo Fiesta

Mesilla gate

Reynold/Griggs Building farther east boasts a rare, stamped metal Italianate storefront, purchased through a mail order catalog and installed about 1890.

The **Maurin Building** on the plaza's southwest corner is New Mexico's oldest known brick structure, built in 1853 by a prosperous French immigrant. He had the habit of keeping large bags of money inside, and was found murdered there, sans loot, three years later. Larceny figures in the history of the **Miranda/Bean Building,** running south on Calle Principal from Calle de Parian. The elder Bean employed sons Sam and Roy in his saloon there, which had a safe where locals kept valuables. A local tale holds that while Sam was away, Roy emptied the safe and skipped. If true, his adult metamorphosis into the unforgiving "hanging" Judge Roy Bean of Old West lore seems more than a little ironic.

Some call the adobe on the plaza at 2355 Calle de Guadalupe the **Governor's Mansion,** because a Confederate governor stayed here for a short time in 1861. It's reputedly haunted—Mesilla folklore tells of an outraged *padrona* who fatally stabbed her naughty son and their maid there. The ill-fated lovers' spirits are said to occasionally break wine glasses. As the manse now houses the wonderfully fancy, antique-filled **Double Eagle restaurant** and its more casual sibling, **Peppers Cafe,** broken glasses are perhaps not necessarily a paranormal occurrence. Waiters, however, report toppled chairs.

The building with perhaps the town's most flamboyant history—the adobe on the plaza's southeast corner—is among its least imposing. For a time it was New Mexico's territorial capitol; then it was a courthouse and jail, where in 1881 Billy "The Kid" Bonney was sentenced to hang for two murders. (He shot his way out with a smuggled revolver.)

Much has changed from the time when Mesilla was known as a town given to fancy balls, cockfights, bullfights, fine hotels, and rowdy saloons. But Mesilla's ambition was always to hang on and eventually become genteel. Hang on it did, and genteel it has become—hence the friendliness you'll feel when you walk its worn brick streets. *Mark Miller*

Travelwise

GETTING THERE

Mesilla is in southwestern New Mexico, about 4 miles southwest of downtown Las Cruces between I-10 and the Rio Grande.
The closest major airport is El Paso (Texas) International, 50 miles southeast. Las Cruces Shuttle Service *(505-525-1784 or 800-288-1784)* makes many runs daily between the airport and Las Cruces.

GENERAL INFORMATION

Spring and fall are the most comfortable times to visit. Mesilla lies at 3,900 feet in high desert country, with 350 sunny days per year. Summers are hot, while winters are mild. There is no visitor center in Mesilla. The **Old Mesilla Association** *(P.O. Box 1005, Mesilla 88046)* publishes a free map suitable for self-guided walking tours, and is available at many businesses on or around the plaza. For additional information visit www.mesilla.com or call the **Mesilla Town Hall** *(505-524-3262)*. For additional information, contact **Las Cruces Convention & Visitors Bureau** *(211 N. Water St., Las Cruces 88001. 505-541-2444 or 800-FIESTAS)*.

SHOPPING

La Posta Chile Shop *(2410 Calle de San Albino. 505-524-3524. Closed Mon.)* Part of La Posta de Mesilla restaurant, it claims to have the Southwest's most extensive inventory of hot sauces, salsas, and chili products.

Mesilla Mercado *(Old Mesilla Plaza. Thurs. and Sun.)* Vendors set up booths to sell food, handicrafts, and other items.

Nambé *(2109 Calle de Parian. 505-527-4623)* Foundry pieces and pottery by the Nambé Mills Santa Fe artisans are sold here.

ANNUAL EVENTS

Christmas Eve Old Mesilla Plaza is transformed into a fairyland by the gentle radiance of *luminarias*—brown paper sacks containing votive candles anchored in sand. Locals and tourists promenade, singing carols.

Cinco de Mayo Fiesta *(Weekend preceding May 5. Old Mesilla Plaza. 505-524-3262)* The celebration commemorates the day in 1862 that Mexican troops defeated a French expeditionary force near Mexico City.

Dias de los Muertos *(Weekend preceding*

Nov. 1-2. Old Mesilla Plaza. 505-524-3262) The "Days of the Dead" commemorate the past lives of relatives, friends, and national heroes.

Diez y Seis de Septiembre Fiesta *(Weekend preceding Sept. 16. Old Mesilla Plaza. 505-524-3262)* The "September 16th" Festival recalls the date in 1810 that priest Miguel Hidalgo y Costilla exhorted followers to revolt against Spanish rule. Women dressed in traditional skirts and men in silver-studded *caballero* suits stroll the plaza while mariachi bands play.

WHERE TO EAT

Double Eagle *(2355 Calle de Guadalupe. 505-523-6700. $$)* Formal dining amid ornate and impressive Victorian antique decor. The Double Eagle features American fare, while the **Peppers Cafe** offers Spanish-Mexican cuisine.

El Patio Restaurante *(Calle de Parian. 505-524-0982. Closed Sat. p.m. and Sun. $$)* One of Mesilla Valley's oldest eateries, serving Mexican food and steaks.

La Posta de Mesilla *(2410 Calle de San Albino. 505-524-3524. Closed Mon. $)* Located in a mid-19th-century building that was once a Butterfield Stagecoach stop, it's known for traditional southern New Mexico dishes and steaks.

Old Mesilla Pastry Café *(2790 Avenida de Mesilla. 505-525-2636. Closed Tues. $)* A popular Southwestern-style breakfast place.

WHERE TO STAY

Mesón de Mesilla *(1803 Ave. de Mesilla. 505-525-9212. $$)* Southwest-style adobe "country inn" with five rooms. Its well-reviewed restaurant serves Continental fare *($$)*.

Patagonia

The jewel of the Sonoita Valley sits among oak grasslands at 4,050 feet between southeastern Arizona's Santa Rita Mountains and the ocher-hued Patagonias, enjoying a reputation as a rural Western-flavored hamlet with an upscale Bohemian flair. A peaceful village of about 1,000 people—many of them artists, craftspeople, artisans, ranchers, naturalists, or retirees—Patagonia's location beside two year-round creeks makes it one of the verdant oases in this semiarid high desert zone, where vineyards and apple orchards stitch green pinstripes across lion-yellow landscapes. Day-trippers come for its galleries and shops and to idle in its restaurants and cafés. Old West history buffs roam back roads in search of ghost towns. Hiking and mountain bike enthusiasts use Patagonia as a jumping-off place to trek the region's network of trails. Savvy sojourners favor the guest ranches tucked away in nearby hills and valleys. And birders travel from afar to study the region's bird-roosting areas, where hundreds of exotic species—and a good many travelers—find refuge. There is no other town quite like it in the Southwest.

The first people to the area were Archaic Indians, sustained by the abundance of game and fish along Sonoita and Harshaw Creeks from roughly 2000 B.C. to 500 B.C. The Hohokam followed, thriving in the same fashion from about A.D. 900 to 1400, as did the Sobaipuri, who greeted the first Spanish missionaries. The Apache prevented permanent settlement until well into the 19th century, when the American military arrived in force.

Patagonia is a relative youngster, established in 1898 alongside the New Mexico & Arizona Railroad and named for its founder, Rollin Rice Richardson, a Pennsylvania-born rancher and mine owner. The following year, the citizens of Rollin voted to rename it after the region in southern South America whose mountains and mines resembled those surrounding the town. Patagonia prospered as a shipping point for ore and livestock. Hotels and boardinghouses sprang up, followed by an opera house, restaurants, and saloons. The mines eventually petered out in 1959 and within three years, the New Mexico & Arizona was out of business and its tracks pulled up. Patagonians, however, were undaunted. The railroad station's grounds were dedicated as **Town Park;** its abandoned depot, completed in 1904, became the **Town Hall.**

You'll find Sonoita and Harshaw Creeks splashing through the central district, where streets are lined with large shade trees. Leave your car to amble among the galleries, shops, and restaurants that make Patagonia unusually sophisticated for such an out-of-the-way place. Many of the vintage mercantile buildings surviving so handsomely are now residences—some of them artist's studios open to prospective patrons.

At the Patagonia-Sonoita Creek Preserve

It's likely you'll hear languages other than English and Spanish, though four of every five Santa Cruz County residents have Hispanic roots. That's because Sonoita Creek creates a variety of habitats as it wanders through its namesake valley, including verdant woodlands and marshes that sustain unusually large bird populations. One result is that this region in general, and the Nature Conservancy's **Patagonia-Sonoita Creek Preserve** in particular, are known to birders and ornithologists worldwide.

Patagonia Lake State Park

The sanctuary, about a mile from downtown, is a veritable Eden in contrast to surrounding landscapes mostly dun-colored and dry. You sense its nurturing quality as you enter its fluttery stands of willow and Fremont cottonwood—many of the latter as old as 130 years and rising up to 100 feet to create ideal perching and nesting places for hawks and herons. Closer to the creek, Arizona black walnut, velvet ash, canyon hackberry, and mesquite thrive. Birders, who make a point of recording their sightings, have so far identified over 160 species here, including the ever popular rose-throated becard. The birds flutter noisily above earthbound neighbors including javelina pigs and desert tortoises.

Mining hamlets—their treasure was silver, lead, and zinc—boomed locally starting in the mid-19th century. **Harshaw,** 10 miles southeast of Patagonia, sprouted about 1873 and by 1890 had a population of 260 and a newspaper reporting on 100 nearby mining operations. Little remains—a few old buildings, foundations, melting adobe walls, and a cemetery. **Mowry,** 5 miles farther on, grew up around a mine purchased in 1860 by a U. S. Army lieutenant named Sylvester Mowry, who renamed the town accordingly. The enterprise ended in 1862 with his arrest for supplying lead for Confederate bullets. Its ruins—decaying walls, scattered metal, and a smelter dump—lie along a gravel road. If you're feeling adventurous, find **Washington Camp** on your road map, about 20 miles south of Patagonia. Once the major service community for Mowry and Harshaw and other towns, it peaked in 1905 with a population of 1,000 miners and their families. The ruins aren't extensive, but there's an aura of Old West romance in all of these historical footnotes.

When it's completed, the largely primitive, often challenging **Arizona Trail** will traverse the state from Mexico to Utah for the pleasure of hikers and rough-terrain bicyclists. The 800-mile path passes through Patagonia. Trekkers often overnight at **Patagonia Lake State Park,** located 7 miles southwest of town. You can swim, fish, or water-ski here, or simply picnic in the shade of campground ramadas, as many do, and savor the pleasures of being happily marooned in this unique Arizona oasis. *Mark Miller*

Travelwise

GETTING THERE

Patagonia is located in southeastern Arizona, 64 miles southeast of Tucson. Most out-of-state visitors arrive via Phoenix Sky Harbor International Airport or Tucson International and rent a vehicle.

GENERAL INFORMATION

Patagonia is a year-round destination. Winters are mild, with occasional rain and light snow from late November through March. Spring is unpredictable, though usually mild and dry with cool nights. Early summer is dry; in July and August, Arizona's "monsoon season" brings frequent afternoon thunderstorms. Fall days are mild and bright. Patagonia's visitor center is located in **Mariposa Books** (305 McKeown Ave. 520-394-0060 or 888-794-0060. Wed.-Mon.). For tourist information, visit the **State of Arizona** website (www.state.az.us) and use the "Community" information button to select Patagonia. The **Arizona Office of Tourism** (800-842-8257) offers a travel kit booklet.

THINGS TO SEE AND DO

Birding In addition to Patagonia-Sonoita Creek Preserve, popular birding spots include: **Empire Cienega Resource Conservation Area** (6 miles N of Sonoita on E side of Ariz. 83. 520-772-4289); **Madera Canyon** (Ariz. 82 N to Sonoita, left on Ariz. 82 for 12 miles. 520-625-8746); and the **San Pedro Riparian Natural Conservation Area** (Visitor center, 7 miles E of Sierra Vista on Ariz. 90. 520-459-2555).

Hiking and Bicycling The Santa Rita and Patagonia Mountains surrounding Patagonia and Sonoita are laced with dirt roads and trails of varying difficulty, from easy to arduous. Consult a topographic map or locally published guides to Coronado National Forest trails.

Horseback Riding Saddle up at Arizona Trail Tours (520-394-2701 or 800-477-0615) in Patagonia for guided horseback day trips.

Patagonia Lake State Park (400 Patagonia Lake Rd. via Ariz. 82. 520-287-6965. Adm. fee) Facilities include picnic ramadas, a swimming beach, and a marina store with boat rentals.

Patagonia-Sonoita Creek Preserve (N. 4th Ave. to Pennsylvania; turn left onto Blue Heaven Rd. 520-394-2400. Closed Mon.-Tues.;

donation) Discover the preserve's pristine character and peacefulness along its footpaths. Guided tours offered every Sat. a.m. No picnicking or camping, pets or horses.

ANNUAL EVENTS

Patagonia Heritage Festival (Mem. Day weekend. Various locations. 520-287-2734) Historic displays depict the town's century-long saga; musicians and other performers.

Southwest Wings Birding Festival (Mid-Aug. Sierra Vista. 520-458-7353) The four-day event features guided birding walks and hummingbird banding demonstrations.

WHERE TO EAT

Home Plate Restaurant (277 McKeown Ave. 520-394-2344. $) Reliable home-style meals.

Velvet Elvis (292 Naugle Ave. 520-394-2102. $) The house specialty is thin, crisp, handspun, stone-fired gourmet pizza.

Wagon Wheel Saloon (400 W. Naugle Ave. 520-394-2433. $) This cowboy bar and restaurant rang up its first sale in 1937 and still serves BBQ ribs, steaks, and hamburgers.

WHERE TO STAY

Circle Z Ranch (1476 Ariz. 82. 520-394-2525 or 888-854-2525. Closed mid-May–Oct. $$$) Arizona's oldest continuously operating dude ranch.

Prescott

Situated at 5,368 feet on a cottonwood basin of creeks and washes, straddled by 1.25 million acres of national forest and wilderness, surrounded by urban parks, and boasting nine historic districts, a lively gallery and performing arts scene, many fine restaurants, and some of the freshest air in the United States, Prescott's only real problem is its spreading reputation. Its head count, nearly 35,000, has doubled since 1970, alarming

some long-time residents. To lifestyle refugees seeking a town neither too big nor too small, however, it's one of the key selling points on Prescott's résumé, whose official nickname is Everybody's Hometown.

The area has always drawn people. Some 9,000 years ago, it supported a population estimated at 100,000, ancestors of the 145 enrolled

Territorial Governor's Mansion at the Sharlot Hall Museum

members of the adjoining **Yavapai Indian Reservation.** The seeds of the town were sown in 1838 by a gold strike on Granite Creek, which runs through town. Local lore holds that the mining camp's first saloon, the Quartz Rock, had one tin cup and two bottles of whiskey. New strikes a generation later induced Abraham Lincoln, seeking revenue for his Civil War-strapped treasury, to push Congress to create the Arizona Territory in 1863. The as-yet-unnamed Granite Creek settlement was designated its capital and named for William Hickling Prescott, a prominent scholar of Spanish, Mexican, and Peruvian history. Alarmed by southern Arizona's Confederate leanings, Congress encouraged the influence of Union loyalists from the Northeast and Midwest. Yankees came in droves, built pitched-roof frame houses along streets lined with trees, and created the most Eastern-looking city in the Southwest.

Prescott, however, was thoroughly Western from the get-go. A chorus line of saloons kicked and shouted along downtown's **Montezuma Street,** starting with the Kentucky Bar at the corner of Goodwin and ending with the Depot House at the Atchison, Topeka & Santa Fe train station. In 1889 capital status transferred for the final time to Phoenix, but Prescott continued to prosper from mining and timber cutting. (It's surrounded by the world's largest stand

Watson Lake and the Granite Dells

of Ponderosa pine.) By 1900 Montezuma Street had so many saloons that
locals called it Whiskey Row. One, **The Palace,** is Arizona's oldest, dating from
1877. Its ornately carved Brunswick bar was transported from San Francisco
by ship to the Sea of Cortez, paddle-wheeled up the Colorado to Ehrenburg,
then hauled here by wagon. As fire swept over Prescott in July 1900, patrons
carried it onto the street and continued their drinking.

Swift rebuilding re-created the local preference for "Eastern" architectural
styles, and Whiskey Row came back as well, its watering holes today elbowed
by restaurants, shops, galleries showing contemporary, Western, and Indian
artwork, and after-hours clubs favoring country-western music.

Start your exploration at Prescott's civic center, **Courthouse Plaza.**
The pale granite Greek Revival-style **Yavapai County Courthouse,** completed
in 1918, is surrounded by three acres of lawns and spreading trees where
you can relax on a bench. The hall of justice is the centerpiece of the **Sharlot
Hall Museum** collection of historic buildings, which includes the 1864 territorial governor's log "mansion," pioneer cabins, and a schoolhouse chock-full
of period artifacts. The **Sharlot Hall Building** exhibits relics of Arizona's prehistoric and Native American cultures, and traces Prescott's growth from gold
camp to three-college town (including four-year Prescott College, one

Steer roping at a Prescott rodeo

of the finest liberal arts colleges in the West).

Put on your walking shoes to explore Prescott's historic districts; the town has eight federally designated ones. The newest is **Mile High Park,** whose bungalow-style houses of stone, pine, and redwood are located in West Prescott, a 1906 subdivision where summer visitors once idylled away pine-scented days in log cabins and tent encampments. You'll also see many lovely examples of vintage architecture in the **East Prescott Historic District** and **Fleury's Addition Historic District.**

While you're touring, have a look at the Indian artifacts and artworks at the **Smoki Museum,** a collection to make an archaeologist's heart go pitty-pat: stone ornaments, bone tools, ancient sandals, a variety of tools, and its pièce de résistance, some 400 whole or reconstructed Southwest vessels and figurines, including many found near Prescott. The Yavapai are represented by a large collection of tribal baskets. Well worth the 5-mile drive from downtown, the **Phippen Museum-Art of the American West,** which resembles a rustic ranch house from Arizona's Territorial era, has an outstanding collection of paintings and artworks by Western artists, and photographs by Edward S. Curtis.

When you've had your fill of antique this and historical that, take a stroll through the brushy hills and prairies of **Pioneer Park,** which overlooks the unusual **Granite Dells** formation. The 5.5-mile **Prescott Peavine Trail** traces an old railroad bed from the bucolic Watson Woods Riparian Preserve to US 89A. The trail has views of Watson Lake, the Granite Dells, old ranch land, and the far-off San Francisco Peaks rising 12,000 feet near **Prescott National Forest,** where in summer hikers and campers escape lowland heat. What recreations you cannot pursue here over four seasons you probably can't find anywhere in the Southwest. Prescott's old-timers, however, would prefer that you not tell anyone.   *Mark Miller*

Travelwise

GETTING THERE

Prescott is located in central Arizona, 96 miles northwest of Phoenix via I-17 and Ariz. 69. Phoenix's Sky Harbor is the nearest major airport, served by Prescott-based bus and shuttle lines. Mesa Airlines *(520-445-7701 or 800-637-2247)*, flying as America West Express *(800-235-9292 or 800-327-7810)*, currently serves Prescott's Municipal Airport, Ernest A. Love Field *(9.2 miles N of downtown Prescott via Ariz. 89)*. Love Field has two rental car agencies.

GENERAL INFORMATION

Prescott enjoys a mild four-season climate. Spring is wildflower season; come autumn, its cottonwoods turn gold. Average snowfall is 21 inches and usually melts within hours; rainfall averages 19 inches per year. Summers are warm, with highs in the 90s. In July and August, the wettest months, afternoon thunderstorms occur often. Obtain visitor information at the **Prescott Tourism Information Center** *(117 W. Goodwin St. at Montezuma St. 520-445-2000 or 800-266-7534)* or contact the **Chamber of Commerce** *(101 S. Cortez St., P.O. Box 1147, Prescott 86302. 520-778-2193)*. Prescott's mile-high elevation and 350 sunny days per year make sunglasses, sunscreen, and a hat advisable.

THINGS TO SEE AND DO

Courthouse Plaza *(Between Cortez and Montezuma Sts.)* Prescott's historical hub, with the imposing hall of justice as its centerpiece. Ask at the nearby visitor center about guided tours of the town and maps of historic districts. The **East Prescott Historic District** is chockablock with 19th-century residences; it's roughly bounded by the Atchison, Topeka & Santa Fe Railroad tracks, and N. Mt. Vernon, Carleton, and N. Alarcon Sts. **Fleury's Addition Historic District**, another collection of old houses, sprawls around Western and Gurley, and along Willow, Grove, and Garden Sts. The **Mile High Park Historic District**, a 1906 subdivision, embraces Oregon Ave.; Gail Gardner Way; Linwood Ave.; Josephine, Shasta, Lindberg, and Mayo Sts.; and Dr. John Flinn Memorial Park on Josephine. Information and maps are also available at Sharlot Hall Museum and City Hall *(201 S. Cortez St.)*.

Phippen Museum-Art of the American West *(4701 Ariz. 89 N. 520-778-1385. Closed Tues.; adm. fee)* Changing exhibitions supplement the permanent collection. The gift shop features work by Arizona artists.

Sharlot Hall Museum *(415 W Gurley St. 520-445-3122. Donation)* The complex of buildings in a 3-acre park includes the Sharlot Hall Building and the reconstructed log-built **Territorial Governor's Mansion**, duplicating the 1864 original.

Smoki Museum *(147 N. Arizona St. 520-445-1230. Mid-April–Oct. Mon.-Fri. and Sun., by appt. rest of year)* Built in 1935 of native stone and wood to resemble an Indian pueblo, it also has a library catering to scholars and history buffs.

Wilderness Recreation The premier outdoor recreation spots hereabouts are in **Prescott National Forest**, known for scenic drives, hiking, backpacking, nature photography, horseback riding, and mountain biking. Ask rangers in the Bradshaw Ranger District *(Visitor Center, 2230 E. Ariz. 69, Prescott. 520-445-7253)* about the Thumb Butte Trail; and the Verde Ranger District *(520-567-4121)* about the General Crook Trail. Depending upon the season, the forest's varied terrain creates opportunities for hang gliding, technical rock climbing and bouldering, and white-water rafting. Local outdoor enthusiasts also recommend the mountains around **Watson Lake** southeast of town.

SHOPPING

Many antique furniture and collectibles stores are located on Cortez St. between Gurley and Sheldon Sts. The Whiskey Row merchant's association publishes a free map and guide to participating businesses.

Merchandise Mart Antique Mall *(205 N. Cortez St. 520-776-1727)* You'll find many retailers in this cavernous building. Quality varies, but the inventory is extensive.

ANNUAL EVENTS

Arizona Cowboy Poets Gathering *(Mid-Aug. Sharlot Hall Museum and other locations. 520-445-3122)* Storytelling in verse and song, Western harmony bands, cowboy singer-songwriters, and cowboy traditions from clothing to fine art. Featured are noted poets selected by a jury, who read from their work.

Christmas Parade and Courthouse Lighting *(1st Sat. in Dec. Courthouse Plaza. 520-445-2000 or 800-266-7534)* The holiday kick-off includes a children's concert of carols, and the transformation of the Courthouse—using spotlights and hundreds of *luminarias*—into a vivid red ornament.

Folk Arts Fair *(Early June. Sharlot Hall Museum. 520-445-3122)* A living history approach offers visitors an opportunity to try their hand at domestic tasks of frontier days, such as candle dipping and wool spinning.

Frontier Days *(Week of July 4. Courthouse Plaza and Yavapai County Fairgrounds. Rodeo information 520-445-3103 or 800-358-1888; Fairgrounds information 520-778-2193. Adm. fee to some events)* Parades, food booths, arts and crafts, entertainment, a fireworks display, a downtown parade, and evening dances. The World's Oldest Rodeo (dating from 1888) is the main event.

Yavapai County Fair *(Mid-Sept. 520-778-2193. Adm. fee to some events)* A traditional get-together with rides, agricultural exhibits, and grandstand entertainment.

WHERE TO EAT

Murphy's *(201 N. Cortez St. 520-445-4044. $$)* One of Prescott's oldest and most popular restaurants, it features fresh seafood, beef, and barbecue. Its building dates from 1892: the tin ceiling is original and the animal head trophies and old photographs complement the rooms.

The Palace *(120 S. Montezuma St. 520-541-1996. $)* Despite its wooly 19th-century personality, it's now a family-friendly restaurant as well.

Peacock Room at the Hassayampa Inn *(122 E. Gurley St. 520-778-9434. $$/$$$)* Regulars come for Continental cuisine, commodious booths, deco touches, chandelier lighting, and friendly service.

WHERE TO STAY

Hassayampa Inn *(122 E. Gurley St. by Courthouse Plaza. 520-778-9434 or 800-322-1927. $$/$$$)* Prescott's grand doyen of hospitality, completed in 1927. Its lobby has that blend of pueblo and art deco details peculiar to the Southwest, as do its 68 rooms. Rates include breakfast in the Peacock Room.

Lynx Creek Farm Bed and Breakfast *(4.5 miles E of town off Ariz. 69. 520-778-9573 or 888-778-9573. $$)* A family-oriented contemporary log lodge, with cabins and a guesthouse near Prescott. Views of the Bradshaw Mountains and Prescott National Forest. Some units with wood-burning fireplaces, kitchenettes, and private outdoor hot tubs and decks.

Marks House Victorian B&B *(203 E. Union St. 520-778-4632 or 800-370-6275. $$)* A Prescott mayor once lived in this finely furnished hillside Queen Anne. Two suites and two rooms, all with private baths. Breakfast is served in a formal dining room.

NEARBY PLACES

Granite Dells *(N of Prescott via Ariz. 89; follow signs)* Hundreds of huge eroded granite rocks squeeze Watson Lake, creating an intriguing labyrinth for hikers and campers.

Granite Basin Wilderness *(Bradshaw Ranger District 520-445-7253)* The most popular of the forest's eight wild areas is only 20 minutes from Prescott. Once there, however, you must travel on foot or horseback. The piney Eden has beautiful vistas, granite boulder fields, some of the best technical rock climbing in America, and several campsites designed for users with disabilities.

Yavapai-Prescott Indian Reservation *(Tribal office: 530 E. Merritt St., Prescott 86301-2038. 520-445-8790)* The 1,409-acre tribal tract draws visitors to its Prescott Resort and Conference Center, which includes a casino.

Moab

The only Utah town on the Colorado River, and the recreation capital of the Beehive State's vast and scenic Canyonlands country, Moab nestles in a valley flanked by steep bluffs on a rugged desert landscape of sand and sagebrush amid spectacularly eroded sandstone formations. Outdoor enthusiasts—river runners, mountain bikers, backcountry hikers in particular—use it as a base camp for adventuring in two of the Southwest's most unusual national parks, Arches and Canyonlands, and the evergreen wildernesses of the Manti-La Sal National Forest, whose mountains spike the eastern horizon.

Mormon pioneers named Moab in 1880 after a biblical reference to "far country" and set to farming and ranching here. For a time more brief than legend suggests, in the late 1800s, the town was a hangout for Butch Cassidy's Wild Bunch and other outlaw gangs. Cow-poking, however, supported most law-abiding local folks until the postwar atomic age set off the Southwest's uranium boom and prospectors blazed the first roads into Canyonlands backcountry—today's "jeeping" trails and mountain bike routes. A few struck it

Western-flavored downtown Moab

rich, but Moab didn't change much, and today a good many of the little city's 5,000-odd working citizens play host, in some way or another, to the thousands of people who come here to hike, pedal, four-wheel drive, and sight-see.

Moab's premier attraction is scenery—massive rock formations taller than the tallest skyscrapers and so vertical they make you dizzy when you squint up at them—and the **Colorado** and **Green Rivers.** Much of this beauty lies within adjoining **Canyonlands National Park** and **Arches National Park.** Wind, ice, and water sculpted Arches, famous for over 2,000-plus stone arches. The Green and Colorado cut the bewildering maze within Canyonlands, best viewed from overlooks in **Dead Horse Point State Park** and Canyonlands's 6,080-foot-high **Grand View Point.** At both you'll find people focusing cameras on the 5,000-square-mile labyrinth, its terraces gradually stepping down to the muddy streams of the Colorado and the Green.

The peaks etching the horizon some 20 miles east are the **La Sals,** rising over 12,000 feet and sheltering, in contrast to the rust-red sagebrush plateau below, an evergreen Shangri-la of meadows, lakes, and streams sunk in the pine, spruce, fir, and aspen of the **Manti-La Sal National Forest.**

You must not fail to take the drive along **Potash Road** (Utah 279) for awe-inspiring close-ups of truly spectacular sandstone and shale cliffs. About 3 miles past the Portal, a notch cut by the Colorado, look for a sign reading "Indian Petroglyphs." Fixed telescopes study rock art scribed into a cliff by the Fremont people, who hunted and farmed these red canyons some 2,000 years ago. Continue to a sign pointing right to "Dinosaur Tracks"—three-toed footprints left by a Triassic creature in mud now uptilted into a vertical rock face.

For a better understanding of Moab's peculiar landscapes, spend an hour at the **Dan O'Laurie Canyon Country Museum** downtown. Exhibits also explain the area's dinosaur days, the lifestyle of this region's earliest inhabitants and the Ute people, whose domain this was. Mining and mineralogy displays recount the frenzied uranium rush.

Some evening when the sky is clear, ride the Moab Skyway Chairlift to the top of the **Moab Rim.** By day, the ten-minute hoist lifts you 1,000 feet to panoramas of the Colorado, the La Sals, and Arches. After dark, stargazers gather to survey the sparkling sky and set up telescopes. There's entertainment waiting downtown— good food, convivial watering holes, musical cafés—but you'll probably find yourself lingering here atop the silent and majestic stone landscape, reminded that the supreme beauty on this earth is wholly natural. *Mark Miller*

Biking Mecca

Given the profusion of sturdy bikes and helmeted pedalers around town, you won't need to be reminded that Moab is America's mountain bike mecca. Its best-known trail— famous among fat-tire aficionados worldwide— is the physically and technically demanding **Slickrock,** an 11-mile loop through a 6-square-mile expanse of undulating petrified sand dunelike terrain just north of town. Locals say Moab's other bike trails are just as scenic; consult a locally published trail guide and consider Hurrah Pass, Porcupine Rim, Gemini Bridges, Poison Spider, Kokopelli's, and the White Rim Trail.

Fisher Towers at sunset, in the La Sal Mountains near Moab

Travelwise

GETTING THERE

Moab is located in southeastern Utah on US 191, 244 miles south of Salt Lake City. Amtrak *(800-872-7245)* serves Green River, 53 miles north. Roadrunner Shuttle *(435-259-9402 or 435-259-7162 in winter)* offers drop-offs and pickups for all sports, parks, hiking and biking trails, and local airports.

GENERAL INFORMATION

Spring and fall bring the most comfortable weather. Spring arrives early, fall commences in October. Summers are hot and dry. Winters are mild, but sudden blizzards can strand hikers. For maps and information, contact the **Canyonlands North Grand County Travel Council** *(P.O. Box 550, Moab 84532. 435-259-8825 or 800-635-6622).* Moab's official website is www.moab.net. Also, visit the **Moab Area Chamber of Commerce's Information Center** *(805 N. Main St., Moab 84532. 435-259-8825 or 800-635-MOAB. www.moab.net).*

THINGS TO SEE AND DO

Arches National Park *(Main entrance, 5 miles N of Moab on US 191. 435-719-2100. Adm. fee)* This park contains more than 950 natural arches—the world's greatest concentration. Rangers conduct seasonal walks, guided hikes, and evening campfire programs.

Back-road Driving Guided tours are offered by Dan Mick's Guided Tours *(600 Millcreek Dr. 435-259-4567)* and Kokopelli Trails & Tales *(2182 Buena Vista. 435-259-5498 or 800-206-3669, ext. 69).*

Canyonlands National Park *(435-719-2313. Adm. fee)* This wonderland of canyon mazes, unbroken scarps, and sandstone pillars is composed of three different districts. The nearest to Moab is Island in the Sky *(30 miles SW via US 191 and Utah 313).* Here, Grand View Point provides a sweeping overview of the park's narrow, interlocked canyons and its wide skies.

Dan O'Laurie Canyon Country Museum *(118 E. Center St. 435-259-7985. Mon.-Sat year-round, call for limited winter hours; adm. fee)* Also featured is Moab's career as a favorite location for Hollywood filmmakers.

Dead Horse Point State Park *(33 miles SW of town via US 191 and Utah 313. 435-259-2614 or 800-322-3770. Adm. fee)* The Main Trail leads to the Observation Shelter, perhaps Canyonlands's finest picnic spot.

Hiking, Backpacking, and River Running Guided trips offered by Adrift Adventures *(378 N. Main St. 435-259-8594 or 800-874-4483)* and Canyon Voyages Adventure Company *(211 N. Main St. 435-259-6007 or 800-733-6007).*

Mountain Biking Unless you're experienced, consult an outfitter. Moab has many; ask at the travel council. Some trails require a permit from the Park Service.

Rock Art Viewing Guided tours in your own vehicle are offered by Canyon Voyages Adventure Company *(211 N. Main St. 435-259-6007 or 800-733-6007. March.-Oct.).*

WHERE TO EAT

Jailhouse Cafe *(101 N. Main St. 435-259-3900. Closed Nov.-Feb. $)* Arrive early at this all-breakfast eatery, or you'll have to wait.

Moab Brewery *(686 S. Main St. 435-259-6333. $$)* A family-oriented restaurant; the lagers and ales are made on the premises.

WHERE TO STAY

Dream Keeper Inn and Retreat *(191 S. 200 East. 435-259-5998 or 888-230-3247. $$)* An acre of shade trees and flower gardens flank this inn.

Sunflower Hill Bed and Breakfast Inn *(185 N. 300 East. 435-259-2974. $$)* Eleven rooms, all with private baths, in two restored vintage buildings on two gardened acres.

THE WEST

Avalon

Santa Catalina Island lies only 22 miles off the southern California mainland, but it feels like a different country. In the town of Avalon, people stroll around enjoying the ocean air and sunshine, slowing down to a pace that belongs more to a European seaside village than to go-go southern California.

In fact, the sight of Avalon may remind you of a color postcard from some picturesque port on the Mediterranean. Sunshine gleams off white-hulled yachts moored in water so blue it looks like Kodachrome. But this postcard is unusual: It has a picture on both sides. That is, once you leave the town of Avalon, the scene changes completely. The land turns wild as it rises toward the mountainous interior. Avalon's cozy bungalows and green golf course give way to dusty chaparral and red earth. Out there, bison roam and eagles soar.

Sailing off Santa Catalina Island

As you cross the channel from overtown (what locals call the mainland), you may be joined by dolphins who surf the wake alongside your ferry. Reaching Santa Catalina, you'll be dropped off on the bayside Crescent Avenue (called **Front Street** by residents). It looks like any American Main Street, with its shops and restaurants—except that you won't see any cars. Most locals get around Avalon on foot. After all, the whole town is less than a quarter of a mile across, with Front Street serving as a communal front yard where people meet, stroll, and gossip. The avenue was designed in the 1930s as a pedestrian promenade, one of the first on the West Coast. Some of the walls, benches, and fountains along Front Street will remind you of an outdoor art fair. They're decorated with ceramic tiles glazed in harlequin colors and whimsically mismatched—geometrical, pictorial, large, small, red, green. The tiles make Front Street look the way Dixieland jazz sounds: improvised on the fly, but hitting just the right note and filled with good spirits.

Down by the waterfront lies the Pleasure Pier, a 1909 landmark that residents call the **Green Pier.** It is painted a riotous shade of green, as tropical as an Amazon parrot. (If you like the color, Avalon's only hardware store will mix you a gallon of Pier Green paint.) The wooden pier serves as Avalon's official weigh station for sportfishing, and you might see a marlin just caught by an incoming boat. Other denizens of Catalina's waters include broadbill swordfish, tuna, and yellowtail. At the pier you can board a glass-bottom boat to the marine reserve at **Lovers Cove.** You'll get a better view in a semi-submersible, which looks like a submarine except that it goes below the water surface only as far as its portholes. But the most eye-popping way to view the underwater world is on a two-person submarine, which dives 40 feet down

Palm-fringed Avalon harbor

Avalon's harbor

but keeps you warm and dry inside a plastic sphere. The craft slowly descends through clouds of tiny fish and past forests of giant bladder kelp, the world's fastest growing plant, which can add three feet of length in a day. Among the coppery fronds you'll spy garibaldi fish of incandescent orange.

Perched on the edge of the bay, the **Casino** is a round landmark resembling a Moorish castle in Spain, with its white walls, red tile roof, and lantern cupola. Despite the name, the Casino has never been used for gambling. Instead, the 1929 building boasts the world's largest dance floor, where 1,500 couples at once swayed to the sounds of Glenn Miller, Tommy Dorsey, and other Big Bands. The ground floor contains the **Avalon Theatre,** the world's first designed especially for talking pictures. Its walls are rampant with art deco murals depicting exotic birds, Indian bowmen, and Spanish galleons on rainbow seas. The artist also worked on Grauman's Chinese Theatre in Hollywood.

Downstairs, the **Catalina Island Museum** displays artifacts from island life, ranging from the bone fishhooks of early Indian inhabitants to memorabilia from steamships that once called at Avalon. The most popular exhibits are pottery and decorative tiles made on the island during the 1930s and now highly collectible. (A single dinner plate may bring $1,000.) Among the historical tales of Avalon's origins that you may stumble across is how chewing gum king William Wrigley, Jr., bought Santa Catalina Island in 1919, sight unseen. Lucky for him, he loved it. He tastefully developed Avalon as a resort playground, leaving such legacies as the Casino. He also brought his Chicago Cubs baseball team to Avalon for spring training on a field he could overlook from his 22-room colonial mansion on a hilltop. With an environmental consciousness ahead of his time, Wrigley protected more than four-fifths of Santa Catalina as a nature preserve.

To reach the island's still wild interior, which locals refer to as "in the hills," you leave Avalon on a rising road lined with pungent eucalyptus trees and follow a summit ridge where bald eagles ride the wind. Bison, which were originally imported in 1924 as movie props for a Zane Grey western, graze on slopes of golden grass. You might also see wild pigs skittering on their spindly legs.

A suggestion before you leave for home: Mail yourself a color postcard of Avalon, just to remind you of the good feeling you had in this little island town. *Jerry Camarillo Dunn, Jr.*

Travelwise

GETTING THERE

Santa Catalina Island lies 22 miles from the southern California mainland and is served by several boat companies: Catalina Express (*1 hour from Long Beach. 310-519-1212 or 800-995-4386*); Catalina Cruises (*1 or 2 hours from Long Beach. 562-436-5006 or 800-228-2546*); and Catalina Passenger Service (*75 minutes from Newport Beach. 949-673-5245*). Island Express Helicopter Service (*15 minutes. 310-510-2525*) provides another transportation option.

GENERAL INFORMATION

Avalon (pop. 3,200) can mushroom to 10,000 people on a holiday or summer weekend. Try to visit midweek or in off-season. Catalina's summer-fall weather averages 76°F; winter-spring averages 63°F. Stop by the **Catalina Island Visitors Bureau** (*P.O. Box 217, Avalon 90704. 310-510-1520. www.catalina.com*) on the Green Pier for brochures and advice on hotel vacancies and packages that include transportation, hotel, and activities.

THINGS TO SEE AND DO

Bicycling Avalon offers level riding—try the shore east to Pebbly Beach or west to Descanso Beach. Most of Avalon's charming cottages are in the canyon bottom. The surrounding hills are steep, though the views make the toil worthwhile. To pedal beyond Avalon, into the island's backcountry, you'll need a permit, which you can obtain from the Catalina Island Conservancy (*Conservancy House, 125 Claressa St. 310-510-2595*), the Catalina Airport (*310-510-0143*), or Two Harbors Visitor Services (*800-785-8425*). Only annual permits are sold. You can bring your own bike cross-channel for a fee. Or contact the visitors bureau about rentals in Avalon.

Boat, Inland, and Casino Tours For tours by semi-submersibles and glass-bottom boats, call Discovery Tours (*310-510-TOUR*), which also offers excursions to see flying fish; inland motor tours to the nature center, horse ranch, and wildlife areas; and a Casino tour.

Catalina Island Museum *(1 Casino Way, in the Casino bldg. 310-510-2414. Adm. fee)* Native American items, historic photos, Catalina pottery, and tiles are on display.

Diving, Snorkeling, and Kayaking
Outfitters offer scuba and snorkel trips and kayak rentals; contact the visitors bureau for a brochure. The underwater park by the Casino permits scuba diving; snorkelers also enjoy **Lovers Cove,** whose friendly fish like frozen peas. SEAmagine *(909-626-6262)* provides high-tech two-person subs for a unique diving experience.

Golf Play nine holes at the Catalina Island Golf Course *(310-510-0530).*

Hiking and Camping A network of trails winds through the island's interior, with camping possible at designated sites. For a hiking permit and a map, call the Catalina Island Conservancy *(310-510-2595).* Camping reservations are made only by mail, fax, or on the web. Contact the Catalina Island Camping Information and Reservation Hotline *(310-510-2800).* Shuttle buses stop at campsites and trailheads *(310-510-2800. Fee. Reservations required).*

Jeep Eco-Tours The Catalina Island Conservancy *(310-510-2595)* offers inland tours that focus on natural history and flora and fauna.

Wrigley Memorial and Botanical Garden *(Avalon Canyon Rd. 310-510-2595)* This Spanish-style memorial honors William Wrigley, Jr., the island's original owner and developer. The garden is devoted to California island endemic plants.

SHOPPING

Shops on Crescent Avenue and adjacent streets sell sportswear, fishing gear, gifts, pottery, and tourist items.

ANNUAL EVENTS

Catalina Festival of Art *(3rd weekend in Sept. 310-510-0808)* Juried outdoor show.

Catalina Island JazzTrax Festival *(Oct. 818-347-5299. Adm. fee)* This three-weekend festival in the Casino Ballroom features smooth jazz.

Catalina Island Museum Tile and Pottery Extravaganza *(All Sept. 310-510-2414. Adm. fee)* Collectible ware

produced on the island in the 1930s is on display at the museum; the museum gift shop sells reproductions.

Catalina Island Silent Film Festival *(Late Spring. Avalon Theatre. 310-510-2414. Adm. fee)* Classic silent films are accompanied by original theater organ.

Fender Catalina Island Blues Festival *(Mid-May. 888-253-8368. Adm fee)* Nationally acclaimed artists play at various venues throughout Avalon. Some concerts are free.

WHERE TO EAT

Avalon restaurants cater to many tastes and budgets. Dress is casual.

Antonio's Pizzeria & Cabaret *(230 Crescent Ave. 310-510-0008. $)* Breakfast, pizza, pasta; some outdoor tables are perched beside the bay.

Avalon Seafood and Fish Market (Rosie's) *(Green Pier. 310-510-0197. $)* A classic pier location for burgers, fish 'n' chips.

Blue Parrot *(Metropole Market Place. 310-510-2465. Closed Jan. $$)* Enjoy steaks, seafood, and pasta, plus bay views.

Catalina Country Club *(1 Country Club Dr. 310-510-7404. $$)* California contemporary cuisine is served in both the dining room and on the patio.

Ristorante Villa Portafino *(101 Crescent Ave. 310-510-0508. $$)* Upscale northern Italian food.

WHERE TO STAY

Hotel Metropole *(205 Crescent Ave. 310-510-1884. $$)* This appealing oceanfront hotel has tastefully appointed rooms with ocean, mountain, or courtyard views; attentive service; and a rooftop spa.

Inn on Mt. Ada *(398 Wrigley Rd. 310-510-2030. $$$)* An elegant but incomprehensibly expensive hideaway in the former Wrigley mansion.

Zane Grey Hotel *(199 Chimes Tower Rd. 310-510-0966. $$)* This friendly, funky hostelry on the hill above the Casino, built in 1926 by the Western novelist, is not for people who want their bedspreads to match. Swimming pool.

Ojai

Ojai lies in a valley that might look strangely familiar if you've ever seen an old California orange crate label. As if printed in soft lithographic colors, green Valencia trees are hung with bright oranges. Under a pale blue sky, country roads wind among the groves against a backdrop of tawny mountains. The town appears in the middle of this tranquil scene, with an arcaded downtown that has only a few blocks of shops and hardly a stoplight. Ojai remains suspended in time and concealed, like Shangri-la, in a valley that some say has a spiritual dimension.

If you linger awhile, you might notice Ojai's major social distinction: a lack of social distinctions. You won't be judged by your car, your money, or your fitness level, the way you are in Los Angeles or trendy Santa Barbara.

To sip a cup of social equality, take a seat at the **Ojai Coffee Roasting Company,** where the air is filled with java steam and lively chatter. Here orange ranchers sit down with artists, meditative mystics with caffeine-wired

Ojai's arcaded downtown

Perusing the goods at Bart's outdoor bookstore

real estate agents, soccer moms with leftover hippies and movie stars. (Ojai is a bit of a Hollywood hideaway.) The cast of coffeehouse characters reveals the town's diversity and its open embrace of all types. In Ojai you can relax and just be yourself.

As a small western town (pop. 8,200), Ojai is not only neighborly but also trustful. For proof, visit the outdoor **Bart's Books,** a local institution that sprawls under a gigantic oak tree. If the shop is closed, it's no problem. Just choose a book from the shelves outside the courtyard and drop your money through the slot in the door. The honor system at work!

How the town developed its unique personality is a topic to explore among the historical exhibits at the **Ojai Valley Museum.** Here you might learn that Ojai meant "moon" to the Chumash Indians, the valley's early inhabitants. But locals prefer an old story that the name of their mountain-ringed valley means "the nest"—the place where the moon settles down after its flight across the night sky. The museum occupies a thick-walled church designed in mission revival style in 1921 by noted architects Richard Requa and Frank Mead. The handsome church was built with the help of philanthropical Ohio glass magnate Edward Drummond Libbey, who took an interest in this dusty California hamlet about 1917 and helped transform it into a place of character.

Another Libbey legacy, downtown's Spanish-style **Arcade** contains shops and galleries of arts and crafts. Ojai boasts quite a few creative people, and you can meet local painters, sculptors, and potters in their native habitats on the annual Ojai Studio Artists Tour in mid-October.

Many artists and writers live in the valley's **East End,** where orange groves, open skies, and rural quiet seem to nurture creativity. An almost palpable feeling of serenity fills the **Ojai Valley,** also attracting people with a spiritual leaning. In the 1920s religious philosopher Jiddu Krishnamurti settled in a ranch house tucked among rose gardens in the valley's East End, his home for some 60 years. "Each time you come to this quiet, peaceful valley," he said, "there is a feeling of strange aloofness, of deep silence and the vast spreading of slow time." Visitors can investigate Krishnamurti's teachings at his old house, now the **Krishnamurti Library.**

On an Ojai hilltop where rabbits scamper through garden hedges stands the 10,000-volume **Krotona Institute Library,** founded in 1926 by the Theosophists, a group that embraces both Eastern and Western wisdom. Yet another spiritual group holds monthly full-moon devotions atop **Meditation Mount,** a perch with an inspiring view over the valley.

Of course, Ojai also offers more down-to-earth pleasures. One joy of the physical plane is hiking along **Shelf Road,** which crosses the flank of the foothills through chaparral and sandstone. Or try biking on the **Ojai Valley Trail,** a conversion of the century-old railroad line that once hauled oranges down to the coast. For boating and fishing there's **Lake Casitas,** surrounded by 6,200 acres of oak-studded hills. In fact, Ojai is a great place to reduce urban stress and, frankly, to enjoy a bit of pampering. Among other treatments, you can have your skin dry-scrubbed with crushed rose petals and then massaged with rose oil at the **Ojai Valley Inn & Spa,** the best of several spas in the valley.

But a luxury lifestyle doesn't really reflect the true Ojai. The valley's personality is more down-to-earth and egalitarian. To discover its essence, step outdoors almost any winter day at sunset and enjoy the **Pink Moment.** After the sun dips behind the hills to the west, people all around town gaze eastward at the sheer face of Topa Topa Mountain. All at once, coral pink light streams across the valley. The mountain face glows, as if illuminated from within. This ancient radiance fills the valley like a blessing and shines equally upon all.

Jerry Camarillo Dunn, Jr.

Travelwise

GETTING THERE
Ojai lies in southern California, 85 miles northwest of Los Angeles and 35 miles south of Santa Barbara. (Both have airports.) There is no public transportation to the Ojai Valley.

GENERAL INFORMATION
Spring and autumn weather is generally mild. Winter is pleasantly cool with some rain. Summer temperatures can reach the high 90s and leave you wilted. In spring the perfume of orange blossoms fills the East End. For information, contact the **Ojai Valley Chamber of Commerce** (*150 W. Ojai Ave., Ojai 93023. 805-646-8126. www.the-ojai.org*). The free "Ojai Valley Visitors Guide" contains a walking map. The Ojai Trolley (*805-640-2562*)

offers inexpensive transportation around town.

THINGS TO SEE AND DO
Backcountry Trips Explore the mountains of Los Padres National Forest with Pink Moment Jeep Tours (*805-653-1321*).

Bicycling The 9-mile **Ojai Valley Trail** is a rails-to-trails conversion of the 100-year-old railroad that once carried trainloads of local oranges en route to markets around the world. Running parallel to Calif. 33 and connecting Ojai with Ventura's Foster Park, it is popular among hikers, bikers, and horseback riders. Rent from Bicycles of Ojai (*108 Cañada St. 805-646-7736. Closed Sun.*).

Camping There are plenty of camping opportunities in the forests and valleys surrounding Ojai, including Rancho del Rey *(805-649-3356)*, in the beautiful Ojai Valley; Lake Casitas (see below), and Los Padres National Forest *(Ojai Ranger Station 805-646-4348)*.

George Stuart's Gallery of Historical Figures *(McNell and Reeves Rds. 805-646-6574. May-Nov. Sat.-Sun.; adm. fee)* Quarter-scale likenesses of personages from Martin Luther to Abraham Lincoln.

Hiking Trails, including **Shelf Road,** are mapped in the "Ojai Valley Visitors Guide," free at the Chamber of Commerce.

Horseback Riding Take lessons or a guided trail ride at the Ojai Valley Inn *(Country Club Rd. 805-646-5511)*.

Krishnamurti Library *(1130 McAndrew Rd. 805-646-4948. Closed Mon.-Tues.)* Books, audio tapes, and videotapes are available on teachings of the late J. Krishnamurti.

Krotona Institute Library *(2 Krotona Hill. 805-646-2653. Closed Mon.)* Books on Theosophy and diverse spiritual traditions.

Lake Casitas *(7 miles W of Ojai, off Calif. 150. 805-649-2233. Camping reservations 805-649-1122. Adm. fee)* This lovely lake offers fishing for trout and bass, boat rentals, camping, picnic areas, and bike rentals *(805-340-BIKE)*. No swimming.

Meditation Mount *(10340 Reeves Rd. 805-646-5508)* Community meditations take place at the full moon; popular sunset viewpoint.

Ojai Valley Museum *(130 W. Ojai Ave. 805-640-1390. Closed Mon.-Tues.; adm. fee)* Exhibits examine local history from Chumash days through early ranching and modern times.

Scenic Driving Meander among the orange groves on a loop drive through the **East End:** Take Ojai Ave. (Calif. 150) east to Reeves Rd. Turn left to McAndrew Rd., where you turn left and continue until McAndrew curves left onto Thacher Rd. Take Thacher west to Carne Rd. and turn left. Go to Grand Ave., turn right, and return to Ojai.

SHOPPING

Shops and galleries are clustered in and near the downtown, mission revival-style Arcade,

built in 1917 by Ohio glass magnate and Ojai philanthropist Edward D. Libbey.

Bart's Books *(302 W. Matilija St. 805-646-3755. Closed Mon.)* Used books are purveyed in an outdoor setting.

Ojai Certified Farmers Market *(Sun. Matilija St., behind the Arcade)* Locally produced oranges, avocados, honey, flowers, and more.

ANNUAL EVENTS

Ojai Festival *(Early June. 805-646-2053)* Launched more than 50 years ago, this outdoor festival has presented some of the world's finest conductors, composers, and performers—from Igor Stravinsky and Aaron Copland to Pierre Boulez and Esa-Pekka Salonen. Adventurous pieces that don't usually appear on regular concert schedules, along with family and children's selections, are played beneath oak and sycamore trees in an amphitheater at Libbey Park.

Ojai Studio Artists Tour *(Mid-Oct. 805-646-8126. Fee)* Take a self-guided tour of studios around the valley.

WHERE TO EAT

Boccali's *(3277 Ojai-Santa Paula Rd. 805-646-6116. $)* This classic roadhouse serves Italian homestyle food.

Maravilla *(Ojai Valley Inn, Country Club Rd. 805-646-5511. Wed.-Sun. $$$)* The Pacific Coast meets Provence in gourmet dishes using local produce, seafood, herbs, cheese.

Ranch House *(S. Lomita Ave. 805-646-2360. Closed Mon.-Tues. Dinner and Sun. brunch only. $$)* Celebrated gourmet dining amid lush plantings, a stream, and an herb garden.

Suzanne's Cuisine *(502 W. Ojai Ave. 805-640-1961. Closed Tues.)* Creative continental preparation of meats, Italian specialties, salads, and seafood, served in the parlor or garden.

WHERE TO STAY

Moon's Nest Inn *(210 E. Matilija St. 805-646-6635. $$)* This B&B is conviently located downtown.

Ojai Valley Inn & Spa *(Country Club Rd. 805-646-5511. $$$)* A top golf resort offering fine dining, swimming, fitness center, and luxury spa on beautiful grounds.

Mendocino

Like Rip Van Winkle, the town of Mendocino appears to have
slumbered for a hundred years and awakened to find itself lost in
time. Built on bluffs beside the Pacific Ocean, the town was settled in
the 1850s by New Englanders whose white clapboard houses still line
the streets. Atop the Masonic Hall the same carved angel has
presided over the town for 150 years. On back streets, wooden water
towers stand like exclamation marks, as if to say "Remember the old
days!" The whole town is on the National Register of Historic Places.

Not that there aren't signs of modern life. In the 1960s Mendocino transformed itself into an art colony after its logging fortunes fell and its walls
began sagging. Hippies arrived, trailing fragrant clouds of patchouli, and the
New Age brought some new life. Now resurrected by galleries, tourism, and a
protective love of its past, Mendocino carries the feeling of the 1850s—and
the 1960s—into the millennium.

Although the sun does shine on Mendocino, many days are foggy. Perhaps

Mendocino's Presbyterian church

Coastline near the Mendocino headlands

this soft white haze, like the blank canvas of a painter, gives rise to imaginative visions. Perhaps that's why so many artists have settled here. All around town, galleries display their work.

Mendocino's artistic phoenix phase began four decades ago, when watercolorist Bill Zacha ran a laundromat and decided to install an art gallery upstairs. (A sign said: "Visit Us During Your Wash Cycle!") In 1959 he founded the **Mendocino Art Center,** which exhibits paintings, weavings, ceramics, and other work by local artists. About his town Bill Zacha once said: "Neon signs, motels, express highways…no sir, you can have them…. I like a town that has peace and dignity and beauty, where you can walk down the street and breathe deep and shout, 'Man! Am I glad I live *here*!'"

Like him, visitors soon slow down to what locals call "Mendo time." Many residents also pursue alternative lifestyles, and bulletin boards around town are plastered with ads for New Age offerings: psychic readings, massages, aromatherapy, numerology, "vibrational kinesiology." There's even an eight-week course in breathing—and you thought you knew how!—taught by Rebecca Aum.

Live-and-let-live sums up Mendocino's philosophy. Every Fourth of July the town cuts loose with a wacky parade whose entrants include the All-Susan Marching Band (composed entirely of women named Susan) and a corps of hemp growers. In Mendocino's backcountry the major cash crop is marijuana.

More attractive (and legal) plants thrive on the broad **Mendocino headlands** that front the town, where you can walk through spring lupines and poppies. Or look offshore for migrating whales. At low tide, clamber down the bluff to tide pools encrusted with sea urchins, crabs, limpets, and other denizens of the not-so-deep. You can also arrange a kayak tour, paddling into sea caves on whose moist walls starfish cling like wallpaper.

Along the ocean side of town runs Main Street. Here you'll find the shingled steeple of the **Presbyterian church,** whose white clapboard walls and neatly trimmed Gothic windows have radiated New England purity since 1868. Nearby stand the **Ford House** and **Kelley House,** both homes of pioneers, as was the gabled **MacCallum House Inn,** with its cottage garden of tea roses.

Main Street is also chockablock with shops. But to discover Mendocino's spirit, wander the backstreets, where community life stands apart from the tourist offerings. White picket fences enclose New England saltbox or Victorian houses and gardens of hollyhocks, nasturtiums, and pear trees. Blackbirds chatter as you pass. You'll see old water towers converted to residences with shingled sides, framed windows, and inside spiral staircases for vertical living.

On a weathered wood fence along Albion Street, you might spy small, faded wooden signs nailed up by two little neighbor girls "In Loving Memory of…" a roster of departed pets, or perhaps just the small friends of two active imaginations: Mr. and Mrs. Fieldmouse, Little Miss Buckteeth, Spot and Speedy, Mr. Mole and Grandfather Mole. It's a storybook sight. On Kelley Street you'll pass **Portuguese Row,** home to families descended from Mendocino's early immigrants. Look for a folk-art garden decorated with abalone shells, highway reflectors, painted wooden daisies, a Polynesian tiki god, and a front gate festooned with badminton rackets. Hey, why not?

Here you discover the artistic spirit and individualism of Mendocino in action. And maybe you also spotted that flyer on a bulletin board in town: "Do Your Own Thing!" it exclaims. "Who Else Can?" *Jerry Camarillo Dunn, Jr.*

Travelwise

GETTING THERE

Mendocino lies on the northern California coast, 160 miles north of San Francisco on Calif. 1. There are airports in San Francisco and Oakland.

GENERAL INFORMATION

Weather can be foggy even in summer, when the average high temperature is 65°F. Pack a sweater. Annual rainfall: 40 inches. For information, contact the **Fort Bragg/Mendocino Coast Chamber of Commerce** *(332 N. Main St., P.O. Box 1141, Fort Bragg 95437. 707-961-6300 or 800-726-2780. www.mendocino coast.com).*

THINGS TO SEE AND DO

Kelley House Museum *(45007 Albion St. 707-937-5791. Daily June-Aug., Fri.-Mon. only rest of year; adm. fee)* Built in 1861 by businessman William H. Kelley, who bought

the entire Mendocino peninsula for $2,650, the house museum features changing historical exhibits.

Mendocino Art Center *(45200 Little Lake St. 707-937-5818)* Exhibitions and classes are offered in ceramics, sculpture, fine arts, jewelry, and textiles. Phone for schedules and registration.

Mendocino Headlands State Park *(707-937-5804)* Bordering town on three sides and featuring cliffside trails, the park includes **Big River Beach,** popular with surfers and kayakers. Occupying the historic **Ford House** on Main Street, the visitor center has natural history displays and a scale model of 1890s Mendocino.

Movie and TV Locations Photogenic Mendocino stood in for Cabot Cove, Maine, in television's *Murder, She Wrote,* and the gabled **Blair House** *(45110 Little Lake*

St.) stood in as the home of Angela Lansbury's character, Jessica Fletcher. *East of Eden* (1954, starring James Dean) disguises Mendocino as Monterey. Couples staying at the **Heritage House** still reserve the rooms where Alan Alda and Ellen Burstyn nestled in 1978's *Same Time, Next Year.*

Ocean Kayaking, Canoeing, and Biking
Explore one of the Mendocino sea caves with Lost Coast Kayaking *(707-937-2434).* Renting a kayak, canoe, or bike through Catch a Canoe & Bicycles, Too! *(707-937-0273)* allows easy access to the Big or Noyo Rivers.

Russian Gulch State Park *(2 miles N of town on Calif. 1. 707-937-5804. Day-use fee)* This luscious park features redwood groves, a beach, and a waterfall trail.

Van Damme State Park *(3 miles S of town on Calif. 1. 707-937-5804. Day-use fee)* Abalone diving *(April-Nov. except July),* trails, river, fern canyon, pygmy pine forest.

SHOPPING

Mendocino features many arts and crafts galleries, where work ranges from fine quality to pedestrian commercial stuff. On the second Saturday of the month, many galleries, artists' studios, and some shops hold evening wine receptions to meet the artists; contact the Chamber for information.

Lark in the Morning *(10460 Kasten St. 707-937-5275)* World music instruments, from Greek bouzoukis to Indian bamboo flutes.

Papa Birds *(45040 Albion St. 707-937-2730)* Purveyor of bird feeders and supplies.

ANNUAL EVENTS
Historic House and Building Tour *(Early May. 707-937-5791. Fee)* Visit some of Mendocino's finest Victorians.

Mendocino Music Festival *(2 weeks in mid- to late July. 707-937-4041)* Orchestral and chamber music, opera, and jazz are presented in a tent on the Mendocino headlands.

Mendocino Whale Festival *(1st weekend in March. 800-726-2780)* This fun festival combines whale-watching with wine tasting.

WHERE TO EAT
Cafe Beaujolais *(961 Ukiah St. 707-937-5614. Dinner only. $$)* Its cuisine is celebrated for the style and variety of its organic produce.

Heritage House *(5 miles S of town on Calif. 1, in Little River. 707-937-5885 or 800-235-5885. $$)* Fine contemporary American cuisine in either the formal dining room or casual bar; top wine list.

Little River Inn *(2 miles S of town on Calif. 1, in Little River. 707-937-5942 or 888-INN-LOVE. $$)* Refined yet unfussy preparation of seafood and meats. The bar's cocktail hour gives guests the chance to mix with locals.

Mendo Burgers *(10483 Lansing St. 707-937-1111. $)* Where townspeople go for grub.

WHERE TO STAY
Heritage House *(5 miles S of town on Calif. 1, in Little River. 707-937-5885 or 800-235-5885. $$$)* This elegant hideaway is set amid 37 acres of gardens and trees and features cliffside cottages, ocean views, double Jacuzzi tubs, featherbeds, and romantic fireplaces. The inn evolved from an 1877 farmhouse.

Little River Inn *(2 miles S on Calif. 1, in Little River. 707-937-5942 or 888-INN-LOVE. $$)* Family owned for generations, this 225-acre resort began as the 1853 home of a Maine lumberman. Many rooms and cottages with ocean views, fireplaces; golf, tennis, day spa.

MacCallum House Inn *(45020 Albion St. 707-937-0289 or 800-609-0492. $$)* Antique-furnished rooms in an 1882 house, with several outbuildings that also room guests.

Mendocino Hotel and Garden Suites *(45080 Main St. 707-937-0511 or 800-548-0513. $$)* In-town rooms and garden suites, done up in Victorian style.

NEARBY PLACES
Fort Bragg *(Fort Bragg/Mendocino Coast Chamber of Commerce, 332 N. Main St., Fort Bragg 95437. 707-961-6300 or 800-726-2780. www.mendocinocoast.com)* An 1850s military post and later a lumber town, blue-collar Fort Bragg has a historic business district with shops, galleries, and restaurants. **Noyo Harbor** is a wonderful working port, with all kinds of sportfishing and whale-watching possibilities. The **California Western Railroad** *(Foot of Laurel St. 707-964-6371. Fare)* runs old-fashioned Skunk Trains on 40-mile scenic steam excursions through the redwoods to the town of Willits.

Downieville

Leave the noise and rush of the California interstates and travel the twisty roads that lead back into the gold rush country, where you'll find the little town of Downieville, perched on a riverbank in the steep canyon confines of the high Sierra. The prospectors who come here now are looking for leaping trout, backcountry trails, and a moment of unbuttoned peace among the old-timers on Main Street's shady benches.

A trestle bridge spans the Downie River just above its juncture with the North Yuba River, and there, if you have any aspiration to continue into northern California's high country, you must wait your turn, because the bridge is only wide enough for one lane of traffic. The narrow bridge provides one assurance that Downieville will likely never be more than the very small town it's always been. Another reason is topography: There is only a small level area in the vicinity were the rivers join, and the rest of the town anchors precariously on steep, forested canyon walls.

Downieville's historic Main Street

The town is built on the mule-team scale of its gold-mining days, with tin-roofed buildings and second-story porches leaning inward along Main Street. The streets aren't getting any wider, but they're getting busier. There have long been visitors with barbed flies in their floppy hats, spending hours on the river angling for rainbow trout. These days, there are also backpackers dropping off the **Pacific Crest National Scenic Trail** for a brew at **St. Charles Place,** and in the winter the RVs towing trailers loaded with snowmobiles. Lately, a swarm of lycra-sleek youngsters have come to ride the trails on bicycles. All of them enjoy a basin of alpine lakes, ghost towns, and trails that mimic the old mining and timber roads. When the outdoor exertions are over, there are peaceful cabins in the woods, or an unhurried meal by the river.

Gold nuggets from the Yuba

What a different scene from the town's heyday, over a century ago, when mines like the **Sixteen-to-One** (recently reopened for tours), the Lucky Boy, and the Ruby lured thousands to these parts. That history is well-displayed at the **Downieville Museum,** with displays of clothing and mine equipment from the 49er era, when gold mines dotted the hills and the town had several hotels and butcher shops. At one point Downieville was California's sixth largest city and in the running to become the state capital. Nuggets as large as 25 pounds were found in Gold Bluff mine, and a monster chunk of gold weighing nearly 50 pounds was found near Gold Lake.

Gold Lake is part of the **Lakes Basin,** a cluster of trout-loaded ponds east of Downieville nestled below the spectacular **Sierra Buttes.** There are lodges at **Sardine** and **Salmon** and **Gold Lakes** where you can rent boats and gear. Or you can drive to Packer Saddle and climb a moderately steep trail to the top of the buttes—the last stretch is up the dizzying stairs of an old fire lookout—or you can unload your mountain bike at the saddle and take an exciting downhill ride through the meadows and forested canyons to Downieville. Inexperienced riders will need a full day, a good supply of water, and a helmet…a little posterior padding wouldn't hurt either.

Some days, though, it's more fun just to hang around town and visit with the locals. Grab a free walking tour map at the visitors kiosk at **Bell Tower Square** and follow shady boardwalks to the museum, the old brewery, the mining equipment on display by Lions Park, the Masonic Hall, and the gallows. If you want a longer stroll, go east on Upper Main Street past Hansen Bridge, the 1849 cabin of town founder William Major Downie, and the pump works, and you'll find forest glades and waterfalls along the river.

Nearby are other charming gold rush towns like **Sierra City,** and over Yuba Pass to the east is beautiful Sierra Valley. This area may be the only place in California that is less bustling, less crowded, and more laid back than it was 150 years ago. What it retains from those days is its air of rustic fortitude, the calloused hands and silver tongues of its old-timers who pass the time on town benches, and a friendly new crop of mountain townfolk, surviving and even thriving far from the busy wheels of modern California.   *Geoffrey O'Gara*

Travelwise

GETTING THERE

Downieville is located in east-central
California, at the junction of the Downie
and North Yuba Rivers on Calif. 49. The
closest large airports are Reno, Nevada, and
Sacramento. From Reno, drive west on I-80
to Truckee, then turn north on Calif. 89
through the Sierra Valley; take Calif. 49 west
over Yuba Pass to Downieville (90 miles).
From the Sacramento side, take I-80 east
to Auburn, where Calif. 49 turns north; at
Nevada City, Calif. 49 becomes a narrow,
twisting mountain road, going north to
Downieville (99 miles).

GENERAL INFORMATION

Summer and fall are favorite visiting times,
though a heavy layer of sunscreen is a wise
precaution in the middle of August. Spring
attracts kayakers during high water, and
anglers once the turbidity clears. Winter has
always attracted cross-country skiers, and
lately an increasing number of snowmobilers
roar along the trails in Tahoe National Forest.
For maps, activities, lodging, and other
information contact the **Downieville
Chamber of Commerce** (*P.O. Box 473,
Downieville 95936. 530-289-3507. www
.visitdownieville.com*). When you arrive in
town between May and October, stop at the
visitors kiosk at Bell Tower Square and pick
up a copy of the walking tour map and
whatever friendly advice you want.

THINGS TO SEE AND DO

Camping There are numerous campgrounds
along the North Yuba River, particularly west
of Downieville, most of them with vault
toilets and potable water. If you don't feel like
sleeping in a tent, you still might want to stop
to picnic. Contact the North Yuba Ranger
Station (*530-288-3231*).

Downieville Foundry Museum (*166 Pearl
St. 530-289-1020. Closed Nov.-March; adm. fee.
Tours by reservation only*) Leonard Kinzler
restored this old foundry, with exhibits on
gold mining and the history of logging in the
1850s and a miniature model of the town as
it was by the 1860s.

Downieville Museum (*330 Main St. 530-
289-3423. May–early Oct.; donation*) In an 1852
building built as a store by Chinese immigrants,
this museum takes visitors back to the days

when Downieville was being carved from the
wilderness. Some Victorian finery is on display,
but it is the pictures of tailings piles, denuded
hillsides, and rampaging floods that capture the
chaotic adventure of gold rush days.

Fishing You can bring your own gear and
fly-fish the pools of the North Yuba, or head
up to the Lakes Basin, where you can rent
boats (and cabins) at **Packer Lake Lodge**
(*Packer Lake Rd., Lakes Basin. 530-862-1221.
Mem. Day–Columbus Day*) or **Sardine Lake
Resort** (*Sardine Lake Rd., off Calif. 49. 530-
862-1196. Mid-May–mid-Oct.*).

Hiking Myriad trails wind through the
Downieville Ranger District of the Tahoe
National Forest, including easy short ones
like the **Devil's Postpile Trail,** or longer
journeys that tie in with the **Pacific Crest
National Scenic Trail** on its route from
Mexico to Canada. Contact the North Yuba
Ranger Station (*15924 Calif. 49, Camptonville.
530-288-3231*). Climbing to the top of the
Sierra Buttes is a difficult, 5-mile round-
trip (watch for snowfields as late as July) that
rewards with a spectacular view. Pick up the
trailhead at Packer Saddle.

Mountain Biking It's the latest craze in
this area, and many bikers take a shuttle
to Packer Saddle for a rough ride down
the mountain trails to Downieville. The
shuttle, along with gear rentals, are
available at Downieville Outfitters (*101
Commercial St. 530-289-0155. Closed
Dec.-March*).

Sixteen-to-One Mine *(Alleghany St., a few miles S of Downieville as the crow flies, but to drive go 20 miles S on Calif. 49 toward the town of North San Juan, then 20 miles E on Ridge Rd. to the mine. 530-287-3330. By appt. only)* This mine has a long history of gold production that continues to this day. Several different lengths and depths of mine tours are available (including the Executive Tour for $500).

ENTERTAINMENT

Kentucky Mine Concert Series On weekends July through August, top-notch entertainment ranging from a cappella singers to Celtic musicians play at an outdoor amphitheater at the Kentucky Mine Museum *(530-862-1310)* in nearby Sierra City.

Yuba Theater *(210 Main St. 530-289-3233)* Hosts performances by the Sierra Turnpike Players and other visiting artists.

SHOPPING

Ruffled Goose *(200 Main St. 530-289-3113)* An eclectic, cluttered, and cheerful gift shop that has lately been advertising a tanning booth. More important, it's one place you can pick up books about the area and local crafts.

Sierra Gold *(204 Main St. 530-289-3515)* Catch a little old-fashioned gold fever, though none of this jewelry is made from the meager flecks collected by amateurs with their dredging machines on the river.

ANNUAL EVENTS

Clampers' Weekend *(Late Aug. 530-289-3113)* E Clampus Vitas is a half-serious organization formed in the mining days to provide winter wood to the widows and orphans of fallen miners. At summer's end they gather for a big blowout, and in the midst of all the fun they don't forget their original mission—in 1998 they gave $700 to the local food bank.

Independence Day Parade *(July 4 weekend. 530-289-3507)* The historic parade, which goes back to mule-wagon days, is followed by a chicken barbecue hosted by the Volunteer Fire Department.

WHERE TO EAT

Forks Riverside Cafe *(310 Main St. 530-289-3225)* The closest thing in Downieville to a posh eatery, with a mix of steak, seafood, and pasta dishes and a river-view patio where you can eat on a nice day.

St. Charles Place *(315 Main St. 530-289-3237. $)* Not a place to eat, really, but a great place to party, as well as a historic building. With poker, pool, and pinball and a loud, friendly crowd on weekends.

WHERE TO STAY

Helm's St. Charles Inn *(459 Mountain House Rd., Goodyears Bar. 530-289-0910. $$)* Once a stagecoach rest stop, it's now a B&B, with antique furnishings in four bedrooms.

The Lure Resort *(100 Calif. 49. 530-289-3465 or 800-671-4084. $$)* Cabins with decks overlooking the river just east of town—an appropriate lodging for fisherpeople.

Sierra Shangri-La *(3 miles E of town on Calif. 49. 530-289-3455. $$)* Cottages and a B&B lodge along the North Yuba, with kitchens and woodstoves in most.

NEARBY PLACES

Lakes Basin Drive east of Sierra City about 4 miles on Calif. 49 to Bassetts, then turn north on Gold Lake Road to visit the cluster of lakes nestled just north of the **Sierra Buttes** *(Beckworth Ranger District 530-836-2575)* for fishing, boating, great hiking, and even swimming, at Sand Pond.

Sierra City *(Sierra County Chamber of Commerce 800-200-4949. www.sierracity.com)* Located 12 miles east of town on Calif. 49, this little town competes with Downieville for being an idyllic mountain retreat town. It features a rebuilt mine and stamp mill at the **Kentucky Mine Museum** *(E of Sierra City on Calif. 49. 530-862-1310. Mem. Day–Sept., weekends in Oct.; donation).*

Virginia City

At dusk a lonesome wind blows off the sagebrush hills around Virginia City and stirs up dust devils on the streets. Gaslights glow outside the Bucket of Blood Saloon, and boot heels echo along the old wooden sidewalks. Squint your eyes a little, and you can almost see the town of the 1870s, when the streets teemed with miners and gamblers, bartenders and preachers, schoolmarms and "soiled doves." One of the most fabulous towns of the Wild West, Virginia City had been created by the richest silver strike in history, the Comstock Lode. Instant wealth transformed miners living in shacks into millionaires whose mansions boasted crystal chandeliers and solid silver door-knobs. Virginia City became a cultured metropolis with an opera house and restaurants that served oysters and French champagne.

Virginia City bathing in a sunset glow

At the local newspaper a young reporter named Sam Clemens first decided to use a pen name: Mark Twain. But even Twain's tall tales couldn't match the sheer vitality and exaggeration of life in Virginia City. When you wake up in the morning at the 1859 **Gold Hill Hotel,** you awake in the past, with all its ghosts. At least, some people believe that two of the hotel's guest rooms are haunted. A departed miner named William still smells up room no. 5 with his cigar smoke, while in room no. 4 a "fancy lady" known as Rosie fills the air with perfume.

In Virginia City the hands of the clock seems to spin backward. You've come to a place that had about 30,000 residents in the booming 1870s, but its peak now is only 800 in summer. In fact, more people lie buried in the **Silver Terrace Cemeteries** than live in town today.

How Virginia City Got Its Name

An 1850s miner named James Finney was better known as "Ole Virginny," either for his home state or for his preference in liquor. One whiskey-soaked night in 1859 he was weaving his way back to his tent, tripped, and dropped a jug of hooch. Ole Virginny watched in dismay as the precious contents seeped into the ground. Making the best of a poor situation, he rose unsteadily to his feet and declared, "I christen this spot Virginia Town!"

If you stroll through the graveyards and read the inscriptions on worn marble headstones, you can decipher the character of the community in its heyday: Most people came from somewhere else, they were ordinary folks such as shopkeepers, and they died too young. An assortment of religious and fraternal groups staked their claims for eternal real estate here, so eight different cemeteries sprawl side by side—for Catholics, city firemen, Odd Fellows, Freemasons, and so on.

Virginia City also had tombs without tombstones—the mine tunnels, sometimes fatal places to work. As you tour the old **Chollar Mine,** picture the days when men labored in shifts around the clock to extract the riches of the fabulous Comstock. They drilled and blasted and hauled ore thousands of feet underground, where temperatures could reach a sweltering 140°F.

A miner made good wages—$4 a day—which he often spent to quench his thirst. In 1880 Virginia City boasted more than a hundred saloons. Men also liked to gamble on just about anything, from the turn of a card to a fight between a dog and a wildcat.

Today you can explore the world of Wild West gambling around Virginia City. The **Delta Saloon** displays an old faro layout, called the "Suicide Table" because three of its owners killed themselves after heavy losses. Exhibits at the **Nevada Gambling Museum** include everything from a wheel of fortune to an 1870s poker room. Look for a cheating device, made of brass levers and wire, called a holdout. Secretly worn on a gambler's arm under his coat, the holdout would slip an ace down his sleeve and into his palm. You'll also see a collection of slot machines manufactured from the 1890s onward, the most beautiful being classic 1930s models rampant with art deco designs, from streamlined eagles' wings to skyscraper shapes of polished aluminum. These days, every saloon in Virginia City has rows of slot machines that are

Piper's Opera House

ablaze with colored lights and chiming with electronic bleeps.

Besides betting and drinking, townsfolk also enjoyed evenings of higher culture. **Piper's Opera House** presented popular touring artists who ranged from the beautiful British actress Lillie Langtry to the American actor-producer David Belasco. In a reflection of the city's class distinctions, mine owners watched the show from exclusive, velvet-draped boxes, while ordinary miners made do with hard wooden seats downstairs—and the town prostitutes had a special section to themselves. When the audience particularly enjoyed a performer, they showed their appreciation by tossing a cascade of silver coins and even ingots onto the stage.

The wealth of Virginia City created a substantial community with the usual institutions of American life. In 1876 the **Fourth Ward School** ranked among the nation's most modern schoolhouses, with central heating, piped-in drinking water, and spring-loaded flush toilets. As you walk the school's worn wooden floors, you'll see rows of wooden desks facing dusty chalkboards and reading lessons that were printed on big manila cards. The school graduated its last class in 1936 and, after decades of silence in its halls, now serves as a local history museum with excellent exhibits.

Soaring above the rooftops of Virginia City, a graceful white steeple marks **St. Mary's in the Mountains**, a church known as the cradle of Catholicism in western Nevada. Inside are carved wooden pews, a baptismal font that was saved from the town's disastrous fire of 1875, and—maybe this won't surprise you by now—a ghost. It's said that people hear the footsteps of a priest who walks across the upper floor. He died long ago. But apparently his tread was distinctive, for he walked with a cane, and on quiet evenings it thumps as he paces.

Is the story true, or only a tall tale? Who knows? But the feeling that the past is very much with you in Virginia City makes a visit all the more fascinating.   *Jerry Camarillo Dunn, Jr.*

Travelwise

GETTING THERE

Virginia City is located in western Nevada, 23 miles southeast of Reno (which has an airport) on Nev. 341.

GENERAL INFORMATION

Virginia City can be quite hot in summer, with temperatures in the 90s. Winter days average 35-40°F, but nights can dip below 10°F. For more information, contact the **Virginia City Chamber of Commerce** *(131 S. C St., Virginia City 89440. 775-847-0311. www.comstocklode.com).* The chamber has a visitor center on C St. in an old train car.

THINGS TO SEE AND DO

The Castle *(B St. 775-847-0275. May-Oct.; adm. fee)* Guided tour of an unrestored 1868 mansion on former Millionaires' Row, filled with antique furnishings and etchings.

Chollar Mine *(Below E St. at town's S end. 775-847-0155. Closed Oct.-April; adm. fee)* Explore a historic mine tunnel.

Fourth Ward School Museum *(S end of C St. 775-847-0975. Closed Nov.-April; donation)* The classrooms of this Second Empire schoolhouse were built to accommodate 1,000 students. Historical exhibits.

Nevada Gambling Museum *(Inside the Palace Emporium on C St. 775-847-9022. Adm. fee)* Vintage gambling devices are on display.

Piper's Opera House *(B St. at Union St. 775-847-0433. Closed Oct.-April; adm. fee)* On exhibit are original scenery, a stage curtain with vintage advertisements, and box seats.

St. Mary's in the Mountains *(E St.)* Local lore says that during the town's 1875 fire, a millionaire mine owner persuaded townspeople to save the mines instead of the Catholic church by promising to finance a new brick structure; this is it, built in 1876.

Saloons There are still a number of working bars on C Street that showcase relics from

the past. The **Delta Saloon** displays the "Suicide Table" and other artifacts. The **Silver Queen** features a portrait of a woman whose gown is made up of 3,261 authentic silver dollars. The **Ponderosa Saloon,** which occupies the 1876 Bank of California building, offers tours of mine workings in the hillside behind the saloon *(775-847-0757).*

Silver Terrace Cemeteries *(Below E St. at town's N edge)* Visit the town's past residents.

Virginia & Truckee Railroad *(Depot at Washington and F Sts. 775-847-0380. Closed mid-Oct.-mid-May; fare)* A vintage steam locomotive pulls open cars and cabooses on a narrated, 35-minute round-trip past ruined mines to nearby settlement of Gold Hill.

The Way It Was Museum *(C St. at Sutton St. 775-847-0766. Adm. fee)* On display are Comstock mining artifacts, scale models of mines, items from daily life, and more.

ANNUAL EVENTS

Comstock Historic Preservation Weekend *(Early May. 775-847-0275)* Historic home and business tours, fashion shows, lectures, art and photography exhibits.

International Camel and Ostrich Races *(1st weekend in Sept. 775-847-0275)* Begun as a hoax, the races are now one of the state's most popular events.

WHERE TO EAT

Crown Point Restaurant *(Gold Hill Hotel, 1 mile S of Virginia City on Nev. 341. 775-847-0111. $$)* French cuisine prepared with Pacific Rim overtones.

WHERE TO STAY

Gold Hill Hotel *(1 mile S of town on Nev. 341. 775-847-0111. $$)* Tasteful lodgings include small rooms in the original stone building (1859) and luxurious rooms in a new addition.

Joseph

Wallowa County, in the high desert country of northeastern Oregon, is a land of epic proportions and spectacular natural beauty. At its heart lies Joseph, a small piece of human history in a landscape of timeless Western grandeur.

As you drive into Joseph, it's not the town so much as its dramatic setting that steals the show. The Wallowa Mountains tower above this community of 1,270 residents like a majestic purple-gray fortress. Although little known outside the region, the Wallowas boast Oregon's largest wilderness (the 358,541-acre **Eagle Cap Wilderness**), which embraces several peaks over 10,000 feet high and more than 50 lakes.

The town, at an elevation of about 4,100 feet, is laid out in a compact grid that begins at the kokanee salmon-filled Wallowa River and ends abruptly in a vast sweep of open countryside. Stretching as far as the eye can see are tawny wheatfields and green pastures with frisking horses, grazing cattle, and glittering streams with names like Lightning Creek.

A handful of sturdy, late 19th-century brick buildings and low wooden

Joseph's main street, dwarfed by the Wallowa Mountains

shop fronts along Main Street lend a classic Old West flavor. The most notable structure, erected as the county's first bank in 1888 (a year after Joseph was incorporated), now houses the **Wallowa County Museum.** It's a delightfully old-fashioned place, the walls a virtual scrapbook of photographs showing Joseph from the pioneering 1870s onward. One room, with a full-size tepee, is devoted to the history of the Nez Perce Indians, the original inhabitants of Wallowa County, and the tragic Nez Perce war of 1877.

You'll learn here that the Nez Perce legacy is a cornerstone of the town's identity. Joseph takes its name from Young Chief Joseph (1840-1904), the revered leader of the Wallowa band of Nez Perce at the time of the tribe's battle with the U.S. Calvary. His equally venerated father, Old Chief Joseph (1783-1872), is buried on a grassy knoll overlooking the tribe's ancestral summer campground at nearby Wallowa Lake.

Nez Perce Defeat

An 1855 treaty allowed the Nez Perce to keep their homeland in Wallowa County. But when the Wallowa band refused to sign a new treaty in 1863, they were ordered off their lands. Angry Nez Perce warriors killed four white settlers, precipitating the Nez Perce war, a 1,400-mile retreat that pitted 800 Indians under Young Chief Joseph against the U.S. military. When he was finally defeated near the Canadian border, Chief Joseph uttered the now famous words: "My heart is sick and sad. From where the sun now stands, I will fight no more forever."

Also on Main Street, a fine collection of Nez Perce baskets, clothing, and household articles is on display in the **Manuel Nez Perce Crossing Museum and Studio.** Here, too, are several 19th-century wagons used by pioneers jolting westward on the Oregon Trail, as well as Western-inspired bronze sculptures produced in its bronze foundry. In recent years Joseph has gained a national reputation as a center for bronze casting, and artists of all kinds have become as much a part of the local scene as the farmers and ranchers who drive in for chicken-fried steak at the **Cheyenne Café.**

In July the entire community celebrates its wild and woolly heritage with Chief Joseph Days. Crowds stream into the outdoor arena on the town's west side to enjoy hard-kicking professional rodeo events. Young women vying to be Rodeo Queen show off their riding skills. The Nez Perce arrive, set up a tepee village, and celebrate with traditional dances.

Quite a different scene awaits about a mile south of town, where peaceful **Wallowa Lake** cups within glacially carved hills. Deer sporting velvet antlers wander among the rustic cabins and lodges in the forest and along the lakeshore. From the lake's south end, you glide up to the 8,200-foot summit of Mount Howard on the glass-enclosed **Wallowa Lake Tramway.** At the top, eye-popping views open up in all directions.

For the folks who live in Joseph, far from the cramp of urban life, these wide-open spaces are a given. But it's not just the silent immensity of landscape that stirs the imagination. The night sky, radiant and pulsating with stars, is also a wonder to behold. *Donald S. Olson*

Travelwise

GETTING THERE

Joseph is located in eastern Oregon on Oreg. 82, 75 miles east of La Grande, Oregon, and 85 miles south of Lewiston, Idaho. The closest major airport is in Lewiston. A car is necessary in this vast, relatively unpopulated area.

GENERAL INFORMATION

The area is generally accessible year-round, but heavy snows can make winter travel daunting. The best months are late May through September. Contact the **Wallowa County Chamber of Commerce** (River St., Enterprise 97828. 541-426-4622 or 800-585-4121). The **Wallowa Mountains Visitor Center** (88401 Hwy. 82, Enterprise. 541-426-5546) has maps of the surrounding area.

THINGS TO SEE AND DO

Boating Rent canoes, rowboats, and paddleboats from Wallowa Lake Marina (Wallowa Lake SP 541-432-9115).

Fishing Rainbow trout, kokanee, and mackinaw reside in **Wallowa Lake;** the **Wallowa River** is popular for spring steelhead fishing.

Horseback Riding Guided day-long excursions and summer pack trips into the spectacular **Eagle Cap Wilderness** can be arranged through Eagle Cap Wilderness Pack Station (59761 Wallowa Lake Hwy. 541-432-4145 or 800-681-6222).

Manuel Nez Perce Crossing Museum and Studio (400 N. Main St. 541-432-7235. Closed Nov.-May; adm. fee) Artifacts represent the tribe that originally inhabited the region.

Wallowa County Museum (110 S. Main St. 541-432-6095. Closed Oct.–Mem. Day) Relics from Joseph's past are displayed.

Wallowa Lake Tramway (59919 Wallowa Lake Hwy. 541-432-5331. Closed Oct.-April; fare) Enjoy spectacular alpine views as you glide up to Mount Howard's summit.

SHOPPING

The bronze sculptures cast in area foundries are prized by many collectors of Western art. **Valley Bronze of Oregon** (307 W. Alder St. 541-432-7441) and **Parks Bronze** (331 Golf Course Rd., Enterprise. 541-426-4595) display works and offer tours of their foundries.

ANNUAL EVENTS

Alpenfest (Late Sept. Edelweiss Lodge, Wallowa Lake. 541-426-4622 or 800-585-4121) Bavarian food, dancing, and an arts and crafts fair herald autumn's arrival.

Chief Joseph Days (Late July. Harley Tucker Mem. Arena. 541-426-4622 or 800-585-4121. Adm fee) The year's biggest shindig features rodeo events and Native American festivities.

WHERE TO EAT

Cheyenne Café (209 N. Main St. 541-432-6300. $) The place to go for home-style cooking; chicken-fried steak is a specialty.

WHERE TO STAY

Collett's Cabins (84681 Ponderosa Ln. 541-432-2391. $) Set among giant pines on Wallowa Lake.

Wallowa Lake Lodge (60060 Wallowa Lake Hwy. 541-432-9821. $$) This 1920s hunting retreat is authentically rustic. The lodge serves hefty portions of classic American fare.

NEARBY PLACES

Hells Canyon National Recreation Area (541-426-5546) The 110-mile-long section of the Snake River from Oxbow Dam north to the Oregon-Washington border is North America's deepest gorge, plunging down for a mile and a half in some areas. To reach **Hat Point,** the most spectacular viewpoint, drive to Imnaha, 30 miles northeast of Joseph on Oreg. 350, and continue another 25 miles east on FR 4240.

Astoria

Lying on the threshold of the sea, where the fabled Columbia River pours into the Pacific Ocean, Astoria traces its roots back to the earliest days of Northwest exploration. With its picturesque waterfront, old-fashioned downtown, and steep streets filled with Victorian houses, it exerts a powerfully nostalgic charm.

Following the course of the mighty Columbia River, the trailblazing duo of Meriwether Lewis and William Clark reached the Pacific near present-day Astoria in 1805. Six years later Fort Astoria, named for its owner, New York financier John Jacob Astor, was established on a hilly, forested peninsula between the river and Youngs Bay. The site of that wilderness fur-trading post—which just happened to be the first American settlement west of the Rockies—is marked in a small park at the corner of 15th and Exchange in downtown Astoria.

It wasn't until the 1840s and 1850s, though, that Astoria really sprang to life as a hard-working port and fishing town. Take a look at the exhibits in the **Columbia River Maritime Museum,** housed in a contemporary wooden building down on the waterfront, and you'll see just how important the Columbia and the Pacific have been to this community—and how many lives they have claimed. Some of the more poignant items on display are the personal effects of passengers who went down in ships snagged on the treacherous Columbia sandbar or capsized in raging gales. A century's worth of rescue vessels attests to the dangers of this rugged coastline, which for years was called the Graveyard of the Pacific.

At the Columbia River Maritime Museum

No matter where you are in Astoria your eye is drawn toward the vast expanse of the Columbia. The sea is 5 nautical miles away, but you can smell its cool, salty breath. Stroll along the waterfront promenade just behind the maritime museum and you'll see a procession of enormous cargo ships, barges, tugs, and fishing and pleasure boats passing up and down the Columbia's deep-water channel to the Pacific. Local anglers cast their lines from the piers, hauling in sturgeon as hungry gulls wheel and cry overhead. Near the old riverfront warehouses the aroma of fresh fish fills the air as the daily catches are unloaded. Chances are, that day's gleaming salmon will appear on the menu at the **Cannery Café** or the **Columbian Café,** two of the best places for fresh seafood.

The fact that this waterfront pedestrian promenade exists tells you some-

The Flavel House, built in 1885

Astoria-Washington Bridge at twilight

thing about the people of Astoria. In the midst of changing times and a changing economy, they are determined to preserve as much of their town's physical
and cultural history as possible. The 1914 wooden passenger trolley that clangs
along the waterfront, past marinas, waterside parks, and old canneries, was
completely restored by local volunteers. Residents are now trying to raise
money to restore the downtown area's Liberty Theatre, a 1920s movie palace.

One town relic, the old **Finnish steambaths,** is still steaming away as it did
when loggers and sailors made up its clientele. If the walls of its sweat rooms
could talk, you'd hear a lot of Scandinavian voices: The immigrants who
settled Astoria came from all over northern Europe and Iceland. Their
descendants put on the big Scandinavian Midsummer Festival every year.

One notch up from the waterfront is the business or "downtown" district,
where you may feel as if you've stumbled across the 1950s. On and around
Commercial Street, the main business artery, small, unpretentious shops sell
everything from fishing tackle to handmade chocolates. **Josephson's** is the last
of the old fish smokehouses.

Astoria's greatest charms are sprinkled throughout the hilly residential
streets above the business district. The Victorian houses built there between
1850 and 1910 give this town of 10,000 residents an architectural cachet
found nowhere else on Oregon's coast. Mostly of clapboard, they range in size
from pillbox to palazzo. Some of the showier Queen Annes and Italianates
have been turned into B&Bs, but for the most part Astoria's Victorians lack
gingerbread detailing and eschew Painted Lady colors. Practical rather than

ostentatious, they were built to withstand gale-force winds and pounding Pacific rains.

Grandest of all is the turreted, Queen Anne-style **Flavel House,** built for Captain George Flavel in 1885. Its hushed, stately rooms, with their carved woodwork and ornate period furnishings, exude a cultured air that was hardly the norm in a raucous frontier seaport once known as the wettest town in the West, and not because of the rainfall. To see how the other half lived, you may want to stroll over to the **Heritage Museum** and have a look at "Vice and Virtue," an exhibition that covers the years from 1890 to Prohibition. Other displays in this disarmingly old-fashioned museum, which was first dedicated as the Astoria City Hall in 1905, interpret the daily lives of the early settlers and Native Americans in Clatsop County.

But if there's anything that approximates hero-worship in Astoria, it's reserved for Lewis and Clark. A painted frieze highlighting the major events of their monumental journey spirals up the sides of the **Astoria Column,** an observation tower modeled after Trajan's triumphal column in Rome. It's perched atop the windy summit of Coxcomb Hill, the highest (and most famous) point in town. From here you can see south across Youngs Bay to distant **Fort Clatsop,** where the explorers spent the rainy winter of 1805-1806, while to the west lie the mouth of the Columbia and the restless Pacific.

It's a vast and inspiring scene, one that generations of Astorians have savored and made a part of their daily lives. Maybe that's why the townspeople chose this spot to bury their time capsule. Many things will have changed in Astoria by the time it's opened in 2044, but the river and the sea will always be there.   *Donald S. Olson*

Travelwise

GETTING THERE

Astoria is located in Oregon's northwestern corner, near the confluence of the Columbia River and the Pacific Ocean. The nearest major airport is in Portland, 96 miles east via I-5 and US 30, from which there is regular bus service.

GENERAL INFORMATION

The weather on the Oregon coast is always unpredictable, but summer and fall are your best bets for mild, clear (or at least rainless) days. The **Astoria-Warrenton Area Chamber of Commerce** (*111 W. Marine Dr., Astoria 97103. 503-325-6311 or 800-875-6807*) publishes a useful information guide and sells a walking-tour booklet highlighting the town's Victorian houses.

THINGS TO SEE AND DO

Astoria Column
(*Coxcomb Hill*) Puff your way up the 164 spiraling stairs and you'll be rewarded with dazzling views of the Lower Columbia region. New York architect Electus Litchfield designed the 125-foot column, which opened in 1926.

Columbia River Maritime Museum
(*1791 Marine Dr. 503-325-2323. Adm. fee*) From fur-trading days to contemporary navigation techniques, Astoria's maritime history is chronicled in exhibits that include the observation tower of a submarine, a U.S. Coast Guard lightship, and personal belongings salvaged from the hundreds of ships that have foundered here since 1811.

Crabbing, Clamming, and Fishing
The beaches and waters of the Lower
Columbia and Pacific Ocean offer plentiful
opportunities for digging razor clams,
catching crabs, and fishing for salmon, tuna,
sturgeon, and bottom fish. Licenses and
equipment can be obtained in local fish and
tackle shops. Charlton Deep Sea Charters
(503-861-2429) offers fishing trips and
scenic boat tours.

Flavel House *(441 8th St. 503-325-2203.*
Adm. fee) A marvelous Queen Anne mansion
in a parklike setting, the house offers a
glimpse of privileged life in Astoria in the late
19th century. The admission price includes
the **Heritage Museum** *(1618 Exchange St.),*
loaded with historic photographs and
memorabilia from the town's early days, and
the **Uppertown Firefighters Museum**
(30th St. and Marine Dr. Call for hours), which
displays firefighting equipment from the late
1800s such as a horse-drawn ladder wagon
and fire trucks used in the first part of the
20th century.

ENTERTAINMENT
Astor Street Opry Company *(Old Finnish*
Meat Market, 279 W. Marine Dr. 503-325-6104)
The perennially popular *Shanghaied in Astoria,* an
old-fashioned melodrama, is performed every
summer by this local company.

Columbia River Coffeehouse Theater
(230 W. Marine Dr. 503-325-7487) Plays and
performances are offered year-round in this
small black-box theater.

SHOPPING
Josephson's *(106 Marine Dr. 503-325-2190)*
One of the oldest commercial smokehouses
on the Oregon coast prepares Columbia
River chinook salmon in the traditional alder-
smoked and lox styles. You can also buy
smoked oysters, mussels, sturgeon, scallops,
and prawns in sealed gift packs.

ANNUAL EVENTS
Astoria Regatta Festival *(Mid-Aug. 503-*
325-6311 or 800-875-6807) The oldest festival
west of the Rockies, this five-day event
features a parade, dancing, ship tours, yacht
races, a salmon and oyster feed, and fireworks.

Astoria-Warrenton Crab and Seafood
Festival *(Last weekend in April. Hammond*
Mooring Basin. 503-325-6311 or 800-875-
6807) This hugely popular festival features

fresh crab and other local seafood, 40
Oregon wineries, arts and crafts, live music,
and much more.

Scandinavian Midsummer Festival
(Mid-June. Astoria High School. 503-325-6311
or 800-875-6807) Astoria's Swedish,
Norwegian, Finnish, Danish, and Icelandic
cultures are represented in a three-day
festival that includes folk dancing, music,
food, craft booths, and a beer garden.

WHERE TO EAT
Cannery Café *(1 6th St. 503-325-8642. $$)*
A former cannery on the Columbia River
has been turned into a bright contemporary
restaurant with wonderful river views and a
seafood-oriented menu.

Columbian Café *(114 Marine Dr. 503-325-*
2233. $$) The atmosphere is cheerfully over-
the-top, but amid the Christmas lights and
kitschy paraphernalia you can dine on fresh
grilled salmon and many inventive entrées.

WHERE TO STAY
Benjamin Young Inn *(3652 Duane St. 503-*
325-6172 or 800-201-1286. $$) Lovers of
grand old houses will enjoy this spacious,
beautifully kept Queen Anne. Graced by
ornate period fixtures, woodwork, and
original furnishings, it has five guest rooms
with views of the Columbia.

Grandview Bed & Breakfast *(1574 Grand*
Ave. 503-325-0000 or 800-488-3250. $$) Nine
eclectically furnished guest rooms in a
century-old house, it offers grand views of
the river, the Coast Range, and the church
spires of Old Astoria.

NEARBY PLACES
Fort Clatsop National Memorial *(Fort*
Clatsop Rd. off Alt. US 101, 5 miles S of Astoria.
503-861-2471. Adm. fee) Set in a lush stretch
of forest, Fort Clatsop is a faithful replica
of the log stockade where Lewis and Clark
headquartered during the winter of 1805-1806.

Fort Stevens State Park *(Fort Stevens Hwy.,*
7 miles W of Astoria. 503-861-3170. Vehicle fee)
Located at the mouth of the Columbia, the
fort was in use from the Civil War through
World War II. In the park you can visit a small
military museum, abandoned gun mounts, eerie
subterranean bunkers, and view the skeleton
of a century-old English four-master
protruding from the beach.

Port Townsend

Washington's Olympic Peninsula is dominated by Olympic National Park, a majestic wilderness of glacier-crowned mountains and old-growth forests. Port Townsend lies just north of the park, on the rocky coastline of the Strait of Juan de Fuca. Full of charm and easy-going sophistication, this historic seaport wafts visitors back to an era when schooners and steamers carried schemers and dreamers to the virgin lands of the Pacific Northwest.

Ann Starrett Mansion and DeLion House

Port Townsend's waterfront

At the end of Quimper Peninsula, a stubby finger of land jutting into the Strait of Juan de Fuca, Port Townsend rises up from the sheltered waters of Port Townsend Bay to a series of high bluffs overlooking Admiralty Inlet, a passageway into Puget Sound and the Hood Canal. Ferry boats, gleaming yachts, and nimble sea kayaks have replaced the multimasted schooners that once dropped anchor here, but the town still marinates in the glow of its rich maritime past.

As proud residents like to point out, Port Townsend was founded in 1851, six months before Seattle, and it quickly became the busiest harbor on the West Coast. But, as they're also fond of relating, Port Townsend's phenomenal boom turned into a big-time bust in 1893, the year an eagerly anticipated transcontinental railroad failed to arrive…it was routed to Seattle instead.

Ironically, it was economic disaster that saved Port Townsend for posterity. Because there wasn't enough money to tear down old buildings or build new ones, the fabric of the 19th-century seaport remained essentially unchanged over the years. Local restoration efforts were bolstered in the 1970s when the lower waterfront area and upper residential neighborhoods were designated national historic districts. Since that time, to the delight of architecture buffs and old house enthusiasts, the entire town has undergone a virtual retro-renaissance back to its Victorian roots. A self-guided driving tour (maps available free from the visitor center) hones in on the town's eclectic array of federal, Gothic, Queen Anne, stick, shingle, and neo-Romanesque structures.

The waterfront area, where the passenger ferry from Whidbey Island chugs regularly in and out of its small terminal, is a perfect place to begin exploring. Water and Washington Streets, running parallel to the harbor, are chockablock with redbrick commercial and civic buildings erected over a century ago when Port Townsend was the official Port of Entry for the Northwest United States. The sailors, immigrants, and brawling adventurers who once jammed these streets would be bewildered by the galleries, coffee shops, and fine restaurants found here today.

For a closer look at the town's colorful past, stop in at the **Jefferson County Historical Museum,** housed in an impressive two-story redbrick building dedicated in 1892 as the City Hall. The judge's bench still presides over the old courtroom, which is filled with area memorabilia, including rare baskets, tools, and carvings collected from the Olympic Peninsula's Native American tribes. Adventure writer Jack London (1876-1916) reputedly got into a brawl and cooled his heels in the gloomy underground lock-up that served as the city jail.

You'll get a more domestic whiff of the past on the bluffs above the waterfront district. In this upper echelon, separated from the rowdiness below, sea captains, merchants, and town worthies built churches and wood-frame houses in a pastiche of styles that grew more ornate and elaborate as the century wore on. The **Rothschild House,** constructed in 1868 and occupied by the same family for nearly a century, provides an intimate peek into the life of a prosperous Port Townsend clan. The little altered interior of this two-story white-frame residence still contains its original furniture and patterned wallpaper; the handgrained woodwork was the work of Chinese artisans. Some of the finest bluff-top homes have been converted into B&Bs.

One thing you'll rarely hear the residents of Port Townsend complain about is weather. Sitting in the rain shadow of the Olympic Mountains, their town receives only a fraction of the precipitation that drenches Seattle and is mild year-round. As a result, people here tend to be outdoors oriented. Many of the community's annual festivals and festivities are outdoor events held in **Fort Worden State Park** at the north end of town. Established in 1896 and in use throughout World War II, the fort is now a 434-acre waterside park with beach walks, picnic areas, a kayaking launch, a marine science center, a lighthouse, and camera-ready views of the San Juan Islands, Admiralty Inlet, and distant Cascade peaks.

Like the rest of Port Townsend, Fort Worden is something of an object lesson in small town pride, ingenuity, and survival. Forming a unique partnership with the state, the community has not only restored the fort's historic buildings, it keeps them alive and in use. The turn-of-the-20th-century houses along **Officers' Row** are used for weddings, reunions, and conferences, an old balloon hangar has been converted into a theater, and the former barracks is now a museum. By carefully restoring and recycling its past, this is one small town that's managed to keep its eyes firmly on the future. *Donald S. Olson*

Travelwise

GETTING THERE

Port Townsend is located on Wash. 20 on the northeastern coast of the Olympic Peninsula, about 55 miles west of Seattle. From Seattle there is ferry service to Bainbridge Island and Kingston, after which you'll need to cross the Hood Canal Bridge. You can also take I-5 to Tacoma, pick up Wash. 16 and 3 north to the Hood Canal Bridge, and follow signs. The Jefferson County airport has charter service to and from Seattle. Bus service is available from the ferry terminals to Port Townsend.

GENERAL INFORMATION

Port Townsend is generally mild year-round and at its sunny best in summer and fall. The **Port Townsend Visitors Center** (2437 E. Sims Way. 360-385-2722 or 888-365-6978. www.ptguide.com) provides a free driving tour map that highlights the town's Victorian architecture and maritime-related culture.

THINGS TO SEE AND DO

Chevy Chase Golf Resort (7401 Cape George Rd. 360-385-0704 or 800-385-8722) Washington's oldest public course (1925) offers 18 holes on a serenely rural course overlooking Discovery Bay.

Fort Worden State Park (Entrance on W St. at Cherry St. 360-385-4730) This lovely waterfront park is a popular spot for concerts, special events, and outdoor recreation. The 1902 **Commanding Officer's Quarters** (Officers' Row. 360-379-9894. Adm. fee) conveys the life of an officer and his family at the turn of the 20th century. The **Coast Artillery Museum** (360-385-4730. Adm. fee) contains military artifacts and photos.

Guided Historical Sidewalk Tours (Meet at Water and Madison Sts. 360-385-1967. Fee) Local historians lead lively walking tours through the Victorian waterfront district.

Jefferson County Historical Museum (210 Madison St. at Water St. 360-385-1003. Adm. fee) The judge's chambers, fire hall, and underground jail in the town's late 19th-century City Hall are all part of this intriguing museum.

Kayaking Guided tours of the area are offered by Kayak Port Townsend (Water and Monroe Sts. 360-385-6240 or 877-578-2252). Kayak rentals are available, too.

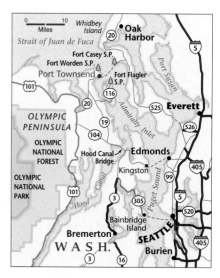

Rothschild House (Jefferson and Taylor Sts. 360-385-7869. Adm. fee) A restored herb garden and rose garden, with old varieties of peonies, roses, and lilacs, adds to the period charm of one of the oldest houses in Port Townsend.

SHOPPING

The town has numerous contemporary arts and crafts galleries. **Ancestral Spirits** (701 Water St. 360-385-0078) specializes in traditional tribal art from the Northwest.

ANNUAL EVENTS

Port Townsend hosts dozens of festivals and events year-round; you can obtain a complete listing from the visitor center.

Jazz Port Townsend (Last weekend in July. McCurdy Pavilion, Fort Worden State Park. 360-385-3102) One of the premier jazz festivals on the West Coast presents concerts by jazz greats and younger artists.

Marrowstone Music Festival (Late Aug. McCurdy Pavilion, Fort Worden State Park. 360-385-3102) Orchestral and chamber music concerts featuring internationally recognized musicians take place on Saturday and Sunday afternoons.

Rhododendron Festival (3rd week in May. 360-385-2722 or 888-365-6978) The week-long festival honors the town's favorite flowering shrub with a senior citizen coronation, a kids' parade, a pet parade, a fish fry, a grand parade, and a marathon run.

WHERE TO EAT

Fountain Café *(920 Washington St. 360-385-1364. Closed Tues. $$)* This small, unpretentious place is one of the best restaurants in town, serving up creative versions of seafood and pasta.

Salal Café *(634 Water St. 360-385-6532. $)* The Salal consistently wins awards for best breakfast in Jefferson County; try the scrambled eggs and oysters or the wild salmon frittata.

Silverwater Café *(237 Taylor St. 360-385-6448. $$)* This friendly establishment is known for its wonderfully fresh seafood, including oysters, salmon, halibut, and crab cakes.

WHERE TO STAY

Ann Starrett Mansion *(744 Clay St. 360-385-3205 or 800-321-0644. $$$)* Built as a wedding present, the 1889 mansion overlooks Puget Sound and is renowned for its frescoed ceilings and free-hung three-tiered staircase.

James House *(1238 Washington St. 360-385-1238 or 800-385-1238. $$)* One of the finest houses in Port Townsend, this splendid 1889 Queen Anne mansion with superb woodwork and Victorian furnishings throughout has 12 inviting guest rooms, most with commanding views of the bay, the Strait, and the distant Cascades.

Palace Hotel *(1004 Water St. 360-385-0773 or 800-962-0741. $$)* Once known as the Palace of Sweets and famous for its ladies of the night, this restored Victorian hotel has many different kinds of rooms, all decorated with antiques and memorabilia.

NEARBY PLACES

Olympic National Park *(Main visitor center, 3002 Mt. Angeles Rd., Port Angeles. 360-452-4501)* Mountains, alpine lakes, wild rivers, hot springs, primitive ocean beaches, and old-growth temperate rain forest are all found in this amazingly diverse national park, a biosphere reserve and World Heritage site spread over some 922,000 acres. For a short but captivating

Ann Starrett Mansion

trip from Port Townsend, follow US 101 west to Port Angeles. Here, follow the sinuous paved road up **Hurricane Ridge,** which puts you on the edge of the park's sawtooth peaks.

Port Gamble *(Kitsap Peninsula Visitor and Convention Bureau 360-297-8200 or 800-416-5616)* Founded in 1853, this tidy village was built by timber magnate Pope & Talbot as a company town; Pope Resources still owns and maintains the townsite, now a historic district. Many buildings date back to the 19th century. Find out more about the town and its setting at the **Of Sea & Shore Museum** *(1 Rainier Ave., above the general store. 360-297-7636. Donation)* and the **Port Gamble Historical Museum** *(Behind the general store. 360-297-8074. Daily May-Oct., by appt. only rest of year; adm. fee).*

Illustrations Credits

Cover

Randy Olson/NGS Image Collection

Frontmatter

1, Tim Thompson. 2-3, John Elk III. 4, Bob Krist. 8, Mark E. Gibson.

New England

11, Dan Beigel (left); William H. Johnson (middle and right). 12, Dan Beigel. 13, Gary Braasch. 14, William H. Johnson. 16, Mike Brinson/Image Bank. 18, William H. Johnson. 21, Paul Rocheleau. 23, William H. Johnson. 25, William Johnson/Stock Boston. 29, Charles Sleicher/Tony Stone Images. 33, William H. Johnson. 35, Kelly/Mooney Photography. 36, Jonathan Wallen. 39, Steve Dunwell. 41, William H. Johnson. 42, William H. Johnson. 45, Jonathan Wallen. 46, William H. Johnson. 49, William H. Johnson. 50, Steve Dunwell. 53, Dan Beigel. 54, Jack McConnell.

Mid-Atlantic

57, Ralph Pugliese, Jr. (left); Jake Rajs (middle); Michael Ventura/Folio Inc. (right). 59, Ralph Pugliese, Jr. 60, Ralph Pugliese, Jr. 63, Scott Barrow. 64, Scott Barrow. 67, Ed Cooper. 68-9, Medford Taylor. 71, Bob Krist. 72, Jonathan Wallen. 75, Gail Mooney. 76, Bob Krist. 77, Mark E. Gibson/Folio, Inc. 81, Walter Choroszewski. 82, Walter Choroszewski. 84, Fred J. Maroon/Folio, Inc. 86, Jake Rajs. 89, Eric Poggenpohl/Folio, Inc. 90, Michael Ventura/Folio, Inc. 93, Michael Ventura/Folio, Inc. 95, Paul Rocheleau. 96, Starke Jett/Folio, Inc. 101, Tal McBride/Folio, Inc. 102, Jeff Greenberg/Folio, Inc. 105, G. P. Cooper. 106, G. P. Cooper.

The Southeast

109, Bob Krist (left); John Elk III/Tony Stone Images (middle); Richard Bickel (right). 111, Kelly/Mooney Photography. 112, Bruce Dale. 114-15, Mike Booher/Transparencies Inc. 116, Tom Raymond/Tony Stone Images. 118-19, Kelly Culpepper/Transparencies, Inc. 120, Chris Ippolito/Transparencies Inc. 123, Mike Booher/Transparencies Inc. 124, Jane Faircloth/Transparencies Inc. 127, William H. Johnson. 129, Bob Krist. 131, Bob Krist. 133, Ron Sherman/Tony Stone Images. 134, Johnny E. Parker. 137, John Elk III/Tony Stone Images. 138, John Elk III. 140, Richard Bickel. 143, Richard Bickel. 145, David Muench. 146, David Muench. 147, David Muench. 149, Patty Tucker. 151, Bruce Newman. 152, William Albert Allard, NGP. 154, Philip Gould. 155, William H. Johnson. 156, William H. Johnson. 159, Neil Johnson.

Great Lakes

161, Daniel Grogan (left); John Elk III (middle); Tom Bean (right). 162, Everett Johnson/Folio, Inc. 165, Mark E. Gibson/Dembinsky Photo Associates. 167, HMS Images/Image Bank. 169, Luciano Duse Photography. 171, Luciano Duse Photography. 173, Fred Hirschmann. 174, Fred Hirschmann. 177, Daniel Grogan. 178, Daniel Grogan. 181, Cathlyn Melloan/Tony Stone Images. 183, Balthazar Korab. 184, Madison Area CVB. 185, Madison Area CVB. 187, Gary Irving/Tony Stone Images. 188, Bruce Mathews/Midwestock. 189, Brian Seed/Tony Stone Images. 191, Tom Bean. 192, Tom Bean. 193, Tom Bean. 195, John Elk III. 196, John Elk III. 200-201, Scott Benson. 202, Tom Bean. 204, Tom Bean.

The Plains

205, Tom Bean (left); Leslie Kelly (middle); Willard Clay/Tony Stone Images (right). 207, Tom Bean (top); Tom Bean (bot). 208, Tom Bean. 211, Leslie Kelly. 212, Leslie Kelly. 215, Tom Bean. 216, Tom Bean. 219, Tim Thompson. 220, John Elk III. 222, Fred J. Maroon/Folio, Inc. 223, Jonathan Wallen. 224, Doris DeWitt/Tony Stone Images. 225, Randy Olson. 227, Wilding Photos. 228, Wilding Photos. 233, Jonathan Wallen. 234, Jonathan Wallen. 237, Jim Argo. 241, Randy Olson. 242, Tim Thompson. 247, John Elk III. 248, John Elk III. 251, Jim Argo. 253, David Sams/Stock Boston. 255, Tim Thompson. 256, Willard Clay/Tony Stone Images (top); Fred Hirschmann (bot).

Rockies and the Southwest

259, Val Burgess (left); John Elk III (middle); George H. H. Huey (right). 261, Bruce Dale. 263, Steve Bly/Tony Stone Images. 265, John Elk III. 268, Pamela Spaulding. 269, John Elk III. 271, Fred Hirschmann. 273, Val Burgess. 275, Val Burgess. 277, Mary Steinbacher. 281, Ed Cooper. 282, Anne Rippy/Image Bank. 285, John Elk III. 286, Bob & Suzanne Clemenz. 288, Jake Rajs. 290, Eric Meola/Image Bank. 293, Chuck Place. 295, Chuck Place. 296, Chuck Place. 299, Michael Nevros. 300, Bob & Suzanne Clemenz. 302, John Elk III. 303, George H. H. Huey. 304, George H. H. Huey. 307, James P. Blair. 308, Tom Bean.

The West

311, Chuck Place (left); Phil Schermeister/Tony Stone Images (middle); John Elk III (right). 312, Jeff Gnass. 313, Chuck Place. 314, John Elk III. 317, Mark E. Gibson/Midwestock. 318, Mark E. Gibson. 321, John Elk III. 322, John Elk III. 325, Fred Hirschmann. 326, James L. Stanfield. 329, Phil Schermeister/Tony Stone Images. 331, Chuck Place. 333, John Elk III. 336, Chuck Place. 337, Tim Thompson. 338, Phil Schermeister/NGS Image Collection. 341, Chuck Place. 342, Walter Bibikow/Folio, Inc. 345, John Elk III. 346, Tim Thompson.

Back Cover

Fred Hirschmann (top); Jake Rajs (bot).

Wood boat show, Port Townsend

Index

National Geographic Guide to Small Town Escapes

Published by the National Geographic Society
John M. Fahey, Jr., *President and Chief Executive Officer*
Gilbert M. Grosvenor, *Chairman of the Board*
Nina D. Hoffman, *Senior Vice President*

Prepared by the Book Division
William R. Gray, *Vice President and Director*
Charles Kogod, *Assistant Director*
Barbara A. Payne, *Editorial Director and Managing Editor*
David Griffin, *Design Director*
Elizabeth L. Newhouse, *Director of Travel Books*

Staff for this Book
Barbara A. Noe, *Editor*
Cinda Rose, *Art Director*
Mary Jenkins, *Illustrations Editor*
Carolinda E. Averitt, *Assistant Editor*
Jerry Camarillo Dunn, Jr., K.M. Kostyal, Mark Miller, Barbara A. Noe, Geoffrey O'Gara,
    Donald S. Olson, William G. Scheller, John M. Thompson, Mel White, David Yeadon, *Writers*
Caroline Hickey, *Senior Researcher*
Josie Dean, Jane Sunderland, *Researchers*
Carl Mehler, *Director of Maps*
XNR Productions, Matt Chwastyk, Patricia A. Healy,
    Gregory Ugiansky, *Map Research and Production*
Richard S. Wain, *Production Manager*
Gillian Carol Dean, *Assistant Designer*
Meredith Wilcox, *Illustrations Assistant*
Deborah E. Patton, *Indexer*
DeShelle Downey, *Project Assistant*
Mary E. Jennings, Victoria Garrett Jones, Keith R. Moore, Mark Waner, *Contributors*

Manufacturing and Quality Control
George V. White, *Director;* John T. Dunn, *Associate Director;* Vincent P. Ryan, *Manager;*
Phillip L. Schlosser, *Financial Analyst*

Library of Congress Cataloging-in-Publication Data
Guide to small town escapes.
    p. cm.
Includes bibliographical references and index.
ISBN 0-7922-7589-6 (reg) ISBN 0-7922-7583-7 (dlx)
    1. United States—Guidebooks. 2. Cities and towns—United States—Guidebooks. I.
National Geographic Society (U.S.)
E158 .G592 2000
917.304'929—dc21
                                            00-035144
                                            CIP